# THE OPENING ACT

# THE OPENING ACT

## CANADIAN THEATRE HISTORY 1945–1953

SUSAN McNICOLL

RONSDALE PRESS

THE OPENING ACT


RONSDALE PRESS
3350 West 21st Avenue
Vancouver, B.C. Canada V6S 1G7
www.ronsdalepress.com

Typesetting: Julie Cochrane, in Granjon 11.5 pt on 15
Cover Design: Julie Cochrane
Front Cover Photo: Bruno Gerussi & Muriel Ontkean in Totem Theatre's *A Streetcar Named Desire*, April 1952, Arngrim Collection.
Back Cover Photos: Thor Arngrim and Norma Macmillan in a Totem Theatre production, Arngrim Collection; Christopher Plummer and Amelia Hall in *Harlequinade*, McNicoll Collection.
Paper: Ancient Forest Friendly Rolland Enviro Satin FSC Recycled — 100% post-consumer waste, totally chlorine-free and acid-free.

Ronsdale Press wishes to thank the following for their support of its publishing program: the Canada Council for the Arts, the Government of Canada through the Canada Book Fund, the British Columbia Arts Council, and the Province of British Columbia through the British Columbia Book Publishing Tax Credit program.

Library and Archives Canada Cataloguing in Publication

McNicoll, Susan
The opening act: Canadian theatre history, 1945–1953 / Susan McNicoll.

Includes bibliographical references and index.
Issued also in electronic format.
ISBN 978-1-55380-113-9

1. Theater—Canada—History—20th century. 2. Canadian drama—History and criticism. 3. Actors—Canada—History—20th century. I. Title.

PN2304.M35 2012 792.0971 C2010-907534-X

At Ronsdale Press we are committed to protecting the environment. To this end we are working with Canopy (formerly Markets Initiative) and printers to phase out our use of paper produced from ancient forests. This book is one step towards that goal.

Printed in Canada by Marquis Book Printing, Quebec

For my father, Floyd Caza,
and all the other journeymen actors
whose passion, commitment and
dedication helped propel Canadian theatre
onto a professional stage

## AUTHOR'S NOTE

Unless otherwise indicated, all quotations are from personal interviews with actors and directors, conducted by the author.

## CONTENTS

# INTRODUCTION

On an afternoon some years ago, I was sitting on the floor of the living room looking through files when some pieces of newspaper fell out onto the carpet. There were five of them from the 1940s and they were yellowed with age. My father, Floyd Caza, had recently died, and these were part of his papers. As I read the clippings, all play reviews of the Ottawa Stage Society and the Everyman Theatre in British Columbia, I became intrigued. They were all connected to my father's time in Canadian theatre, when he worked alongside actors such as Christopher Plummer and Arthur Hill. I knew he had been an actor at one time but had never really given it much thought beyond that.

The general consensus has been that theatre in Canada, in any professional sense, began with the Stratford Festival in 1953. Yet these clippings pre-dated the festival by several years. At first I thought it must be amateur theatre, done as a hobby, but the reviews indicated otherwise. As an ex-newspaper reporter, and a long-time lover of theatre, my curiosity was piqued. I looked at the clippings in my hand and decided I wanted to know more, much more, about this period of time in Canadian theatre.

Floyd Caza, the actor whose death was the catalyst for *The Opening Act*. He is giving his best William Holden impression in this publicity shot, c. 1950. (MCNICOLL COLLECTION)

*The Opening Act* evolved from those five pieces my father had cut out of newspapers all those years ago.

In recent years, I am happy to say, a number of volumes highlighting various theatres of the post-war period have been published, but back when I began my research there were almost no books on the subject. Finding little pre-Stratford material, I had to start from scratch. And I did it with no Internet, which, looking back, I have to admit may not have been a bad thing. It forced me to interview actors from that time, most of whom have since died, and to go to the source documents directly in order to discover the history for myself. It was not long before I realized my father had been involved in an exciting time in Canadian theatre, a time of incredible growth.

There had been earlier professional theatre in Canada, but it had been sporadic, scattered across centuries. By the early twentieth century there were some homegrown professional acting troupes, particularly in Montreal, but the majority of theatre in Canada was provided by touring companies from England and America. The Depression in the 1930s put an end to most professional theatre and while amateur theatres still existed, they were spread across Canada and had no cohesive force. At the end of the Second World War, no professional companies existed in Canada presenting traditional dramatic theatre.

After the war, in 1946, a new kind of theatre company sprang up, especially in British Columbia, Ontario and Quebec. They set out to be professional—paying the actors and providing the public with top-notch performances. One company led to another and professional theatre burst onto centre stage in Canada with incredible speed. It became clear to me that the modern era of professional theatre in Canada began, not in 1953 with Stratford, but during this post-war era. It did not take me long to decide there was a book here to be written about bringing professional theatre onto the Canadian scene.

In my naivety I didn't expect the manuscript to be a long one and thankfully had no idea it would take so many years to finish. I applied for, and received, a Canada Council grant, and with that help I spent most of the next year at the Toronto Public Library reading every issue of *Saturday Night* and any major newspaper or other magazine in the country from 1945 to 1953. The people in the theatre division were invaluable to me as they gave me files of the individual companies. At the same time I compiled a long list of actors from the era and started to track them down.

Determined to write a comprehensive history covering the entire country, I made a two-week trip out to Vancouver, the city that eventually became my home. I spent as much time in the old Vancouver Public Library as I could, met with actors, and made a side trip to Los Angeles for an interview with Arthur Hill. Unfortunately, the Maritimes did not have any homegrown professional theatre in the early post-war years. Newfoundland did have the London Theatre Company, started by Leslie

Yeo in 1951, but all the actors were brought over from England. Yeo himself had come to Canada four years earlier with Britain's Alexandra Company, which performed in Newfoundland for the 1947–48 winter season.

That first year of research helped crystallize in my own mind what I wanted to achieve. The focus would be professional theatre, although this was a little complicated as the line between professional and amateur theatre often blurred. Many of the little community theatres often did excellent work, but the sheer number of them simply prohibited inclusion. I decided that if the actors were paid to perform, then the group was professional, and that became my standard for inclusion in the book. I veered from this course only twice. The Montreal Repertory Theatre only occasionally paid *one* of the performers in a production, never all of them, but it was a very important long-standing group in English Quebec. The other large concession I made to my mandate was the chapter on the Dominion Drama Festival. While I wanted the book to reflect professional theatre, I felt I could not entirely overlook the impact of amateur groups on the growth of professional Canadian theatre. The Dominion Drama Festival was important because it not only gave Canada's actors an extra outlet for performing, but also presented many Canadian plays, thereby giving exposure to our fledgling playwrights.

The next step was to choose the order in which to introduce the theatres. I decided to start on the West Coast and move east, which seemed less complicated than trying to attempt a chronological sequence because so many theatres opened at the same time. It was also, I confess, the direction my father followed during his career as an actor.

I then had to decide which years to include in the book. Luckily, with the exception of Theatre Under the Stars, which started out in 1940 as professional in intent but amateur in reality, the new birth of Canadian theatre began following the Second World War. So, 1945 seemed a good starting point, and Stratford in 1953 was the perfect bookend.

One final decision had to be made. How was I going to deal with theatres that operated during the post-war years but continued on after 1953? Some theatres began and ended during the time period so they were easy to include. But others were less clear, such as the two French Quebec theatres, Théâtre du Nouveau Monde and Théâtre du Rideau Vert, which both continued past the 1950s. I decided to include any professional theatre that operated during my time frame, but the focus of the book would remain on the 1945 to 1953 period, with a preamble of any earlier influences or a short follow-up of the subsequent years.

When Stratford began in 1953, to be followed by the regional theatre boom in the 1960s, it was only because of the many qualified people who had acquired their training and experience through the theatres of the post-war years. Of the sixty-five actors at the Stratford Festival in 1953, all but four were Canadian, either by birth or training.

Without the earlier years of professional theatre that provided a pool of experienced Canadian actors, Stratford's first year would have had an entirely different look, and certainly not a Canadian one. The 1945–53 period was short but the impact it had on professional theatre in Canada cannot be overstated. The rapid growth during those years was all the more remarkable because it happened over such a brief period of time.

The people who laid this professional theatre foundation were as diverse and dedicated as any of Canada's other pioneers. I felt Canada owed it them to record their voices for posterity, and I set out to do that in *The Opening Act*.

The close to fifty interviews I conducted were crucial, because they give the flavour of those years. It was important that readers should have a view of the times through the eyes of those who lived it. Many of the theatre people from the period stayed on the stage while others became better known in movies, television and writing: Robertson Davies, Timothy Findley, Elwy Yost (Ontario's man at the movies), Arthur Hill, William Shatner and Christopher Plummer, to name a few. Much of the material from the interviews is included in the separate chapters, but to keep the biographical material from being intrusive, I have also included some excerpts from the interviews as well as historical material in an appendix of "Theatre Vignettes." Some of these are brief while others are longer, with the individuals talking about their childhood and what they did in later years.

It was remarkable that so many men and women suddenly decided in 1945 that they were going to be the ones to bring theatre to Canada—permanently. They strove with hope and determination towards the creation of a lasting professional theatre in Canada. They succeeded but, as will be seen, the road they travelled was far from easy.

CHAPTER ONE

# THE BEGINNINGS OF CANADIAN THEATRE'S RENAISSANCE

"[Canadians] have never been without theatre and it's my contention that the theatre is a natural expression of society. . . . Wherever you set people down, some theatrical expression will emerge."

—HERBERT WHITTAKER

Just as homegrown professional theatre in Canada did not spring fully formed from the Stratford Festival, the early post-war flurry of professional theatre activity was not the first seen in Canada. Most of the earlier theatre in the nineteenth and early twentieth centuries, however, was amateur and sporadic. That, in turn, was preceded by decades of amateur theatre brought from Europe, thought at first to have begun with a production of *Le Théâtre de Neptune en la Nouvelle-France* on November 14, 1606, in Port Royal (once the capital of Acadia and now a small community in the western part of Nova Scotia). It has been recently discovered, however, that there was an even earlier European theatrical event, in 1583, when explorer Sir Humphrey Gilbert had a small group of entertainers on his ship perform during anchorage in St. John's, Newfoundland.

Of course, for hundreds of years prior to the arrival of the European amateur theatres, there had been what is sometimes referred to as paratheatre among North America's indigenous peoples. These were performances, often spiritual, involving rituals and dancing enacted in elaborate costumes and frequently using sophisticated stage effects.

For traditional European-style theatre, one can look to the mid-eighteenth century, which saw a good deal of "garrison theatre," a term used to describe the theatrical activities of the British and French army and navy personnel stationed in the territory that would become Canada. While residents of the early colonies were not involved in these productions, they were beneficiaries of the theatres built by soldiers for their own performances. For example, in Halifax the soldiers built the New Grand Theatre, which opened in 1789 with a production of Shakespeare's *Merchant of Venice*.

The first professional theatre group to play in Canada was The American Company of Comedians in Halifax, Nova Scotia in 1768. By the 1780s, amateur theatres had begun to spring up in Newfoundland, followed quickly by companies in other colonies. These performances usually took place in town halls or taverns, typically with all-male casts. Often the biggest obstacle theatres faced at the time came from the church, both Protestant and Catholic, which still often compared theatres to brothels.

By the mid-nineteenth century, most Canadian towns had a stage, but few had real theatre buildings. The stage usually consisted of a raised platform at the end of a long room in the town hall. Some cities, however, had buildings resembling real theatres and they began bringing in professional companies, the majority from Britain. Canadian-born actor Graves Simcoe Lee was a member of one such company, and he wrote what is said to be the first play by a Canadian seen on a Toronto stage. *Fiddle, Faddle and Foozle* opened April 9, 1853, at the Royal Lyceum Theatre.

At the beginning of the twentieth century, resident and travelling companies from Britain, the United States and France were providing most of the professional theatre in Canada. There were often numerous travelling companies performing across Canada at the same time. With little local competition, touring in Canada was a profitable venture. One successful homegrown enterprise during this period was headed by Nova Scotia-born Harold Nelson Shaw. Shaw's self-proclaimed "all Canadian" company toured extensively, and successfully, throughout Western Canada from 1902 to 1910.

In its approach to theatre, Quebec was far ahead of other provinces. The period of 1898 to 1914 is often described as the "golden age" of theatre in Montreal. Not only was there a growing amateur movement, there were numerous professional theatres, and companies such as Théâtre des Variétés and Théâtre National were filling the seats. However, the boom ended with the First World War.

As the 1920s drew to a close, aspiring actors were still turning to amateur theatre, such as the burgeoning Little Theatre Movement, for their instruction, as it was often the only place to gain a training in theatre. The Margaret Eaton School of Literature and Expression in Toronto began classes in drama in 1906, but there were few other training opportunities until the Banff School of Fine Arts opened in 1933. As there was no other way to obtain experience, most learning occurred on stage, in front of an audience.

The travelling companies had sometimes given work to Canada's few professional actors, but once the Depression arrived even those theatres disappeared. After that, as a result of the great distances dividing parts of Canada, it seemed as though radio would be the only available means for the public to be exposed to drama or comedy, and the only source of work available to actors.

One exception to this disappearance of professional theatre was John Holden, who was courageous enough to set up a professional Canadian theatre company at the height of the Depression, in 1934, and managed to keep it alive until he left to fight overseas in 1941. By that time Theatre Under the Stars (TUTS) in Vancouver was into its second year, but it quickly became a summer theatre that presented only musicals, focusing more on singing and dancing than dramatic theatre. It also did not initially pay its actors.

If there was no professional theatre, there was, however, still amateur theatre. Herbert Whittaker said that when the Depression came and theatre companies left, "instinctively, people turned to their own, made their own theatre." In fact, amateur theatre was especially strong during the 1930s, aided tremendously by the Dominion Drama Festival, which began in 1932 to showcase little theatres across the country. In fact, many saw amateur theatre's growing influence through the Festival as a sign that Canada was finally ready to create its own Canadian national drama. Harley Granville-Barker was a well-known British actor, writer, and also an adjudicator for the Festival in the 1930s. In 1936, he wrote in *Queen's Quarterly* that Canada's fledgling actors and writers were ready and waiting, and if a national theatre scene was not established, Canada risked losing them to London, New York and Hollywood. And it would be our loss, he added.

It was into this environment in 1945 that a diverse band of people came together to return Canadian theatre to a professional status. First there were those who were already professionals prior to the Second World War, including Robert Christie, Jane Mallett, John Holden, Cosy Lee and Peter Mews. Mews (who later became identified with Matthew in *Anne of Green Gables*) was also part of a second group that played a role in theatre's development—those who had appeared in various musical revues (traditionally shows consisting of a series of topical sketches, songs and dancing) that entertained the war troops, both in Canada and overseas. Two of the companies, the Army Show and Meet the Navy, provided work for actors like Robert Goodier, Barbara (Davis) Chilcott, John Pratt and Peter Mews. Although hired by the Army Show as an actor, Mews also made another major contribution. He had trained as a designer prior to the war and when the large Army Show needed to be broken down into five smaller ones, Mews helped design the various sets.

Without a doubt, however, the largest collection of people to contribute to the post-war professional theatre boom in Canada came from the universities. "It was so exciting because things were happening," one of those students, actor David Gardner, said. "We were young and it was young and there was a marvellous feeling of being in the centre of something that had never happened in this country before. Everything we did was new and yes, there was a juice in the air that was marvellous."

In addition to the regular students, a number of returning soldiers used their Department of Veterans Affairs credits to attend university and, while there, became involved in theatre as an extracurricular activity. This created an advantageous situation in which the university drama groups had actors of varying ages and experiences to choose from. "[The returning veterans] were older than the average student and they did things very fast and learned things fast because there was a sense of urgency to it all," said Joy Coghill, who worked with a number of post-war theatres. "Having survived the war . . . if someone wanted to be an actor, a writer or a painter, by God they were going to do it. . . . What you chose to do, you didn't do lightly."

Many, surprisingly, chose the stage. Members of all these groups cared passionately about Canadian theatre. If there were no theatres, they would start them, and they refused to take no for an answer. Some held other jobs (including appearing in radio plays) but most worked full-time in the theatre. They put in twelve to sixteen hours a day on a regular basis, with little expectation of financial reward. There was a tremendous sense of camaraderie, and after their "regular" working day ended, they often stayed together and drank well into the night. It was, said Christopher Plummer, "a drinking era." With only a few hours sleep, they rose and went to work again.

Most companies were set up as repertory theatres—a resident group of actors staging a different play every week. They barely had time to take a breath between productions. "Sometimes you did quite phenomenal work because there was no time to waste," said Joy Coghill, who directed and appeared in thirteen plays in thirteen weeks one summer at the International Players in Kingston. "Usually in rehearsal what happens is that there is an initial reading where you actually grasp it in that moment. Then it takes you all the rest of the time to come back to feel that thing you discovered in the beginning. But when you only have six days you don't have time to go down and come back. You just get it, learn it and get it again and that's all there is."

"They were the cramming years," Christopher Plummer said of his time with the Canadian Repertory Theatre. "It was the best, the best training, in front of the public. You learn a lot more there than anywhere else. . . . Weekly rep was unbelievable. It was horrendous because we had matinees [too] you know. It was also great. One was young, you could do it." Weekly rep also taught actors the art of ad libbing. "People became masters of making it up when they didn't know what they were supposed to do," Coghill said. "People would say, 'excuse me a minute,' and rush off stage and look at their lines which were pasted on the outside of flats. Or they would have a book sitting beside them and as they were acting in the scene they would be 'presuming a piece of business' by looking in a book but they were actually reading their part."

Sometimes it was not only their lines they forgot, but their accents and their cues as well. Gertrude Allen was playing in J.M. Barrie's *Dear Brutus* for the Canadian Repertory Theatre, while also rehearsing every afternoon with a broad Welsh accent for *The Late Christopher Bean* by Sidney Howard. One night Allen was horrified in the middle of *Dear Brutus* to find she was talking with a strong Welsh accent. And once, in *See How They Run* by Philip King, Christopher Plummer heard his cue a moment too late and dashed onto the stage through the nearest opening he saw. This happened to be a cupboard on the set, which he totally demolished in the process, adding an unscheduled laugh to the comedy.

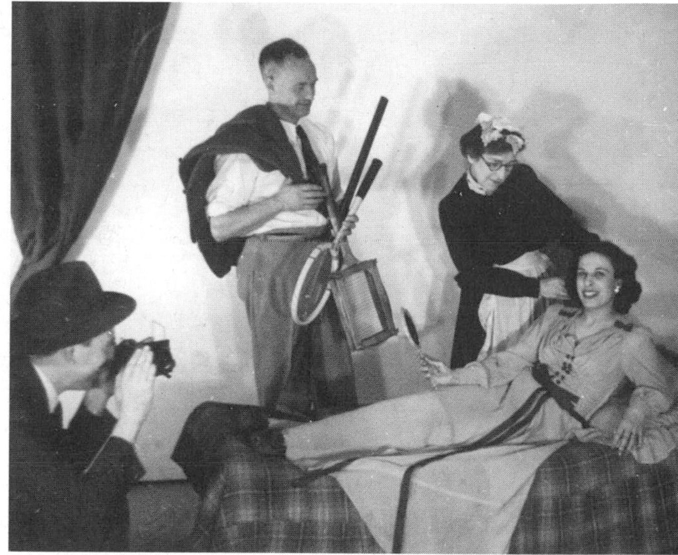

A group of actors in the Ottawa Stage Society setting up one of their scenes for a publicity photograph, c. June 1948. (MCNICOLL COLLECTION)

Just as the actors did not have weeks to prepare, neither did the directors. As a result, companies often purchased their scripts from Samuel French, Inc. Beginning in 1830, American Samuel French and his partner, British playwright and actor Thomas Lacy, pioneered the concept of providing published scripts to theatrical groups. These scripts also included the blocking for the plays, usually taken from New York's Broadway or London's West End productions. Joy Coghill recalled, "Usually you used the blocking that was in [Samuel] French's script, because there wasn't time to redo it all and the blocking was written on the sides, so you would arrange the floor plan as close as you could to the stuff written down in the brackets in French's scripts." This system was also invaluable to theatres that brought a star or well-known name in to play the lead. They had often played the role before, using French's blocking, and showed up only for the dress rehearsal. The play had already been blocked and rehearsed and the star would then just slip into the ready-to-go production, with Canadians filling all the other roles.

The Samuel French system also created problems for theatres, however. French sent out a kit, which included only one complete version of the play, as well as the pages for each character. Because of the cost to the theatre, actors received only these pages, not a full copy of the play. As a result, they memorized only their own lines and cues and, other than their own cue, they rarely knew what the other characters were saying. "You would get this very intense listening," Coghill said, "because I would be listening like mad to you, because my life depended on hearing the cue and coming in quickly with mine because they were usually comedies and they had to go fast."

Many of those who were involved with the early companies were young and idealistic, and hoped the theatres would flourish, creating a permanent, professional Canadian theatre. "It was a time in life when one was just sort of pressing on with a faint glow of hope on one's face, looking towards a very insecure future," Stratford's best-known actor, William Hutt, remembered. "Nonetheless it was exciting, simply because we never knew how far it was going to carry us all."

Initially, the companies they began did not carry them as far as they hoped. The wonderful beginning that each group embarked upon was too soon crushed, usually due to a mountain of debt. Actress Dorothy Davies was in on so many of these beginnings in British Columbia that she began to wonder if she was a jinx. Davies recalled that every time she turned around somebody was saying to her, "We are going to start a theatre and we feel it would be wonderful if you would be a part of this . . . because this is really going somewhere." Then the theatre folded. After being in on this enthusiastic beginning numerous times, Davies wanted to tell them perhaps they should try someone else.

It is hard to comprehend how most actors eked out a living in the late 1940s and harder still to understand how any company survived those pre-grant days. Most theatres managed to limp through only one or two years before folding. The lack of financial backing was the single biggest obstacle facing Canadian theatre. Many of the theatres were financially supported by the individuals who organized the group in the first place, people like Vancouver's Sydney Risk of the Everyman Theatre and Montreal's Open Air Playhouse's Rosanna Seaborn. Some theatres had "angels"—private individuals who quietly supported a theatre financially but stayed out of the day-to-day management. The only other outside financial help came from the occasional sponsoring of theatre productions by a Rotary or Kiwanis club. Clearly, it was obvious to everyone in theatre that government help was needed. Even before the war was over, in June 1944, actor David Gardner recalled that "there was the great march on Ottawa with the Arts and Letters Club, the Dominion Drama Festival, and John Coulter and people like that, to try and do something about the arts [when] the war ended."

With theatres calling out for financial assistance, in 1949 the government asked future Governor-General Vincent Massey to head a Royal Commission to look into the national development of the arts, letters and sciences, and suggest ways the government could encourage organizations in those fields. During the two-year study, Massey and four colleagues travelled nearly ten thousand miles across Canada, hearing briefs from various cultural groups. The majority of the briefs contained impassioned pleas for assistance, none stronger than those from the country's fledgling theatres. Theatres needed money to make rent and to pay their actors a living wage. Dorothy Somerset, a major theatre force in British Columbia, summed up the lot of the actor in Canada when she wrote in her brief that "Canada's theatre artists are almost destitute. There are very few acting companies to provide them with careers or professional opportunities."

Theatre people also stressed in their briefs that it was vital the government build theatres. After securing financing, theatres needed a location, but few found a permanent home. The Royal Ontario Museum was used by many Toronto theatres, while others operated out of high school auditoriums, town halls and makeshift theatres converted from spaces meant for other functions. The theatre community, along with many other artist groups, helped propel the commission to issue the most crucial recommendation in the 200,000-word Massey Commission report (Royal Commission on National Development in the Arts, Letters and Sciences). Released in May 1951, the report proposed "that a body be created to be known as the Canada Council for the Encouragement of the Arts, Letters, Humanities and Social Sciences."

The basic idea of a Canada Council seemed simple enough but, interestingly enough, it was an action in the United States that forced the government's hand when, in 1956, the Rockefeller Foundation announced it would soon end the many scholarships it provided in Canada in the fields of social sciences and humanities. With the loss of these U.S. funds, the Canadian government realized it had to act. In March 1957, the House of Commons adopted a bill establishing the Canada Council for the Arts, Letters, Humanities and Social Sciences. The Council came into being partly because of what the Royal Commission saw and heard in the comments and briefs from Canada's early theatre pioneers. The Canada Council's formation was too late, however, to save most of the theatres recorded in this book.

In addition to their financial woes, Canadian actors had no union during the early post-war period. Although a number of companies, such as Theatre Under the Stars in Vancouver and the Niagara Falls Summer Theatre, eventually followed the standards set by the Actors' Equity Association in the United States in 1913, actors were not unionized in Canada until after the opening of the Stratford Festival. According to Vernon Chapman, there had been a meeting in 1951 to discuss the feasibility of inviting the American union to organize performers in Canada. Among those in favour of the idea were Donald and Murray Davis of the Straw Hat Players and Michael Sadlier from the Peterborough Summer Theatre. In opposition to the plan were Vernon Chapman, Drew Thompson, Dora Mavor Moore, the International Players, and the New Play Society. The proposition was defeated, and a Canadian branch of Actor's Equity did not open until 1955.

Despite the long days, forgotten lines, terrible stages and low pay, actors, directors and other theatre professionals persevered because many of them believed they were involved in a special time for Canadian theatre. "Looking back, one, or at least I, was very hopeful. . . . I don't know why really, because one was perfectly dropping dead from what one was trying to do," Amelia Hall said about the efforts to bring professional theatre to Canada. She was involved with many of the early post-war theatres, most notably the Canadian Repertory Theatre, which she ran for a number of years.

"[We] thought we were doing a very important job," said another Canadian Repertory Theatre alumni, Peter Sturgess. Charmion King, who performed with many of the post-war Ontario theatres, agreed, "There was a tremendous amount of enthusiasm, and we started feeling that we could do it, that we were capable, and that we had talent. That was all that really mattered."

Others, while they hoped for the best, were too busy with mere survival to see what was taking place in front of them. "Working too hard to know," said Joy Coghill, that "we were pulling rabbits out of the hat all the way along."

"We were always conscious of the fact there should be a theatre, hoped there would be," remembered Sam Payne, one of the rare actors in those days who moved back and forth between theatres in British Columbia and Ontario. "However, I wasn't aware of pioneering and all that. We were simply involved in keeping going. When you were in a company, working most of the time under poor conditions, salary and space wise, you did your best. We had youth on our side which always helps."

"I wasn't going around deeply thinking 'we are pioneers' . . . I didn't think that at all," said Christopher Plummer. "In fact it was only a few years later I realized that we were unique. I think I was pretty selfish so I was really thinking of my own success more than what we were all trying to do. I was . . . fighting to be accepted."

Plummer wasn't the only one fighting for acceptance. In addition to bringing theatre to the major centres and smaller towns across the country, actors were also trying to bring an air of respectability to their chosen profession. Some theatres still came up against churches that viewed theatre, and all those involved with it, as sinful. Acting in general was not seen as a noble, or notable, profession. "You go, you're part of a rowing team or something like that and everybody adores you when you come home, but nothing much ever happened, at least in those days, when you did anything in drama," said Dorothy Davies, describing the attitude of the times.

This disregard for actors is illustrated by a 1953 incident involving Amelia Hall. She had been chosen by Tyrone Guthrie to be in Stratford's first season and had, subsequently, received high praise for her two roles. Because of Amelia Hall's contribution to theatre in Canada's capital, Ottawa Mayor, Charlotte Whitton, wanted to honour Hall by presenting her with a city-crested signet ring. Whitton was opposed in her motion by a city alderman, who pointed out that Hall was not an athlete. Feeling it would detract from civic honours to sports champions, the alderman scornfully asked,

A glum-looking Christopher Plummer, starring in the Canadian Repertory Theatre's 1950 production of *The Glass Menagerie*, with Amelia Hall and Janet Fehm. (MCNICOLL COLLECTION)

"What championship did Miss Hall win?" The mayor withdrew her motion. When they heard what happened, however, local athletes donated a sum of money, which was then presented by the mayor, along with some gifts, to Hall at Stratford.

Acting wasn't even recognized as a valid profession during the early post-war years. When questioned by the public about their careers, and they replied they were actors, many were asked, "Yes, but what do you do during the daytime?" or, "What do you do for a living?" David Gardner discovered the extent of this attitude first hand when he filled out his income tax form at the end of 1951, a year in which he had toured and performed with a theatre in Ontario. Gardner recalled what happened:

> At the end of that year I submitted my expenses, my income tax expenses for touring, for hotels, meals out, etc. as a touring actor. "What category are you?" I was asked. "Actor," I replied. My income tax form was returned to me saying "we have no category for actor in this country at this time so we have taken your expenses and we have re-classified you as a travelling salesman," which was not far off! Again, an indication of where we were in this country, professionally speaking.

The push towards professionalism in Canadian theatre involved not only those appearing on the stage but also those behind it. Paul Kligman recalled:

> We were in a learning process. The performances were there . . . I don't think we had to take a back seat to anyone in presentation. By that I mean design and creativity. We were more inventive in many ways than our counterparts in both New York and Great Britain simply because they had greater amounts of money available to them in order to do some of the magic that only theatre can do.

Directors, playwrights, stagehands and set designers were all working towards a higher level of excellence. And with a growing professional theatre scene and more productions to be reviewed, critics also had to learn their craft. Herbert Whittaker was one of the major critics of the day, and his growth as a critic included ten years at the *Montreal Gazette*. Whittaker learned his craft by being immersed completely in the Quebec theatrical scene, starting as a costume and set designer, before quickly moving on to directing. His involvement in all areas of the theatre gave him a more rounded look at the Canadian theatre scene than that of Nathan Cohen, the other major critic of that generation. While Cohen was seen as controversial, Whittaker was perceived as being gentler in his criticism of the actors, no doubt the result of his experience backstage.

Any overview of early post-war theatre would be incomplete without mention of the types of plays performed, and the Canadians who wrote some of them. Most of the summer repertory theatres relied solely on comedies, often farces, and thrillers, as murder mysteries were then called, and seldom did they vary that format. When they did, audiences, who were generally on vacation and looking for fun, stayed away. Among the most popular summer plays were the following:

| | |
|---|---|
| *Personal Appearance* | by Lawrence Riley |
| *Private Lives* | by Noël Coward |
| *See How They Run* | by Philip King |
| *Papa Is All* | by Patterson Greene |
| *While the Sun Shines* | by Terence Rattigan |
| *Night Must Fall* | by Emlyn Williams |

Whittaker recalled that the winter theatres had the opportunity and inclination to be more daring, as their patrons tended to crave more intellectual fodder:

> There is a strong Canadian character as you know and it is someone intellectual who is not overly passionate but is not insensitive to sentiment. And it has an appreciation of good words. I think that is something of a distinctive thing that our language is still a matter of concern to us. So plays that reflect that—I remember early productions in

> Toronto of *The Cocktail Party* [by T.S. Eliot] and one I did myself of *The Family Reunion*, another Eliot play. These were well suited to the theatre public. The Jupiter Theatre did Christopher Fry's *The Lady's Not for Burning*, first with Chris Plummer and later with Patrick McKnee. They were the kind of plays we wanted to see . . . they satisfied the audience need.

The post-war period was also the first time that Canada began to seriously produce its own plays. The Carnegie Foundation and Samuel French, Inc. had both made early attempts to encourage playwrights in Canada in the 1930s; the former started a playwriting competition in Alberta, while Samuel French launched a Canadian Playwrights series, offering up a range of one-act plays. In spite of these efforts, however, the plays were slow in coming. "There was always an effort, underlined, to have plays about the Canadian scene as such," Whittaker said. "It's taken years because unless you have a remunerative theatre you don't develop professional playwrights. Unless a playwright is working steadily at his craft and seeing his performances staged, he doesn't thrive and doesn't come to fulfillment."

Authors such as John Coulter (best known in Canada for his *Riel* trilogy), Herman Voaden, Elsie Park Gowan and Gwen Pharis Ringwood were already established playwrights prior to the Second World War. Their plays had been seen on many amateur stages across the country, and they had written numerous plays performed successfully on radio. While the number of new theatres springing up following 1945 gave them more of an opportunity to see their plays staged, it was still not easy to be a playwright in Canada, as Robertson Davies wrote to Amelia Hall in 1946:

> Writing plays in Canada is rather like growing oranges in Canada—it can be done if you are prepared to take an immense amount of trouble and fight a hostile climate and provide answers to all the people who want to explain to you that it is really cheaper to get all your oranges from the States. A performance of a play is immensely valuable to a playwright, because it gives him a chance to see what can be made of his play on the stage, how it appeals to an audience, and where he made his mistakes.[1]

Although his success as a novelist has overshadowed his earlier work, back in the 1940s and '50s, Robertson Davies was better known for his newspaper column, *The Diary of Samuel Marchbanks*, in the *Peterborough Examiner*, and as a playwright. As Samuel Marchbanks, Davies sometimes wrote about the plight of those in the theatre:

> Now what is the Canadian playhouse? Nine times out of ten, Fishorn, it is a school hall, smelling of chalk and kids, and decorated in the early concrete style. The stage is a small, raised room at one end. And I mean room. If you step into the wings suddenly you will fracture your nose against the wall. There is no place for storing scenery, no place for the actor to dress—and the lighting is designed to warm the stage, not to illuminate it.[2]

During those early years, Davies wrote *Overlaid*, *Eros at Breakfast*, *The Voice of the People*, *At the Gates of the Righteous* (all one-act plays), as well as *Fortune*, *My Foe*, *King Phoenix* and *At My Heart's Core*. In addition to Robertson Davies, among those helped most by post-war theatre were Lister Sinclair, Ted Allan, Morley Callaghan and Paul Gury. Sinclair and Allan produced numerous radio plays but Davies was the most prolific as far as theatre was concerned. Most of his one-act plays were seen at the Dominion Drama Festival, which helped to encourage Canadian playwrights, albeit at an amateur level.

At the professional level, however, it was the New Play Society that was most supportive of Canadian playwrights. In 1949–50 they staged an all-Canadian, five-play season. By comparison, out of the forty or so full-length plays at the Dominion Drama Festival that year, only six were Canadian, along with six one-act Canadian plays. Beginning in 1948, the New Play Society also staged the wildly popular yearly revue *Spring Thaw*, a series of skits about current events in Canada. Writers and actors contributed sketches that poked fun at themselves, other Canadians and various institutions. For the first time, Canadian playwrights began to allow Canadians to see their own culture reflected back to them. Mavor Moore recalled:

> What happened with *Spring Thaw*, and . . . other Canadian plays, all of which incidentally made money or broke even, [the audience] found themselves on the stage. [We] came to naturalism very late. The reason was that until after World War Two we had not really had a chance to see ourselves on stage. Not that there hadn't been Canadian plays. There had, and important ones which reflected us. But they tended to be literary plays or educational plays, which had not found an audience at all, even in the heyday of Hart House. *Spring Thaw* actually made fun of the better-known people in business and society and so on. They had to come and see it, see what people were laughing at. So for the first time we found this broad popular audience.

Totem Theatre in British Columbia had great success when they staged *A Crowded Affair*, written by Totem's own Norma Macmillan, a comedy about a British Columbian family. The theatre had three very good weeks of business. Macmillan said at the time that Canadians should enjoy plays about themselves, and that it was "good for us all" to laugh at ourselves.

Because of the success of their *Spring Thaw*, in 1949, the New Play Society transferred Morley Callaghan's *To Tell the Truth*, a Canadian play, from a very successful run at their usual location in the Royal Ontario Museum to the much larger Royal Alexandra Theatre. "It made, as I recall, $57," Moore said. "It made the transfer to the Royal Alex, which had housed only one Canadian show ever, and that was with *The Dumbells* [A group of Canadian soldiers turned singers near the end of World War One]. There had never been a Canadian play at the Royal Alexandra. That was the sort of breakthrough we were making to a different kind of audience and without, we thought, lowering our standards."

Other groups, such as the International Players and Jupiter Theatre, staged the occasional Canadian play but most summer theatres avoided them, as did the Canadian Repertory Theatre. "People might criticize me for not having done more Canadian plays because I only produced two in five years," Amelia Hall said, "but you had to do things, anything, that you thought would get people into the theatre. Of the two Canadian plays we did, they stayed away in droves from one. They came to the other because it was by Robertson Davies and they knew he wrote funny stuff in the newspaper every weekend."

Canadian plays to stage, money to operate, and theatres in which to perform: those were the immediate concerns in the post-war years, but without an audience everything else was for naught, and it was here that the actors faced their biggest obstacle. Selling less than 80 to 90 percent of the seats was a death knell for a theatre. "The big struggle at the Canadian Repertory Theatre and any other theatre at that time," Amelia Hall said, "was to make people aware of theatre, to think of it as something that was exciting, something you wanted to attend." Herbert Whittaker commented that the theatres of the day "had a common enemy, which . . . was the apathy of the public. You had to say, 'I will be heard. I must be paid attention to.' You were fighting not only for your own chance to be heard and seen, and the chance to do what you wanted most to do, but you were saying there must be a condition of theatre in this country more widely recognized than it is. In a sense, without knowing it, [the actors] were saying, 'don't settle for something that comes in a can or is tuned in by a button on a radio machine. Just wait for us, wait for us to come and perform for you.'"

And perform they did.

CHAPTER TWO

# EVERYMAN THEATRE

"We joined as I'm sure everybody else in that group did, with the same thought in mind—maybe this would be the beginning of theatre. It certainly didn't fail for any lack of enthusiasm on our part."

—ARTHUR HILL

At the end of the war in 1945, British Columbia had no professional theatre other than Theatre Under the Stars (TUTS), strictly a summer musical theatre. The province, however, had a strong tradition of amateur theatre. Both the Vancouver Little Theatre Association (founded in 1921) and UBC's Players' Club (1915) were active and vibrant theatre groups with good attendance. (The latter is still running today.) The Victoria Little Theatre Association started in 1931 and in the following year the British Columbia Drama Association (later Theatre BC) began its yearly festival of presentations from community theatres. There was also radio drama, which began in British Columbia in 1927. The arts in general were also represented by the Vancouver Symphony, founded in 1930, and the Vancouver Art Gallery in 1931. Professional ballet (1951) and opera (1960) would come later, although groups from outside Canada did perform earlier. Consequently, by the end of the war, Vancouverites were already exposed to a variety of the arts, but they were still waiting for the first traditional professional theatre to appear. That wait ended in 1946 with the opening of Everyman Theatre.

If there was one post-war group that was the epitome of what theatre in Canada in the late 1940s and early 1950s was trying to do, it was Everyman Theatre. Everyman toured, staged Canadian plays, often charged only 25¢ a seat, and operated an acting school. They also had alumni that left a permanent mark on the Canadian theatre scene's history, actors such as Arthur Hill and Ted Follows. The theatre's brochure stated the company's goals:

> The primary aim of the Everyman Theatre is the establishment of a highly trained, purely Canadian, professional company in Western Canada. Such an idea is the logical outgrowth of the Canadian amateur theatre movement. The Everyman Theatre offers young Canadians who wish to make drama their life work a chance to do so without leaving the country. It encourages not only the interpretative artists . . . the actors, but also the creative artists . . . the playwrights. By visiting the hamlets, towns and cities of the West, Everyman hopes to bring theatre right to the people, at prices which enable every person to attend.

It was the only theatre of the time that did it all.

The catalyst and chief financier for Everyman, Sydney Risk, was born and raised in Vancouver, and had for many years been pushing for a repertory theatre in Western Canada. After graduating from the University of British Columbia (UBC) in 1930, Risk continued to work there with the Players' Club, the university's extracurricular theatre group. In 1933 he went to England to gain further experience in professional theatre. Risk trained at London's Old Vic theatre school under the direction of Tyrone Guthrie, and then worked with a number of repertory companies. He came to admire the way they operated—maintaining a permanent company while providing an important training ground for young British actors. One company Risk worked with was the Everyman Theatre, a name he would eventually use for his own company.

Risk returned to Canada in 1938, and the following summer joined Dorothy Somerset to teach at UBC's Summer School of the Theatre. Risk also began teaching with the University of Alberta's Extension Department. There were no drama departments as such in those days; theatre was extracurricular.

Risk also spent six summers as head of the theatre division of the Banff School of Fine Arts. While there, he actively started the final drive towards his own theatre, picking out potential talent from his classes. Two of his Banff students from the summer of 1946, Ted Follows and Floyd Caza, found themselves, a month later, members of the theatre group Risk had worked towards for fifteen years. Risk dipped into the Banff pool to find one other member for Everyman, Lois McLean.

"I met him when I attended the Banff School in 1944 and 1945," McLean said, "and worked with him when he became Drama Advisor at the University of Alberta." McLean was also one of a group of students, under the name Provincial Players, that Risk toured around Alberta in the summer of 1946. She had nothing but praise for

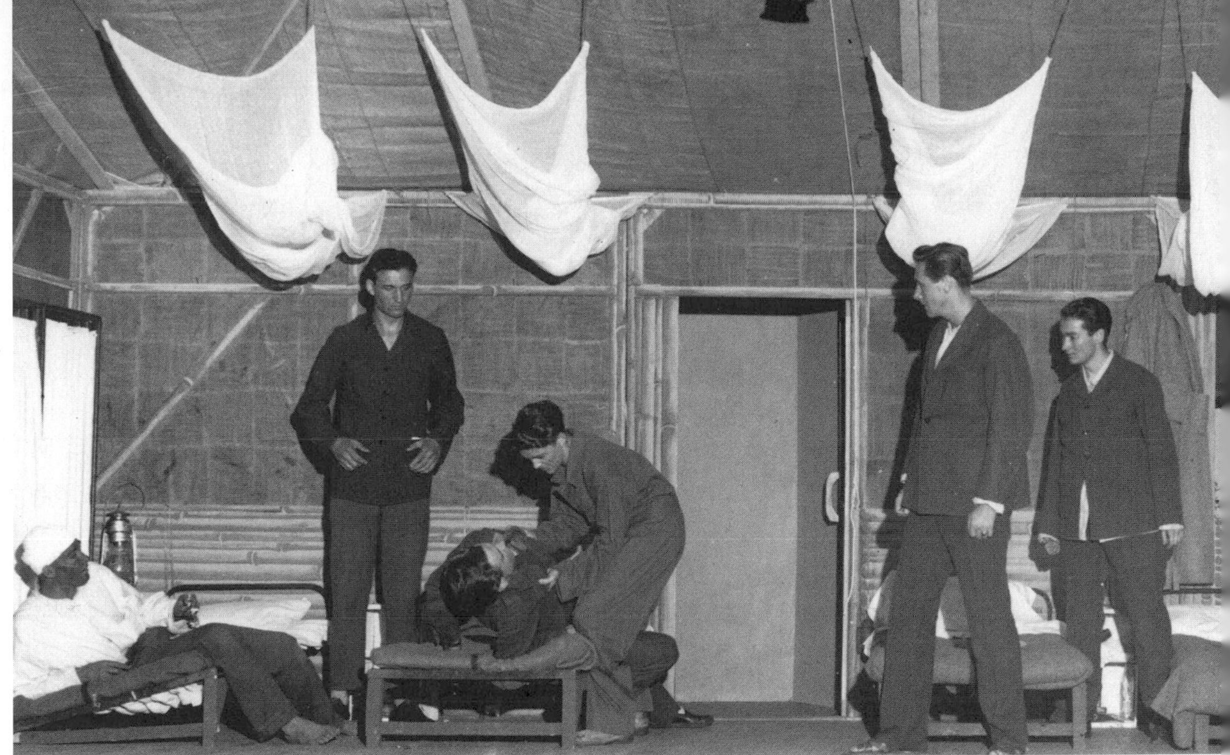

Floyd Caza (far left on bed) and Ted Follows (bending over centre stage) during a 1946 amateur production of *Stampede* at the Banff School of Fine Arts. After the performance, Sydney Risk asked both to join his Everyman Theatre. (MCNICOLL COLLECTION)

Risk. "He was a wonderful teacher . . . taught us as much as we would have learned in a regular drama program."

Two others joined Risk as founders of Everyman. George Brodersen, a professor of English at the University of Manitoba, had long been part of Manitoba's amateur theatre movement and provided some of the financial assistance needed to get Everyman off the ground. He also did most of the advance work for their first big tour. The third founder was the highly respected Dorothy Somerset. She was a member of the Extension Department at UBC, where she had managed to establish a few short drama courses and also promoted extracurricular drama activities. Her biggest contribution in this area was in 1938 when she founded the Extension Department's Summer School of the Theatre. Somerset ran Everyman's studio group of younger actors in training, some of whom in later years appeared with the theatre group.

The first members of the group came together in September 1946. In a typical "cut costs" fashion, this meeting took place at a cottage belonging to Risk's parents in Gibsons Landing on the Sunshine Coast. Money was a problem from day one for Everyman, with Risk and Brodersen's initial investment of $6,000 eaten up much faster than anticipated. They were determined to be professional, however, and the actors joining the group signed contracts and were paid salaries. Initially this was $10 a week with their rooms, when they had one, and meals provided free. Once on tour, the actors were supposed to receive $20 a week and another $20 for food. Often the money ran out before they were paid.

The Gibsons Landing cottage became the workshop and living quarters for the group. It was a communal effort, and everyone pitched in doing different jobs, whether it was secretarial, housekeeping or publicity. Rehearsals were in the morning and afternoon at the local community hall. After dinner at night they sat around the fireplace reading plays and discussing theatre. In addition to Risk, the theatre at this point consisted of nine actors: Lois McLean, Esther Nelson, Hilda Nual, Shirley Kerr, Floyd Caza, Ron Rosvold (who dropped out after a couple of months), David Major, Drew Thompson and Ted Follows.

Most of the group came either from little theatres or the Banff School of Fine Arts, but at least one was chosen as a result of auditions. "I still remember the audition I took," David Major said. "We had to do an improvisation. I remember how elated I was when I received this letter one morning saying I had been accepted by the group."

The name "Everyman" was chosen by Risk partly because of the English connection but also because the theatre stood for every man. All actors in the group were equal; there were no stars. Their longer name was The Western Canada Repertory Company. Everyman's inaugural play was Oscar Wilde's *The Importance of Being Earnest*, which they planned to tour throughout the Fraser Valley in the fall of 1946. Their transportation, such as it was, became the most irritating and sometimes frightening aspect of both that autumn tour of the Fraser Valley and their January to May 1947 tour of the four western provinces. In an effort to keep travelling costs down, Risk, with some financial contributions from the young members of his company, bought an old twenty-six-seat RCAF bus. It was cut down to twelve seats with the spare space made into a kitchen where cooking was done on a gasoline pressure portable stove. The bus was nicknamed "Agatha" and its life was to be much shorter than anyone anticipated. The group also had a second-hand twelve-ton truck, "Miriam," that carried the scenery, props and luggage.

In addition to rehearsing *The Importance of Being Earnest*, the group spent seven long weeks prior to their first tour making their own sets, costumes and furniture. They also studied the theory of drama and stagecraft, did body movement and voice exercises, all the while managing daily chores of cooking and cleaning. By November 1946, Everyman was ready to make its debut in Gibsons Landing, and it did so amidst opening night trials that included Floyd Caza ripping his pants, Sydney Risk losing the coloured slides for his lamps and an unofficial appearance by a mutt named Jigs who could not be kept off the stage by its owner, a little girl in the audience. When the dog was put outside, it went around the back and made a spectacular re-entrance via the stage door, to great applause.

Later in the month the company took to the road for the short tour of Fraser Valley towns from Ladner to Agassiz, and then back to West Vancouver. They returned to Gibsons Landing before Christmas in order to add two new plays to their repertoire, and four new members to the theatre.

The first of these new actors was Murray Westgate from Regina, Saskatchewan, who became involved in theatre through an amateur organization, even though he was studying commercial art at the time. After war service in the Navy he "was in the throes of trying to get re-established." All he knew was that he wanted to be a professional actor, and he was not going to be one if he stayed in Regina. Seeing an article on Everyman Theatre in a national magazine, he took a chance and wrote to Sydney Risk. "I knew they were only paying $10 a week and were a co-operative effort," Westgate said. "By George, Sydney Risk wrote back and said, 'Sure, come on out.'"

The next two to join were Arthur Hill and his wife Peggy Hassard. In the fall of 1946 they were asked by Risk to come and watch a production of *The Importance of Being Earnest* in West Vancouver, with the idea that if they liked what they saw, they would join Everyman. Born the son of the town's only lawyer in Melfort, Saskatchewan, Arthur Hill had been studying law at UBC prior to the war. After service in the Air Force, he returned to UBC and to the Players' Club. Peggy Hassard had done some amateur theatrics under Sydney Risk before and was also busy in radio. "I had made

In the fall of 1946, five Everyman Theatre actors offer their rogue gallery imitation as though in a police lineup. Left to right are Floyd Caza, Ted Follows, Ed McNamara, Murray Westgate and David Major. (MCNICOLL COLLECTION)

my stand in every direction of the theatre," Hassard said. "I had been interested in it from the time I was about seven or eight, and had always studied with the whole idea that I wanted to go into theatre."

Both she and her husband went to see the Everyman production. "It seemed to be on a pretty good scale," Hill said. "The sets were certainly impressionistic. They seemed to know what they were doing." Hassard added, "I think we caught some of the fire that Sydney had and felt it should be helped along." They accepted Risk's invitation.

The fourth addition to Everyman was Ed McNamara. Born in Chicago, he had held a number of different jobs and was something of a drifter until he came to Canada in 1939 to join the Canadian army. After he left the service, McNamara continued to take odd jobs and finally became involved with theatre early in 1946. He joined Everyman in December of that year.

For two weeks prior to Christmas, the group worked on Anton Chekhov's one-act comedy *The Marriage Proposal* and the Canadian play *The Last Caveman*, by well-known radio dramatist Elsie Park Gowan. First performed by the Edmonton Little Theatre in 1936, *The Last Caveman* was re-written by the author at Risk's request, keeping in mind the actors chosen to play the characters. Gowan dedicated the revised version to the Everyman actors who performed it. Her play went together with the Chekhov play as a twin bill, alternating with *The Importance of Being Earnest* on the other nights.

The choice of plays was somewhat unusual. Arthur Hill and Peggy Hassard felt Risk should have picked plays better suited to the audiences of small western towns. Hassard thought the Wilde play was a particularly poor choice. "Imagine farm folk," she said, "who worked hard for a living all day, going to listen to folks . . . talking about some subject they don't even understand."

"*The Last Caveman* . . . was all right but I don't think the audience got engaged with it," Arthur Hill said. "It was chosen because it was Canadian and by someone he knew. I liked her [Gowan] very much indeed, she was a lovely person. But the fact of the matter is, if you're going out to try to sell a theatre then you bloody well better get the best plays you can find that really grip your audience. . . . They loved *The Marriage Proposal*, but then Chekhov is superb."

January 1947 arrived and the plays and players were ready for the long tour. The first stop was Abbotsford, forty miles from Vancouver in the Fraser Valley, which they reached on icy, wind-swept roads that were a warning of things to come, as the West suffered through the worst winter in recorded history. The world premiere of *The Last Caveman* by a professional company was successful and the group left for the town of Hope. They were by this time, however, beginning to have grave doubts about the safety of their converted bus, which had a gaping hole in its floor and a broken heater. The doubts turned into abject horror on the third day when they reached the

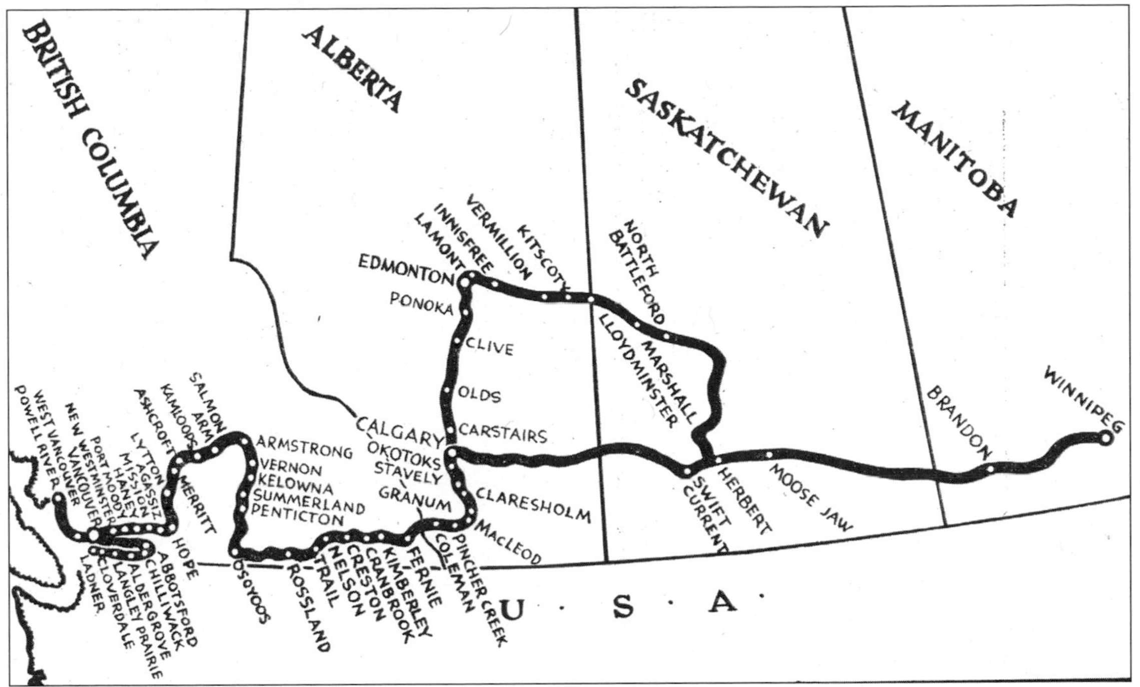


A map showing the gruelling touring route taken by Everyman Theatre during the coldest winter in recorded history. Yet they missed only one performance. (MCNICOLL COLLECTION)

Fraser Canyon which, in spite of its great beauty, had at that time a treacherous road with narrow steep bends. The crew joked at breakfast about it being "their last ride together."

Most of the driving was done by Sydney Risk, in charge of the bus, and Floyd Caza and Ed McNamara, alternating at the wheel of the accompanying truck carrying the stage scenery. The truck was definitely the safer bet. The bus was "just ornery, wouldn't steer properly, stop properly, and the engine finally conked out and all our prayers were answered," Arthur Hill said. The actors would never have to travel in it again. "We didn't even mind that it conked out on a very high road in the mountain," Peggy Hassard added. The place of its demise was, appropriately, Hell's Gate. Two of the men walked the few miles to Boston Bar and found someone to take the group to their next stop. Their ride ended up being in an open garbage truck. Lois McLean wrote of the tour that the driver "swerved round the Hell's Gate curves at a great pace after informing us that his brakes 'ain't too good, or too new.'"[3] The group made it, cold but alive, to Lytton, where they had to wait for a while before the truck arrived, making the curtain more than an hour late. It was the first time Everyman almost missed a performance but it certainly was not the last.

The day after the Fraser Canyon adventure, minus the two men still driving the truck, the members of Everyman took the train to Ashcroft, only to find they had to perform in a small room with no raised platform. Their solution was to secure four large tables together, and these served as their stage. The next night found them in a huge auditorium in Kamloops, and this diversity in stage conditions plagued them throughout the tour. Hill said that "the difference in quality between one town and another was unbelievable."

Some of the places were so cold there was frost around the doorways and the actors had to rub the makeup in their hands just to get it soft enough to put on their faces. Eventually the group became accustomed to adjusting their sets and themselves to fit whatever facilities were available. Their sleeping quarters were also precarious at best. The men had a room only every second night and on the alternate nights they slept on the stage in sleeping bags. Sometimes a few of them who had rooms would sneak the others in late at night. The rental rooms were not in five-star hotels either. "Some of them were beer parlours, as we used to call them," David Major said. "They had hotel rooms upstairs and they were pretty noisy." Lois McLean was in charge of finding the hotels they slept in, and once made a disastrous choice. She explained:

> There was an interesting experience at Trail [in B.C.]. I was in charge of booking hotels ahead. I used a rather old hotel guide, which seemed to work well—except in Trail. Floyd and Sydney ran upstairs in the chosen hotel, only to come tumbling down saying, 'No, no! It's now a brothel!' . . . I didn't live that one down for some time!"[4]

Everyman was rarely able to anticipate the type of reception they would receive in each location. In some towns, with only a population of fifty, they would play to a large audience because people in the neighbouring communities would come to see the plays. Then, in a large town, they would be in competition with another event and the audience was almost non-existent. "There was a curling bonspiel [tournament] on one night and we were in a small hall," Murray Westgate recalled about a town in Saskatchewan. "The stage was about the size of a table. . . . There were more people on the stage than in the audience. Then another person from the bonspiel would come over to watch the play. It was weird and the dressing room was cold. The windows were broken and the grease paint was hard as rock, frozen, as we were trying to put our makeup on. And there was only one bare bulb in the back behind the stage."

In addition to performing, all the actors had backstage responsibilities. Esther Nelson was in charge of lighting and her assistant was Ed McNamara, one of the more colourful members of Everyman. With a restless nature which he never lost, McNamara was not an easy assistant for Esther Nelson because he was easily distracted. "He always had visions of being a song and dance man," Murray Westgate said. "Whenever we were in an empty hall in the afternoon, setting up lights or something, Esther had a time getting him [to work]. He'd be singing 'if you knew Susie like I knew Susie,' and tap dancing across the stage pretending he was in front of an audience doing his thing."

Floyd Caza was the stage manager, a job he held later with other theatres in the East. Hilda Nual and Peggy Hassard were in charge of wardrobe while the props were handled by Murray Westgate. His was a difficult job as they were forever repairing the easily broken pieces of period furniture needed in the Wilde play. "We would tape up the legs and paint them white with scenery paint," Westgate said. "It was a very fragile thing, and we'd say, 'Now when you go on stage, don't sit on it, just pretend you're sitting.' They would just barely sit on it and do their lines. It would have fallen apart if they had really sat down."

The costumes were seldom cleaned because Everyman was never in one place long enough to have them done. "We had formal dress with white-winged collars," Westgate said. "You wouldn't get a chance to get the makeup off the collars so you covered it with white makeup so it wouldn't look so bad on stage."

Everyman was a remarkable group of people, Westgate said, but there were still days when one of them would say, "How did I get into this?" or, "If I could, I'd quit tomorrow." Ted Follows remembered one especially depressing morning when money had run out and the group debated whether to carry on. They did. Whenever one of them was down, someone else was always there to pick them up again. As could be expected, there were some flare-ups but these were short-lived and members of the group remember mainly the camaraderie between them all, the feeling they always had each other's backs.

"At Cranbrook, I wasn't playing that night so I took the cash box and returned to our hotel room," McLean said. "Two rowdy drunks followed me up the stairs. I managed to get into the room and lock the door. They banged on it and demanded entrance to see what was in the box. No phone in the room. The knocking subsided and I heard Sydney tapping at the door. I let him in." When McLean told him what had happened, Risk, who was a physically slight and delicate man, said he would go back to the theatre for reinforcements. On going out he met the two men who had returned and subsequently tried to throw him down the stairs. Risk escaped and finally made it back to the theatre. "So we all went and got some of the pipe irons we used to screw together to make the framework [for the curtain on stage]," David Major remembered. "We were going to find these people who did it and went marching down the street of this town with these iron bars. We never did find them. It was most fortunate for everyone!"

To break the monotony of the long tour the actors often played jokes on each other. In *The Last Caveman* there was a scene in which the father, played by Major, asks his son, played by Follows, to get him their gun. This often took the latter some time to do because Major usually hid it somewhere off-stage. One time he tied it so tightly to a doorknob that "his son" nearly didn't make it back on stage in time. "I thought, 'God, what have I done, he's not going to come back,'" Major said. "Another time, Ed McNamara wore gloves and there was a scene where he had to get some matches and a glass off this table so we glued the matches and glass of water to the table. However, the glue wasn't quite dry and all the matches stuck to his gloves. We had a hell of a time."

Their sturdy truck finally succumbed to the elements near Okotoks, Alberta, when the temperature dropped to forty degrees below zero. It was picked up a couple of months later when spring came to the prairies and Everyman was on its return trip to Vancouver. After losing the truck, the entire group took the train exclusively, using the 150-pound allowance to transport the scenery in the baggage car. Some of the group travelled with the scenery because they usually had only about five minutes at their stop to get everything off the train. One day some of the actors were sitting on a long box in the baggage car and found out on their arrival that it contained a body on its way to a crematorium.

One of the most amazing aspects of the tour was that in spite of the inclement weather, Everyman, often performing seven times a week, missed only one engagement. They were in a day coach on their way from Moose Jaw to Moosiman when the train was stopped by sixteen-foot-high snow drifts. They were told the tracks would be cleared soon and that the "train could leave at any time and not to go away." The train did finally leave—after the company had spent two days sitting in the day coach with no electric light and washrooms that were frozen up. They sped past Moosiman and staggered off the train in Brandon, Manitoba, more than fifty-four hours after boarding. There they performed all three of their plays in the City Hall theatre, ate, packed up the sets and props and then, still without sleep, took the train to Winnipeg at half-past five the following morning.

With every bad experience or frustration the company encountered, there was an amusing one as compensation. At one school matinee the curtains closed after the second of three acts of *The Last Caveman*. After a brief intermission the curtain opened and the cast began the final act, when suddenly somebody realized there was nobody out there. Because they had staged three scenes, the audience, thinking those were the three acts and the play was over, had all gone home!

The actors especially liked towns which gave them receptions that included food. "We didn't get that well fed on our $10 a week," Murray Westgate said. "Whenever the local people entertained us we just made pigs of ourselves. They'd be passing round the sandwiches, cakes and coffee and we were just diving into it because we were all so hungry."

For sheer colour and pageantry a small town in Alberta, Mundare, won the prize. It was predominantly Russian and "all the buildings had onion-shaped domes," Westgate said. On their arrival the actors were picked up by a horse and sleigh which transported them and the sets to the hall where they were to perform. On the way they saw something distinctive. "The tradition in the town, which went right back to Russia," recalled Arthur Hill, "was that on occasions like that at nightfall, maybe an hour before the performance, there was someone like a town crier with a bell, who went through the town."

"The hall was full," Murray Westgate said. "It was covered with sawdust and there was spitting tobacco on the floor. The audience loved [the play]. I don't think they understood a word of it but they loved it. It was quite memorable." *The Marriage Proposal* was especially popular in towns such as Mundare with large Russian or Ukrainian populations. The cast would get unexpected laughter whenever the words "kopek" or "rubles" were spoken.

Everyman was never on a strong financial footing at the best of times, and as the tour continued the circumstances worsened. Risk lost a great deal of his own money and some of his parents' as well. George Brodersen and Dorothy Somerset had also contributed money to Everyman. Meetings were frequently called when the situation became especially bleak. "The memory I don't want to have dropped was the fact that we were forever having crisis meetings," Arthur Hill said. The actors themselves even helped out whenever they could. "At North Battleford [in Saskatchewan], we didn't have enough money to buy our rail tickets onwards," Lois McLean said. "I sold my new portable typewriter, given to me by my parents on graduation, for $150, which went a long way towards purchasing the tickets."

With his many years of experience in theatre in England and his teaching in Canada, there was no doubt Sydney Risk was well qualified to run the theatrical side of the group. He also had many connections with people in the towns throughout the western provinces, and he had George Brodersen doing excellent advance work for him. The one thing Risk was not, however, was an astute businessman. He was so determined to bring theatre to the masses that ticket prices were kept unreasonably low.

"Sometimes we'd give matinees for I think about a thousand students or more, I forget exactly," David Major said. "He was charging them something like fifteen cents or a quarter—some ridiculous amount. We used to say to him that even if you get a million people in here you will never make any money charging that. However, that was the whole idea, to bring theatre to people who hadn't had it before, and they wanted everyone to be able to afford it."

Everyman arrived back in Vancouver in late April 1947. Soon after they appeared at the York Theatre in East Vancouver for a week where *The Last Caveman* received three curtain calls. They immediately prepared themselves for a short tour of Vancouver Island. At that point, some cast members decided to part company with the group, Arthur Hill and Peggy Hassard among them. "We could see Everyman was not really going to be what we had hoped for," Hill said. "We were just going through the motions. It did not come as a great revelation at the end."

The tour of the Island had been added to the original itinerary and both of them decided they had given enough and wanted to go back to working for the CBC in Vancouver. They were soon to leave Canada for other shores. "I think somewhere early on if you were interested in theatre you certainly had to look toward London or New York to see what was going on," Peggy Hassard said. "You hoped that it might happen in Canada but still, in the back of your head, you knew if you really wanted to strike out you would have to go away. I don't think we really felt it [Everyman] had failed. I think we had gone into it knowing it was going to be for a few months. It wasn't something, at least in my mind, that I expected would just go on and on."

"We were all eager people who wanted to have this [theatre] happen," Hill added. "If it had happened, really happened, we might never have gone to England. When you're that age you have hopes for your own country. Naturally you assume that whatever advances made are going to happen while you're here. . . . You know, when you're all under pressure, you go through terrible fallings out and coming togethers and all the rest of it. It was formative, absolutely formative, there's no question about it. You find that later in your life you make decisions about people based on things that happened there."

With Hill and Hassard gone, in late spring 1947, Everyman undertook its planned tour on Vancouver Island. They crossed on a paddle steamer and did a short circuit there. The lack of available theatres plagued them on the Island, as it had throughout their previous long tour. One night they played in an army drill hall that would normally hold four thousand soldiers but as the audience numbered only one hundred, they curtained off one end of it to make it more intimate.

After the Vancouver Island tour, it was unclear whether Everyman could continue. Risk knew that it was important for Everyman to hold on to a core of actors who, having gained experience, would pass their knowledge on to new members, but he had lost Hill and Hassard and now his advance man, George Brodersen, had left him as well. Moreover, no one could go on subsidizing his theatre, either directly out of their pockets or by taking abysmally low salaries. And Everyman still had no building to work from, which presented endless problems.

Risk was not one for quitting, however, and during the summer of 1947, Everyman found some new recruits; they also added George Bernard Shaw's *Arms and the Man* to their repertoire. They finally obtained permission from UBC to use some army huts on land it owned at Little Mountain. Risk hoped one of these could be turned into a theatre for performances but this was not feasible, although it did prove valuable as a workshop. One of the new recruits, Lillian Carlson, was a product of UBC's Summer School of the Theatre. In addition to her work with Everyman, she appeared with

Theatre Under the Stars, Totem, Vanguard and Avon Theatres. By the fall of 1947 the only original members of Everyman still with Risk were Lois McLean, David Major, Floyd Caza, Murray Westgate and Esther Nelson.

Their second season opened with a student matinee performance of *The Importance of Being Earnest* at Richmond High School and an evening performance at the same location for the general public. Risk had sought, and received, permission to use school auditoriums, a move which did a great deal to save Everyman from immediate extinction. They also staged *Arms and the Man*, taking both productions on a fall tour of the Fraser Valley and the Okanagan. At this point Murray Westgate bowed out of the company. He had become involved with radio, and his allegiance now lay with it, but he also felt the second year of Everyman was different from the first. "I could see the writing on the wall," Westgate said. "It wasn't going to work. I think Sydney lost all his money. He never made a cent. . . . The idealism was gone in the second year."

In spite of a dwindling cast, Everyman still toured the Fraser Valley and the Okanagan in the fall of 1947, but found its financial instability necessitated abandoning a four-province tour similar to their first one. Even the shorter tour added to the company's already heavy debt, and in order to try to bring money in and save the theatre, plans for a Vancouver playhouse were sped up. They planned to open in February 1948 with a repertoire of seven plays. All this exercise did was tip the financial scales even further against them, and February, instead of being the month of hope, almost saw the death of Everyman. Those running the group were deeply discouraged for a time. They retreated to lick their wounds and search for new opportunities. It was certainly the end for most of the cast members who had been with the group from its beginning. In spring 1948, David Major left for England and Drew Thompson and Floyd Caza moved east.

Despite all odds, by the late summer of 1948 the fortunes of Everyman had once again improved. Risk realized the group's best chance for survival was to abandon his plans for a permanent playhouse and continue his affiliation with the school system. They would choose two or three plays each season, at least one of which was suitable for elementary students, plus one for high school students and the general public. Risk found sponsors for the first two plays, scheduled for the fall of 1948. The adult play was the previously performed *Arms and the Man* and, for their first foray into children's theatre, Everyman picked *The Emperor's New Clothes*, written by a specialist in young people's theatre, American Charlotte Chorpenning. They chose this play because it had previously been mounted at UBC's Summer School of the Theatre. With the university's permission and cooperation from the Vancouver Little Theatre Association, Everyman obtained the use of the costumes and settings from the previous production. They also used most of the original UBC cast, augmented by members of their own group. This was another turning point for Everyman as it changed, for a time only, from semi-professional to mainly amateur. Most of the actors came from UBC's Players' Club or Summer School of the Theatre.

Ticket selling and advertising became easier and less expensive through the school system. This, in addition to the now basically amateur status of Everyman, kept operating costs at a minimum and made the theatre competitive for the public's entertainment dollar by being able to charge low admission prices. Seats ranged from 25¢ to 75¢. Everyman paid all expenses and received 80 percent of the first $100 collected and 50 percent of the remainder. The rest went to the play's sponsors.

For two seasons Everyman continued to present plays in this fashion and worked towards being a completely professional theatre again. In October 1949, they presented Chorpenning's dramatization of *Little Red Riding Hood* for the first time, and they also staged *Noah* by André Obey. As an amateur group, Everyman presented the latter at the 1950 British Columbia regional finals of the Dominion Drama Festival and, winning there, went on to represent the province at the national finals. Present in the cast were Thor Arngrim (of later Totem Theatre fame), Lillian Carlson, Ron Wilson, Peg Dixon and original Everyman member Lois McLean. They did not win at the nationals and, when they returned to Vancouver, Sydney Risk, who had not been well for some time, was forced to rest for a number of months.

The Dominion Drama Festival had brought Everyman back into prominence on the Vancouver theatre scene, and while convalescing, Risk began to look again for a building to house his theatre. This time he was successful. Although little more than an old dance hall above a grocery store, a tiny theatre on Main Street in Vancouver finally gave Everyman a home. Planning a larger repertoire than in previous seasons, with five adult and three children's plays, Risk opened in January 1951, with Ibsen's *Ghosts*, which was, proclaimed the *Vancouver Sun*, "a sterling performance." The play starred Joy Coghill, an individual who spent the next two seasons giving her heart and soul to Everyman. Although she appeared in some adult plays with Everyman, Coghill's main love was their children's division, and it was with her as artistic director that the group's theatre for young people became a driving force. (Years later, in 1953 Coghill would found Holiday Theatre, the first professional children's theatre in Canada. She acknowledged that her time heading up Everyman's Children's Theatre gave her the groundwork for Holiday Theatre to be a success.)

In Everyman's first season in the Main Street theatre, beginning in January 1951, Coghill did two children's shows—the previously successful Chorpenning adaptation of *Little Red Riding Hood* and a version of *Hansel and Gretel* written by a theatre member. The latter was so popular it was held over and a projected third play had to be cancelled. Among the Everyman adult plays that year were a Canadian premiere of

Jean Paul Sartre's *The Flies* and a play directed by Coghill that produced the biggest hit of Everyman's first season in their new theatre—the musical melodrama *Will the Mail Train Run Tonight?* (also known as *Love Rides the Rails*). The year had built a foundation under the group's feet and it was a busy time, Coghill remembered:

> We cleaned, we answered the phone and we did, of course, the rehearsing and acting, the making of costumes. We learned by a very, very tough apprenticeship. It taught us a lot. We didn't get paid. We did everything and then we divided the profits at the end of the week on a space that only held 125 people as I remember [it actually held only 100] . . . some weeks only $10.

Performances ran from Wednesday to Saturday, and there were also classes in speech and movement taught by Dorothy Somerset and Joy Coghill. In the fall of 1951, Everyman produced T.S. Eliot's *Murder in the Cathedral* (originally written to be performed in Canterbury Cathedral in 1935). At the invitation of a minister, Everyman staged a special presentation of the play at a local church in December 1951.

Ron Wilson and Joy Coghill starring in Everyman Theatre's production of Ibsen's *Ghosts*. (COGHILL COLLECTION)

The 1951 season was a success but the roller-coaster ride of Everyman was heading downhill again in 1952 when they learned their theatre building was too old and was now slated for demolition. In September 1952 they took over an old building on Hastings Street called The State Theatre. It was yet another beginning for Everyman. Dorothy Davies was asked to play Lady Macbeth in a large production of Shakespeare's play. "[Risk] had a very good company of young people," Davies said. "He took over a theatre and fixed it and cleaned it up. It was changed from a burlesque house into a legitimate theatre."

It was renamed the Avon Theatre. To acquire it, Risk entered into a special arrangement with the owners of the building. He agreed to renovate the building and share some control of Everyman, and in return received a low rent and financial investment in the company. The deal, the details of which have never been revealed, would ultimately bring an end to Everyman Theatre.

Because of the agreement, Everyman had to abandon the use of the repertory system with its resident cast. Gone also was the intimacy between actors and audience as they now performed in an eight-hundred-seat theatre. The previous close-knit feeling within the theatre group vanished as the business of making money became of foremost importance. In addition to Dorothy Davies, the *Macbeth* cast included

Juan Root as MacDuff and a top United States actor of the day, Dean Goodman, was imported for the lead role.

Packed houses greeted almost every performance in the two-week run and it appeared as though Everyman might at last be assured of stability and a permanent place on Vancouver's theatre scene. A one-week run of Oscar Wilde's *The Importance of Being Earnest* followed, directed by Risk and starring London actor Richard Litt. Another imported talent, Zasu Pitts, starred in their next production, *The Late Christopher Bean*, a Sidney Howard adaptation of a French play by René Fauchois. Crowds were good but none equalled the earlier *Macbeth*, and Everyman also faced stiff competition for the public's dollar that autumn from Totem Theatre (see Chapter Three). Costs were up and revenues down.

Then in November 1952, the group presented a double bill that would once again set Everyman on the brink of collapse—Christopher Fry's *A Phoenix Too Frequent*, starring Dorothy Davies, and *Down in the Valley* by Kurt Weill. Others in the casts were balladeer Ed McCurdy, Jimmie Johnston, Jessie Richardson and John Emerson, and there was an additional expense which accounted for the high production costs—a fifteen-piece pit orchestra, conducted by Laurence Wilson, needed for *Down in the Valley*. Everyman staged two more plays before Christmas 1952 but rumours of financial problems were so rampant that Risk had to issue a statement in December to assure the public the theatre would carry on.

"By the time Christmas of 1952 came, things were not going well at all, and Sydney had a lot of bills," Dorothy Davies recalled. "That was when we decided to do *Tobacco Road*." This decision would lead to enormous notoriety for Everyman in 1953. The issue turned into the biggest censorship case of the post-war theatre scene in Canada.

*Tobacco Road*, a Jack Kirkland adaptation of a novel by Erskine Caldwell, originally opened in New York to poor reviews in 1933. Neither the critics nor the audiences liked it and even if it did survive, censorship problems seemed a certainty with its gritty and earthy depiction of poor tenant farmers. Then sociologists began pointing out that the play was a realistic portrait of life among impoverished whites in Georgia, and it seemed the tide might be slowly turning in its favour. To keep the play going on Broadway, the cast took a salary cut, but *Tobacco Road* was still in jeopardy until it was taken over by a cut-rate ticket agency. From then on everything was positive and the play finally closed in New York after a monumental 3,182 performances. In the beginning, *Tobacco Road* was staged as a serious drama but as time passed much of it was played for the humour.

Although the play became popular in New York, it was not to be as lucky on the road, where it was banned in many cities. In 1935, the mayor of Chicago saw a performance of *Tobacco Road* after it had been running in his city for five weeks. Horrified, he immediately cancelled the theatre's licence. A number of appeals were launched but none was successful, and the play was not staged again in the windy city.

In spite of its chequered career, *Tobacco Road* had at least two runs in Canada prior to the Everyman 1953 fiasco in Vancouver. The Niagara Barn Theatre staged the play in September 1951 and the International Players of Kingston in the late spring of 1952. The latter not only performed *Tobacco Road* without incident, it was also the greatest financial success for the group up to that time.

Everyman Theatre opened *Tobacco Road* to capacity crowds at the Avon Theatre in Vancouver, on Wednesday, January 7, 1953. It was announced as "Adults Entertainment only," with no one under eighteen allowed into the theatre. "It was a good show," said its director Dorothy Davies. "It looked nice and had good colour." Davies was the first woman in North America to direct *Tobacco Road*, and, at the time, she had doubts about whether she was perhaps a little too prudish to do justice to the script.

Davies need not have worried about her supposed prudery getting in the way; opening night reviews for *Tobacco Road* in Vancouver proclaimed that the play was "enacted with realism and convincing sincerity." The setting was felt to be authentic, and many of the actors turned in outstanding performances. One interesting casting note was that of Jim Peters, who played the female role of Grandma. The play was nearing the end of the first week of its run when one or two members of the audience complained to the police about obscenity in the production. In those days if anyone filed a complaint against a certain show, the police would be obliged to send a couple of officers to view a performance.

The officers attended the production on Wednesday, January 15, and the next morning Everyman received a warning from city police morality officers. The message was clear: clean up the production of *Tobacco Road* or close the doors.

What was causing the commotion? The setting was a squalid shack where Jeeter Lester lived with his wife, mother and two of his many offspring. It was set in the back country of Georgia, on land once used for the profitable raising of tobacco, but which became desolate ground when it was poorly cultivated for the growing of cotton. The various members of the family were dressed in filthy, torn garments as worn-out as the rented land they lived on. The characters sit around lazily, taking verbal, and sometimes physical, pot-shots at each other. Two of the children are still at home. Ellie May is an eighteen-year-old woman with an attractive figure but also a harelip which causes her to talk with difficulty. Most of the time she does not make anything more than animal-like guttural sounds. Dude, sixteen, is a slow-witted boy with nothing but hatred and contempt for almost everyone around him. The only genuine feelings of caring shown are between Ada, Jeeter's wife, and Pearl, their twelve-year-old daughter who Jeeter married off to the neighbour, Lov, in exchange for $7.00. Another neighbour,

Sister Bessie Rice, a somewhat unorthodox preacher of forty, takes it upon herself to marry Dude Lester in spite of their age difference.

The dialogue of *Tobacco Road* is liberally sprinkled with "go to hell," "shut up," "By God and by Jesus," "goddamn you" and the occasional "son-of-a-bitch"—strong language for a play in 1953. There are also numerous references to various family members sleeping around, especially Jeeter and Ada. Jeeter is informed during the course of the action that Pearl is not, in fact, his daughter. In spite of all these obvious insults to common decency, it was the events that were implied rather than overt that precipitated the obscenity trial.

"After the police sent people on the vice squad to look at the show," Dorothy Davies said, "they decided that Jeeter was urinating on the stage and that sexual intercourse took place on the stage." While the script does not call for intercourse to take place on stage, it does call for two scenes which involve sexual teasing or, at the most, are a crude form of foreplay. One involved Ellie May and Lov, the sex-starved husband of Pearl. In another incident, Bessie gets Dude sexually aroused during a scene before their marriage. Both of them call for a great deal of rubbing and petting but nothing beyond that. Nevertheless, the detective and the policewoman who viewed the show on behalf of the police department described the show as "lewd and filthy."

Everyman producer Sydney Risk appeared with a delegation before Vancouver's mayor Fred Hume to protest the police order of "clean up or close down." He also met with City Prosecutor Gordon Scott. Risk declared that the theatre would continue to run *Tobacco Road*, even if it was ordered to close or was faced with prosecution under the Criminal Code of Canada. The night following the visit by the vice squad, Risk spoke to the audience to tell them he thought people should be allowed to decide for themselves what they wanted to see in the theatre. He received thunderous applause. Newspapers, magazine editorials and letters of the day supported Risk's view. After his speech, it became clear to authorities that Everyman was not going to pay any attention to the police edict and would continue to stage the drama without changing anything. At the time, Risk said, he had been told it didn't matter if they cleaned up the play; they would be charged anyway. The morning of January 17, Gordon Scott confirmed charges would be laid. The only questions left were who would be charged and when.

The answers were not long in coming. That night police were standing by, waiting to arrest five of the cast members when the first act was over and the curtain came down, but the curtain never came down that night. The actors stalled the action of arrest by merely dimming the lights. Faced with having to make the arrests on stage in front of some one thousand patrons, the police waited. During the second act the cast made entrances and exits through carefully calculated routes, thwarting the police in their efforts. The management asked technicians, stagehands and even reporters, to jam the wings, making it even more difficult for the officers to reach the actors they wanted to arrest. Police called for reinforcements, and at the opening of the third act they marched out on to the stage and made the arrests. The audience screamed and jeered, some shouting "Gestapo," even as Sydney Risk tried to keep them calm.

Taken into custody at that time were Douglas Haskins (Jeeter), Douglas Hellier (Lov), Ted Babcock (Dude), Tamara Dlugo (Ellie May) and Louise DeVick (Sister Bessie). They were taken to the police station at ten in the evening and were finally released two hours later on $100 bail each, paid by theatre operator Charles Nelson. In the meantime, patrons at the theatre were given free coffee and impromptu entertainment by the remainder of the cast with the help of two fellow actors in the audience—John Emerson and Bruno Gerussi. Those arrested arrived back at the theatre close to midnight to finish the third act, and were greeted with a screaming ovation from the audience, only a few of whom had left.

The five actors had been charged with being in an indecent show, for which they could be jailed and fined $20. The following day Charles Nelson, director Dorothy Davies and producer Sydney Risk were charged with permitting an indecent show. Earlier in the day, Everyman obtained a Supreme Court injunction to prevent further police raids on the Avon Theatre. They had learned that the police would likely repeat Friday's raid and then oppose the granting of bail. The City Prosecutor's office moved to have the injunction set aside. As might be expected, the controversy had created huge lines at the box office and a phone that never stopped ringing. However, a few days later Everyman set aside the injunction and announced the play would not be performed again until the court case was resolved.

The trial for the first of the defendants, Douglas Hellier, began in Police Court on January 28, 1953. The author of the novel on which the play was based, Erskine Caldwell, flew in to be of any assistance he could to the defence. The book, which he had written twenty years earlier, was removed from newsstands in Vancouver the week prior to the trial. Caldwell said Jack Kirkland's play was faithful to the novel in all respects and told the court that *Tobacco Road* had been performed somewhere in the world at least once every twenty-four hours since 1933. The court was also informed that the play had been included in a book of the twenty best plays of American theatre.

Most of the legal proceedings consisted of the prosecution bringing in witnesses to call the play "filth" and the defence countering with people stating that they were not corrupted by the performance. Crowds at the trial were large, and it was front page news in all the papers. Letters to the editor, which came in great numbers, were greatly in favour of *Tobacco Road*. Six witnesses were called at the trial for the Crown to say the play was obscene but defence responded with twenty-one witnesses, including clergymen and university professors. Both Sydney Risk and Dorothy Davies were called as defence witnesses for Hellier's trial. Davies, who actually received some

Erskine Caldwell, who wrote the original novel, is surrounded by the cast of *Tobacco Road* in 1953. Caldwell flew to Vancouver at his own expense to testify on their behalf during the largest censorship trial in Canadian theatre history. (*VANCOUVER SUN*)

phone threats throughout the trial, was on the stand for almost two hours and took complete responsibility for anything her actors did on stage.

Douglas Hellier was found guilty of participating in an "indecent, obscene and immoral" performance, as were almost all the others in the final judgement brought down by Magistrate W.B. McInnes, who said the play catered "to the lower instincts" of the audience. The only one to escape the guilty rap was producer Sydney Risk. Charles Nelson, charged as manager of the theatre, was fined $50 or thirty days in jail. Dorothy Davies faced a $20 fine or ten days in jail, as did the remainder of the defendants. In each case the fine was the maximum allowed under the Criminal Code at that time.

Naturally, an appeal was launched immediately. A committee was formed by prominent Vancouver citizens to raise money for the appeal. All the profits Everyman had made with *Tobacco Road* had been eaten up by the trial. The actors convicted did not even have enough money to pay the fines, let alone to cover an appeal. Charles Nelson paid the total of $170 for the entire group.

The appeal lasted for only slightly more than three hours in County Court on March 17, 1953. The hearing was the first time during the case that the real issue of what was at stake was named. The prosecution chanced to use the word "censorship" and Judge J.A. McGeer, who presided over the proceedings, immediately said, "Ah, the ugly head of censorship." The judge threw out the convictions on the basis that the defence witnesses who had seen the play were a good cross-section of society and had not found the production obscene. No sooner were the convictions thrown out of court than the management of Everyman announced it might reopen *Tobacco Road* after Easter in order to clear up its debts.

Between the closing of *Tobacco Road* in January and Easter, Everyman had staged a number of other plays and had also taken *Tobacco Road* on tour to Victoria and then Seattle with Bruno Gerussi in the role of Skeeter—all the while the obscenity case was before the courts. In Victoria there was opposition from the Catholic Women's League and the production, staged at the York Theatre, lost money. Everyman's financial situation was worsened by the stay in Seattle, where they received poor reviews and even poorer audiences. Plans for an extended tour were shelved. The regular schedule continued in Vancouver with Moss Hart's *Light Up the Sky*. "That was a production we did with very much the same people and much the same problems in the play that are in *Tobacco Road* actually," Dorothy Davies said. "But nobody notices it when you dress beautifully and you're drinking champagne. It is only when you look wretched and poor it causes great offence."

A Crown appeal was made a month later to the British Columbia Court of Appeal to reverse the decision which had thrown out the convictions. This appeal, a test case against only one of the seven, Douglas Hellier, was successful and the conviction stood.

The issue had finally reached its conclusion. An appendix to the story, however, reveals "how quickly they forget." A year and a half after the *Tobacco Road* debacle, Dorothy Davies directed a production of Arthur Miller's *The Crucible*, which represented British Columbia at the Dominion Drama Festival. Davies won the Louis Jouvet Award as best director. In recognition, the Vancouver City Council awarded her a civic medal, the first one to be given to an artist. "One year I'm having all this [the obscenity charges] done to me," Davies said, not missing the irony, "and then all of a sudden I become a hero."

*Tobacco Road* was not yet put to rest in Vancouver, however, as it was staged again at the Avon theatre to good crowds. But while the play continued on, it was not presented under the banner of Everyman Theatre. Sydney Risk pulled his support and, at the end of the 1952–53 season, left the partnership and the Avon, taking the name of Everyman with him. Being in a partnership with businessmen took too much control of the theatre out of his hands. Risk did not like the commercial direction in which the company was moving, and he resented the implication in the press that *Tobacco Road* had been staged for publicity purposes only. The mounting debt also played a role in his decision. Risk chose to let his long-time dream die and retired the name "Everyman Theatre," for which he owned the copyright.

At its best, Everyman Theatre had been "the kind of theatre which if it had existed when I was starting out, I would not perhaps have had to go so far from my own country to get experience and earn a living," Risk said in the Everyman Theatre program for the 1946–47 winter tour. Sydney Risk's role in the development of professional theatre in Canada would not be forgotten. The Jessie Richardson Awards that honour the Vancouver theatre community named an award after him—the Sydney J. Risk Prize for Outstanding Original Script by an Emerging Playwright.

CHAPTER THREE

# TOTEM THEATRE & THEATRE UNDER THE STARS

"The shows were of a very high level . . . maybe just a notch or two below what you would see on Broadway in those days."

—PAUL KLIGMAN ON THEATRE UNDER THE STARS

The other major post-war theatre in British Columbia was actually started by two men who had worked with Sydney Risk and his Everyman Theatre—Thor Arngrim and Stuart Baker. They founded Totem Theatre in 1951 but before they reached that point they worked with a number of other theatres, both amateur and professional. One of these theatres was considerably smaller than Everyman and certainly survived for a much shorter duration, but as with all the theatres, it gave Arngrim and Baker valuable experience.

The Island Stock Theatre Company was formed by Juan Root, and its home was on Bowen Island, a short ferry ride from Vancouver. In the summer of 1947, Root's company hit the road, or more accurately the water, for a ten-week tour of small towns and resorts. They played in nearby Gibsons Landing on Mondays, Horseshoe Bay on Tuesdays and Wednesdays, Deep Cove on Thursdays, and Fridays found them back at home on Bowen Island. They also appeared once in Vancouver.

It was a combination repertory company and school. "Juan Root was an American actor who had a scheme," Sam Payne recalled. "In America they took on students who paid a fee to come and act," while the balance of the company consisted of professionals. Root decided to follow this path, and among the professionals who appeared with his company were Sam Payne, Frank Lambrett-Smith and Dorothy Davies.

They all lived in cottages on Bowen Island, travelling mostly by ferry, "a very small ferry," Dorothy Davies remembered. "The result was that, as you had to take good care of your costumes and scenery, those things had the major area on the ferry, and the actors hung on to the outside as well as they could. It was quite amusing."

It could also be dangerous because ferry travel in those years was a little rough at the best of times. During one particularly stormy trip, the boat was also carrying a number of American tourists, including a mother with a child who was seven or eight years of age. Thor Arngrim recalled, "She turned to me, terrified, and she said, 'you will save my child.' I was only sixteen. I had to tell her the truth. I said, 'I won't be saving your child because I'll be drowning. I can't swim.'" He remembered thinking no one would be helping him either because they would be busy saving the scenery. "Keep it up high and dry; to hell with the actors. You can always get more actors!"

The company's financial situation was precarious at best. "We were not being paid toward the end [of the summer]," recalled Dorothy Davies. "We more or less finished off because we had a commitment to the audience, not a contract." The company succeeded in offering a tour of the Vancouver suburbs and nearby resorts that fall, but that was the end of it.

However, among the students with the theatre were two young men who, four years later, left their mark on Vancouver's theatrical landscape when they began Totem Theatre. "In the Island Theatre were Stuart Baker and Thor Arngrim," Davies said. "They were very young and inexperienced but they did a lot of work to try and make [Juan Root's theatre] go."

"They came as students," Sam Payne said. "They were only about eighteen or nineteen. One day Thor said to me, 'You know I'm going to run my own company one day and you can be in it.' I said, 'Just let me know,' and that's what happened." Arngrim and Baker met at a Vancouver Little Theatre audition. They knew instantly they were destined for friendship. "Yes, right away, totally," Arngrim said. "Stuart was really, intensely involved in the theatre psychologically; he was in the theatre, radio, and he was recording. And he wanted to do things. And he wanted to produce, write. . . . It was a miracle. I thought at the time, 'This is so bizarre to meet someone that you connected with on this level.' You could go for years and never meet anyone like that."

The two men had taken very different routes to that Vancouver Little Theatre audition. Thorhallur Marven Arngrimsson was born as Wilfred James Banin in Regina on November 25, 1928, and was adopted from a Salvation Army orphanage as a youngster by the Arngrimssons, an Icelandic farming family from Mozart, Saskatchewan. He knew from the beginning that he wanted to be involved in acting, starring in every

A collage of photographs of Thor Arngrim (left) and Stuart Baker, the two young men who founded Totem Theatre and kept it going for three years in spite of numerous obstacles, c. 1952. (ARNGRIM COLLECTION)

production at his one-room school and even creating elaborate lighting for the productions with gas lamps, apple crates and reflectors. "I was always very into producing the overall picture," he said.

His parents took him to all the touring shows. Understanding that small town life was not for him, they gave him their blessing when he left for Vancouver at sixteen.

He wasted no time and found a job selling stoves at Spencers. "I didn't know one end of the stove from another," Arngrim said laughing, "but they were very good, very generous to me. They let me get off for radio shows, unheard of really, and I bought tickets to everything, went to every damn play, the Boston Pops, I spent all my money that way."

Arngrim joined Juan Root's company and worked with Sydney Risk's Everyman Theatre (appearing at the Dominion Drama Festival with them), and a number of other groups. "I worked everywhere in town. There's not a company I didn't work with. Stuart [Baker] did too," Arngrim said. "That's one of the things that had an enormous bearing on our [future] company."

Like Arngrim, Stuart Baker didn't arrive in Vancouver until his teens, but he had much farther to come than his eventual partner. Baker was born in Australia and moved to Kent, England, with his mother a couple of years later. In his later career he would perform under the name Stuart Kent, taken from his childhood home. As a teenager he appeared regularly on radio as a juvenile voice. In 1940 he was sent to relatives in Vancouver to escape the German air raids. At eighteen he joined the Canadian Army and on his release chose to stay in Canada. He returned to radio and also auditioned at the Vancouver Little Theatre where he met Arngrim. Following a production with UBC's Summer School of the Theatre, the two men were asked to join Sydney Risk's Everyman Theatre. It was with him that Arngrim and Baker learned everything about how to run (and how not to run) a theatre.

Risk was also the one who tapped into their public relations talents. "I just had a sense for [promotion]," Arngrim said. "It was Sydney that said, 'Can you do publicity?' And we just said, 'Oh yeah sure, we can do that.' We actually made some money doing that. That's how we survived as actors. We did publicity for a lot of acts and theatres."

The final push towards their own theatre happened in 1950 when they joined Yvonne Firkins' latest venture, the Vancouver Stage Society. "She was an amazing woman," Arngrim said. "She was a very good director but she was very, very difficult. . . . She was more neurotic and created more big scenes than the actors did."

Baker was in the first (and as it turned out, only) production by Firkins' group, Moss Hart's *Light Up the Sky*, beginning October 2, 1950. It was arena-style theatre, where the audience sits on three or four sides of the stage, and it was a critical success although a financial failure. The thirteen performances attracted only about nine hundred patrons. Firkins' expenses totalled $2,100 but the box office take was only $1,120. Most groups begun by Firkins broke up under "less than harmonious circumstances," and the same happened with this one, Arngrim said. However, it provided the young men with the final push towards their own theatre. Firkins' plan had been to set up a permanent company, and the theatre community had been counting on her success. When she failed, they were disappointed and restless. Since many of them were actors wanting to appear professionally, some of them began talking to Baker about the possibility of restaging *Light Up the Sky*.

"Everybody was very frustrated," Arngrim recalled. "So we picked up on that whole tone. . . . Stuart and I just said, 'Oh, let's do something.'" And without another thought, that is what happened. "I mean it was ridiculous how easily Totem Theatre started," Arngrim said.

By 1951, Arngrim and Baker, tagged "The Gold Dust Twins" by the press, were finally able to put all their years of training to good use when they began Totem Summer Theatre on a hope and a prayer. Right from the beginning Arngrim said they knew the kind of theatre they wanted to create:

> A permanent theatre that would be . . . something that the community would really respond to and they would be proud of. I mean it would be their theatre. We thought it was very important to be inclusive, to be one with the acting crew, but also with the community itself. That we were part of it and so were they. Because without them there would be no theatre.

The initial plans called for a summer repertory company, but they had a multitude of problems to overcome if they were ever to see their dream realized.

The biggest of these was money. After months of work they were able to get $500 in backing from the Youth Music League, and this was used to pay advance royalties on three of the comedies planned for the summer company. They also received support from the Community Arts Council of Vancouver. Nevertheless, they needed a larger influx of capital if they were to move forward. They approached Valdi Grimson, a wealthy, retired farmer from Saskatchewan and a friend of Arngrim's family. They were looking for a donation. "He was very rich and he was interested," Arngrim remembered. "But he said, 'Well, I'd like to help you but it'll have to be a loan.' Oh my God, a loan. Can you imagine a loan? This is summer theatre. He was crazier than we were."

Theatres, especially summer ones, had a reputation for leaving unpaid bills in their wake so the odds of the farmer ever seeing his money again were slim. Arngrim and Baker were determined, however, not to follow the trend. "Stuart and I pledged to each other, unless this is absolutely a disaster we have to pay all the creditors," Arngrim recalled. They survived past that first crucial year, Arngrim said, because they knew how to "put up a good front."

The two men had done a great deal of radio work, performing and also writing radio scripts. "They were terrible," Arngrim said laughing when he described the scripts they turned out. "They were pseudo suspense pieces, dramas, murder mysteries, all those simply dreadful bizarre shows. But everyone wanted to be in them because everyone wanted to act in something."

Because of their knowledge of the radio crowd, Arngrim and Baker turned to them to find most of their actors. At first it looked like they might have trouble getting any established actors. Arngrim was only twenty-two and Baker twenty-six. They had been told that their age would be a huge obstacle, that they would never get the co-operation and support of the older, more experienced acting community in Vancouver, one that would deem them too young to run a legitimate theatre. Another problem was Arngrim had heard that certain actors were not willing to work with specific directors or actors:

> I thought it was . . . silly, and so stupid. We said we're going to work with everybody. And we quickly gathered up people who would not speak to each other. We did and it worked. . . . They said, 'Oh, those boys are such upstarts. Can you imagine? They've asked Doris Buckingham [star on CBC radio and of Theatre Under the Stars] to do the play. She'll never do the play.' I said, 'She's gonna do it. It's a play. Come on. It's a job'. . . . Doris was thrilled to be in a play. She said, 'Thank God you asked me!' But everybody was like that. They were thrilled to be asked.

The cast list for their first production reads like a who's who of post-war British Columbia theatre professionals and proves they did, indeed, get support. Among company regulars that summer were John Emerson, Betty Phillips, Peg Dixon, Babs Hitchman, Sam Payne and Murray Westgate. Another actor to appear with them was Frank Lambrett-Smith, whom Arngrim had known for a long time, having appeared with him when he took his Shakespeare productions to schools and local halls. In 1947 Arngrim approached Lambrett-Smith to appear in the opening production for Totem Theatre. It was directed by Dorothy Davies, who also starred with Totem in a number of plays during the theatre's first two seasons.

Arngrim and Baker called themselves the producers and referred to all their cast as stars, even the less well-known members. "We just pretended we were stars," Arngrim said. When people said that they could not refer to the actors as "stars," Arngrim replied, "We can say anything we want. Who's gonna stop us?" It was funny because the local media, newspapers, they just bought it. They liked it because it was exciting for them to consider our actors stars. Up until then, that hadn't happened."

Totem even had the support of Vancouver's other open-air venture, Theatre Under the Stars (TUTS). Doris Buckingham, wife of TUTS producer Bill Buckingham, appeared in a Totem play that first summer, in spite of the fact the group was potential competition for her husband's company.

Later in the summer, Totem was joined by a young actress, Norma Macmillan, who became one of the leading ladies in the company and much more than that to Thor Arngrim, although they were not impressed with each other at the beginning. "I didn't think she was serious about theatre at all," Arngrim said of the woman who

As seen in this cover of the 1952 production of *Tony Draws a Horse*, Arngrim and Baker spent a great deal of money on publicity, which included paying an artist to create covers for each play. (ARNGRIM COLLECTION)

later became his wife. "I thought she was just a socialite playing, and she thought I was just an affected actor." It was not long before their opinions of each other changed. In addition to acting, Macmillan became the secretary, ticket seller, and the unofficial third producer of Totem.

In the beginning, Arngrim and Baker had hoped to find an indoor venue for their theatre. When they could not find one, Arngrim remembered performing outdoors at Ambleside Park in West Vancouver with Juan Root's company, and he approached the West Vancouver Parks Board. They were delighted to have the theatre perform there and gave the area to Totem rent-free, but that was as far as the help went. The two men had to start from scratch on what was once "a soccer field," as Dorothy Davies called it. They bought lumber on credit and went to work building a proscenium stage with the audience sitting directly in front. There was a roof over the stage along with an adjoining building to house a dressing room, props, etc. Eight hundred seats were rented, and they also enclosed the entire area with fencing to ensure people paid to see the show.

Totem had to borrow furniture and costumes from West Vancouver merchants as well as to overcome opposition from cinema owners and amateur theatrical groups concerned with losing their own audiences. Finally, however, Arngrim and Baker launched into rehearsals. When salaries were so abysmal, it was remarkable that so many theatre people, who by 1951 had a number of years' experience behind them, were willing to pitch in and help. The actors and backstage crew shared equally in a divvying up of box office receipts, less expenses, in lieu of salary. As audiences increased over the season, the actors' "take" rose from $10 to $36 a week. One reason Arngrim and Baker believed a number of theatres folded quickly was that they offered salaries that could not be supported by the theatre's income. By tying salaries to box office receipts, the producers hoped Totem stood a better chance of survival.

To keep expenses down, the two men personally took on as many of the jobs around the theatre as they could. In addition to performing themselves, they handled the business end, public relations, casting, the building and even the cleaning of sets. They also knew the value of publicity. A third of their $6,000 loan from Grimson was spent on lavish souvenir programs and advertising, and their publicity efforts usually brought high returns. They also involved the media by sending out letters and making phone calls. Baker wrote all the publicity material, including the elaborate and slick programs they sold to patrons for 25¢.

From day one, Baker wrote frequently to Margaret Ness, who covered entertainment at *Saturday Night* magazine, one of the largest national general interest publications in Canada at the time. "For the past week Thor and I have been literally living out at Ambleside Park, in a corner of our theatre building," Baker wrote to Ness on July 5, 1951. "It's a bit chilly—camping out—but this makes it much simpler since there is so much work to be done all the time." Ness promoted them frequently in the magazine, so Baker's constant communications with her paid off.

The first result of their efforts was on July 2, 1951, when the first of a scheduled eight plays, *Light Up the Sky* by Moss Hart, opened at the Totem Summer Theatre. It starred Frank Lambrett-Smith, Bea Lennard, Babs Hitchman, Betty Phillips, John Emerson and an unknown Canadian talent with some American experience, Bruno

Gerussi, who later became one of the most recognized television faces in the country in *The Beachcombers*. Almost 350 patrons attended opening night. But the second night gave them pause to wonder if they had been completely insane to undertake this venture. Wind and rain continued throughout the day and the temperature cooled. Baker started to talk about having to refund money to the one hundred hardy souls who braved the weather to attend. Then they came up with a solution. "We said, 'Hey, let's take down the fence.... We're going to have the first legitimate drive-in theatre,'" Arngrim remembered. "So we took down the fence and all the cars drove in where the seats [normally] were, and parked. They didn't hear a word, all these windshield wipers going. They stayed though, nobody left." Car horns were heard at the conclusion of the play instead of clapping.

Reviews were excellent and the theatre was even mentioned in *Billboard* magazine, quite a coup at the time. The audiences were enthusiastic, but when the first show ended a week later, Totem had added another $1,000 debt to their start-up loans. The remaining eight weeks proceeded, with some shows doing better than others. Mary Chase's *Harvey* and Brandon Thomas' *Charley's Aunt* were popular and held over a few extra days. This resulted in one of the original eight plays being cancelled.

Prior to the final play of the summer, *Born Yesterday* by Garson Kanin, Arngrim and Baker admitted they would be lucky to break even financially for the season, as they were considerably in debt. They had intended to enter a float in the Pacific National Exhibition parade, which would cost $500, but rather than cancel it, the two men decided they were so broke they might as well go ahead. Denis Johnston described it in *Theatre and AutoBiography*:

> For the float they had a large stork built of papier-mâché, holding in its beak an oversized diaper in which reclined the star of *Born Yesterday*, the attractive Lillian Carlson, dressed only in a swimsuit and a fur coat.[5]

It would not be the last time they used beautiful actresses for what they called "leg art" to promote Totem. When the float succeeded in drawing large crowds to Totem's last production, Arngrim and Baker were able to clear all debts, including the repayment of all loans. In total, fifteen thousand people attended the seven plays over eight weeks. Although this represented only 35 percent of capacity, it was enough to keep the theatre above water. They even had a small profit, with which they purchased a typewriter!

There was another "profit" that came from the first summer, as Baker explained in a letter to Margaret Ness of *Saturday Night*: "The double success, both artistic and financial, convinced some important folks that Totem was a worthwhile venture, so that from now on we have substantial backing to continue, and also to guarantee set salaries for all."

Thor Arngrim and Norma Macmillan hamming it up during a rehearsal for a Totem Theatre production. They would later marry. (ARNGRIM COLLECTION)

Mother Nature had been remarkably kind to them in that 1951 summer with only the one semi-rainout, but they realized they were going to have to find an indoor home if they were to survive. The margin for error was non-existent in outdoor theatre. In October they announced they had found a venue, one with a thrust stage, very unusual for that time, although much more common fifty years later. It was a "semi-in-the-round arena theatre," said Dorothy Davies. "It had a bit of a backdrop but then the stage went out into a big room. They built the seats out [from the three sides of the stage] for the people to sit."

It began as an empty meeting hall—"only four walls" as Arngrim described it—in a three-storey building at the corner of Dunsmuir and Beatty streets in downtown Vancouver. "It was opposite the bus terminal, where all the buses left for the outlying areas," Arngrim said. "It was a great location." It was owned by the International Brotherhood of Electrical Workers. "We have the ground floor, in the newly remodelled auditorium," Baker wrote to Ness, "which the union have recently had soundproofed, repainted, with a private wide entrance onto Dunsmuir installed, a box office, cloakroom and the usual toilet facilities."

They also had office space on the top floor, next door to some music studios of the BC Institute of Music. The building had one more major feature that Arngrim and Baker used to full advantage. A door off Beatty Street led downstairs to the Press Club where members of the press could grab a drink. They negotiated with the club to allow Totem's patrons a temporary membership. Because there were few places in town to get a drink, this was an added attraction, Arngrim said, "especially to the men who were dragged to the theatre by their wives." It was also convenient that the press was only a few steps away, given the theatre's relentless desire for publicity. "Some say it is typical of Arngrim and Baker to get near the Press!" Baker wrote to Ness.

They had to build everything from scratch: the thrust stage (the playing area was twenty-five feet by thirty feet), and all the platforms for the seats around three sides of it. "The [biggest] challenge was the back stage," Arngrim said. "There wasn't any. Everything was built just right there on the stage because it was three sided. . . . There was this tiny little space for a communal dressing room that was also the sound and the board area too. It all happened there."

With a seating capacity of 378, it was one of the largest semi-in-the-round arena theatres in North America at the time. They had wanted a completely circular, four-sided, arena theatre but ran into problems with the building inspector and had to abandon the plans. Ticket prices were $1.25 and $1.50 which included the horrendous 17.5 percent amusement tax levied by the B.C. provincial government. A government official was actually there to collect the money every night after the play began. Rent for the first year was $800 a month, jumping to $1,000 in year two. Actors were paid from $30 to $75 a week.

Arngrim and Baker did a great deal to support other organizations in the city with donations and help. In one of their programs, they talked about what they had done in the community in the previous year:

> During the past year, the theatre has contributed to the Thetis Club's "Shower of Dimes" for the crippled children; and to the Civic Ballet Society, donating a night's proceeds and publicizing their campaign to send Vancouver dancers East for the Festival. We have also been happy to donate proceeds to The Community Chest's Red Feather campaign, to acknowledge the wonderful work done by Alcoholics Anonymous, to open the Community Arts Council Week. . . . The cast and management arranged that one night would be a benefit for [actor] Ian Dobbie, who had literally had all his wardrobe stolen while working at the theatre.

They also supported other arts groups in the city, even accepting ads in their programs for other theatres, which was never done at the time because it promoted the competition. They felt all the arts should be tied together and supportive of one another. For the two years that they called the Dunsmuir building home, they displayed the works of different Canadian artists in their lobby. As the plays changed so did the artists. It was one of their ways of giving back.

The fact that the building was owned by a labour union slowed the building progress down because each job had to be carried out by a different union and all the work had to be co-ordinated. They could not simply bring in a few construction people to have it all accomplished at once, and paying union wages meant that the costs rose. Having the downtown location also increased the level of fire regulations, and new wiring had to be installed. The electricians didn't finish their work until 7:15 p.m. opening night.

While all the building work was taking place, Arngrim and Baker were busy choosing the plays for the season. It was not easy, partly because the plays had to be available through Samuel French, Inc. in order to obtain the scripts; they also had to choose plays that had success with audiences of the era. "Choosing plays for me was a very tense time," Arngrim said. "It is hard to keep track of quality plays. . . . There were not many available. . . . We were doing a play a week. You are going to go through the good plays really fast."

Then they made a move halfway through their first winter season that added considerably to their inventory of good plays and gave them an edge on their competition, groups such as Everyman Theatre and Theatre Under the Stars. "I said, 'I think we should go to New York and talk to Audrey Wood,'" Arngrim said, referring to Tennessee Williams' agent. The idea was to acquire first Canadian production rights for all of his plays. When they met with her, "she liked the way we talked," Arngrim recalled. "She thought it was going to be good. She knew the list of plays we had done. She had confidence we would do the Williams plays well. She wasn't going to let us have them otherwise." They succeeded but the rights came with a high price. "Tennessee Williams was so hot, it was very high royalties. It was well worth it though," Arngrim said.

Arngrim also had an interesting experience the one and only time he actually met Williams. They were sitting in the back seat of a car, going through the Lincoln Tunnel connecting New York and New Jersey, when suddenly Williams became hysterical and tried to open the door and jump out of the car. Arngrim and another passenger in the car had to hold him back until they were through the tunnel. Arngrim later discovered that Williams suffered from severe claustrophobia.

In spite of having paid for the first Canadian production rights to all of Williams' plays in Canada, it turned out that, unknown to them, *The Glass Menagerie* had already been performed a number of times, twice by the Canadian Repertory Theatre alone. Whether Audrey Wood was aware of this or whether Samuel French, Inc., the company responsible for sending the scripts and collecting royalties, knew about the arrangement between Wood and Totem is unknown. It is also possible that Totem bought the rights to all Williams' plays that had not already been performed in Canada up to that time.

Choosing plays was not only difficult; the results were often not what were expected. "Some of them were a surprise," Arngrim said. "The plays you really liked and which you thought were good were often not well received. And then a play you did not like very much and you thought, 'is this any good?' the critics loved it, the audiences loved it."

They chose to open their first indoor season on November 20, 1951, with S.N. Behrman's comedy *Biography*. With a winter season following the summer one, Totem officially became a year-round repertory company, only the second in Canada (the first being the International Players in Kingston).

Once again Dorothy Davies was involved but this time as an actress, not the director. "She was a *star*," Arngrim said. "With Dorothy Davies you always got Dorothy . . . busy [on stage] and a lot of stuff going on but it was all good . . . audiences loved her. It was marvellous to work with her. Her energy and the commitment to either doing the role or directing meant that people came to a play simply because she was in it. She had that ability. There were only a handful of people in our group [who could do that]—Dorothy Davies, Sam Payne and Norma [Macmillan]. They were audience favourites."

The directing honour for *Biography* went to Phoebe Smith. Another major player in B.C. theatre, Smith spent many years developing a noteworthy reputation on the London stage before coming to Canada in the 1930s, where she not only acted but directed with the Vancouver Little Theatre and most other post-war groups in the province. Smith always referred to Arngrim and Baker as "the boys."

It took the actors time to get used to the new style of theatre. During the blackout

Wally Marsh reaching protectively for a glass animal held by Norma Macmillan in Totem Theatre's *The Glass Menagerie*, c. 1951. In order to maintain authenticity, they broke whole sets of the glass animals for each performance. (ARNGRIM COLLECTION)

ending of scenes, one actress, unused to not having a curtain and moving around in the darkness, had to crawl off the stage on her hands and knees. The audience was also often a little too close for comfort. In *Biography*, Dorothy Davies' character was constantly smoking but every time she put a cigarette to her lips, some chivalrous man in the audience stepped on stage to light it for her. And during the run of *The Glass Menagerie*, a coat rack, on stage only as a prop, was used by the audience to hang their coats.

During the summer, Totem gave audiences a diet of comedies only, but the two producers went further out on a limb in their winter season with what Dorothy Davies called "an interesting series of work." There were Canadian premieres of *Come Back, Little Sheba* by William Inge and Jean-Paul Sartre's controversial *No Exit*, a major hit. Most of the productions received rave reviews by critics such as Stanley Bligh of the *Vancouver Sun*, who called *Biography* an "historic occasion for Canadian theatre."

As mentioned earlier, Arngrim and Baker knew how to keep the press engaged and were the first actively to foster a strong relationship with reporters and columnists. A couple of journalists wrote that Baker and Arngrim spent more time at the newspaper offices than at their own theatre.

"They had a point," Arngrim laughed. "They were so good, though, because we really did get them involved. They were so supportive. . . . Local newspapers would call us when they needed filler, a human interest story, and they could count on us. We would tell them a story and if we didn't have one, we would make one up."

Most of the time that wasn't necessary. On February 19, 1951, the final dress rehearsal for Noël Coward's *Private Lives*, which was opening that night, was underway. Meanwhile a fire had broken out and smoke was rising from the building. Arngrim and Baker, who were not in the production, saw the fire as they were heading across Cambie Bridge towards the theatre, and Arngrim recalled the following conversation:

> "Oh God, I think it is our place. Do you have a nickel?" Or whatever it was for a phone call. "We've got to call the press." Stuart said, "Shouldn't we call the fire department?" and I said, "We *will* call the fire department but we'll call the press first because we want the press there when the fire department arrives." So that is how we thought. . . . You could smell the smoke and so they came and took pictures and there was Phoebe Smith, the director, and all the actors standing in the middle of the theatre. We wouldn't want them to stop rehearsing so we told them—just keep rehearsing. And we told the press, "Oh yes, the show will go on." So we had all that fabulous coverage.

The fire actually did a great deal of damage to their office, which was uninhabitable for at least two weeks. However, in true theatre fashion, the show did, in fact, go on that night.

To promote Totem, they handed out many complimentary tickets—to cab drivers, hotel concierges and university students. They gave special group rates, anything to get an audience into the theatre. When the Sadler's Wells Ballet was in town threatening to pull customers away, Totem simply placed an advertisement for their current production in the Ballet's program, which drummed up good business.

The two producers decided the first Tennessee Williams' play they would tackle was *A Streetcar Named Desire*, even though everyone told them it was impossible to stage, even more so in their semi-arena-style theatre. Undaunted they went ahead, building a two-storey set with a spiral staircase. The technical work for the show took so long the actors could rehearse only three of the eleven scenes on the actual set, putting an end to rehearsal only an hour before opening. It was not only the first Canadian staging of the play, but also the first time it had ever been done on this type of stage. The "adults-only" play had heavy advanced sales, making it an instant hit. *A Streetcar Named Desire* ran for a record-breaking four weeks, almost unheard of for a serious play in those years. The play was also the Totem debut of the two actresses

Muriel Ontkean, as Blanche, seductively sprays perfume in the direction of Stanley, played by Bruno Gerussi, in *A Streetcar Named Desire*, Totem Theatre, April 1952. (ARNGRIM COLLECTION)

playing Stella and Blanche—Lorraine Foreman and Muriel Ontkean. The pivotal role of Stanley, one that had just recently exploded onto movie screens with Marlon Brando, went to Bruno Gerussi.

*A Streetcar Named Desire* was the biggest of Gerussi's early successes. "I had the privilege of working with Bruno when he was young," Arngrim said. "He was marvellous. He was exciting. Today most people . . . only know Bruno from *The Beachcombers*. He was not a hack back then. He may have become a hack, I don't know because I didn't watch him on *The Beachcombers*, but he was anything but then. He was vital, imaginative and very intense. Fabulous, animalistic, sexual qualities. . . . He did *The Little Foxes* [by Lillian Hellman] and *The Glass Menagerie*—he was marvellous in all of them. He could be temperamental but I didn't find him worse than any other actor."

The movie version of *Streetcar* was so famous that it presented an amusing problem for Totem's two young producers. The manager of the Orpheum, a large movie house, saw Totem's presentation of the play and threatened to sue them for stealing the story from the movie. It took some time for Arngrim and Baker to convince him that *Streetcar* had been a play before it was made into a movie and that they did, indeed, have full rights to use it.

The play was directed by Ian Dobbie who also happened to be an electrical genius. In England, Dobbie had spent many years learning different aspects of the theatre business. During the Second World War, he was trained as an electrician until the Army found out he was an actor and sent him off to do Army shows. In 1948 he came to Canada and some two years later joined Totem Theatre where his electrical expertise was as much valued as his directing. Lighting an arena-style stage presents numerous problems, as the actors' faces must never be in shadow whichever way they face, and the audience must never have lights shining on them. "He was very clever with lighting and managed to do some very effective things," Dorothy Davies said.

Totem's winter season was an unqualified success although the harried young producers were always hard at work. They gave it everything they had and also spent a great deal of money to make things on stage highly realistic. They broke collections of glass animals nightly in *The Glass Menagerie* and used real and lavish food when the script called for it. They believed maintaining authenticity was essential in that style of theatre and even put food on the stage table before they would put it into their own mouths. Once in a while they would combine the two. Already thin, Thor Arngrim had lost weight during Totem's early struggles and was forever trying to gain back pounds. After each performance of *The Voice of the Turtle* by John William Van Druten, Arngrim took the eggs from a breakfast scene that were mixed but never cooked, beat them with milk from a working refrigerator on the set, and drank the eggnog.

Because the 1951–52 winter season had been such a hit, Totem Theatre launched directly into its second summer. The group stayed at the arena theatre rather than battle any summer elements. They also added air conditioning—at least a kind of air conditioning. At one point during the summer it became very hot. "Stu and I wanted to attract the audience, convince them it was a cool place to go," Arngrim said. He saw that air conditioning had become the rage in theatres back east and was trying to think of a way to bring it to the theatre on Dunsmuir. He came up with a reasonable facsimile. In the attic of the building, directly over their office and the adjacent music studios, was a giant fan that blew air into ductwork leading to a grille at the back of the theatre. "I thought if we put a block of ice in front of the fan, it would be like air conditioning," Arngrim said. "So we did, and it worked. And yeah, we were able to advertise it [as air conditioned]!"

The system worked remarkably well, except on one occasion. An accident involving the ice one day may well have ended the music career of a young student in one of the music studios next to the office. Arngrim remembered:

> The guy would have to deliver this ice you know, as late in the day as possible so the block of ice would last. And one day the tongs slipped and he lost the block of ice. It slid off the fan and it came crashing through the ceiling into the room where a singing student was having her first lesson. It was just surreal: the ice was lodged [embedded] in the piano. Their door was closed, and there was a cloud of dust that came under the door. There's a scream and then the door flies open and here's the vocal coach just ashen white. These two people trying to deal with it, this huge block of ice stuck in the piano. Can you imagine?

The block of ice notwithstanding, Totem had a successful 1952 summer season, with *Clutterbuck* by Benn Levy and George Bernard Shaw's *Pygmalion* as the highlights.

The staging of *Clutterbuck* saw the reuniting of Gay Scrivener and Sam Payne. Scrivener, who had gone to England and made a name for herself, was back in Canada on holiday and joined Totem for the one play. She and Payne had been teamed together in 1938 when they appeared in London's West End in *Judgement Day*, adapted from a play by Austrian playwright Ödön von Horváth. Sam Payne spent winters working with the Canadian Repertory Theatre in Ottawa but always returned to Vancouver for the summers. "I didn't like to stay in Toronto and Ottawa in the summer," Payne said. "I did two summers [there] and it nearly killed me. I couldn't stand the heat."

Payne had roles in a number of the plays, including Henry Higgins in *Pygmalion*, Totem's 1952 closing production of the summer. Dorothy Davies played opposite him as Eliza. Payne had a certain charm and audiences adored him, but he was notorious across the country for not being able to remember his lines. "He was just incredible," Arngrim said. "Sometimes he would just speak gibberish but the audience would be

One of the stalwarts of the Totem Theatre era, Sam Payne laughs and points a finger at Thor Arngrim in a scene from *Hay Fever*, c. 1951. (ARNGRIM COLLECTION)

spellbound. He did it with his voice. . . . I remember in Victoria we had this fellow actress who was the prompter and she sat in a fireplace. And he couldn't hear [her] so he took the poker and gave her a jab and said 'speak up you dizzy bitch!' He actually physically poked her with the poker. . . . He could not remember lines. That is why radio was perfect for him." Payne was remembered for taking his script and actually counting the words. "Words, a lot of words," he was often heard to say.

That summer of 1952 also provided another milestone when the *Financial Post* reported that the formation of Arngrim and Baker Productions Ltd. made Totem the first incorporated legitimate theatre company in Canada.

Following *Pygmalion*, Totem immediately began its second winter season with J. Hartley Manners' *Peg O' My Heart*, starring Norma Macmillan, whose various jobs with the theatre now included house manager, box-office worker, makeup assistant, typist, cleaning lady, musical arranger and frequent actress. She had become indispensable.

*Tony Draws a Horse* by Lesley Storm was presented as Totem's first birthday attraction in November 1952. To ensure good crowds they pulled another one of their legendary publicity stunts. A nightclub act called *Lady Godiva* was appearing in town and Arngrim had an idea. "There was an actress who played Lady Godiva at a supper club called the Cave. She had a specially trained horse," Arngrim remembered. "We did a whole promotion around it, and on opening night the horse came to the play. The horse sat in the front row, just for a photo op." They had the horse come in down the aisle and take its seat just before curtain time and the crowd roared as flashbulbs went off. "It attracted a lot of attention," Arngrim understated.

Totem continued to be covered extensively by the press, the critics attending most of the plays. Sometimes they even got a review when no one from the press attended! Critic Ada McGeer occasionally counted on Totem to write the review for her, or at least to supply the main points. Arngrim recalled, "I think one of her relatives was a mayor and her husband was a judge [provincial court judge James McGeer]. She was very big at the CBC. She was a statuesque woman . . . a real character. She was on the jury for auditions at the CBC and then she was a critic for one of the local papers [the *Vancouver Sun*]. She'd be so rattled and confused that sometimes she didn't get to the play and she'd call up and say, 'Is Norma there? I can't get over there. What's it [the play] like? Is Sam [Payne] good?' 'Yes, oh well, just give me a little description.' So she would write a review from that. She was a marvellous character. She was not the only critic that wrote a review without coming to the play."

At Christmas 1952 they staged Wayne and Shuster's *Mother Goose* pantomime, starring Barney Potts and Lorraine Foreman. They performed it at the Georgia Auditorium and created an elaborate set, including "a 'strobe' number in the Haunted Castle scene—a ballet of bats and spiders," Baker wrote to Margaret Ness. In addition to in-

During their production of the pantomime *Mother Goose*, Totem Theatre gave all the children a cut-out theatre, complete with figures they could cut out and place in the theatre. It was a huge hit. (ARNGRIM COLLECTION)

tricate sets and one of their usual artistic programs, they also gave a cut-out theatre and characters from the pantomime to the children in the audience to build and colour in. With all the extra costs, including a cast of fifty (mostly TUTS performers), Totem lost a great deal of money on the production, but luckily their main theatre was doing well and they could absorb the loss.

Looking at the production figures, one can see that in the first year alone, more than sixty thousand patrons saw the twenty-two indoor productions during Totem's first full year. Most of the shows ran two weeks, nine were held over for a third, and one show ran for four weeks. Tennessee Williams continued to be an audience favourite as crowds flocked to see the group's production of *Summer and Smoke*. Financial conditions improved for the company in spite of high overhead. Most of the plays they chose were new on the market and royalties to secure them cost an average of $200 per week. By the fall of 1952 in the second year, the rental for the auditorium reached $1,000 a month. Salaries started at $35 a week for actors and $50 for directors, but this was only for the time the show was playing. No one received a cent for rehearsal. Still, the future looked bright and the two young men began to talk about building their own theatre. Sadly, it would never happen.

Totem's lease with the International Brotherhood of Electrical Workers, who owned the building, was due to expire May 31, 1953. The two producers assumed it would be renewed, but in March, Baker and Arngrim were informed that was not possible. The union wanted the space for their own uses. Moreover, the building was no longer able to meet city building fire and safety regulations required for theatres. If that was not bad enough, the city also notified Totem there were no other available buildings that did. Although Totem obtained a lease extension to August 31, 1953, and they were able to stay for the summer, it made little difference to the theatre's ultimate fate. A three-week presentation of *Gigi* by Anita Loos closed out Totem's golden period. With no theatre to perform in, they were now struggling to survive.

"The company and the theatre operation itself has fortunately always been quite successful—both artistically and 'dollar and cents'-wise," Baker wrote in a letter to Margaret Ness. "But now the company may have to disband if we cannot find a place to continue operations." Totem had the support of the media and the public, and there were many ideas thrown around as to where they could go. There was talk of an amphitheatre being built in Ambleside Park. "Stuart and I had no interest at all [in the park] but the media and different people kept bringing it up, including the Park Board," Arngrim said. There were some exceptions to the support, however. "I remember there was a woman on the Park Board who got up at a meeting and said she didn't want those damn actors because they would be fornicating in the bushes. You know those actors."

They started a massive publicity campaign to raise $150,000 to build their own theatre but this fell well short of its goal with only $10,000 collected. Arngrim wanted to let the theatre go at this point and walk away, but Baker and Macmillan persuaded him otherwise. They moved their operation to the York Theatre in Victoria.

Their new location had already been home for a year to Ian Thorne's York Theatre Company. The formation of that group was announced with great flourish in the summer of 1952; Thorne was bringing live theatre back to Victoria after twenty-five years. The building he chose had been a theatre earlier in the vaudeville days and had an excellent stage with eight hundred seats.

Thorne, a post-war arrival from the English theatre, placed ads for actors in papers all down the West Coast and the response was phenomenal. More than 250 arrived in Victoria to audition, with a scant seven men and four women being chosen. Only five of the eleven were Canadian. In spite of capital and a location, Thorne's group did not last even a year, but the building itself provided a place for Totem to hang its hat.

Totem's *Gigi* closed in Vancouver on August 8, 1953, and opened a week later in Victoria. While the media were supportive, there was one thing that Totem lacked—an audience. "One thing I didn't like about Victoria," Arngrim said, "was their audiences were very unsophisticated. . . . If the horse show was on, there'd be nobody at your theatre. And then the next night you'd be sold out, and then the following night the symphony's on, and they'd all be at the symphony. . . . They'd go to all of [the events]."

Totem was forced to bring most of the actors from Vancouver, increasing their costs. The audiences became smaller and smaller. The plays that sold well were potboilers and light British comedies. Arngrim was again close to having had enough. He wanted to present more meaningful plays, and he told Stuart, "You know, if this is what's going to work, I don't think I'm really terribly interested in this. I'd make a buck to pay for the [more interesting plays]. But if we're getting to the point where nine out of ten of them would have to be of this calibre. . . ."

Totem's letterhead still read "The Living Theatre in the Canadian West" but the pulse was weak. The theatre was in Victoria for only three months before the media began to report on their financial plight. It would only get worse. In February 1954 Arngrim collapsed and was hospitalized for a week. It was the stress, he said, of working at something he no longer believed in.

The highlight of their time in Victoria was *A Crowded Affair* by Norma Macmillan, starring Sam Payne and Gay Scrivener who were reunited once again. Written a few years earlier, the comedy was set in Victoria, which brought in the crowds. Because of its successful three-week run, the producers decided to have a one night presentation of it on May 17, 1954, at the Georgia Auditorium, at the corner of Denman and Georgia in Vancouver. At the same time the rest of the crew was staging Totem's last play in Victoria, *Rope* by Patrick Hamilton.

As far as Arngrim was concerned this was to be the end of Totem, but the night in Vancouver was such a triumph that they were approached by the man running the

Thor Arngrim pours himself a drink in the thriller *Rope* by Patrick Hamilton in the last play presented in Victoria by Totem Theatre in 1954. They had also staged it in the 1951–52 season in Vancouver. (ARNGRIM COLLECTION)

auditorium, asking them to present a series of plays there that summer. Again, Arngrim was not enthusiastic about the idea but Baker and Macmillan definitely were, so he decided to go along with them. "He made us an offer we couldn't refuse," Arngrim said, "and what the hell, why not do the season? And it was an opportunity for all the actors to work."

It was an eight-hundred-seat theatre, however, and impossible to fill night after night. The debts began to rise. One of the few successful plays in the nine-play summer season was *The Man Who Came to Dinner* by George Kaufman and Moss Hart. As in their earlier production of it, the play starred John Emerson.

Emerson was one of those multi-talented individuals who so often gravitate towards a theatrical career. In addition to acting, he was an accomplished pianist, violinist, and writer, as well as the head of a successful company of singers. He also read poetry to a national radio audience in *John Emerson Presents*. A popular figure on the Vancouver show business scene, Emerson was well known in both radio and theatre circles for his polished wit and smooth flair for subtle comedy. And for his reputation!

"Oh my God, he was crazy," Arngrim laughed. "I loved John Emerson. A lot of people didn't like John a lot, and he drove them crazy because he was very temperamental, but he was *funny*. . . . He'd forget a line, and then someone would give it to him and he'd do it. And then he would be gone along two speeches and he'd remember what he'd forgotten and say, 'Wait.' And he'd go back."

In the lead up to the opening of *The Man Who Came to Dinner*, they had another problem with Emerson because he did not think his name was big enough on the marquee. "He was wonderful in [the play] but he was an egomaniac, and there was this very small marquee at the Georgia Auditorium, very small. 'We don't control the marquee,' I told him. 'We're renting the venue. It can't be any bigger. That's as big as the letters are on the marquee.' But he wouldn't stop. So Stuart and I went out and got a huge banner, about thirty feet long and twelve feet high and painted, 'Starring John Emerson' and hung it on the side of the auditorium. Just covered the side of the auditorium." Emerson told them it was "'just a tad too big.' I said, 'Well, you wanted big.'"

The production would also give Arngrim a chance to perform one last big publicity stunt. In the play, a radio personality called Sheridan Whitehead receives a number of crazy presents from his equally crazy Hollywood friends at Christmas. While the play was running, there was a circus in town and with it was Alberta Slim, a country and western singer. He had with him an elephant and trainer, and this gave Arngrim an idea. The elephant, named Suzie, could be one of the gifts, he decided:

> [Alberta Slim] had this elephant and its trainer was meant to bring it down the aisle. It was just a sight gag. Everyone would freak out when here comes this thundering elephant . . . and then it just ends and [Suzie] leaves and people just have a huge laugh. Then the play continues like nothing has happened. But no, this man wanted the elephant to perform so he would get it to perform [in the theatre]. We said, "Stop, stop, stop, no more. If you do that we'll just cut the elephant. We don't want a performance by the elephant." It would have ruined the gag. He was very unhappy, sulky. So I said, "Look, ok, I don't like to do it but you can have the elephant perform outside the theatre. Stand outside the theatre and perform." Well, of course, it worked. It was fabulous. . . .

> That was fun because Theatre Under the Stars had a special bus, a free shuttle bus to their shows that left from outside our theatre, so a lot of people who had not necessarily purchased tickets yet [for TUTS], and who were going to do so at the gate, got off the bus because they wanted to see the elephant again. It was hilarious.

TUTS' loss was Totem's gain, but it was not nearly enough. Arngrim and Baker had seen the writing on the wall for some time.

Arngrim said it was a shock to the public and to the media because they expected them to continue as always, but "we knew that summer," he said, "knew it back in Victoria actually. We knew it was over because we were there!" Their intense ambition and abundant energy were not enough. Totem's ultimate failure to survive did not lie in a lack of talent or audiences but in a lack of suitable buildings.

Looking back, Thor Arngrim said the years with Totem were really an amazing time. "People asked me silly questions such as, 'Those must have been really wild times?' I'd say, 'I don't know what you're talking about.' We were working so hard. Maybe every few weeks someone would give a party but it was very low key. It wasn't nearly as wild as people all thought it was. You were dropping dead from doing it. But it was so much fun. I would not have done anything different looking at it all fifty years later. I wouldn't have missed that for anything. It was all terrific."

❧

There was one other major theatre in Vancouver at the same time as Everyman and Totem. This was Theatre Under the Stars or, as it was known by its initials—TUTS. Although TUTS presented only musicals after its first year, it is included here along with more traditional theatres for two main reasons. The first is financial. TUTS gave employment to a number of serious actors who also sang and danced. Once TUTS began to pay performers, it was another source of income for actors at a time when it was hard to find money in any type of theatre. TUTS also quickly became professional. Any form of theatre that was professional was another step forward for Canadian theatre.

What began in Vancouver as a modest undertaking in 1940, with the actors being given only streetcar fare in lieu of salary, soon became a shining light among Canada's summer theatres. The three figures who came together to create a theatre in Stanley Park, recognized as one of the great green spaces of the world, were Basil Horsfall, E.V. Young and A.S. Wootten. They founded the Theatre Under the Stars Society, and they did it with the wholehearted co-operation of the Vancouver Board of Park Commissioners (as it was then called).

With their backgrounds, Horsfall, Young and Wootten seemed in many ways the ideal trio to promote such an endeavour, which in its first summer attracted some thirteen thousand people to ten performances. Basil Horsfall, who had been given a guest conductorship with the International Opera Company in Europe, was musical director for TUTS productions from the beginning until his sudden death in 1950. E.V. Young had started his career as an actor in St. James Theatre in London, England, and A.S. Wootten was a Park Board superintendent who understood the added charm of Stanley Park, the location they had chosen for their outdoor theatre.

The venture had been preceded by an experiment in the late 1930s, when Horsfall, Young and Stanley Bligh, among others, staged a few Shakespearean plays at Brockton Oval in Stanley Park. However, the facilities were inadequate and the audiences sparse. As a result, Horsfall began looking at the possibilities of using the Marion Malkin Memorial Bowl, also in Stanley Park, for productions. At first, the Park Board was unwilling to risk the necessary funds, which were estimated to be $3,000 for 1940. Then Vancouver City Council guaranteed $1,000 and, with this backing, the Tourist Association also donated $1,000. Faced with this pressure, the Park Board was finally prevailed upon to risk the remaining thousand.

In a brilliant publicity move, Totem Theatre had an elephant come down the aisle as part of a scene in *The Man Who Came to Dinner*. (ARNGRIM COLLECTION)

This scant amount was a far cry from the $250,000 budget for a season only thirteen years later. Expenses for the 1940 summer exceeded the revenue, but the Park Board decided to go ahead for a second summer anyway, with one major change. The Board felt TUTS would succeed better with one person at the helm so the triumvirate production committee was abandoned, although all three men stayed closely involved during the early years in one capacity or another. In their place the Board hired Gordon Hilker.

Theatre Under the Stars was an unusual theatre, not only because it was outside and had a large seating capacity of more than four thousand, but because it was formed during the Second World War when even many amateur theatres were struggling to survive. By the time the war was over, TUTS was well on its way to becoming the most elaborate and durable summer theatre in the country. They managed to overcome the fears of Vancouver residents, worried over the possible damage to their natural resource, Stanley Park. In a pre-TUTS 1939 incident, an undetermined number of save-the-park vigilantes infiltrated a crowd of some ten thousand people attending a one-night concert in Stanley Park. They armed themselves with shovels and wire-cutters and tore down the fence that enclosed the performance area. It was a great credit to TUTS when it opened the following year that the people of Vancouver saw that it harmonized with the beautiful setting in Stanley Park, and they did not try to pull down the barriers.

TUTS did not start out to become a musical company when it opened in the summer of 1940. "We did Shakespeare's *As You Like It* and *A Midsummer Night's Dream* and selections from opera," said first-year performer Sam Payne. "The plays didn't take as well as the operas so they decided to drop the straight plays." From the second summer on, they staged only light comedic musicals and operettas, augmented by a chorus and a corps de ballet. Their subsequent speedy success was likely due to the fact that it was wartime, and people wanted something to entertain them, something light to take their minds off the hostilities.

Playing outdoors presents certain problems at any time but Stanley Park had its own eccentricities. Payne described the performing area of TUTS as follows:

> The theatre is quite large and you have to project more. You often felt as though you were shouting your head off. And you had to play large. Of course, in musical comedy you do anyway. It was great fun. There's a zoo nearby. We played to the accompaniment of seals honking and monkeys screeching. [Before the dressing rooms were built, the performers] dressed in the monkey house. I remember one time before the Bowl was added to, we were doing *The Firefly* and I was playing the sort of hero parts in those days. It was pouring with rain and the orchestra was crammed onto the stage with the cast just trying to do the play. I was clasping the heroine fondly to my chest and her wig went flying off into the crowd.

As Payne stated, actions and words were often punctuated by sounds from the nearby zoo or a passing ship in Burrard Inlet. Sometimes the cast took advantage of such interruptions. In one musical a man fakes his own death to escape his wife, and when she comes into money, he reappears to try to plant the idea in her head that her husband might be alive. She insists her husband did die and the two are arguing when the blast of a freighter's whistle is heard. The actor ad libbed, "There, he's calling to you now," and the audience roared with laughter.

Another tie-in to the script was that Vancouver used a muzzle-loading cannon, which fired every night at nine o'clock. "It happened in one of the romantic comedies," Sam Payne said. "It was *Blossom Time* or something. We'd have a gun and point it at the villain and right at that point, bang it went. Much applause and laughter from the audience. It was fun and people liked it."

Audiences for TUTS increased each year. By 1945 more than one hundred and forty thousand people watched the six shows staged that season, shows that included *The Vagabond King*, Oscar Straus' *The Chocolate Soldier* and *Rio Rita*. The average price of admission was 62¢. The productions were elaborate, and the company had 127 players, only five of whom were not Canadian. The few non-Canadians each year were usually Americans imported for starring roles. Among the early Canadian performers were Barney Potts, Betty Phillips and Larry McCance. McCance was one of the founding members and an active participant in TUTS for two summers until he joined the Royal Canadian Air Force in 1941.

The stage on which the productions were mounted was originally a small concert bowl donated to the City of Vancouver in 1934 by a former mayor, W.H. Malkin. This early stage was poor and its backstage facilities almost nonexistent. It was enlarged twice for TUTS through the years. Some of the audience sat on deck chairs or benches while the rest spread blankets on the grassy slopes. With an operating surplus acquired during the early years, much needed lighting equipment, scenery pieces and costumes were purchased. For a number of years TUTS also took their shows on the road to Portland and Seattle.

The Board of Park Commissioners, which played such a large role in the creation of TUTS, also did a great deal to improve the acting and singing of provincial talent. In 1944 the Board set into motion the British Columbia Institute of Music and Drama, whose sole purpose was to provide free training in all branches of the theatrical arts to promising young talent throughout British Columbia. In addition to lectures, students were given practical classes in dancing, balancing exercises, stage movement, speech, makeup and ensemble singing. The students frequently went on from the Institute to play parts in the TUTS productions.

One actor with TUTS for many seasons was Paul Kligman. Between 1946 and 1952, he appeared in twenty-five musicals, playing "mostly the heavy comics." He remarked, "We did everything from early kinds of musicals like *Desert Song* and *Chocolate Soldier* . . . right up to the era of *Finian's Rainbow* and *Wizard of Oz*, which were the current hits. We also did a revival of an early [George] Gershwin show that very few people realized he wrote. It was called *Song of the Flame*. . . . I enjoyed that very much."

The TUTS' version of *Song of the Flame* was scheduled to go on tour and then open on Broadway, but it never made it quite that far. "We made the unfortunate mistake of trying to follow the first tour of *Oklahoma* across the country," Kligman said. "They took all the money and we followed into a town and died simply because they had cleaned out the town."

Pay varied at TUTS from actor to actor, but after its first few tentative years, it was generally a good salary for the time period. As an example, in 1949, the last year he performed with the group while living in Vancouver, Paul Kligman made slightly less than $200 a week. When he returned from Toronto in 1952 to star with TUTS in three musicals, he was paid $1,150 for four weeks of work.

The quality of the shows was always good. "Their ability to costume, design and produce the shows was of a very high level," Kligman said. The durability and high standard of TUTS was such that it fast gained an international reputation for excellence, and young talents flocked to audition for the chorus of the company. In 1951 more than four hundred showed up to auditions while only twenty-four were chosen. While the majority of applicants, who had to be at least fifteen-years-old, came from British Columbia, there were some from as far away as Los Angeles, Toronto and New York City. Most members of the chorus had opportunities throughout the season to perform small parts in one of the productions.

Rehearsals at TUTS went on from ten in the morning to ten in the evening with only two meal breaks, and this continued for a couple of months before the opening. Once the season was underway the cast performed in the evenings. In the mornings and afternoons they would rehearse for the following week's performances, a routine followed by most summer companies in those years. Dress rehearsals sometimes took place at midnight, after a performance was over, and did not end until almost dawn.

As dancing and movement in TUTS shows were intricate, it was expected the organization would hire someone very talented to be their choreographer. And they did. Born in England, Aida Broadbent lived in Vancouver from the age of two until thirteen, when her parents moved to California. From 1946 into the 1960s, she always stopped whatever she was doing to return to Vancouver in the summer to produce the dance sequences in the TUTS musicals. The remainder of the year Broadbent did shows for many stars, including Jimmy Durante. In 1949, when Durante was starring at the Pacific National Exhibition in Vancouver, he was so impressed with the TUTS dancers he took them all down to Dallas to appear in his show at the State Fair.

Of all TUTS graduates, it was perhaps the dancers who achieved the greatest success beyond the confines of Stanley Park, foremost among them Lois Smith and David Adams. Another member of TUTS to achieve recognition was soprano Betty Phillips, a Vancouverite who received training in classical singing. She performed on many CBC radio shows including her own, *Betty Phillips Sings*. She was with TUTS for many seasons.

By the late 1940s, production costs were nearing $20,000 per week but the low overhead allowed TUTS to keep its head above water. Ticket prices ranged from 35¢ to $1.75 in a 4,600-seat capacity area. Salaries for stars and supporting players ranged from $200 to $500 a week.

In 1949 TUTS became the subject of controversial debates among Park Board members. The main issue was the British Columbia Institute of Music and Drama, which, as mentioned earlier, the Park Board had established in 1944 to teach young actors and singers. An organization of music and drama teachers threatened the Park Board with legal action, claiming they did not have the legal power to run an educational institution. But it was not the only reason that the Park Board came to the decision that TUTS was becoming too big a responsibility. During those years, each season of TUTS seemed more successful than the one before and, with continuing prosperity, the operation simply grew too big for the Board to handle properly.

It took them almost a year before final decisions were made, but the Board turned TUTS and the Institute over to the non-profit Vancouver Civic Theatre Society, giving them some financial assistance for the remaining few months of 1949. The Society was incorporated in 1950, and after that it was on its own.

In that same year, attendance rose again, and TUTS set two records: 4,411 patrons came on one night to see *Sweethearts*, with music by Victor Herbert and lyrics by Robert B. Smith and Harry B. Smith. Fred De Gresac was responsible for putting dance and music together into a story. The run of *Chu Chin Chow* garnered an attendance of 34,584. It was written by Oscar Asche, who was better known on the British stage as an actor. The $20,000 surplus recorded at the end of the season showed that the Vancouver Civic Theatre Society had made some wise choices. One of the wisest was to hire Bill Buckingham.

The lives of Bill Buckingham and his wife Doris were deeply entwined with TUTS for many years. Bill graduated from UBC in 1927 and was called to the bar in 1931. He practised law and did radio work on the side until 1948. He was heard on *Farm Broadcast* for many years with two of his fellow TUTS performers, Dorothy Davies and Jimmy Johnston. First acting in TUTS shows and then directing them, Buckingham finally took over as production manager in 1955, a position he was to keep for the next five years. Doris Buckingham held the performing record for longevity with the company. She starred in nineteen of the twenty-three years TUTS operated, while also appearing with other theatres and on CBC radio.

Management had set a policy that the seasons would run from the last week in June until mid-August, and they stuck with this even though they were sometimes tempted to extend a successful show beyond the end of a season. One such time was 1951 when they closed out the summer with a three-week run of *Brigadoon*, playing to sold-out houses of the musical every night and drawing 74,086 patrons. The weather had cooperated to such a point that summer that TUTS had not cancelled a single performance. They decided, however, not to push their luck and ended the season after the scheduled run of *Brigadoon*.

Prior to the 1952 season, the Malkin Bowl was enlarged to the tune of $20,000, much of which was given by W.H. Malkin, the original donor. Six productions were staged in what was an adventurous season with three major highlights. They opened June 23, 1952, with the first of these, a production of *Timber!*—the first all-Canadian musical—written, produced and performed by Canadians. It had three collaborators in Vancouver: pianist Dolores Claman, who composed the music, along with Doug Nixon and David Savage, who wrote the story and lyrics. In 1968 Claman wrote the original theme for CBC's televised *Hockey Night in Canada* show. Doug Nixon was

The TUT's cast of the musical *Brigadoon*, which had a successful three-week run at the end of the 1951 summer, pulled in more than 74,000 patrons. (VANCOUVER PUBLIC LIBRARY)

more involved with radio, and later television, than the stage. He worked at radio stations in Edmonton and Vancouver before joining the CBC. It was in Vancouver that Nixon met his *Timber!* collaborators.

*Timber!* was about the local lumber industry, a lusty story of a group of loggers hitting town for a party. At the centre of the epic was a young high rigger whose job it was to scale a tree, lop off the top and the surrounding branches, and then secure cables between the tree and an engine so as to make it easier to pull out the logs. His was the most glamorous and dangerous job and one which modern machinery has largely eliminated. In *Timber!* the high rigger falls in love with the daughter of a timber baron, who tries to keep the couple apart. Through the efforts of the other loggers, the young lovers are reunited, and the script called for this meeting to take place, appropriately, in Vancouver's Stanley Park.

Just as the New Play Society's *Spring Thaw* revues in Toronto were a success because Canadians recognized themselves on stage, so *Timber!* produced a similar response in British Columbians. The audience laughed and applauded at every opportunity and the production drew more than fifteen thousand people in four nights. Its authors made $1,000. A slightly abridged version of *Timber!* was also heard on CBC's *Wednesday Night* on July 2, 1952, with most of the performers repeating their stage roles. These included Don Garrand as the high rigger, Jacqueline Smith as his young love and Frank Wade as her father. Other notables were Len Hayman, Lorraine McAllister, Thora Anders and the ever-popular Barney Potts.

The 1952 season also included the biggest production in TUTS' history. It was the first time *The Wizard of Oz* would be seen on stage in Canada, and it had the largest cast TUTS had ever assembled, led by Jacqueline Smith as Dorothy and Paul Kligman, Jerry Stovin and Barney Potts as her three unusual companions. Aida Broadbent created four original numbers for the show, and it took Gail McCance and Charles Baker two full months to design and complete the set. A stage turntable was used for the first time, as was an elaborate snow scene. The director was Jimmie Johnston who had begun working as an actor for TUTS after he returned from the Royal Canadian Air Force. He continued to act with the group until 1949 when he also began to direct. Between 1949 and 1963 he directed close to fifty musicals for the company.

TUTS followed *The Wizard of Oz* with the popular *Finian's Rainbow*, which managed to create an unexpected stir. As was seen with the Everyman Theatre, it was very easy for a private citizen to complain to the police about a production of a play they thought was obscene. Because of this, most theatre groups in Canada were extremely careful not to have anything in a production that might offend anyone in the audience. In one of the climactic scenes of *Finian's Rainbow*, a leading character unearths the pot at the end of the rainbow, and it turns out to be a chamber pot. In this staging of the musical, the pot was there, large as life. Some complaints of vulgarity were made to police, who passed them on to TUTS manager Bill Buckingham. Although they decided not to change the scene, when the play was restaged in 1956, they decided to leave out the actual pot and just have the actress pretend to find it, thereby eliminating a small issue before it could become a big one. The productions in 1952 brought in audiences totalling 166,417.

Rain always played a larger part in the operation of TUTS than management liked, but since it was an open-air venture, the elements were bound to have a key role. Although the Vancouver Civic Theatre Society was a non-profit organization, it nevertheless had to keep a large operating surplus in case the coming season suffered a series of rainouts. In 1953, for example, Mother Nature smiled down in such a way that an all-time attendance record was set; the profit for the summer was so high that bonuses were given to both the performers and production crews.

The next two summers, however, saw rain followed by more rain and the cash surplus of the group plummeted from $94,800 to $9,000. After a 1955 loss of $60,000, the company took out an insurance policy to protect it from mammoth losses due to precipitation. Rain continued to plague TUTS through the 1950s but it was something the company and audience seemed to accept, and on occasion the show even went on in the rain at the request of the audience. It seemed the lure of TUTS was not only the pleasure of the productions themselves but also the chance to spend an evening sitting in the summer night air. Illustrating this was an indoor 1956 Christmas presentation they did of *The Wizard of Oz*, which failed miserably at the box office.

By 1959 the financial situation was looking so precarious that management decided to explore the possibility of a retractable roof for their location, but they were met with opposition from many sources including the Board, which still controlled Stanley Park, the site of the Malkin Bowl. Ideas for the roof were scrapped. Following heavy losses that year, TUTS was under the gun once again in spite of the insurance policy. Yet things improved in 1960 with a rain-free and successful season. In the following year, however, they had to pass the hat to get even two shows into production. And the mounting debts in 1962 and 1963 finally led to bankruptcy, and the end of the theatre that began in 1941.

An actor who was with TUTS in 1940 and for many summers after, was also there at the end. "When it finished I was in the last show, *Carousel*," Sam Payne said. "So I can say I was with TUTS pretty well from the beginning to the end."

In 1969, another group, Theatre in the Park, began presenting musicals at the Malkin Bowl, and in 1980 they renamed themselves Theatre Under the Stars, bringing back the famous name. They closed down for the 2006 season to "re-group," returning the following year. They are still carrying on in 2012. The name may have continued, but after 1963, any vestige of the original TUTS was gone.

CHAPTER FOUR

# THE LITTLE THEATRE MOVEMENT & THE DOMINION DRAMA FESTIVAL

"The little theatres in those days attracted all the people who would have been professional actors—if there had been a professional theatre."

—HERBERT WHITTAKER

It was the amateur theatres that held the stage until Canada was ready for professional theatre. In the early post-war years, the roads of amateur and professional theatre were often intertwined and the distinctions between them unclear. In fact, several groups such as Everyman, Totem and Theatre Under the Stars found some of their actors from the amateur ranks so it is important to consider the amateur and its role in Canadian theatre. It provided much experience to the young actors in the country who had nowhere else to learn their trade and, in addition, most of theatre's teachers at the time were connected with amateur theatre in one way or another. And, while amateur theatre did not directly create professional theatre, it certainly encouraged a readiness for it by keeping the public's interest in theatre alive.

In fact, most of Canada's early exposure to the footlights was community or local theatre, which in the twentieth century became known as the Little Theatre Movement. Although it later became a term to describe amateur or non-professional theatre, little theatre was originally an international movement against the mass-produced, coarse, professional theatre presented to the public around the turn of the century. The

Little Theatre Movement reached its peak in Canada in the 1920s and '30s when movie houses and the Depression had combined to wipe out most professional theatre that existed up to that time. Even the road companies from other countries stopped touring for many years. Without the strength of little theatres during the ensuing years when this country's stages were dark, the return to professionalism in post-war Canadian theatre would have been a much slower and more difficult process.

If Canada had a unifying national theatre during that time, it was supplied by the various little theatres, theatre guilds and drama groups across the country. They kept the public's appetite for drama alive, maintaining its habit of attending theatre. But, just as important, they also did this without sacrificing quality. "You see, at that time it was almost impossible to draw a line between the professional and high amateur," Herbert Whittaker said. Community theatres, he argued, have been around in one form or another as long as people have inhabited Canada.

The vast majority of amateur theatre groups began between the two world wars. From Vancouver's Little Theatre, formed in 1921, to St. John's Players in 1937, the entire country was blanketed in a network of these theatres. Among them was the London Little Theatre, which had almost eight hundred members in its first year, 1934–35. Located in the Grand Theatre, downtown in the city of London, Ontario, they gave only five performances (one for each of five plays) in their first year. Fifteen years later, membership was an astounding 10,636 and the group was giving nine performances for each of the six plays a season. More importantly, they now owned the Grand Theatre, having purchased it in 1945. The group won top honours at the Dominion Drama Festival (DDF) in 1936 with *Twenty-Five Cents* by W. Eric Harris, and won again in 1948 for their production of George Bernard Shaw's *Saint Joan*.

There were many other successful groups. To name only a few: Woodstock Little Theatre, which went from four hundred members in 1946 to two thousand in 1951; the Negro Theatre Guild in Montreal, which won a DDF award in 1949; Trinity Players, which formed around the turn of the twentieth century and went on to become Montreal's longest running amateur theatre; the Ottawa Drama League, which was a very active group, winning a number of DDF awards; and Toronto's Belmont Group Theatre, which was organized in 1942 by Ben and Sylvia Lennick. Later on the Lennicks appeared frequently with Wayne and Shuster.

Some of the amateur theatres are still operating in the twenty-first century, including the Vagabond Players and Winnipeg's Le Cercle Molière. The Vagabond Players formed in 1937 in New Westminster, British Columbia, and staged four to eight plays a year. In 1951, with the help of the city, they took a gamble and borrowed $1,600 to remodel and equip a building in Queen's Park that they had previously used as a storage area. They opened with *Strange Bedfellows* by Colin Clements and Florence Ryerson, playing to packed houses for eleven performances, which was enough to pay off the

The Little Theatre Club of Saskatoon presented three one-act plays, including this one, *Good Night Please*, c. 1946. Shown third from the right is Floyd Caza. (MCNICOLL COLLECTION)

debt. During the next twenty years, their Vagabond Playhouse added a new stage, dressing rooms, wood paneling and a lounge. They made numerous appearances in the Dominion Drama Festival, winning the regional award for best entry in 1958.

Le Cercle Molière, a French-language theatre in Winnipeg, celebrated its seventy-fifth anniversary with a 2001–02 season composed entirely of Franco-Manitoban plays. By that time it had been a professional company for twenty-five years, with a budget in 1985 of close to $400,000. The group was started by a French teacher, André Castelein de la Lande, and a circle (hence the name) of Molière admirers. It was under Arthur Boutal that Le Cercle's reputation for quality emerged. He was artistic director from 1928 until his death in 1941, at which time his wife, Pauline Boutal, was so determined to keep the company going she became the artistic director herself. The group also won many DDF awards including individual ones won by Pauline Boutal.

Another amateur group which, although it did not evolve into a professional theatre, planted the seeds for one, was Workshop 14, the forerunner of Theatre Calgary. A latecomer to the little theatre scene, Workshop 14 was not formed until 1944 but quickly made itself known. It won more regional and national awards than any other amateur group of the time. In the ten years following the 1949 revival of Alberta's regional drama festivals, Workshop 14 won the best play award nine times. It began when Betty Mitchell, teacher of drama at Western Canada High School, was approached by some of her former drama students. They wanted to continue their studies with an eye towards the professional stage. At the outset, Mitchell picked plays that were not too taxing for the fledgling thespians. The royalties for her first choice, *Papa Is All*, by Patterson Greene, were paid by twenty-five members of the group itself, and the production was successful enough to pay for a second one. They were on their way.

Workshop 14's headquarters were two rooms in Western Canada High School, supplied by the Board of Education. The group was initially called the Fourteen-Fifteen Club after the numbers of the two rooms they occupied, becoming Workshop 15 and finally, a year after their inauguration, Workshop 14. As the years passed they began staging plays with more substance, and at the 1949 Alberta regional finals for the DDF, adjudicator Robert Speaight said their presentation was "the best performance of Ibsen's *Hedda Gabler* I've ever seen and the best I am ever likely to see."

In the previous year Workshop 14 had moved from the school to the Old Barn, which was actually the second storey of an aging building, and they moved yet again in 1956. In 1965 they amalgamated with the Musicians and Actors Club to create the MAC 14 Club which ultimately became Theatre Calgary. Among those that came out of the early Workshop 14 years were Conrad Bain of later television fame in *Maude* and *Different Strokes*, Myra Benson, Ron Hartmann, Irene Prothroe and Gordon Atkinson. The theatre did a great deal for prairie theatre, and during its early years gave several small scholarships of $200 to members "to enable them to continue their studies in dramatic art," according to one group's report to the Royal Commission in 1949. "Such awards have been made on condition the winners would return to Canada and impart their knowledge to others," their report added.

Workshop 14 was not the only amateur group which boasted an impressive alumni. The Vancouver Little Theatre Association also possessed a remarkable graduate list. Arthur Hill and his wife Peggy Hassard, John Drainie, Sam Payne, Ed McNamara,

Paul Kligman, Joan Miller (first female winner at the DDF), Fletcher Markle and Barbara Kelly all performed with the Vancouver Little Theatre.

The university theatre groups were another avenue of training for amateur actors at that time. Among these was the well-known Hart House, used by University of Toronto students. There was also a strong drama group at Queen's University in Kingston, Ontario. The University of British Columbia had an amateur theatre group that was second to none. "The Players' Club when I was at university was absolutely first rate," said one of its most famous alumni, Arthur Hill. "We did difficult work, we did it well and it was all extracurricular. A lot of producers, good actors [were there]. John Glen went on to be an actor in England. Lister Sinclair was in the Players' Club. . . . Pierre Berton was also at the university and wrote very good reviews of plays."

The University of British Columbia's Summer School of the Theatre was also very active. Under the directorship of Dorothy Somerset, students worked with various teachers and staged plays at the university. "It was the place where [young actors] emerged with some sort of opinion, given from some professional that she [Dorothy Somerset] had brought in, as to whether we had the right to go on in this business," Joy Coghill said.

Universities from all parts of Canada, while they did not offer credit courses in theatre in the immediate years following the war, strongly supported extracurricular drama groups that operated during the school year. Some even organized summer theatre companies (often travelling ones) for the students, in order for them to gain experience. Four of these operated out of institutions in Saskatchewan, Alberta, Ontario and Nova Scotia.

The Western Stage Society was the most elaborate of the four and was made up of eight University of Saskatchewan students (one was Frances Hyland, who went on to star at Stratford and appeared in the *Road to Avonlea* television series). Although not actually part of the university, the group was managed by the campus drama department. In its first season of 1948 the group travelled to more than sixty cities, towns and villages from the United States border to Flin Flon, Manitoba. They covered almost ten thousand miles in a large car, pulling a trailer carrying the sets and props. Obtaining their operating funds from box office receipts and program advertising, the students were given a salary plus living and travelling expenses, making them, financially at least, professional actors. They performed a modernized version of Molière's *The Doctor in Spite of Himself* and some scenes from *A Midsummer Night's Dream*. A successful second season followed, and in their third summer they gave more than ninety performances in eighty-three cities before a lack of money forced the group to close the season early.

In 1946, a number of students from the University of Alberta formed the Provincial Players and took to the road at the end of the school year with three plays under the sponsorship and direction of Sydney Risk, who at that time was the head of drama at the university. They appeared in thirty towns and were successful enough to warrant a second season, which was financed with a loan from the University Student's Union. Directed by Robert Orchard, the six-member group was not financially successful but nevertheless survived. By 1950, the University of Alberta was one of the backers of the theatre, which started touring in May of that year, appearing in twenty-eight Alberta centres including a two-thousand-seat outdoor bowl in Medicine Hat. They finished their summer, which had consisted of three one-act plays by Robertson Davies, in Banff where the students received scholarships to attend the Banff School of Fine Arts. The group lasted only one more summer.

Another group of students, this one from the University of Western Ontario, joined forces with a few other Londoners and formed a theatre in 1950 which operated for a number of years. Campus Players '50, which became Circle Theatre the following year, performed out-of-the-ordinary plays such as *Sit Ye Doon* by hometown resident Bill Digby.

There was little homegrown theatre activity in the Maritimes in the early post-war years but there was one group of university students, under the auspices of the Nova Scotia Drama League, which in 1950 attempted to change that. A borrowed station wagon and theatre equipment, and a provincial grant and monies from various individuals, all culminated in a summer tour. Harold Sipperall, a professor at Acadia, brought together the best actors from Mount Allison, Dalhousie and Acadia universities. Financially, everything was done on a professional basis with the cast being paid for three weeks of rehearsals and two months touring. They staged Ibsen's *Ghosts* and the thriller *Angel Street* by Patrick Hamilton, as well as a series of one-act plays. Although the audiences were not large, the enthusiasm for the performances was strong and the group did encourage theatre in the Maritimes.

In addition to the little theatres and universities, there were also a few individual training schools for aspiring actors: Dora Mavor Moore's, which opened in 1950; a school run by Sterndale Bennett (a man that Vernon Chapman said has not been given enough credit for his contributions to Canadian theatre); and institutions such as the Royal Conservatory of Music, which gave drama classes, and The Academy of Radio Arts.

The biggest of the teaching schools, however, was the Banff School of Fine Arts. In 1932, the University of Alberta, with the aid of a Carnegie grant, added Fine Arts to their Extension Department. Elizabeth Sterling Haynes was named Director of Drama and promoted theatre all across Alberta, pushing for a permanent training centre. She recommended Banff as the site to the director of drama, A.E. Corbett. With Haynes as instructor, the Banff School of the Theatre, as it was then called, opened in 1933 with 102 students, each paying a $1.00 registration fee. Only 25 students had been planned for, so it is safe to say the school was an instant success. By 1936 the name was changed to the Banff School of Fine Arts, with Senator Cameron as director, and Haynes and Ted Cohen in charge of production. Art, music and ballet departments were all added that summer, and in 1937 the course expanded from four to six weeks and scholarships were added. In 1949, because of rapid growth, the school temporarily had to bring in a ceiling of six hundred students. Sydney Risk, recruited from the school when he was forming his Everyman company in 1946, and Ted Follows and Bruno Gerussi were two early Banff alumni.

Working within all the mentioned training grounds were many mentors who supported both amateur theatre and actors, and in the process helped keep theatre alive in Canada. "They were nearly all women of strong character with some social position who, if they didn't have money themselves, had access to people with money so that the patrons could support something that obviously enhanced the community," Herbert Whittaker said. "Martha Allan [of the Montreal Repertory Theatre] was almost a prototype of the people who were behind the successful community and little theatres across this country."

Although he would have been much too modest to admit it, Herbert Whittaker was one of the mentors himself. Alongside Charles Rittenhouse, he helped introduce Montreal's high school students to theatre, encouraging young actors such as Christopher Plummer. Madge and Filmore Sadler then took many of these students to the Brae Manor Playhouse in Knowlton, Quebec, for the summers. Eleanor Stuart taught voice in Montreal. On the French side, Father Émile Legault was encouraging actors in his Les Compagnons, as was Ludmilla Pitoëff with her company. Kingston had William Angus who headed drama at Queen's University, while the Maritimes were blessed with Harold Sipperall and Donald Wetmore, the latter being a playwright as well as an educator.

Toronto's young actors came under the tutelage of Robert Gill, Sterndale Bennett, Dorothy Goulding, Dora Mavor Moore, Josephine Barrington and Clara Salisbury Baker. Baker joined the Conservatory of Music in 1938, becoming the head of speech and drama there in 1940. Baker's students included Amelia Hall, Toby Robins, Kate Reid and Barbara Hamilton.

In Western Canada, the active theatre women who influenced the lives of so many young actors with their teaching included Betty Mitchell (Workshop 14), Dorothy Somerset (UBC Summer School of the Theatre), Jessie Richardson, Elizabeth Sterling

Haynes, Florence James and Mary Ellen Burgess. One of the best-loved promoters of British Columbian theatre, Jessie Richardson came to Canada as a war bride in 1919. From the time she appeared with the Vancouver Little Theatre in the 1930s, Richardson remained active in every aspect of the theatre for the balance of her life.

In 1929, Elizabeth Sterling Haynes was one of those that founded the Edmonton Little Theatre and helped begin the Alberta Drama League. Haynes will best be remembered for her role in the formation of the Banff School of Fine Arts. Florence James taught at Saskatchewan's Summer School of the Arts, at the Banff School of Fine Arts, at the Regina Little Theatre, and in 1953 she became the drama consultant for the Saskatchewan Arts Board. In addition to being a teacher, Mary Ellen Burgess was involved with community theatre through the years and obtained training herself at both Banff and Columbia University. Both Florence James and Mary Ellen Burgess were tireless leaders of amateur actors in Saskatchewan. Joy Coghill said that the impact of the many women who taught and nurtured young students was immense: "This marvellous thing that these ladies did—they laid the seed of it all. Their influence was on so many people."

Besides a fervent belief in theatre, one other thing that these women all had in common was their support for what was arguably the most important development for early amateur theatre, the Dominion Drama Festival. Some of them were among the organizers of the DDF itself, founded in 1932, and many actually served on the Festival's executive committee at one time or another. The DDF was the meeting point for the network of little theatres and community theatre groups springing up across the country, "a national checkpoint," Herbert Whittaker said. It was not only a nationwide contest but for many years the only major force unifying theatrical interests from all regions of the country. It also gave French and English drama groups, who previously had little contact, the chance to appreciate the work of performers in another language.

The size of Canada made interaction between theatres very difficult and tended to make regions more self focused. Herbert Whittaker commented on this isolation of theatres:

> A direct result of isolation was that a great many people didn't bother thinking about the achievements elsewhere. It was probable that they were just as concerned with their own achievement in theatre in Winnipeg and Vancouver as they were here [Toronto]. It's a country that's never been prone to the Broadway syndrome—because we realized that these places, centres, are far apart and that they need their own theatre, and everybody there that has theatrical instinct and interests tends to join that one and adhere to it. The only counter-acting element there, in that respect that I can think of, was the Dominion Drama Festival and its exchanges of area. At first all the final festivals were

held in Ottawa and then they started to go to different parts of the country in recognition of the size and need of the country.

The Massey Commission in 1951 stated in part that "nothing in Canada has done so much for the amateur theatre as the Dominion Drama Festivals."

The DDF was not the first drama festival in Canada but it was the first to attempt to cover the entire country. There had been competitions such as the Alberta Drama Festival in 1930. There was a French competition in Quebec organized in 1908 by Paul Cazeneuve. The largest of the pre-DDF festivals, the Earl Grey Musical and Dramatic Competition, began in Ottawa. It was established in 1907 by the then governor-general of Canada, Earl Grey, who was also responsible for football's Grey Cup, although his loyalties lay much more with the arts than athletics. There were two presentations, one for drama and one for music. The trophy given was of a man and a woman, representing respectively music and drama, with a fence between them suggesting that each had its own territory. However, both figures had one foot on the lowest rail of the fence to indicate that their territories nevertheless overlapped. The first two competitions were held in Ottawa, with subsequent ones in Montreal, Toronto and Winnipeg. Unlike the later DDF, there was no regional weeding out process, the quality of presentations ranged widely, and some of the judges were quite brutal in their comments. The festival ceased when Earl Grey's tenure as governor-general ended in 1911.

While many people were involved in the formation of the Dominion Drama Festival (sixty at the first meeting in October 1932), it was the formidable head of the Montreal Repertory Theatre, Martha Allan, who worked closely with Governor-General Lord Bessborough to get it off the ground. She stayed involved in it until it stopped for the duration of the Second World War.

When they held that first meeting in 1932, Allan and Bessborough could not possibly have imagined the impact the Dominion Drama Festival would have on theatre in Canada. A system of regional eliminations began in February 1933, the first year of the Festival, which had a budget of $10,000. Adjudicators chose the best play in each region and that play would move on to the finals. By the time those took place in Ottawa in April 1933, 110 plays from eight provinces had been narrowed down to 24. At the opening of the festival, Lord Bessborough said the "spirit of a nation, if it is to find full expression, must include a National Drama."

There were only three prize presentations that first year: The Bessborough Trophy for best presentation at the Festival and two Festival plaques, one each for French and English, given to the best presentations, excluding the Bessborough Trophy winner. The Masquers Club of Winnipeg, the Vancouver Little Theatre Association and L'Union Dramatique de Québec were the three victors. In the ensuing years other awards were added, including ones for male and female performances, best director and best Canadian play. John Coulter, Gwen Pharis Ringwood, Martha Allan, Paul

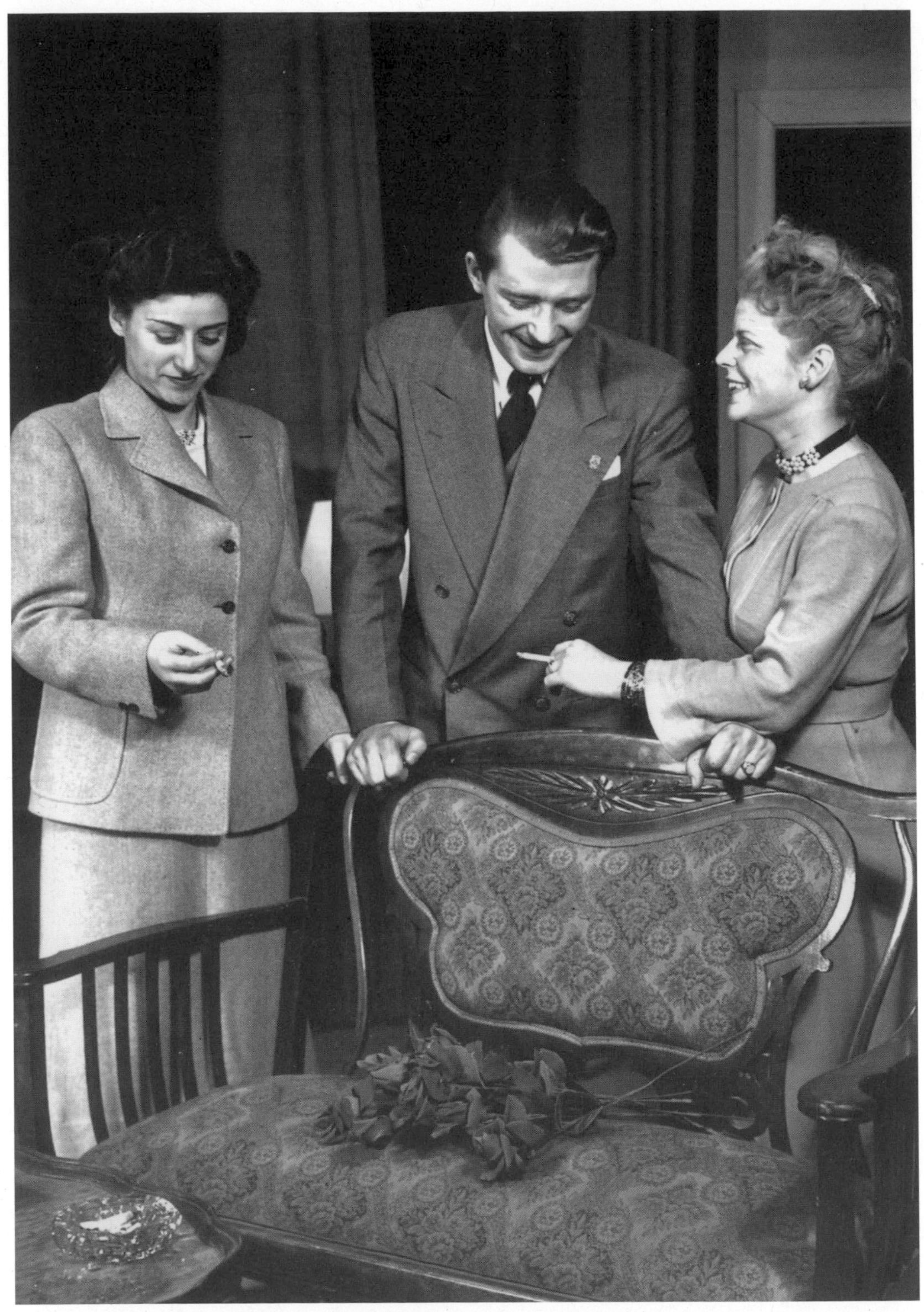

Sonya Britton, Floyd Caza and Joy Coghill laughing during a rehearsal for *The Silver Cord*, which was the Vancouver Little Theatre entry into the 1948 Dominion Drama Festival. (COGHILL COLLECTION)

Gury and Robertson Davies were among the winning playwrights. It was really one of the first efforts in Canada to encourage indigenous playwrights. In the early years only one-act plays or scenes from full-length ones were presented at the festival.

At the start, the amateurism of the festival was emphasized. Under DDF rules, only the directors were allowed to be professional. No actor who intended to continue on at a professional level was allowed to appear. They could perform, however, if they had given up acting and turned to another profession. It quickly became difficult to draw the line as many groups, such as the Montreal Repertory Theatre and Les Compagnons de Saint-Laurent in later years, actually paid some of their actors to appear with them, thereby invalidating their amateur status. Finally in October 1947, the DDF Committee capitulated, and the rule limiting professional actors from competition was deleted.

The DDF committee suspended operations for the Second World War from 1939 to 1947. A number of provincial festivals in 1946, primarily in the West, led the way for the revival of the DDF the following year. Full-length plays were now accepted, and by 1950 the DDF no longer allowed one-act productions in the finals.

During the five or six years following 1948, the level of competition at the DDF was unbelievably high as the actors who appeared were among the best Canada had to offer. The regional battles were often fiercer than the national one. Herbert Whittaker recalled:

> There were a great many community and amateur groups in their drama festivals at that time and they reached an extraordinarily high standard because of it. There's also the fact that the Royal Alexandra had never stopped bringing in productions and I think it [Toronto] was the only town in the country that had an unbroken road company tradition. While those road companies were not always of high standard there were enough of them to have people know what high standards were in the theatre, so that various amateur and academic theatres were really in a very high state of production. And their preliminary festivals here [in Ontario] were amongst the highest in the country.

The 1948 final was significant because it was the first time a group (Les Compagnons de Saint-Laurent), in spite of solid acting performances that won them individual awards, was severely reprimanded and basically disqualified by the adjudicator. He criticized the cuts they did on the text of a play, which basically resulted in censorship—Les Compagnons was run by Jesuit priests.

Although an effort was made in the beginning to have all areas of the country evenly represented in the DDF finals, the invitations were soon offered more on merit than location. Of the twelve plays invited to the final in 1949, six were from Ontario, three from Montreal and one each from New Brunswick, Alberta and British Columbia. An illustrious group of actors appeared that year, including Denise Pelletier, Roger Garceau, Denyse Saint-Pierre, William Hutt, Ted Follows, Eric House, Anna Cameron and

Kate Reid. The bilingual adjudicators for the finals continued to be people well thought of in their field and brought in from outside Canada. The 1950 choice was the French-born director Michel Saint-Denis who had overseen the DDF in 1937 and subsequently went on to help in the formation of Canada's National Theatre School in 1960. The 1950 festival was hosted by Calgary, which was celebrating its seventy-fifth anniversary; it was only the second time the DDF had been held outside Ontario. Saint-Denis called those who filled the 1,400-seat theatre "one of the best theatre audiences I have known." The theatre was sold out for five of the six nights of performances.

By the 1960s most of the adjudicators for the regional finals were Canadian. They included David Gardner, Robert Gill, Esse W. Ljungh, Betty Mitchell, Herbert Whittaker, Walter Massey and Norma Springford.

When it came to the question of its value to Canadian professional theatre, the DDF in the post-war years had its supporters and its detractors. Some saw the theatre community's focus on the DDF, an amateur festival, as a blockade in the way of professional status, in spite of the fact the acting standards of the festival were so high. Actors struggled to be paid in those years, if only a token, in order to help Canadian theatre out from under the cloak of amateurism. "I had an absolute loathing for the amateur from very early on," said Christopher Plummer, who nevertheless did work with groups such as the Montreal Repertory Theatre and the Shakespeare Society. "I thought, why am I not getting paid for this? Why am I not professional? The Montreal Rep[ertory Theatre], although I loved it, it smelled of amateurism. . . . I couldn't wait to get out of that wrap."

Others who hoped to go on as professionals felt differently and saw amateur theatre and the yearly festival as a stepping stone to be used for experience and exposure. Virtually all the actors who emerged from the post-war years to make their mark had graced the stage of some amateur theatre. "I used to be in them," recalled Sam Payne. "That [DDF] is one thing that helped to foster talent or keep it going. They were sort of under semi-professional standards." It was these high standards of competition that kept many actors returning to perform in DDF if they had the opportunity. "We had all grown up with amateur theatre," Donald Davis added. "We had all been involved, one way or another, with the whole Drama Festival syndrome which went right across the country and which was the highlight of the year. And some mighty fine stuff I saw in the years of the DDF. In those days the distinctions between professional and amateur and community and so on, weren't finely drawn."

Appearing in the DDF also gave many actors confidence. "I don't really believe in [competition] but the DDF did some things in that survivors went on into the profession," said Joy Coghill who was in the 1948 finals with Sidney Howard's *The Silver Cord*, presented by Vancouver Little Theatre. "All those people who became our stars all won a DDF here or there and that gave them the courage to go on."

One of those people was John Colicos, who won the best actor award at the DDF in 1951 for his performance in the women's University of Toronto Alumnae Drama Club's production of Shaw's *In Good King Charles's Golden Days*. It was not long before the young actor was achieving international recognition. Colicos was directed at the 1951 DDF by Herbert Whittaker, who won the Louis Jouvet Directing Award for this effort. It was in that year also, however, that the cracks began to show in the Festival. Following the 1952 DDF, in order to "avoid collapse of the Festival," whose operating costs had risen sharply, the executive committee recommended acceptance of $15,000 from Calvert's distillery plus an extra $2,300 in cash awards. In exchange for this, all previous prizes were replaced by the Calvert trophies. The DDF had gone commercial and this loss of tradition bothered many people. But costs had risen, and the emergence of professional theatres had drained many actors and resources that prior to this had gone to the amateur theatre.

Looking back, one can see the zenith of the DDF was reached in the early post-war years and, as the 1950s drew to a close, the influence of the Festival on theatre diminished rapidly. Professional actors no longer appeared in amateur productions and the newly formed Canada Council (1957) funded only professional involvement. As a result, any impact the DDF might have on professional theatre in Canada was now over even though the organization would survive in some form for almost two more decades.

From 1961 to 1965 the DDF was run by the Canadian Association of Broadcasters, but the organization's debt continued to increase every year. There was one major highlight in the 1960s, during Canada's 1967 centennial year, when the DDF held an all-Canadian play festival in St. John's, giving indigenous playwrights a boost. Sixty-two Canadian plays were presented in all regions, with six full-length ones chosen to compete in the finals.

Nevertheless, the DDF had lost its direction and seemed to be floundering to find a way to survive. A reorganization to try to save the Festival took place in 1970. It was renamed Theatre Canada and continued to present amateur productions but all elements of competition were removed. There was little bite left in this remnant of the DDF, and Theatre Canada was finally closed in 1978.

Ultimately, the Dominion Drama Festival had served as a valuable stepping stone on the road to professional Canadian theatre. In the early years it gave a focus to amateur theatres, and they were one of the few places that young actors could gain experience. The DDF brought together all the regional amateur and semi-professional theatres across the country into one central location. Not only did it allow the actors to have exposure and experience, but it also gave them an opportunity to see that they were not alone, that others were fighting all across the country, just as they were, to create professional theatre in Canada.

CHAPTER FIVE

# RADIO DRAMA & JUPITER THEATRE

"It was one of the proudest, golden times of our kind of identity and creativity."
—CHRISTOPHER PLUMMER

From the moment in 1923 when radio in Canada began, drama played an important role. Radio presented plays, including many Canadian plays, from coast to coast, and in the early years following the Second World War, it had the added benefit of giving actors a lucrative way to make a living while continuing to act on stage.

Although it was not the only city involved, Toronto was by far the largest radio centre in the country, and that message was not lost on actors in other parts of the country. "Every year there was always an exodus from Vancouver to Toronto where the major work was being done, where strawberries were really being picked," Murray Westgate said. Toronto appeared to be the land of milk and honey, or as close to it as any actor would find in Canada's pre-television days. It was not because of theatre but because radio, or more specifically radio drama, was a real financial pull. "I think the reason the push [for actors] came in Toronto," Donald Davis said, "was because of the Canadian Broadcasting Corporation, because of radio. If you wanted to earn some money in the theatre, in English-speaking Canada, you came to Toronto." Davis talked of radio and theatre almost interchangeably and, in a way, he was right. Radio drama productions at that time were very sophisticated, with elaborate music and sound effects, and actors who were highly skilled with voices trained for the theatre. Not only did radio drama give Canada's struggling acting community some financial stability; it also made an enormous contribution to the field of drama and offered exposure for Canadian playwrights who sometimes took their radio scripts and expanded them into stage plays.

The Canadian Broadcasting Corporation, a Canadian Crown corporation commonly known as the CBC, was not the first broadcasting network in Canada. It had a predecessor, one owned by the Canadian National Railway. From 1923 to 1932, CNR Radio (officially the Canadian National Railways Radio Department) broadcast entertainment and information to its train passengers, and was the first national radio network in North America. As broadcasts could be received by anyone living in the coverage area of the numerous station transmitters (plus the CNR rented time on private radio stations), the network was able to provide radio from Vancouver to Halifax. The first private station to broadcast in Canada was XWA in Montreal on May 20, 1920. By 1929 there were at least sixty such stations. The programming was produced in English, French and, occasionally, in some Aboriginal languages.

Right from the beginning, drama had been a major part of CNR's mandate as they broadcast plays from 1925 on. It was during that year that the first Canadian play was broadcast in Canada—*The Rosary* (author unknown) in Moncton, New Brunswick. From 1927 to 1932, an anthology series, including some Canadian works, was heard in Vancouver. The productions included Shakespeare, adaptations from American and European plays, and some original Vancouver dramas. The "Romance of Canada," a series of twenty-four plays based on Canadian history written by Merrill Denison, was broadcast by CNR Radio. The series was produced in Montreal (1931–32), with Tyrone Guthrie directing the first season and Rupert Caplan and Esmie Moonie the second.

CNR closed down in 1932 and a year later most of its assets were sold to a new government agency, the Canadian Radio Broadcasting Commission (CRBC). The CRBC became the first public broadcasting network and continued to broadcast many dramas until, in November 1936, it became the Canadian Broadcasting Corporation.

In 1939, the CBC hired Andrew Allan as a producer in Vancouver where he established himself admirably in radio drama. As a result, in 1943 the CBC appointed Allan head of radio drama in Toronto. In the ensuing years he would make radio drama a truly nationalistic expression of the time and move it into what has been called the "Golden Age of radio." Radio connected all the different regions of the country in a way that theatre always had difficulty doing, and from the beginning radio in Canada made drama its own. Radio drama shares many of the same techniques as the stage, minus the visuals. Good actors were essential for radio drama, and they in turn needed radio for the good money it offered. But actors also wanted to be involved because the radio drama produced in Canada during the 1940s and '50s was known as the very best in the world. Theatre actors also believed work in radio drama helped improve their stage talents. Christopher Plummer commented, "It helped me with my voice, it helped me be conscious of a kind of orchestral rhythm which is essential to an actor, particularly if you are doing the classics. And we did classics [on radio] as well as original plays."

Toronto may have been the largest, but there were also solid radio communities in Vancouver, Winnipeg, Montreal and Halifax. In addition to Andrew Allan, some of the other producers who gave much to radio drama across Canada were J. Frank Willis in Toronto, Rupert Caplan, working mostly out of Montreal, Doug Nixon in Vancouver, Stephen Appleby in Halifax, and Esse Ljungh in Winnipeg and later Toronto. Ljungh's story is particularly interesting. He was originally from Sweden, and in 1927 headed for a job in Chile as a correspondent and translator. A revolution there left him looking for work in Canada, where he found his true vocation. Ljungh's radio work in Winnipeg and Toronto was renowned and included *The Gallant Greenhorn* by Ray Darby in December 1947, numerous plays in the acclaimed *Stage Series* and the opening production of CBC's *Wednesday Night*. "He was marvellous too in a kind of weird, undisciplined, much freer way [than Andrew Allan]," remembered Christopher Plummer. "He was, I thought, terrific."

It was during the years following the Second World War that radio drama reached new heights in Canada. The most famous of the shows were the above-mentioned *Stage Series* and CBC's *Wednesday Night*. Andrew Allan produced the *Stage Series* from 1944 to 1955 when Esse Ljungh took over from him. Ljungh also produced many of the CBC *Wednesday Night* dramas.

There was great geographical diversity in the plays produced in Canada during the post-war period. As an example, excluding CBC's *Sunday Night* and commercial shows, a breakdown of the three hundred English plays produced nationwide during the 1948–49 season shows the following: sixty from Vancouver, forty-seven from Winnipeg, sixty-five from Montreal, twenty-five from Halifax and 103 from Toronto. It was also in radio, more than in the theatre, that Canadian playwrights were able to thrive by having their works produced. During the same 1948–49 season, among those who had original plays produced under the *Stage Series* were Robertson Davies, Len Peterson, Lister Sinclair and Tommy Tweed. On the French side (Radio-Canada), there were some dramas produced in Quebec but serials were much more popular than straight dramatic plays. There were on average, in the post-war years, from ten to fifteen serials a day on French language radio.

Toronto was still the Mecca for radio drama, however, because aside from copious productivity, the city also had one thing going for it after the Second World War that no other place in Canada or the world had—a perfectionist by the name of Andrew Allan. It was as producer of the *Stage Series* in Toronto that Allan will best be remembered. In the beginning, the series was not always popular with a public that was longing for a diet of boy-meets-girl fluff. They certainly did not get that from Allan. The plays he produced made them think, with broad social themes and endings that were anything but standard fare. He was not interested in pat resolutions to plot lines and wanted to show people as they actually lived. Audiences eventually came around, and Sunday night productions were enjoyed right across the country. They were said to have a national audience second only to Saturday Night Hockey broadcasts. The productions were huge in scope and, counting Lucio Agostini and his orchestra, there were often as many as seventy-five people working on one show.

Lucio Agostini wrote the scores for all the *Stage Series* plays and he was a master at it. Five or six days before rehearsal, Allan would go over the play with Agostini and explain what he wanted from the background music. He would then not hear the score until the first run-through with the cast. Agostini, who also composed and conducted music for other CBC shows such as *Wednesday Night* and *Ford Theatre*, gave an explanation for this in the CBC *Times* for December 24–30, 1950. "Andrew knows music and the mood of the play thoroughly," he said, "and his explanations are so precise that it's impossible for the musical director to write a bad score."

Rehearsals for the *Stage Series* were generally at night. Betting pools at $1.00 a person were frequently set up around what ungodly hour in the early morning the actors would be allowed to go home. Allan wasted no rehearsal time, however, and started each one by explaining the mood of the play. He often told each actor what clothes his character would be dressed in so they would better understand the physical aspects of the individuals they represented.

Allan's adherence to detail and his expectations of excellence from everyone involved led to high quality performances time and time again. "He was a genius at what he did," Christopher Plummer said. "I put him in the same class as I do [Tyrone] Guthrie and all the great directors. In his own medium he was, to me, in their class ... one of the best in the history of radio."

There was no question Allan was a genius. There was also no question he was a difficult man to be around if you made a mistake. Part of the reason for this was Allan's desire for flawless productions, but there was another practical reason—everything was recorded live. There could be no going back over parts of a script in which a mistake had been made.

One near miss happened during the final rehearsal of T.S Eliot's *Murder in the Cathedral*. It involved Sam Payne. "Andrew had got six silver trumpets for the balcony

Andrew Allan (right foreground) listens to a group of actors performing in his famous *Stage Series*. In the post-war years Canada was known for producing the best radio drama in the world, c. late 1940s. (MCNICOLL COLLECTION)

in this theatre where we were recording it," recalled Payne. "Every actor had to have his shoes off and there had to be dead silence. . . . That day I had picked up an alarm clock I had fixed. I had a little suitcase . . . put the clock in it and sat it on a seat in the theatre. . . . Yes, it happened. The alarm went off. Thank God it was only a rehearsal but Allan still tore a strip off me from here to there."

With everything going out live, precision and timing were key. A major disaster, caused by another producer, J. Frank Willis, was narrowly avoided one night by a quick-thinking assistant. In radio dramas, the producer was responsible for holding his arm in the air and bringing it down, thereby giving everyone the cue for the production to begin. Willis was a congenial and well-liked man, known for his spontaneous sense of humour, but on this occasion it is doubtful he was trying to be funny, as Christopher Plummer explained:

> I wish I had been in the show where he threw a cue out to a massive radio production, where the orchestras were in two studios, a chorus in a third one and the actors in the fourth. One of those massive Wednesday night series. He got so drunk at dinner that he came back and as he threw the cue for this massive show to begin he just fell backwards. He never finished the gesture so Alice, his secretary, quickly finished it for him. But he just disappeared backwards. The poor actors looking up at the control booth just saw nobody there at all.

Considering it was all live, the truly amazing thing was that disasters did not happen more often.

Willis was not the only drinker in the group and most of them also smoked to excess. "The radio crowd, we worked for years in radio, they were all, most of those people, heavy drinkers, and a lot of smoking," Thor Arngrim said. "You would go into a sound stage, and you couldn't see—it was like a nightclub, a cabaret. And then fluorescent lighting, the worst lighting in the world for reading on white paper. And then all the smoke, cough, hack. How people kept from coughing during a broadcast I have no idea. I look back and wonder how we managed. The musicians also smoked. . . . I guess when Andrew said you don't cough, you don't cough!"

On the job Allan used Mister or Miss with his performers but was on a first name basis with all of them away from the set. The air of formality that surrounded him at work led some to describe him as cold and aloof. It was certainly wise to stay on his good side. Even though actors might have been nervous about making mistakes, they all wanted to work with him, for he was undoubtedly the best.

"He was a hard disciplinarian," remembered Lister Sinclair, who had at least fifty of his scripts produced by Allan. "He was very much a perfectionist in some ways and totally indifferent in others. . . . One of the things he used to say you must have, first of all, to be a director was authority . . . not really authority in the sense of bellowing and stamping about in jackboots but certainly in the sense of being able to have things done your way."

"If you weren't up to it, you'd had it with Andrew," Sam Payne said. "You had to keep on your toes, which is good. I've always contended, along with ninety thousand other people, that Andrew was one of the great directors of our time. . . . Radio was in its zenith and I was very lucky because Andrew was very good to me."

He was good to a number of actors and kept a strong nucleus of them employed during the late 1940s when, as mentioned earlier, there were few opportunities in Canada for even good actors to make a living. His reputation among other CBC producers was such that if an actor had Allan's approval, it frequently led to the actor finding work with all the other producers. Paul Kligman, who had done radio work with Esse Ljungh in Winnipeg and Doug Nixon in Vancouver, remembered being ecstatic when shortly after he arrived in Toronto, Allan offered him a small role in an upcoming *Stage Series* production. "Of course I danced about that," Kligman said. "The trick in those days was that if Andrew Allan rehired you for a second show the other producers would start to do so because it meant he approved of your quality and he was the leader of the band."

The *Stage Series* was certainly the most prestigious radio drama show but there were many other series widely listened to, and they kept actors busy. Shows such as *Wednesday Night*, *The Carsons* and *The Craigs*. While *Wednesday Night* did not have the stature of the *Stage Series*, its shows were the same high calibre and actors wanted to appear on it. Although Allan was sometimes involved, in fact the largest number of the plays on *Wednesday Night* were produced by Esse Ljungh. He and Allan did not get along, and he was known to refer to Allan sarcastically as "The Legend." The two men fought for actors and plays, and they had a completely different style of producing. Many actors preferred Ljungh simply because he was less rigid and allowed emotions to rule the action, whereas Allan felt that the words and language should dictate the flow of a play. In addition to a wide variety of plays, the majority Canadian, *Wednesday Night* performed a yearly presentation of a full-length Shakespeare play. In 1951 it was *Hamlet* with a cast that included John Colicos, Frank Peddie, Lorne Greene, Tommy Tweed, Joy Lafleur and Robert Christie.

With so many opportunities for actors with *Wednesday Night*, the *Stage Series* and other radio shows, radio drama sometimes kept actors from venturing very far from the "radio cities." "For all of us in those years, running through this was the fact you were working on radio," Dorothy Davies said. She played the role of Mary on the serial *The Carsons*, one of the CBC *Farm Broadcasts* that focused on rural life. "That was the important thing that held you here [in Vancouver], particularly a few, a very few of us who were fortunate enough to be on the Farm broadcast because that was a steady income."

Radio drama was also an important outlet for Canadian playwrights, at a level no other medium before or since has been. CBC radio, both in French and English, gave playwrights national exposure and some financial security. The 1949–51 Massey Commission states "the work of the Canadian Broadcasting Corporation has fully demonstrated that we suffer from no lack of playwrights . . . where opportunity exists for their abilities." Even in the mid-1940s the average pay for a half-hour radio script was $70 to $75, good payment at the time. The network, year after year, showed its support for homegrown writers. In a "Canadian content" move, spearheaded first in Vancouver and then Toronto by Andrew Allan and other producers, 80 to 100 percent of the plays produced each year in the 1940s and early '50s were written by Canadians. Many of these were adaptations of other works. In the first seven weeks of the 1951 *Stage Series*, all of the plays were adapted from either novels or stage plays. Among the writers who contributed were Allan himself and Lister Sinclair. Including school broadcasts and documentaries, Sinclair had approximately seven hundred of his scripts on the air throughout his career, and in those days he received $100 for a half-hour script. "I looked over some of the early ones. I think they are very much *pièce d'occasion*, occasional pieces in the eighteenth-century term," Sinclair said. "Often they have a lot of vitality during the occasion and none whatsoever afterwards. A lot of them were written in the war context."

Among other Canadian writers frequently heard on the radio were Len Peterson, Fletcher Markle, Robertson Davies, Allan King, W.O. Mitchell and Tommy Tweed. With the well-known, distinctive twang in his voice, Tweed was one of the stars of Canadian radio drama, not only as an actor but as one of its most prolific writers. One of the strangest pieces he wrote was a history of Canada, which he called *England's Frozen Asset*.

The one ongoing radio series that probably captured the hearts of listeners more than any other was *Jake and the Kid* by W.O. Mitchell. It starred John Drainie in the role of Jake, the laconic, argumentative, storytelling chronicler of the everyday doings of the mythical town of Crocus. John Drainie was the cream of the crop when it came to actors in radio drama. The talents of the man that Herbert Whittaker called "the best radio actor that the continent had ever produced," included an uncanny knack for doing different accents and an ability to play a wide range of ages. He was often known to put in extra rehearsal time developing characters. "John was able to make a script sound the way you should have written it," said Lister Sinclair. "He had an extraordinary sense of what the nuances were and of what you were trying to convey. . . . He didn't play against lines, he played very much with them."

In addition to Drainie and Tweed, there were many other highly skilled radio actors at the time, including Bernard Braden and his wife Barbara Kelly, Lorne Greene, Ruth Springford, Jane Mallett, Barry Morse, Don Harron and Christopher Plummer. Plummer felt he came in at the end of the golden age of radio. "That was the closest thing that Canadians ever got to forming a unique kind of repertory group, and identity," Plummer said. "All those plays by those talented Canadians . . . they were so damn good, all of them." Almost every top actor who appeared on stage also showed up on the airwaves.

The need for trained radio personnel following the Second World War was so great that it prompted Lorne Greene, theatre actor and Canada's leading newscaster, to open a school, the Academy of Radio Arts. Greene was to news casting what Drainie was to radio drama. His reading of the news to Canadians during the war earned him the nickname "The Voice of Doom," and his was the most-recognized voice in the country. When Greene became convinced of the need for a training centre, he set up the Academy in an old twenty-two-room Victorian mansion on Toronto's Jarvis Street in 1946, at a cost of $50,000. The $400, six-month course included production, direction, speech, acting, announcing, writing and sound effects. Production and direction were taught by Andrew Allan, while other teachers included Mavor Moore, Esse Ljungh, Fletcher Markle, Lister Sinclair and Greene himself, who taught, not surprisingly, announcing. In spite of a reputation for self-importance, Greene was also very kind. More than once he allowed deserving students to attend the school even though they could not afford to pay. Obviously, this did not help the bottom line. Financially a failure, with losses of $3,000 to $5,000 a year, the school nevertheless graduated nearly four hundred students, and almost all found employment because of high demand. Graduates included Fred Davis, Murray Chercover and Leslie Nielsen. As a result of mounting losses, however, Lorne Greene was forced to close the school in 1952.

In the fall of that year, the core of stage and radio actors were also in on the birth of television in Canada. The Montreal station had a two-day jump on Toronto when it opened on September 6, 1952. From the outset, drama played as big a role in the new medium as it had in radio. In its first six months CBC television theatre presented nine comedies, three mysteries, five dramas and three romantic comedies. Among them were Ibsen's *An Enemy of the People*, Shaw's *Candida* and *The Playboy of the Western World* by J.M. Synge.

The first Shakespeare ever seen on Canadian television was *Othello* in February 1953, starring Lorne Greene in the lead role. As in radio, everything in television's early days was live and always difficult for the actors. "It was certainly my first television. Frightening beyond belief," remembered Christopher Plummer. "You didn't have an audience, there was no time, you bumped into each other. You bumped into cameras, it was a disaster. But everybody acted very earnestly and I played two parts." An Austrian actor, Joseph Furst, starred as Iago in that first televised Shakespearean production, and his performance was stored away in the mind of a young actor in the cast, to be resurrected in the distant future. Twenty-nine years later on Broadway, when he won acclaim and a Best Actor Tony Award nomination for the role of Iago opposite James Earl Jones' Othello, Christopher Plummer would use some of what he saw in that 1953 production. "I remember very clearly, Lorne of course, but even more clearly Joseph Furst," Plummer said. "He was a rather fascinating Iago. And I remember using—I now confess—two of his bits of business in my own performance on Broadway thousands of years later. They always stuck in my mind as being extremely daring and very good and I must admit they were not my own, they were his."

Although television gave the actors another outlet for their talents, it temporarily had a somewhat negative effect on theatre because it was easier for the public to sit at home with the new toy than to make the effort to go out. In time, though, it actually had the result of encouraging the public to go to the theatre. This was felt first and most strongly on the French side. "It's very strange what happened in Montreal," said Jean-Louis Roux, who was seen on both the French and English versions of *La famille Plouffe (The Plouffe Family)*. "Little by little the people who were watching television wished to see the actors in the flesh and I think that for many years it attracted people to the theatres."

⁂

Just as television tended in time to lure audiences back to live theatre, many of the actors were restless to return to the stage. The question, however, was where to find the stage. Except for *Spring Thaw*, the New Play Society had ceased operations for a time, so actors in Toronto had lost their main venue for continuing their stage work. They were looking for another, and the radio actors in particular began to talk about the possibility of forming their own theatre. Jupiter Theatre, incorporated as a non-profit organization in 1951, came into being as a result of these talks among the radio actors and their desire to perform on stage. Paul Kligman was one of them:

> Jupiter came about probably because of a lot of chatter that was going on at the time, that there was no theatre to speak of, of any consequence, in Toronto. Certainly not anything that was native, but there were a lot of plays worth doing that were avant-garde of their day, that we thought should be seen. It started with conversations around the CBC radio building [on Jarvis Street], usually in the canteen, with John Drainie, Lorne Greene, George Robertson and myself as a very, very new person to the scene. Then there was a woman by the name of Edna Slater, a very sharp lady who was in public relations. Glen Frankfurter was another, and one of the writers that I started to socialize with, Len Peterson. We kept saying, "Why don't we try to get a theatre going."

This group of people finally came together one evening in John Drainie's living room to form Jupiter Theatre, and they became its board of directors, with Drainie as chairman. The name was inspired by Orson Welles' Mercury Theatre, as the group hoped to start the same type of theatre with Canadian playwrights and actors.

Jupiter's importance to Canadian theatre lies in its progressive objectives. It would not only present important plays from around the world but also give Canadian writers encouragement to turn their talents to the stage. In addition to getting radio actors back onto the stage, Jupiter hoped to establish a professional theatre "which eventually would be self-sustaining and sufficiently remunerative to Canadian artists" to stop their departure from the country to look for greener fields. They wanted to provide this medium not only for actors and writers, but also directors and technical people.

Their first challenge was to find an acceptable stage on which to perform. In the end they used one that had been utilized by the New Play Society and others—the Museum Theatre at the Royal Ontario Museum. With a four hundred-seat theatre in which to perform, the organization now turned its attention to financing. "We thought that Drainie and Lorne and Glen Frankfurter [being in the advertising business], certainly were in a position to talk to some important people about putting money in," Paul Kligman said. "It wasn't going to require a lot and we could get it off the ground."

Even though it was television's *Bonanza* that later made him an international celebrity, Lorne Greene was still enough of a star in Canada back in 1951 to help inaugurate Jupiter Theatre. "It was using the force of Lorne Greene's name really, to walk into an office and say to somebody, 'How about putting a couple hundred dollars into the show,'" Paul Kligman said. "And literally that is all it was. Nobody came up with thousands. I think even Lady Eaton helped, but again it was a nominal amount of money. And the kind of money we raised, at best, was something in the neighbourhood of $2,000."

Among those who contributed financially were poet E.J. Pratt, director Esse Ljungh and actor Budd Knapp. The board members also each contributed $100. The next decision for the board was which plays to stage. Jupiter wanted the theatre to be bold in its choice of plays and to support Canadian playwrights—but only if the product was good. The theatre's first press release on September 29, 1951, stated, "Jupiter Theatre doesn't intend to produce plays just because they are by a Canadian. Every play, Canadian or foreign, must meet a certain high standard." It was, nevertheless, the case that of the fifteen plays produced by Jupiter in total, four were Canadian.

Finding a play for their opening production—one on which they could agree—was a lengthy process, and they ultimately did not go with a Canadian one. "They started off, because they were expert actors in one sense of the word, with a very advanced and very revolutionary new work—Bertolt Brecht's *Life of Galileo*," Herbert Whittaker said. The play had been translated and adapted by actor Charles Laughton, in collaboration with Brecht. Laughton happened to be performing at Massey Hall in Toronto prior to Jupiter's opening, and he gave a one-man reading of *Galileo* for the cast to help them better understand the work. The director and set designer was Herbert Whittaker.

The critical role of Galileo was given to John Drainie. "His performance in *Galileo* was a very expert one that came oddly close to the Brechtian concept," Whittaker said. "I say 'oddly' because, as the director I can't say that it was a deep experience with Brechtian presentation that I brought to it. Drainie's restraint, his use of the voice rather than the body, the way in which he held a thing in balance was a very fine performance."

Whittaker had a large cast to fill but many of the roles were small, and this did not please one particular newscaster. Lorne Greene had developed a reputation for being aloof and full of his own importance. Indeed, when once asked to nominate the best newscaster in the world, he said, "Lorne Greene, of course." When Whittaker chose his cast for Jupiter's first production, he gave one of the smaller roles to Greene, in spite of the fact that Greene was a co-founder and backer of the theatre.

Greene is reputed to have said, "Mr. Whittaker, I think you might have given me a better part to play." Whittaker replied, "God perhaps." And Greene boomed back, "Yes, that would be better."

Other members of the cast, in addition to John Drainie in the lead, included Margot Christie, David Gardner, Hugh Webster, Margot Lassner, Doug Haskins (later to be involved in Everyman's *Tobacco Road* trial in Vancouver) and Donald Glen, who handled three roles in the production.

If they were superstitious or believed in omens, the group might have had reason to be apprehensive on December 14, 1951, the opening date for *Galileo*. Toronto suffered one of its worst snowstorms in decades, and radio stations were urging everyone to remain at home. Luckily for the new theatre, the public, particularly the radio community, turned out in force despite the weather. The critics in Toronto's three daily newspapers were supportive, although Nathan Cohen was not completely on board. In the January 1952 edition of his own magazine, *The Critic*, Cohen wrote that "Toronto needs at least one drama company capable of speaking boldly and forthrightly on meaningful issues."[6] He hoped that Jupiter would be that theatre, but when it came to reviewing *Galileo*, he called Herbert Whittaker's set design "serviceable" and wrote that "the Jupiter production lacked the intellectual multiplicity of the text."[7] The audiences, however, were large and Jupiter Theatre was well on its way to success.

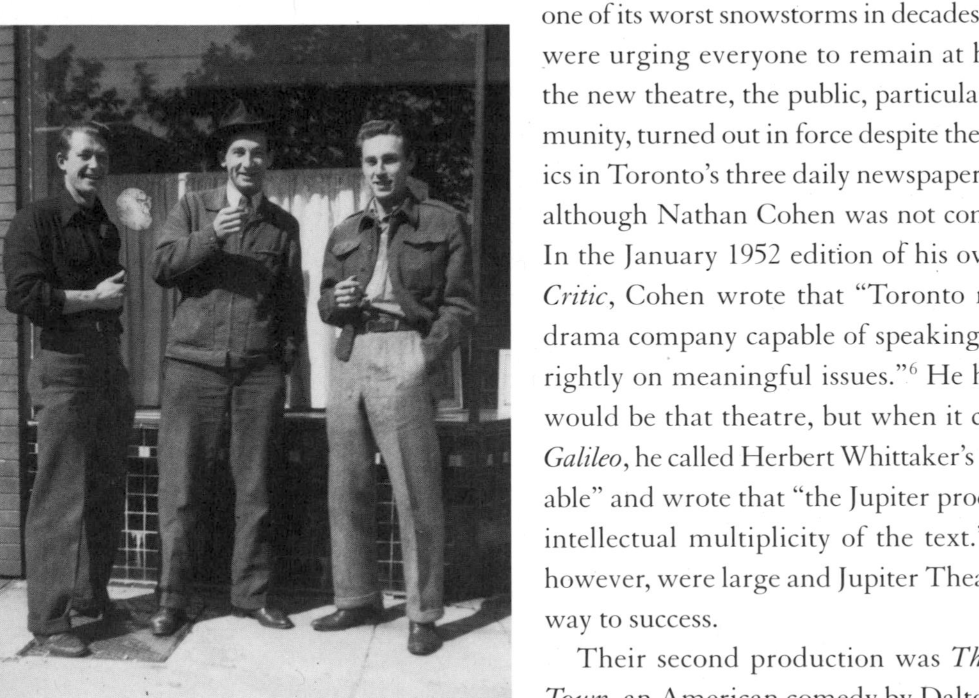

Ed McNamara, who starred in Jupiter Theatre's *The Biggest Thief in Town*, is shown here flanked by Floyd Caza (left) and David Major. (MCNICOLL COLLECTION)

Their second production was *The Biggest Thief in Town*, an American comedy by Dalton Trumbo, which ran for the last week in January and the first in February, 1952. Directed by Roberta Beatty, the play was a critical and commercial success. In the cast were Ed McNamara, Norman Jewison, Gerry Sarracini, Ruth Springford and

Alex McKee. The lead role went to Budd Knapp, who, in addition to the stage, worked in television and film but was best-known as an excellent radio actor.

The theatre's first two productions had attracted more than five thousand patrons and their subsequent play was to prove theatre-goers would support something of quality written by a Canadian. Lister Sinclair originally wrote *Socrates* for radio (performed on the *Stage Series* in 1947 and 1948) and then adapted it for the stage. It was chosen from more than a dozen plays submitted by Canadian writers. The action of the play takes place during the last three days of Socrates' life. In it there are two groups, one trying to have Socrates condemned and put to death for the corruption of youth, and the other, his friends, who are trying to take him far away and out of danger. Socrates refuses to leave and chooses to die for his principles. The play was directed by Esse Ljungh.

In addition to choosing plays, Jupiter's board of directors had another function unequalled in any other theatre, as Paul Kligman recalled:

> One of the unique features of Jupiter which had not occurred in theatre up to that point, certainly not in Canada, and has not really occurred to any great degree since, was the fact that each one of the directors was expected to produce one of the plays that we would choose. In other words I would be put in charge of production and had to worry about who would be cast, the director, the monies to be handed out and so forth. . . . I chose *Socrates*. . . . We had incredible co-operation from the design and the costumes communities. Suzanne Ness [other sources list the costumes being done by Barbara McNabb] did the costumes for *Socrates*, many, many costumes of togas. Lorne Greene's father had a shoe factory and gave us the sandals for nothing. Ness was busy block painting on cloth to create the togas and the right look. I think we did the whole costumes, and it was an enormous task, for something like $27.

The distinguished cast included Christopher Plummer, Robert Christie, Paul Kligman, David Gardner, Murray Westgate, Alex McKee and Frank Peddie, one of that era's top radio actors, as Socrates. The production of *Socrates*, February 22 to March 1, 1952, turned out to be the hit of the season, with close to a thousand people turned away, which was very gratifying for Canadian playwrights. Singled out in particular by the critics for excellence were Peddie and Plummer. While Herbert Whittaker called it "a clever, even brilliant work," Nathan Cohen was not as kind, even going so far as to call Sinclair "the peddler of shopworn cerebral cogitations." Cohen would later regret those words.

Jupiter closed out their four-play season with *Crime Passionnel* by Jean-Paul Sartre. Originally hoping to have Montreal actor Pierre Dagenais as director, Jupiter had to settle for New Yorker Edward Ludlum. He directed a cast which included Don Harron (fresh from foreign success), Lorne Greene, British actress Honor Blackman, John Drainie, William Needles and Ed McNamara. Once again the reviews were excellent with one reviewer saying there was not an inferior performance in the entire production. The theatre's first season, with forty-one performances in all, was an unqualified success.

Because there was not much remuneration for the Jupiter actors, the critical accolades were important. The small salaries also meant many continued to do other work during the day so rehearsals usually took place between ten in the evening and one in the morning. Most of the actors felt it was worth it. "Now those four plays—in no way would they have appeared on anybody's slate," Paul Kligman said. "To this day they have been avoided by the community. We took those on as being important plays and they were highly successful."

Perhaps the most amazing statistic from Jupiter's first season was that the group very nearly broke even financially, a definite victory in those years. "We got a lot of things done for a nickel and dime," Kligman said. "We certainly couldn't pay salaries to any great degree but the acting fraternity and sorority turned out. I don't think we had any major refusals. They were paid mostly honorariums and, in a couple of cases, a little more was paid simply because of the stature of the people." Actors such as John Drainie and Lorne Greene were among those who received more, Kligman said.

In their second season Jupiter became much more ambitious, with seven shows and one hundred and three performances. They opened with Eugene O'Neill's *Anna Christie* in October 1952. Kligman recalls how he was not pleased with the new direction:

> Unfortunately they started to think along the lines of being successful commercially as well as artistically and were afraid of producing a losing year. So we went into a few productions . . . which I don't think we should have done. It was at this time George Robertson and I felt the pressure of the fact we were starting to deviate from the original thinking. We chose to withdraw as directors and resigned.

The others continued, however, and *The Money Makers* by Canadian Ted Allan was Jupiter's next offering. It was about an idealistic Canadian writer and his wife who move to Hollywood where they fall prey to the influences of the entertainment capital. The play depicted many of the same cultural differences that remain today. The cast included Kate Reid, John Drainie and Lorne Greene. A week after the show ended, the CBC filmed *The Money Makers* for television with the same three actors in the lead roles. It was the first time a Canadian stage play was seen on TV. Both Whittaker and Cohen liked certain aspects of the play, and Cohen called Ted Allan "a new and stimulating playwright."

*The Show-Off* by George Kelly and Tennessee Williams' *Summer and Smoke* were also staged that year with the latter being particularly successful. Aileen Seaton was in the pivotal role of Alma Winemiller, with Murray Davis, Kate Reid, Katherine Blake and Barbara Hamilton also in the cast. The three biggest hits of the season, which saw attendance top thirty-three thousand, were *The Money Makers*, and two Christopher

Fry plays, *The Lady's Not for Burning* and *A Sleep of Prisoners*. The latter was staged at St. Andrew's Church, the first time Jupiter appeared outside the confines of the Museum Theatre.

Fry wrote *A Sleep of Prisoners* especially to be performed in churches in order to bring deeper meaning to the biblical incidents which illustrate his story. Don Harron, Leonard White, W. Brodie and Patrick Macnee (of later TV *Avengers* fame) made up the cast. The Canadian premiere of *The Lady's Not for Burning*, with Christopher Plummer, Don Harron, Eric House and Katherine Blake, drew more than 6,500 people in its two-week run. It was so popular, in fact, that a repeat performance of it was given at Hart House at the University of Toronto. It was performed after the conclusion of Jupiter's second season with Patrick Macnee replacing Christopher Plummer.

Their second season had one dismal failure, and it turned out to be Jupiter's third Canadian play. *Blue Is for Mourning* was written by controversial drama critic Nathan Cohen who, given all his vitriolic attacks on actors and playwrights, should have known anything less than perfection would see him crucified. He didn't even come close.

Cohen was known for his biting criticisms but he cared very much about the arts, and from 1950 to 1954 he sporadically published the *The Critic*, with articles (many of which he wrote) covering all aspects of the arts from radio and theatre to ballet and opera. The magazine also contained film reviews by Gerald Pratley and book reviews by Robert Weaver. In this, his own publication, he did temper some of his criticisms but still wrote comments such as "most of the talent in Toronto is rudimentary, tentative and inexperienced" and "what we have . . . at best is a reasonable supply of potential professionals."

It was this supply of "potential professionals" that would mount Nathan Cohen's play, *Blue Is for Mourning*, which opened ominously on Friday 13, February 1953. In *The Critic* he had lamented the shortage of competent Canadian directors, so when Jupiter brought up an American, Jerome Mayer, Cohen may have thought he would get a break. Being the playwright, rather than the critic, brought out another side of Cohen, cast member Eric House recalled:

> Strange sight at rehearsal of Nathan sitting in the front row watching. Here was a play about Cape Breton, where Nathan comes from, and about mining which he was very familiar with. Then this New York director is coming up and telling him, "No, this isn't right," not understanding all the nuances, not giving him [Cohen] a chance. And Nathan sitting in the front row accepting it, saying, "Yes sir, no sir." I couldn't believe it. I was mad because I didn't agree with the directing most of the time. I thought, "Why the hell doesn't he say something and stand up for his own play." But he didn't. He was cowed completely and by the time it opened he was running away from it.

More than likely Cohen sensed what was coming. In the cast with Eric House were Cosy Lee and American actor Donald McKee. The play was roundly panned by the critics, although Paul Kligman said it was a much better play than Jupiter's presentation showed it to be. The criticism came from many sources but perhaps the most scathing came from Lister Sinclair, who filled in for Cohen on CJBC's *Views the Shows* that week. He had been critically trashed in the past by Cohen and was not going to miss this opportunity to return the favour. "[Cohen]'s written this play and God, after knocking everybody, including Lister Sinclair's play," Eric House said, "they asked Sinclair if he would like to review it and he said, 'Would I?' He really did a job on it." Sinclair said in part of his review that "in the program we're told that *Blue Is for Mourning* is to be the first part of a trilogy. I can only hope that Mr. Cohen will not harden his heart and carry through his dread resolve."

He didn't. Nathan Cohen left the writing of plays to others and went back to being a critic. Even with the failure of *Blue Is for Mourning*, Jupiter's deficit at the end of their second season was small, but it would not remain that way for long.

Jupiter's third season was fraught with financial woes from the beginning as the group decided to move from the Museum Theatre. They planned three productions at the Royal Alexandra Theatre and five at Ryerson, including three Canadian ones. The theatre at Ryerson was semi-circular, with a vaulted ceiling, pillars and stained-glass windows. A slightly elevated platform took the place of a stage and there were no curtains. Their previous successes with Christopher Fry led Jupiter to open with Fry's adaptation of *Ring Round the Moon* by Jean Anouilh. This Royal Alexandra production was followed by *Right You Are, If You Think You Are* by Luigi Pirandello and Lister Sinclair's *The Blood Is Strong*, both at Ryerson.

Sinclair's story of Scottish settlers in Cape Breton Island, Nova Scotia, in the 1880s began (like *Socrates*) as a half-hour radio play, broadcast February 2, 1945. *The Blood Is Strong* proved popular with audiences and critics but it was not enough to stop the bleeding. The top actors were being paid as much as $135 per week, creating much larger budgets than in previous years. What turned out to be Jupiter's last production, Noël Coward's *Relative Values*, was presented at the Royal Alexandra in January 1954. Even Coward's name wasn't enough to attract the much-needed audiences. In Jupiter's last season, actors included John Colicos, Frank Peddie, Ruth Springford, Douglas Rain, Toby Robins, Jane Mallett and Josephine Barrington.

In February 1954, it was announced that Jupiter was closing down after an abbreviated season in order to reorganize itself. Accumulated debts now totalled $10,000. Lorne Greene and the other directors tried to find ways to overcome this by finding another location for Jupiter. That never happened. Founded by radio actors looking for a way back on to the stage, Jupiter's brief success helped to foster a space for Canadian content in traditional professional theatre. Paul Kligman later declared, "I still say it was the most incredible start any theatre in Toronto ever had."

CHAPTER SIX

# THE NEW PLAY SOCIETY

"They were professional performers with no theatre to come back to [after the war] but determined to carve a professional career for themselves."

—MAVOR MOORE

Ontario was the most prolific of the provinces in terms of the number of theatres it turned out in the post-war years. One of the earliest, and most successful, was the New Play Society, spearheaded by a woman whom Lister Sinclair called "the gentle, genial steamroller." Dora Mavor Moore was one of Canada's true theatrical matriarchs, and when she began the New Play Society in 1946, it was the culmination of a natural progression from a lifelong love of theatre to the development of an amateur theatre and finally to the creation of her own professional theatre.

Born in Scotland in 1888, Moore came to Canada four years later when her father, James Mavor, became a professor at the University of Toronto. Among his friends were George Bernard Shaw and Leo Tolstoy, and his daughter learned early on about the importance of drama and literature.

While enrolled at the University of Toronto, Dora Mavor Moore discovered academic courses were not for her. What interested her was acting, and Moore quickly turned to the theatre. Graduating from the Margaret Eaton School of Literature and Expression in 1911, Moore won a scholarship to study at the Royal Academy of

Dramatic Art (RADA) in London, England, and had the distinction of being the first Canadian alumna of that great institution. On returning to Canada she joined the Colonial Theatre Stock Company in Ottawa. From there she went to New York and then toured with the Ben Greet Pastoral Players. In Canada, Moore married clergyman Francis Moore in 1915, and they went overseas. While in England she met up again with Ben Greet, who was then director of the famous Old Vic Theatre Company in London, and Moore became one of the first Canadians to star at that theatre.

Returning to Canada once more, she began to teach theatre, or "dramatic expression" as it was then called, to young people. It was something that continued to bring her joy all her life and, indeed, Moore later formed a theatre school as part of the New Play Society. She plied her early teaching talents at the Margaret Eaton and Forest Hill Village schools, the University Extension Players and Victoria College at the University of Toronto, all amateur groups. Among her work in the 1930s was the founding and directing of the Hart House Touring Players, counselling drama at summer girls' camps, adjudicating drama festivals, directing with the Toronto Public Library Dramatic Club, and teaching speech at the YWCA.

Throughout this period she also travelled and studied overseas. It was during her travels that, in 1937, she met W.B. Yeats, an old friend of her father. In addition to being a renowned Irish poet and dramatist, Yeats had played a major role in the foundation of the Irish Dramatic Movement in 1899, the main purpose of which was to present Irish plays with Irish content, performed by Irish actors. Moore was his guest for a week, and it was on her return home from that inspiring meeting that she began the long struggle to help bring the same professional, homegrown theatre to Canada.

Most of all, Moore loved teaching and guiding young people, and it was to them she turned on her arrival back in Canada following her pivotal visit with Yeats. With the help of her sons, Moore bought an 1840s farmhouse with a barn attached to it, a building which became very useful a few years later. In 1938 she helped found the amateur group, the Village Players, which was composed mostly of Moore's students from Forest Hill High School and the University of Toronto. For the next couple of years, this ensemble of unpaid actors toured high schools, staging mostly Shakespearean scenes and occasionally full plays. The Second World War took its toll when many actors left to enlist, but Moore somehow found enough replacements to keep going and was also able to find a permanent home for the Village Players, right in her own backyard—literally. The barn which stood on her property in northwest Toronto was renovated to fit the need.

"It was a real barn," said her son Mavor Moore. "My brother who was an engineer and thus an electrician, my younger brother who was hefty and did most of the toting, and I . . . we built a theatre in the barn but the stage was extremely tiny." The seating capacity could be stretched only to eighty, there was no electricity, and it was lit by coal-oil lamps. Because it was unheated, the barn could be used for performances only in the summer months. In winter, when the group toured schools, a wood stove warmed up the barn enough for the actors to use it for rehearsals and to make the props and costumes. Among its contributions to Toronto theatre, the Village Players can number the first Canadian presentations of works by Spain's Federico Garcia Lorca and also scenes from Bertolt Brecht's *The Private Life of the Master Race*. Among the many people who acted with the theatre between 1938 and 1946 were Mavor Moore, Peter Mews, William Needles, Lloyd Bochner, Vernon Chapman, Pegi Brown, Barbara Kelly and Don Harron. It was a diverse group of people, Mavor Moore remembered:

> The Village Players itself had been a combination of three sorts of people. There were the people who started with my mother touring Shakespeare around the high schools in the late 1930s. These were the kids who had come out of her high school classes. A lot of them were at the university where she had also directed. They were, in fact, students with an ambition to become professional but at that time they were not. Mixed with them was a second group, of whom my mother herself was one, which is to say professionals who had been working in and around Canada since the First World War. Among them were some real old pros. They had done very little during the thirties because there was very little [professional] theatre. But the third group which joined the Village Players in the barn on Bathurst Street included those radio professionals who wanted to qualify themselves to work in the theatre as well. This included everyone from Andrew Allan down. His whole troupe—Bernard Braden, Barbara Kelly, Lister Sinclair, Lorne Greene, Fletcher Markle and a little later on, Don Harron.

"The war ended for me in January 1945, when I was put on the reserve list," Don Harron recalled. "At one point I was taken to see an evening of one-act plays by Mrs. Dora Mavor Moore. And afterwards I met her and her eyes gleamed because I was a male who wasn't in service at the time. So she said to come and read for a part in *Charley's Aunt* [by Brandon Thomas], a troop show going to hospitals. There was a very strong radio community at that time—Bernard Braden, Bud Knapp, John Drainie, and most of these people were in this production. . . . I [was] embarrassed reading in front of these people, not because I was in awe of them but because I was bad, although I'd acted before. I was a professional actor on radio when I was eleven."

However bad his reading was, Dora Mavor Moore hired Don Harron for her Village Players. One year later, in the fall of 1946, his professional stage career also began with her when Moore took the nucleus of the Village Players, added another group of actors to it, and gave birth to the New Play Society. The added actors came from the Forces shows during the Second World War, actors with no theatre to return to in Canada. The decision to turn the Village Players into a professional group was the result of a vote taken at a meeting in early 1946. It was close, with almost as many against

Dora Mavor Moore was the epitome of many women of her generation who gave so much to theatre in Canada. Not only did she found the New Play Society but she ran a school to encourage Canadian talent. (MCNICOLL COLLECTION)

the idea as for it. But Moore went ahead anyway, using her own savings and $2,000 in war bonds donated by her sons. As the barn on Bathurst Street was obviously too small for a professional theatre to survive financially, a search began for possible locations.

"The only available small theatre—you didn't want one that was too big—was the one in the Royal Ontario Museum," Mavor Moore said. "They were looking for a tenant at that time because they had set up a department called University Extension, whose job it was to get the public into the museum. So they liked the idea of the public coming to see plays and getting used to coming to the Museum."

"The New Play Society was done on a tiny little stage at the Museum before they converted it," Peter Sturgess said. "The thing was like a postage stamp. About ten steps and you were across the stage. However, they did the most remarkable things there, they really did. And of course, Mrs. Moore was used to theatre and she knew exactly what she wanted. Remarkable woman."

The theatre, which seated slightly more than four hundred people, became the New Play Society's home in spite of its cramped twenty by twenty-one foot stage. The theatre paid the Museum $100 a night in rental fees. One advantage of the location was that it was non-union, which allowed Mrs. Moore to bring in any musician or crew she wanted without worrying about union rules. She was not so lucky at the Royal Alexandra Theatre a few years later when she was forced by a musicians' union to pay them for a non-union show in which they were not needed. In a classic Moore anecdote, she exacted revenge by forcing them to play during intermission.

The name of the New Play Society was somewhat ambiguous. "You could never figure whether it was going to be about new plays or a new society for putting on old plays," Don Harron said. "It sort of wound up being a bit of both." A number of the new plays also came from Canadian playwrights. "We wanted particularly to do Canadian plays, though oddly enough when the title was picked the 'new' was not meant to apply to the plays but to the Society," Mavor Moore recounted.

As with most other theatres that sprang up in Canada's post-war years, the New Play Society wanted to start a professional but non-profit theatre. Nobody, it seemed, ever expected to make a buck—and they were certainly correct in their assumption. The theatre planned to present modern classics, established masterpieces, Canadian plays and also hoped to bring in productions from outside Toronto. When one recalls the impact the visit with Yeats had on Moore, it is not surprising that she chose to open not only with an Irish play, but with one that had been performed at the Abbey Theatre in Dublin—*The Playboy of the Western World* by J.M. Synge. A capacity audience greeted the theatre's opening night on October 11, 1946, and critics wrote glowing notices. One was especially pleased with the efforts to produce "the true lilt and cadence of an Irish countryside," as the *Globe and Mail* reviewer wrote. The talented cast included Pegi Brown, Peter Mews, William Needles, Charmion King, Vernon Chapman and Don Harron, with the last two singled out for praise in the newspapers.

Each play ran Friday and Saturday nights, for two weeks. During the first six-play season, actors were paid only $15 per production, which came to $3.75 per night. They received nothing for rehearsals. Strindberg's *The Father* was their second play, and then sticking with her mandate to offer dramas from other lands, Moore brought a Chinese play to the Museum theatre. *Lady Precious Stream* by Hsiung Shih-I was staged in Chinese by the Gin Hong Sing Dramatic Society in authentic Chinese dress and was remarkably well-received by the audiences. In November 1946, Mavor Moore returned to Toronto, and he undertook not only the direction of the play but the management of the company. "I joined her at once and, matter of fact, it was a good thing all around," Mavor Moore remembered, "because she had bitten off really far more than she could chew trying to run [a theatre]." Vernon Chapman, who spent a number of years as Dora's assistant whenever Mavor was not in town, agreed:

> She was marvellous at training people and she had, herself, in comparison to the amateur companies of the day, a very professional attitude, but I don't think she had the ability to concentrate on one particular thrust for a long period of time to see it through. Other things would happen and she would get side-tracked. . . . She did start the [New Play Society], got it going, but then Mavor came in and added a certain business or practical side to it.

*The Circle* by Somerset Maugham was their next production and starred a number of radio personalities, including Bernard Braden and his wife Barbara Kelly, Jane Mallett, Peter Mews, Lloyd Bochner and Vernon Chapman. The radio community had an even bigger role in the following play. Directed by Andrew Allan, Eugene O'Neill's comedy *Ah, Wilderness!* had a cast led by Budd Knapp, Don Harron, Claire Murray, Tommy Tweed, Arden Keay and Lloyd Bochner. Allan brought to the stage the same excellence he displayed in radio directing, and *Ah, Wilderness!* received high critical and public approval. In his review for *The Canadian Jewish Weekly (Vochenblatt)*, Nathan Cohen wrote that "it was the best-acted, best-directed amateur production we have ever seen in Toronto." Except for the fact that he got the "amateur" part wrong, it was probably one of the nicest things he ever wrote as a critic throughout his career. He did add, however, that he was disappointed that "a group of such obvious talents as the New Play Society should waste them on a such a weak play."

The New Play Society closed out that first series of plays in December 1946, with the *Coventry Nativity Play* starring Mavor Moore, Pegi Brown, Vernon Chapman, Peter Mews and Charmion King. It also received rave reviews. The New Play Society season had been, if not a financial success, at least a critically triumphant one. Buoyed by this fact, it was announced prior to their Christmas show that a second six-play series would begin in February 1947, with James Bridie's *Mr. Bolfry*. All productions would now be presented for three nights, Thursdays through Saturdays. James Bridie was an alias for Osborne Mavor who happened to be Dora's cousin. The cast was led by Mavor Moore in the title role, supported by Pegi Brown, Ruth Springford, Babs Hitchman and veteran actor Frank Peddie.

The New Play Society then presented, in succession, William Saroyan's *The Time of Your Life*, *This Way to the Tomb* by Ronald Duncan and a translation of the popular Russian comedy *The Government Inspector*. The fifth production in the series gave fulfillment to the theatre's mandate to stage worthy Canadian plays. Lister Sinclair's *The Man in the Blue Moon* had an extremely large cast and was directed by the author himself. The cast included John Drainie in the lead, with Jane Mallett, Budd Knapp and William Needles. The performances were lauded, Drainie's in particular, although Nathan Cohen, in his role as the CBC radio theatre critic, referred to the plot as being "confused." The New Play Society closed out its second series, and their first full winter season, by bringing the talented and established French Canadian group from Montreal, Les Compagnons de Saint-Laurent, to the Museum Theatre. They presented two Molière comedies in French, *Les Précieuses ridicules* and *Le Médecin malgré lui*.

The second series of plays had added to the New Play Society's growing reputation for staging important plays with high quality production values, but it still had an uphill climb financially. Some excerpts written in a letter by Dora Mavor Moore to the theatre's honorary treasurer in March 1947 clearly show the progress made and the problems ahead:

> The Society has had an altogether extraordinary success artistically . . . and we believe that its continuance is of the utmost importance to Canada. For the first time we now appear to have established a Canadian "theatre" which can hold its own professionally with that of other countries. . . . However, the grind financially has been uphill . . . we hope to finish this second series without too great a deficit. As things stand now, I shall be personally responsible for whatever deficit there is. I have already put my meagre funds into this venture, because I believe that its continued success is vital to our cultural life. If this society fails, the possibility of keeping our artists in Canada, and making a Canadian contribution to the world's dramatic art and literature, will be set back many years.

The theatre's management clearly hoped that the next year (with a third and fourth series of plays) would at least bring them solvency. If, however, the opening rehearsal for the fall series of 1947 was any indication of the way fortunes were to go, the season would be a trying one. Dora Mavor Moore failed to see a wire on the set and had a bad tumble. After the fall, she led the cast through a rehearsal of more than three hours, only finding out after she returned home that she had two broken ribs. Undaunted, she carried on with the season.

Mavor Moore played an interesting role in one of the second season productions. The group staged George Bernard Shaw's *Candida*, which starred Jane Mallett in the lead with the part of James Mavor Morell played by Mavor Moore. Shaw had taken the name of his old friend, Professor James Mavor, and used it in the play. Having his grandson Mavor Moore play the part so many years later was too good to pass up for the New Play Society. Other productions that season included Shakespeare's *Macbeth* and *The Tempest*, *Charley's Aunt*, Lillian Hellman's *The Little Foxes*, and *Amphitryon 38*, written by Jean Giraudoux and staged by the Montreal Repertory Theatre.

Dora Mavor Moore had personally campaigned to bring *Amphitryon 38* from Montreal to Toronto, just as she had brought in the Chinese theatre and Les Compagnons de Saint-Laurent during the previous seasons. Nevertheless, there were arguments between Moore and the Montreal Repertory Theatre on almost every aspect of the production. While the play was a critical success, it was a financial failure, and put a damper on Moore's enthusiasm to bring in any other outside shows. In fact, in a December 1947 letter to Amelia Hall, Moore said the theatre was unable to bring an Ottawa Drama League presentation to Toronto because, while it had been critically applauded, the Montreal Repertory Theatre play had lost $700 as a result of the low attendance.

On the other side of the spectrum, the *Macbeth* production, under the direction of

Mavor Moore, was enough of a success to be taken on a short tour. Many actors appeared more than once throughout the second season, including Drew Thompson, Pegi Brown, Peter Sturgess, Margot Christie, Ruth Springford, Alex Mckee, Don Harron and the man who would later become synonymous with the role of Matthew in *Anne of Green Gables*—Peter Mews.

In the Spring of 1948, Mews and a number of others in previous casts were to become involved with a project that would become the New Play Society's biggest calling card—*Spring Thaw*—and it is worth pausing for a moment in the history of the New Play Society to look closely at the development of *Spring Thaw*. It materialized from a stroke of fate. The fifth production in the theatre's fourth series of plays was to be a Hugh Kemp stage adaptation of Hugh MacLennan's novel *Two Solitudes*. When it became obvious the script would not be forthcoming in time, members of the group scrambled to come up with an alternative and decided on a revue. Radio's Andrew Allan suggested the name *Spring Thaw* during a coffee break at the CBC. In the program Allan was thanked "for his invaluable advice and assistance in launching *Spring Thaw* on its way."

A number of people supplied sketches, ideas or music, including Mavor Moore, Don Harron (who would contribute a great deal during the ensuing years), Tommy Tweed, Jane Mallett, Peter Mews, Lucio Agostini, Eric Christmas and Lister Sinclair, who wrote the words to the opening song, *We All Hate Toronto* ("Where the bloodstream is blue and Sundays are too"). Why did the name fit so well? The program explained it:

> When *Spring Thaw* comes all sorts of things appear . . . the birds, the flowers, that old shovel you lost under the snow, holes in the road, and so on. But most particularly, mankind becomes touched with a strange lightness in the heart and the head, and therefore, without another word of excuse, we begin our revue.

It was the only year where there was actually a tenuous storyline tying together the different sketches. Revolving around a strike in a department store, twenty sketches (separated by Mavor Moore's invention of a ten-second blackout) were performed by actors that included Don Harron, Frosia Gregory, Alfie Scopp, Jane Mallett, Peter Mews, Connie Vernon, Drew Thompson and Eric Christmas. *Monday Morning*, *You're Always in Love in the Springtime*, *It'll Never Get Well if You Picket* and *I Haven't Anywhere to Go* were some of the skits. The first *Spring Thaw* opened on April Fools Day 1948 and ran for three nights.

The theatre was packed and the revue an instant success, although an accident on the second night sent a cast member to hospital. One of the sketches near the end of the show, *Lecture on Music*, was performed by Connie Vernon. It was decided the number would be danced, and the most energetic part involved Peter Mews and Drew Thompson lifting Vernon overhead. They slipped and she hit the ground head first and the tiara she was wearing left a nasty gash in her head, which needed stitches.

After that first year it was always arranged for *Spring Thaw* to close out the New Play Society season. Its run was extended each year, two weeks in the second year, more the third and so on, leaving in its wake performance records for all-Canadian productions. In 1956 it was performed 104 times, and even this was eclipsed the following year. The name *Spring Thaw* was copyrighted on the suggestion of Vernon Chapman. He recalled how it happened:

> This one year there was a danger this rival revue was being created. I told her "if other people are going to do this we had better get the name copyrighted." And that kept the New Play Society and Mrs. Moore going. . . . It was my idea.

It was during the 1950s that *Spring Thaw* was at its height of popularity, and proved beyond doubt that Canadians loved self-directed humour. The audiences laughed at the portraits of themselves and their neighbours that were being played out in front of them on stage.

In the 1952 *Spring Thaw*, the fifth sketch was called *Th'Ex* and introduced a character from rural Ontario, lost at the Canadian National Exhibition and looking for his friend who went by the name of Charlie Farquharson. This Parry Sound farmer, who in later appearances took his friend's name for his own, had a permanently stunned expression on his face and a strong accent. He hit home with the audience, which convulsed with laughter throughout Don Harron's four-minute sketch.

Harron, who was the creator of the character, had tried the persona out on a number of occasions. In 1942 Harron had spent six months working on a farm in southern Ontario, and Charlie ended up being a compendium of the people he met and worked with there. He first tried the accent out in the 1949 New Play Society production of *The Inheritance*, but nobody noticed it. When a four-minute monologue was needed to fill a gap in the 1952 *Spring Thaw*, Charlie Farquharson was born.

Although Don Harron appeared under many guises in the early *Spring Thaws*, as both actor and writer, from the first year in 1948, the revues really revolved around Canada's premiere comedienne of the time, Jane Mallett, who not only starred in the shows but also contributed material. By 1952 Mallett was receiving $100 a week to star in *Spring Thaw*. She was guaranteed four weeks, eight shows a week with the option of the show continuing beyond. In that year, a hundred thousand people saw *Spring Thaw* in its five-week run. Besides Mallett, other performers in the early years were Peter Mews (often also responsible for designing the sets), Don Harron, Vernon

Chapman, Eric Christmas, Lou Jacobi, Pegi Brown, Mavor Moore, Norman Jewison and Dave Broadfoot.

A number of comic sketches (many politically incorrect and of questionable taste) included the following:

• Frequent appearances by Peter Mews as the jowly John Diefenbaker ("You may remember my recent Bill of Rights" he'd say, "Well . . . forget it"). Mews appeared in almost all the *Spring Thaws* in the first two decades.

• An Eskimo ballet with bundled up actors pirouetting on snowshoes.

• *The Red Choux, a ballet*, conceived and danced by Connie Vernon and Peter Mews, described as follows in the program: "Minnihuhu, a beautiful but illegitimate princess, has been turned into a totem-pole by her furious father, Hukami. She is bored. A neighbouring totem (in reality young Prince Happy Paddle) realizes it is her birthday and wants to make her a present of a red cabbage (choux) he happens to have with him. . . ." It was a parody of the big movie hit *The Red Shoes*.

• Gerry Sarracini as the Sicilian bandit Taranna in a mock operetta *La Traviesti*, about the forthcoming amalgamation of Toronto with its suburbs. The skit also featured a long-gowned Jane Mallett as the spirit of amalgamation, complete with dove and outstretched finger!

• Furred and gloved matrons of Montreal's Westmount forced to don helmets and fight off the French Canadians.

• Jane Mallett doing a perfect imitation of a know-it-all radio commentator who will not stop talking and get off the air (it was so spot on that many thought it was a take-off of announcer Kate Aitken; the theatre feared it might be sued but it was not).

• A 1949 portrayal of skater Barbara Ann Scott as a piping-voiced ninny, too ladylike to be true, which caused a columnist for the *Toronto Telegram* to call for the show to be closed on the grounds of bad taste.

• Jane Mallett reciting such suggestive lines as "this afternoon I had a tramp in the woods." In another skit she also portrayed Ottawa mayor Charlotte Whitton, who roared with laughter when she attended the show.

• Barbara Hamilton playing a strung out Gertrude to Robert Goulet's Hamlet in Don Harron's Shakespeare take-off, *Something Is Cool in Denmark*.

Financially, *Spring Thaw* was a monumental success although it did lead to some disagreement in the New Play Society offices because Dora Mavor Moore felt the skits in *Spring Thaw* were too much of a departure from the artistic aims of the theatre. In spite of her objections, the season-ending skits continued year after year far beyond the time frame of this book, though eventually under new management.

By 1961 the financial outlook for the New Play Society, which was now mostly devoted to the operation of Dora Mavor Moore's school and the presentation of *Spring Thaw*, was bleak, for they were almost $15,000 in the hole. "They were deeply in debt and the only asset they had really was the title of *Spring Thaw* which hadn't had a very successful production the previous year," Mavor Moore said. "So I raised the money to buy the title of *Spring Thaw* and the price paid for that got the New Play Society out of debt."

Mavor Moore produced a number of the *Spring Thaws* after 1961, just as he had done in earlier seasons. In the years he did not run the show, he simply leased it out to other producers. The tone of the revues changed, however, as the show toured the country in the late 1960s and the humour became more national than local. Eventually *Spring Thaw*'s original concept had changed far too much for Mavor Moore, who still owned the rights to the name. Dave Broadfoot, who had portrayed a politician, the member of Parliament from Kicking Horse Pass, said that they took away its "Canadianness," and it did not work anymore. Moore let it die after the 1971 show, only to allow its rebirth again in 1980, with Wayne and Shuster and Pierre Berton contributing some of the material.

Returning now to the history of the New Play Society as a whole, one can see that the early success of *Spring Thaw* brought more than financial rewards for the theatre. The fact that it was drawing large audiences to an all-Canadian production caused many people to see The New Play Society in its early years as the signal hope for Canadian drama. Don Harron said that "the success of it [*Spring Thaw*] encouraged us to say, 'Oh my God, the era of Canadian theatre has dawned.'" He used the word "us" quite justifiably, for the New Play Society had decided for the first time in the 1948–49 season to hire a permanent company of actors, bringing others in for one or two shows only. Besides Harron, the other permanent actors included Pegi Brown, Toby Robins, Lloyd Bochner and Robert Christie.

Surprisingly enough, even with the new permanent company of actors, the New Play Society decided to make the 1948–49 season shorter than the previous two. They staged five plays plus *Spring Thaw*, about half as many as it usually performed. The productions were generally of a serious nature, as before, and they now lasted a week, with Wednesday nights dark. This was because many of the radio actors worked those evenings in the *Wednesday Night* drama series.

They opened that season in the fall of 1948 with a staging of Maxwell Anderson's *Joan of Lorraine*, with Mona O'Hearn and Lorne Greene in the lead roles. The armour worn by Greene took three people hours and hours to knit, using heavy string and then painting it silver. Other actors included Lloyd Bochner, Alfie Scopp, Peter Sturgess and Pegi Brown. Brown was in both of the next two productions, Shaw's *You Never Can Tell* and *Storm in a Teacup* by James Bridie. Many of the theatre's stalwarts appeared in the two shows with the addition of Toby Robins, a high school student. Robins went on to become an accomplished actress, starring at Stratford in *Cyrano de Bergerac* opposite Christopher Plummer, and was one of the first hosts on television's *Front Page Challenge*.

For their second Canadian play, the New Play Society chose *To Tell the Truth* by Morley Callaghan. He had written it ten years earlier but put it away when he had trouble getting it produced. When he was asked for a play to stage, Callaghan quickly retrieved it. The show provided another first for the group, as the play's run at the Museum Theatre in January 1949 proved so successful they decided to move it into much larger quarters at the Royal Alexandra Theatre for a second run in February 1949.

Nevertheless, most of their productions continued to be staged at the Museum Theatre where their potential take on a performance night in 1949 could reach $730 at the top while their operating costs per night were in the $370 range. The theatre was the subject of articles in five national periodicals as well as newspaper pieces across Canada, Britain and the United States. Even Nathan Cohen, in the *Canadian Jewish Weekly*, referred to the contribution the New Play Society was making to Canadian theatre, citing that "productions are of a remarkably high standard," although, like Dora Mavor Moore, he was never a big fan of the *Spring Thaw* revues.

The 1949–50 season was the most enterprising the theatre undertook during its history, as *Spring Thaw* and five of the ten regular productions were Canadian. Mavor Moore's *Who's Who*, *The Inheritance* by Harry Boyle, *Narrow Passage* by Andrew Allan, John Coulter's *Riel* and the Morley Callaghan play *Going Home* were the home-grown contributions. It was the success of *Spring Thaw* and Callaghan's previous *To Tell the Truth* that encouraged the New Play Society to go ahead with such an ambitiously "Canadian" season. They felt a broader, newer type of audience was out there, waiting to be tapped. Mavor Moore remembered:

> The audiences were, in the early days, more or less the intelligentsia and those members of the upper middle class and even occasionally what passed for high society with an intellectual and artistic bent. That's how it began, because the plays we were doing were by no means thought to be popular. Things like Strindberg's *The Father* and *The Playboy of the Western World*. These, you know, were not designed to make money. . . . We began to get through to a popular audience and without, we thought, lowering our standards, without doing anything which was designedly commercially popular.

Part of the challenge facing the New Play Society at this time was that they tended to take on a little more than they could comfortably handle. The productions lasted a week, sometimes two, and rehearsal time was still not long enough to do justice to the plays. They did have a number of successes in the season that began in September 1949 with Mavor Moore's comedy *Who's Who*, which, years later, he admitted was autobiographical. "There had been a one-act version of *Who's Who*, which I had done before I went overseas, with the Arts and Letters Club," Moore said. "This turned out to be the first act of the final version."

On opening night, they ran into an obstacle that couldn't be predicted. "The play opened the same night the *Noronic* [ship] burned in Toronto Harbour," cast member Don Harron remembered, "so although the reviews were good they were buried." *Who's Who* had a stellar cast, including Lorne Greene, Toby Robins, Kay Hawtrey and Alex McKee.

"He was a marvellous actor who was an old radio actor who rarely did theatre," Harron said of McKee. "He was the man who walked up from the audience and interrupted the play saying, 'What's going on here?' People believed him, that he really was an average citizen and they tried to shut him up!" Also in the cast were Margot and Robert Christie, whose daughter is entertainer Dinah Christie.

Robert Christie directed the successful 1949 New Play Society production of *The Inheritance*, a story about the conflict between two generations of Southern Ontario farmers, which had played previously on radio's *Stage Series*. Vernon Chapman, who had just returned from a year in England, was in charge of props. He had been persuaded back into the theatre by the persistent Dora Mavor Moore, who had a tendency to get whatever she wanted. Chapman recalled:

> I was so broke when I got back from England I had to take two jobs. One was in the daytime, the other in the evening. I will never forget Mrs. Moore coming down to see me while I was selling tickets. There was a lineup of people. She got in the line and stood in front of the wicket and talked me into going back to work for the New Play Society, holding up all these people. She was marvellous. . . . One thing about Mrs. Moore is that people had great loyalty to her and great respect for her. She could not have run the New Play Society had she not been a penny pincher, but because she had to pinch pennies, people sometimes got annoyed and said, "Well, we're not going to play here anymore."

Her penny-pinching led to an actor's revolt in one production. The money for props was always scarce, which presented a problem with *The Inheritance* as the farm family frequently came together around the dinner table which meant a tremendous amount of food was needed. Chapman said:

> There was no water backstage at the Museum Theatre. Since we had no money to run these shows, Mrs. Moore decided that we should have, for example, instant mashed potatoes that we could warm up with warm water we got from the washroom of the foyer. They had a turkey dinner so I asked her what we were going to do about it. We couldn't afford to buy a turkey. She and the secretary went home and they moulded a turkey out of mashed potatoes which they put gravy on and baked in the oven. It looked great but

> the poor actors after they had gone through a couple of meals of these interminable potatoes had trouble even speaking. They objected so strenuously I went to Mrs. Moore the following day and said, "I am not going to be responsible, I will not serve them instant mashed potatoes anymore," because I got the blame for it of course, being the prop man.

Chapman reported that they managed to persuade her to buy the turkey, but noted that they had "to stick the pieces back on because we couldn't afford a new turkey each night."

One of the more successful ventures the New Play Society undertook was for Christmas in 1949, when they staged a pantomime, something they would continue to do in future holiday seasons. The pantomime is traditionally a Christmas entertainment based vaguely on a fairy tale, with added popular songs of the day and topical humour. The 1949 pantomime was *Mother Goose*, compiled by Mavor Moore and staged by Eric Christmas, who came to Canada in the late 1940s and subsequently went on to success with the CBC and on Broadway. Mavor Moore had to take over the staging of the show because his mother, Dora, and Eric Christmas did not get along. The choreography for the show was the first work done in Canada by Betty Oliphant, who, with Celia Franca, later founded the National Ballet School of Canada. Future pantomimes were *Babes in the Wood* (in which singer Gisele MacKenzie made her first professional stage appearance), *Peter Pan* and *Cinderella*. All were sponsored by the Riverdale Kiwanis.

"[*Peter Pan* in 1952] was probably one of the most expensive Canadian productions up to that time, about $30,000," Vernon Chapman said. "The Kiwanis did very well out of the first two but I don't think, I recall, they made much money out of *Peter Pan*. . . . It was the first venture for Canadian entrepreneurs into this calibre of production, certainly since the war."

Andrew Allan's *Narrow Passage*, a play Don Harron referred to as "a Canadian Ibsen," was performed in January 1950, but it was not as popular with critics as *The Inheritance* had been. A month later the group was to stage its most controversial and troublesome production of their history—*Riel* by John Coulter. He subsequently wrote two other plays about Riel. Originally from Ireland, Coulter wrote numerous plays and worked tirelessly for many years to help establish a national theatre in Canada.

Coulter is best known, however, for igniting the Riel controversy. Up to this time, Louis Riel had largely been seen in English Canada as a traitor. Coulter set about showing other sides to him. Being one of the first to present a more heroic side to Riel, Coulter was not thanked for it by many at the time. In addition to its run with the New Play Society, *Riel* was produced a year later as a radio play and, in the late 1970s, the story emerged as a television miniseries.

Riel's story was a difficult and lengthy subject even for a miniseries, so it is not surprising that *Riel* was nearly impossible for Coulter to construct into a single play. It was divided into two parts, the first rebellion in 1869 occupying Part I, with the second half of the play concerning itself with the second rebellion in 1885. The staging, partly because of the huge cast and the scarcity of rehearsal time, caused director Don Harron a great deal of anguish. "My wife remembered me saying, 'I'm going to get ulcers,' because I was worried about everybody's parts," Harron said. "I also played in it. Not very well. Bob Christie sort of saved the show."

Robert Christie was the technical production supervisor for *Riel* and also played the part of Sir John A. Macdonald, a role he became identified with and played many more times in his career. The cast included Harron as Thomas Scott, Margot Christie as Riel's mother, Pegi Brown as his wife and Mavor Moore in the demanding title role. "I remember when Mavor was Riel and not being there for most of the rehearsals," Harron said. "We were lying under the floorboards giving him his lines."

Directed by Dora Mavor Moore, *King Lear* followed the *Riel* production. It also had a large cast, led by Mavor Moore who had laryngitis for the entire production. The last Canadian play of the season was *Going Home* by Morley Callaghan.

Dora Mavor Moore loved teaching theatre so it was inevitable she would open her own school, which she did in 1950. The New Play Society was one of the first Canadian acting companies to have a school connected with it. On more than one occasion, Dora Mavor Moore said that she was not only teaching those who would make the theatre a career, but helping prepare them for life by promoting self-expression. Students of all ages attended the school, which had courses in acting, speech, makeup, mime and direction. When the school finally closed in 1968, its enrolment was at two hundred and it had nine teachers. "I drew up the curriculum," Vernon Chapman said. "I taught the history of the theatre and speech. It was purely an evening course. One of the reasons for it was to get money."

It didn't work out that way, and the school was financially supported mainly by the *Spring Thaw* revues. Besides the school, the New Play Society was involved in many other projects through the years in its support for Canadian plays, playwrights and directors. It sponsored a series of lectures given by Andrew Allan, Lister Sinclair, Mavor Moore, Herbert Whittaker, Nathan Cohen and Robertson Davies. In 1959 they presented a Director's Stage Series that saw plays by André Obey, Bertolt Brecht and Jean Anouilh, with directors including Herbert Whittaker, George McCowan and Leon Major.

Although 1949–50 was to be the last of the formal "series," the New Play Society did continue, although *Spring Thaw '51* was the only show the following year. For the holidays that year they presented a pantomime, and three months later, in 1952, staged Shaw's *Arms and the Man*, directed by Earle Grey and starring some old regulars—Don Harron, Robert and Margot Christie, Toby Robins and Pegi Brown. It was the theatre's fiftieth production.

Dora Mavor Moore continued to be the fierce emotional force behind the theatre, even though others ran it for her. She showed this clearly in a 1951 incident. As long as they were struggling, the tax man left them alone, but as soon as it appeared (incorrectly) that the New Play Society might actually be making money, the theatre was threatened with a business tax by the City of Toronto. Dora's lawyer felt she could present the theatre's case more powerfully than he could, and so Moore faced down city council herself. It took only twenty minutes for her to have the theatre excused from the tax.

In 1953 the New Play Society became incorporated as an educational, non-profit organization with a board of directors and Dora Mavor Moore as managing director. Only the Christmas pantomime and *Spring Thaw* appeared on the boards in the 1952–53 season. The Museum Theatre had now become a union building and so the theatre began to look around for another home as Moore was not prepared to live under union demands. It was at this time she became involved with the growing plans for a festival at Stratford, Ontario. Vernon Chapman recalled:

> Mrs. Moore became wildly enthusiastic about the idea [Stratford]. So much so that the plans we had for the New Play Society got temporarily shelved. We had then almost found a home. It was to be a converted skating rink. I designed the seating and it would have been flexible as an arena theatre or a proscenium one.

Chapman recalled that they even had a program to raise funds but once Dora Mavor Moore became interested in Stratford she seemed to lose interest in the New Play Society. "I began to see that it was not going to happen so I quit late in 1952," he said.

Despite that loss of interest, however, the autumn of 1953 found the group back on stage for a somewhat extended season, staging six regular plays plus the Christmas pantomime and *Spring Thaw*. Included was another Canadian play, *Mistress of Jalna* by Mazo de la Roche which, although it had become a hit in London's West End, did not do as well back home. The action was set earlier in time than her more famous *Whiteoaks*.

The financial deficit at the end of that season ended any attempts for future long series of plays, but the New Play Society did continue with *Spring Thaw* and the occasional play. One of these was *Sunshine Town* by Mavor Moore. It was presented on both CBC radio as *The Hero of Mariposa*, on CBC-TV as *Sunshine Town* and at the Royal Alexandra Theatre in 1955. Another adaptation, by Don Harron, of Earle Birney's novel *Turvey*, was presented by the theatre in 1956–57 at the Avenue Theatre. These two plays and others were critical successes but financial disasters, and the theatre made the decision that in the future they would concern themselves only with *Spring Thaw* and the school. The New Play Society, which had been inactive in recent years, formally surrendered its charter in 1971.

The New Play Society made a remarkable contribution to Canadian theatre by staging the plays of so many Canadian playwrights. There were many who contributed to the theatre through the years, people such as Mavor Moore, Vernon Chapman and Peter Mews, but the one and only constant was Dora Mavor Moore. She was honoured on more than one occasion for her devotion and contributions to theatre. In 1967 she was given the Centennial Medal for services to the nation and in 1970 became an officer of the Order of Canada. The Dora Awards, honouring the best in Toronto theatre, are named after her and rightly so. For her, professionalism was the key, and she would take no wavering from its ideal, even if it was in a light vein.

One of the funniest stories about her involved Ted Follows and the 1949 pantomime *Mother Goose*. Follows had had to turn down the part of the goose that laid the golden egg in the pantomime, but he paid a visit backstage during the run. He said he was persuaded, as a joke, to don the papier-mâché, goose-shaped shell and to appear on stage that day. In spite of the fact that only his shins and feet were visible, Follows did not fool one particular member of the audience—the theatrical matriarch herself. Moore swept backstage afterwards, crying "Who's in the goose tonight, who's in the goose?" She never missed a thing.

CHAPTER SEVEN

# THE OTTAWA STAGE SOCIETY & THE CANADIAN REPERTORY THEATRE

"The Canadian Repertory Theatre in Ottawa produces a play a week throughout the season, giving great pleasure to its supporters and saving Ottawa from the dubious distinction of being the only important capital without a theatre."

—ROYAL COMMISSION ON NATIONAL DEVELOPMENT IN THE ARTS, LETTERS AND SCIENCES, 1951

A single dollar bill. This constituted the financial resources of what became the best-known of the pre-Stratford theatre groups: the Ottawa Stage Society and its successor, the Canadian Repertory Theatre. Hugh Parker bought one hundred one-cent stamps and sent out letters to a hundred of Ottawa's top citizens. They were asked to purchase $6.00 season tickets, good for the six plays he hoped to stage in 1948. If the single response Hugh Parker received to his letters was any indication, the Ottawa Stage Society would have been over before it began. Not to be discouraged, with the $6.00 he received, Parker sent out six hundred more letters and eventually had enough money to start.

Hugh Parker was a natural choice to establish a theatre. He had started as a stage-hand in England when he was fourteen years old and wrote his first operetta four years later, followed by several radio and stage plays. During the Second World War, Parker was a member of the Royal Air Force (RAF) stationed in Patricia Bay, British Columbia. He wrote and directed the show for the town's centennial in 1943, and also produced and directed the RAF *Smile Show*, which first toured the province and then down the West Coast of the United States. During this time, Parker saw a need for professional theatre in Canada. In 1944 he was posted back to England but returned to Canada two years later and began working towards his dream for a national theatre. Initially his aims were four-fold: "to provide popular drama at popular prices," "to extend hospitality to leaders in the arts who visit this country," "to encourage the professional stage in Canada" and "to provide encouragement for talented members of amateur organizations."

The last aim Parker had addressed even before his theatre began. In 1947 he worked with the amateur theatre, the Ottawa Drama League, staging a traditional English Christmas pantomime for them. Written by Parker himself, *The Crystal Garden* had an enormous cast of one hundred, one of whom became the Ottawa Stage Society's leading lady—Betty Leighton. However, it was not going to be easy to find other actors for his new professional enterprise. Far away from the theatrical centres of Vancouver, Toronto and Montreal, an Ottawa theatre would have to fight for more than just an audience. Toronto was still the main pull for most stage actors because there were more professional theatre groups within reach of the city than anywhere else in Canada, even if most operated only in summer.

Parker had one piece of luck when the Dominion Drama Festival took place in Ottawa that spring of 1948. Derek Ralston and Floyd Caza came east in a Vancouver Little Theatre production of *The Silver Cord* by Sidney Howard, British Columbia's entry at the 1948 Festival. Parker was impressed with what he saw and, once the Festival was over in April, he asked them to stay and join his new theatre, the Ottawa Stage Society, which he hoped to get underway in May. They were the only Canadian-born actors in the original seven-member cast.

Parker's most urgent need at the start was a resident director. Malcolm Morley, described fondly as a fussbudget and a bear of a man by those who worked with him, was a transplanted Englishman with vast directing credentials. He first came to Canada as an adjudicator of two Dominion Drama Festivals prior to the Second World War. Although British-born, Morley made his first stage appearance in New York and did not appear in London until ten years later. He worked extensively in England before returning to Canada where Parker persuaded him to become the resident director of the Ottawa Stage Society.

"I'd like to give Hugh a pat on the back for his courage," Morley said in Ottawa's *Evening Citizen* newspaper. "He's doing what so many people have been talking about—and he's doing it on a very practical basis."

As was the case with other groups, Parker's long range plan for the theatre was to offer a career in Canada to professional actors who, due to the lack of opportunity here, inevitably had to seek their fortunes further afield. Dreaming big, Parker also hoped to establish theatres in Toronto, Vancouver, Winnipeg and Montreal. Both the Ottawa

It was this production of *The Silver Cord*, presented by the Vancouver Little Theatre at the Dominion Drama Festival in Ottawa, which brought Derek Ralston and Floyd Caza east, where they then joined the Ottawa Stage Society. (COGHILL COLLECTION)

Stage Society and the Canadian Repertory Theatre (generally known as the CRT), employed many talented Canadians, including Christopher Plummer, Donald Davis, Ted Follows, Anna Cameron, William Shatner, George McGowan, Sam Payne, Derek Ralston, Jack and Alicia Ammon and Barbara Chilcott. David Haber and Silvio Narizzano worked both as actors and directors. In addition, six CRT alumni appeared in Stratford's first season in 1953: Amelia Hall, Betty Leighton, Bea Lennard, William Hutt, Eric House and Richard Easton. An amazing amount of talent passed through the two theatre groups between 1948 and 1956 when the last sputtering of the CRT died out.

Malcolm Morley arrived at the beginning of May 1948, and the cast immediately went into rehearsals for their May 10 opening of a Terence Rattigan play, *While the Sun Shines*. Very much indicative of the type of play popular at the time, the comedy was filled with love and mistaken identities. The Earl of Harpenden puts up an American airman, Lieutenant Mulvaney. The Earl arranges for Mulvaney to date an ex-girlfriend, but the airman mistakes the Earl's fiancée for the ex and they fall in love. Confusion and mayhem ensues. In the seven-member cast were five actors from

Britain: Betty Leighton, Reginald Malcolm, Robert Le Main, Joanna Baker and Bryan Herbert. They joined Floyd Caza and Derek Ralston.

The auditorium in La Salle Academy, a Catholic boys' school run by the Brothers of the Christian Schools, was not Hugh Parker's first choice as a theatre for his group. The truth is, it would not have been anyone's first choice. It was difficult enough to be starting up in a non-theatrical centre like Ottawa, but to choose a building off the beaten track seemed like suicide.

"Ottawa has always been a difficult theatrical town, simply because its main concern is government," William Hutt commented. "In those days when legit theatre was embryonic to say the least . . . if the United States Ambassador came to see something they would hesitate, quite understandably, to take him to a rather seedy high school auditorium to see Canadian theatre."

The lack of a home for the theatre had already held up plans for some time. When Parker's negotiations for the use of the Ottawa Little Theatre building fell through, the authorities of the La Salle Academy came forward to offer their auditorium, which seated seven hundred and had an adequate stage. A deal was struck. Although frequent efforts were made to find a more suitable location, the Academy was the only home the Ottawa Stage Society would ever know. The facilities were basic and needed a great deal of work before opening night. The cast's dressing rooms were dirty and messy but, still, it was home.

"The smell of the joint" is what Christopher Plummer, who joined in the fall of 1948, remembered most about the theatre:

> The smell. It was exciting though because . . . it smelled like a dump but that is where the theatre was so I associated the theatre with that smell, a real reeking old musty smell. And the backstage area, that tiny hallway, and the curtained-off dressing rooms [downstairs] where we had to change into our one or two suits that we made versatile by reversing the collars when we played ministers . . . I remember it as if it was yesterday. The building and the horrors.

The cast also shared the spotlight with a rat they named Oscar. Betty Leighton said, "He used to come and sit in the footlight [troughs] quite often. If he sat and cleaned his whiskers for a while, then we figured we weren't doing too badly."

Leighton joined the theatre at $50 a week, a higher salary than anyone else received. And Oscar the rat's days were numbered when a few months later a resident cat joined the company. The feline created other problems, however, when she appeared on stage during a performance. Amelia Hall said that many times an actor picked up the cat mid-scene and gently handed her off to the stage manager in the wings.

Hugh Parker had hoped to open his new venture with Noël Coward's *This Happy Breed*, but was unable to secure the rights to produce the play, apparently because it had not yet been performed on the New York stage. His alternative, Terence Rattigan's *While the Sun Shines*, was eventually successful—but not on the first try. Parker tried to ensure an opening night success by having prominent people in the audience but failed. "I know Hugh worked very hard to have the governor-general come but he wouldn't be associated with anything that hadn't been proven," Leighton said.

Apparently the governor-general was not alone in his concerns, for the Ottawa Stage Society opened with only twenty-nine paying customers. The group did not despair and in the second week of their scheduled six-week season, they hired more actors and presented Esther McCracken's comedy, *Quiet Wedding*. Audiences began to grow and on the Saturday evening of their third week, during the run of George Bernard Shaw's *Pygmalion*, the theatre was sold out, and they turned away one hundred people. The Ottawa Stage Society also began to attract an unexpected group to their productions. The balcony seats were so inexpensive that teenage boys began bringing their girlfriends to the theatre instead of the movies.

In the theatre's *Pygmalion* production, Malcolm Morley played Alfred Doolittle, his role in the original London production of the play and one that the playwright Shaw had wanted to see Morley in. *Pygmalion* was followed by Gerald Savory's *George and Margaret* and Terence Rattigan's *Flare Path*, the theatre's first attempt at a more serious play.

For the final production of the short six-week first season, Parker and Morley chose a Canadian play by Catharine Brickenden, *A Pig in a Poke*. One of Parker's goals for

Betty Leighton (far left) and Derek Ralston (third from the left) were among the cast of the Ottawa Stage Society presentation of *A Pig in A Poke* by Canadian Catharine Brickendon. The play closed out the theatre's first season in July 1948 to rave reviews. (MCNICOLL COLLECTION)

the Ottawa Stage Society was the encouragement of homegrown writers, and this farce, set in rural Ontario, was the first step towards achieving this goal. The critics were supportive of *A Pig in a Poke*, including Herbert Whittaker who made a trip from Montreal to review the play for the *Montreal Gazette*. He viewed the success of the Ottawa Stage Society's first season with great hope. "Their hard work and the response of the public to it indicate that Canada's capital city is ready to support its own professional theatre where larger cities have failed," Whittaker wrote.

An increasing audience and the fact they were now being touted as a tourist attraction led management to announce a second six-week summer season. Parker chose to open with Noël Coward's popular *Private Lives*, followed by Agatha Christie's *Ten Little Indians*. They also decided on a rerun of *While the Sun Shines*, hoping to bring in better crowds this time. The governor-general, Viscount Alexander of Tunis, and Lady Alexander were finally persuaded to attend, now that the theatre was "proven."

J.B. Priestley's *Laburnum Grove*, Edward Percy and Reginald Denham's *Suspect* and *Arsenic and Old Lace* by Joseph Kesselring rounded out the series, which ended the last week of July 1948. The theatre's members then had a seven-week break to reflect on their successes. The Ottawa Stage Society had a great deal to be proud of: their sixty-six performances in twelve weeks had been seen by 25,000 people. For many of the actors, their time off was a busman's holiday as they took the production of *Laburnum Grove* to Toronto.

Malcolm Morley had to leave a month before the end of the season because of prior commitments to other theatres in Quebec. It was during this time that he worked with a young actor at both Montreal's Open Air Playhouse and Brae Manor in Knowlton, Quebec, and later persuaded him to come to Ottawa. "I was urgently called in to take over from someone who was sick [at Brae Manor]," recalled Christopher Plummer. "It was as Falkland in *The Rivals* [by Richard Sheridan] and I didn't know one line. Malcolm was pleased that I managed to ad lib my way out of trouble. He realized that I could do it so he hired me [for the Ottawa Stage Society], but as a stage manager." This was definitely not Morley's best move. The stage manager's job was a demanding one, especially in a fledgling group where one had to build sets and scrounge props and costumes. Plummer wanted no part of it. "He soon found out I was hopeless as a stage manager," Plummer said. "I was a prop man for about twenty-four hours and then they fired me. Torture. I was there to act. Then suddenly they put me in as Falkland again, a part I now knew from Brae Manor. I was off to the races."

Although Plummer was only eighteen years old at the time, his vast talent was already evident and he became a favourite with the audiences of the Ottawa Stage Society, quickly starring in leading roles. Plummer was not the only new addition to the group, as Eric Workman, Ivor Jackson from Newfoundland and Montreal's Richard Barclay also joined at the end of the 1948 summer.

A scene from *Laburnum Grove* by the Ottawa Stage Society, a production that was so successful it was taken to Toronto. Included are (far right) Derek Ralston and (second left) Betty Leighton, c. 1948. (MCNICOLL COLLECTION)

The fall season opened in September with Norman Krasna's comedy *John Loves Mary*. The Ottawa public was delighted to have the group back, for a love affair had developed between the actors and the audience. Part of this was definitely fostered by the repertory system, which would see an actor in a small character role one week and then in a romantic lead the next. The other reason was that audiences felt they were part of something. "A very, very tight community," Betty Leighton called it. Whatever the cause, there was a special bond between the public and the performers. Christopher Plummer recalled the relationship:

> I certainly felt a rapport in Ottawa. We all did because we became a family. We had a pretty good cast in those days. They were damn good actors all the way down the line. . . . Everybody got to know us in the audience. We were very close. We knew almost everyone in that audience personally by the end of our stay there. They would always ask us out to their homes.

Loyal patrons sent care packages of bread, coffee and sugar to the actors. "They were great," Leighton remembered. "You know, I was in Calgary some time ago. I got a note backstage saying, 'You won't remember us but we saw all the early Stage Society shows.' They came back to see me and they listed plays I had completely forgotten. It meant so much to them in those days."

Feeling as though they were part of a family, members of the audience did everything they could to help out their "relatives." Often items from their homes ended up in a production. The cast scrounged costumes, props, whatever was needed. Department stores donated furniture and furs. It was not all altruistic. Colonial Furniture sold nine Kroehler beds after one appeared in a bedroom scene in *Nina* by Samuel Taylor. The actors also used their own resourcefulness. "I remember I had a black net overdress," Leighton said. "It was given to me by the wife of the Adjutant General of the Canadian Forces. I used to put different under-pinnings under this black net thing to make it look different. She also gave me a velvet evening coat she'd had since the thirties. There was no money. We had to be ingenious." Leighton had her own fan club. "I had a little Scottish lady who organized a few people. They used to give me, on opening night, a silver teaspoon or something. And on special occasions, like my five hundredth performance [Leighton was the first to achieve this milestone], the lady presented me with Shelley tea cups."

The actors returned the affection not only with their performances but by trying to talk to as many of the patrons as possible. "The people who weren't working [in the current show] often used to go along the line and sell tickets," Leighton said. "Because the box office was very small and it took a long time for everybody to get through, they would chat with the people."

Local retailers often helped with supplies and props. One department store, Charles Ogilvy, gave them a huge box of remnants of upholstery and drapery material. "We used to cover the same old Salvation Army sofa until finally the back legs broke on stage during a show," Leighton said. Although neither remembered which play it was, Peter Sturgess also recalled the incident. "Derek Ralston was an English cop, with ruddy big boots on and a helmet," Sturgess said. "He was supposed to sit on the sofa, take off his helmet and wipe his brow because everyone is giving him conflicting reports." Leighton continued with the story, "Derek made the entrance and there were already three of us sitting on [the sofa]. He sat down, the back legs went and we all went back with legs up in the air. It was crazy and stopped the show for ten minutes."

"All the audience could see were these legs waving up in the air," Sturgess concluded. "They were hysterical. As was always the case in those moments, I had the next line and I couldn't get on. Every time I tried to say the next line another gale of laughter would come up."

Working in a repertory theatre such as the Ottawa Stage Society had its rewards, but it was not an easy life and definitely not for the faint-hearted. An average week in repertory would exhaust even the toughest of mortals. From fall through spring the group played Monday through Saturday, changing to a Tuesday start for June and

Actors roll the dice during a scene from the Ottawa Stage Society's inaugural production of *While the Sun Shines*. From left to right: Derek Ralston, Floyd Caza, Brian Herbert and Robert Le Main. (MCNICOLL COLLECTION)

July. Monday night would be the first performance of the current play followed by rehearsal on Tuesday morning for the following week's production. Rehearsals usually ended near three in the afternoon, and then in the evening the second performance of the current play took place. This continued all week. They rarely left the theatre before midnight. Somewhere in there the actors had to find time to learn lines, which usually meant they did not get to sleep until two or three in the morning. The actors were also young and many went out drinking after the evening shows.

They had virtually no days off and Sunday was the busiest day of all. In the morning the staff took down the scenery of the previous week's play and put up the sets for the new one. The stage crew, led by stage manager Floyd Caza, lighting man Roy Sylvester and Ruth White in charge of decor, were the busiest at that point. The cast arrived and costume fittings began. Finding the right outfit for each actor, and dealing with the meagre supplies they could beg, borrow or steal, was an endless procedure. Finally they were able to begin the dress rehearsal, which frequently ended at three on Monday morning. Then they were at the theatre again later that morning for a final rehearsal for the production that night.

On one particular weekend, the theatre was not available to them on the Sunday so they took down the set after the Saturday evening performance and put up the new one, leaving the theatre at six on Sunday morning. They had to have their usual Sunday dress rehearsal from one to seven on Monday morning instead, followed by the final rehearsal at two in the afternoon later the same day. After a short break, they were back for the evening performance. It was not uncommon for them to work sixteen- or seventeen-hour days.

While the actors and management were working long days on the stage, designer Penny Sparling was working just as hard and long under it in the cellar. From England, Sparling had extensive experience with the Old Vic theatre before becoming a scenic artist with the Liverpool Repertory Theatre. Her expertise allowed her to create and reuse flats over and over again. Amelia Hall recalled:

> The flats at the Stage Society had so much paint on them that it would "go cancerous" and peel off. Normally flats are discarded when they reach this point of deterioration, but there was no money for new flats and Penny conceived the idea of scrubbing them down with hot water . . . as Penny . . . splashed about with hot water on the ageing flats it ran off on the dirt floor and formed mud![8]

Not to be deterred, they laid planks down on the mud floor. Then they were able to wash down and reuse the flats repeatedly.

It was back-breaking work, in more ways than one, as Betty Leighton discovered. In a scene from Noël Coward's *Private Lives*, Leighton's character asks to have a love seat moved. During the dress rehearsal director Malcolm Morley decided he did not like the love seat in question, so between the rehearsal and the opening, Floyd Caza had to go out and find another one. He was able to find only a very heavy Victorian one and suggested changing the script so that Leighton could be asked to help him move it. This seemed agreeable except time did not permit any tryouts and that night Leighton suffered a severe back injury "helping" to move it and could barely stand up for the rest of the performance. The only way she staggered through the week was by going for heat treatments every day. She also had to drop out of the next production. As compensation for her suffering, Parker raised Leighton's salary to $60 a week, very good theatre pay for the times.

In January 1949 Peter Sturgess joined the theatre and became a permanent fixture. Coming from England in 1947 to a country he said he was not sure had a theatre industry, Sturgess met Dora Mavor Moore in Toronto and appeared in a number of her New Play Society productions, one of which was directed by Malcolm Morley, who extended an invitation to join the Stage Society. Sturgess turned it down at first but boredom some months later led him to phone Morley, and his relocation to Ottawa followed. He became a strong character actor in what he called "a magnificent company." Others who joined in early 1949 were Joyce Spencer, John Atkinson, Gertrude Allen and Sam Payne, who quickly became popular with audiences and critics alike.

Payne had been living in Toronto, appearing mainly on radio. "One or two friends of mine were in Ottawa at the time in the Stage Society," Payne said. "I went down once or twice to see them and then they asked me to come and play there." Payne had been doing well in radio and was not sure about the move, but there was a temporary lull so he decided to go for one or two shows. He never returned to Toronto.

As successful as they appeared to be, clouds were moving in on the Ottawa Stage Society. Except for a few financial patrons the theatre was basically on its own, and in spite of often having solid crowds, expenses had been outstripping revenue in the summer days of 1949. The Ottawa Stage Society was in jeopardy and pleas were issued to the public. One such request was a letter mailed to subscribers and other supporters, which said in part:

> You will no doubt have heard that the Stage Society is facing the end of its run in Ottawa. . . . We have built up, by infinite endeavour, a stock of scenery as well as lighting equipment, furniture and properties. . . . Our future now rests with you and those other friends who wish us to succeed in our effort for the Theatre in Canada. . . . We have been forced to let certain commitments slide in the hope that with leniency on the part of our creditors and an increase in audience attendance, we should eventually be able to meet our obligations. This has not worked out as we hoped. We are now faced with closing our doors on July 23rd unless a deficit of $3,000 is met before this date. . . . Will you help the permanent theatre in Ottawa to continue? You will be doing a great thing towards that goal on which so many eyes are fixed—The National Theatre of Canada.

Crowds picked up and in late July the group staged *Room Service* by Allen Boretz and John Murray. A play about a Broadway producer trying to bring a sure-fire hit to the stage while beating off such bothersome details as no backing, no money and debts piling up clearly brought the message home to audiences, but it did not seem to matter. The debts continued, and bills were not being paid. Trucking companies would no longer move stage furniture, and Samuel French, Inc. refused to send any more plays until they were paid the royalties owing.

Finally in August 1949, Hugh Parker stopped asking for money because he realized that, for him, the end had come. One of the backers of the group, Violet Southgate,

This distressed looking trio of Derek Ralston, Robert Le Main and Floyd Caza play in a scene from *While the Sun Shines* with the Ottawa Stage Society in May 1948. (MCNICOLL COLLECTION)

had filed a writ for recovery of two loans totalling $1,300, making the end inevitable. Parker was bankrupt.

"I'll never know why those rotten people forced Hugh into bankruptcy," Leighton said, "because he would have made a nice theatre for them. We were looking for properties [to buy] when they forced him into this bankruptcy. . . . As far as I know he owed some money to a lumber company and he had a note from a lady whose husband was keen on getting the whole thing civic. That's how it all happened."

But it wasn't over just yet. La Salle Academy temporarily waived the rent due and many of the actors worked without salary, managing to keep the theatre going for a few more weeks. They worked hard, but they were fighting a battle they simply could not win. On September 10, 1949, the theatre gave its last performance of *We Proudly Present* by Ivor Novello, with most of their regulars in the cast.

The Ottawa Stage Society was by no means a failure. Out of its ashes was to rise a group that holds a hallowed place in the annals of Canadian theatre history.

The Canadian Repertory Theatre Society Incorporated was formed in September 1949, a day before the last performance of *We Proudly Present* by the Ottawa Stage Society. A three-man advisory committee, consisting of Malcolm Morley (who directed and produced), Eric Workman and Reginald Malcolm, would run the group. Hugh Parker had no involvement with the new theatre but most of the actors from the Ottawa Stage Society signed new contracts with the CRT, although some salaries were lower. The objectives of the group were fairly straightforward and much along the lines of their predecessor: to be a non-profit organization establishing a professional theatre in Ottawa, leading to a National Theatre. Any profit would be used to support and encourage promising amateurs and later to open a school.

They also operated out of the La Salle Academy, setting up a schedule of thirty-five weeks a year, which left the actors free to work in the country's growing summer theatre industry. There were two major angels of the CRT at the beginning—newspaper publisher Harry S. Southam and Ottawa businessman Charles Southgate (ironically the husband of the woman who filed the earlier writ against Parker). Southgate continued his backing throughout the CRT's six years of operation. He was the ultimate theatre supporter in those pre-grant days, not only for his money but for his enthusiasm. Sadly, there were too few like him.

Opening night for the CRT was October 1, 1949, and the production was Esther McCracken's *Quiet Weekend*, a sequel to her *Quiet Wedding*, which had been presented to Ottawa audiences by the Ottawa Stage Society shortly after its inception. The cast included Betty Leighton, Eric Workman, Gertrude Allen, Derek Ralston, Reginald Malcolm and Sam Payne. For the second play, J.B. Priestley's *An Inspector Calls*, Anna Cameron joined the CRT and later starred in many of their first season productions.

Although a "Sold Out" sign had been put up at the CRT's opening night, it was not up often enough in the early months and the deficit rose. The operational loss for the first eight weeks was $2,000. It could not have been known at the time, but the fortunes of the CRT were to improve dramatically in December 1949 with the arrival of Amelia Hall, described by Christopher Plummer as "Canada's Helen Hayes."[9] Until her departure from the group in 1954, Millie, as she was known to her friends, was the CRT's most tireless workhorse. Hall recalled how it all happened:

> I had been offered a job teaching class for the Montreal Repertory Theatre. I had been there two days when I got a call from Malcolm Morley. . . . He was phoning me to see if I would go and play in *Arsenic and Old Lace*, just for the one play. I decided to do that and he kept keeping me on. I got paid $28 a week.

She went for one week and stayed four years, never taking a vacation. While the first play was easy for Hall, the second, *Outward Bound* by Sutton Vane, was not. It was the first time she had learned such a demanding and difficult role in only six days, and she felt on trial. Derek Ralston helped her get through. "He was a most generous actor, and always so well prepared, that he gave me the confidence I needed."[10]

In the first two months Hall concentrated solely on acting. That changed in February 1950 when a major reorganization took place. "While Malcolm was still there, he was the director," she said. But then in mid-season Malcolm Morley's mother became ill and he returned to England. Hall said, "I had known Malcolm Morley for some years and I felt he wasn't happy working in Canada. I knew the CRT wasn't going to last long if he stayed because he obviously wasn't giving it his full attention. They wanted the theatre to be run by younger people and for Canadian people. So what happened was Malcolm left, quite amicably I think, because he sent many kind words from England on various occasions afterwards."

Hall was asked to take over the running of the CRT, to both direct and star in productions. After telling them she would take the job only if she had someone to share it with, Sam Payne was asked to join her and he accepted. It was a successful partnership for the CRT, with Bruce Raymond added as the business manager. Although all three ran the company together, the lion's share of the work was done by Hall, who received $45 a week while the lead actors were paid $40. The first show under their management, *The Glass Menagerie* by Tennessee Williams, saw the return of Christopher Plummer to the La Salle Academy stage after a six-month absence.

Plummer had been fired previously by Malcolm Morley, whom he called "a sweet, old sheepdog of a man." In the brashness of youth, Plummer had spoken out when he should have exercised restraint. "Poor Malcolm, just trying to get the god-damned play on," Plummer said. "I was simply insolent beyond belief. I remember Malcolm firing me and saying, 'I think you will have some success in your life. A lot of failure and some success. You will taste both.'" Plummer, who was nineteen years of age when Morley fired him, decided the sooner he could be successful the better, and with a letter of introduction to Robert Whitehead, he headed for New York and Broadway. "I stayed in all sorts of joints," he said. "I wandered about New York and got into trouble. I had a good time." Broadway, however, would have to wait. Robert Whitehead didn't have anything to offer him at that time and radio auditions came to naught. Quickly running out of money, Plummer recalls saying, "To hell with this. I am not going to conquer Broadway. I better go back to where I am employable.'"

Plummer was not long back in Canada before the CRT restructuring took place. "The first thing we did," recalled Amelia Hall, "was bring Chris Plummer back.... Chris was an actor who could give headaches to management, which was why Malcolm did not want him back, but, as a member of the Stratford Board of Governors once remarked to me, 'When I see him on stage I don't give a damn about the headaches!'"[11]

Christopher Plummer, as Romeo, clutches Amelia Hall to his breast in the 1950 CRT production of *Harlequinade* by Terence Rattigan. The play involves a professional theatre company performing *Romeo and Juliet*. (MCNICOLL COLLECTION)

Hall, Derek Ralston and Janet Fehm joined Plummer in *The Glass Menagerie*, directed by Sam Payne. Plummer appeared in many productions that year including *Harvey* by Mary Chase, Terence Rattigan's *The Browning Version* and his last show with the CRT, *A Murder Has Been Arranged*, a mystery by Emlyn Williams.

Earlier on with the Ottawa Stage Society, Plummer had become a matinee idol, and word of his return to the CRT had spread. As soon as he began to walk down the aisle and up towards the set, the applause began. Sam Payne said that a tumult was caused in the theatre "when the lights went up on Chris."

Betty Leighton still returned frequently to star. Derek Ralston, until he finally left in May 1950, chalked up more than 550 performances with the Ottawa Stage Society and the CRT. Others who starred early on with the CRT were Joanna Baker, Gertrude Allen, Bea Whitfield, Peter Sturgess, Lynne Gorman and John Atkinson, who later took over as business manager from Bruce Raymond. The CRT helped launch the careers of many fine actors, but many successful directors, designers and stage managers, including David Haber, also got their start there.

Choosing what plays to stage was difficult for the CRT, as it had been for its predecessor. Hugh Parker had learned quickly with the Ottawa Stage Society which plays were popular. He explained the process in an article that appeared in Ottawa's *Evening Citizen*, December 3, 1948:

> If there is one question asked more than another it is: "Why don't you do such and such a play?" . . . There must be a very definitive affirmative answer to each of the following questions: Can the books be obtained? Can a release on the play be secured? Can it be cast with the available personnel? Can it be staged, that is, is it too costly? Are the technical requirements possible? And, finally, is it "box office?" . . . Ottawa is, apparently, not yet ready to assimilate the more serious dramatic fare. Farce, comedy and mystery are the ingredients, at the moment, of the happy box office recipe.[12]

The CRT also began with the lighter plays, but once Amelia Hall arrived, the fare became a little more varied. Nevertheless, they were still limited by what was available and what they could afford.

The management of the CRT did something else that was innovative with their choice of plays. Shortly after they began, they asked their patrons what plays they would like to see and then tried to accommodate their choices. The first of these was *The Heiress*, a play based on Henry James' *Washington Square* and written by Ruth and Augustus Goetz. After repeated requests, and in spite of the royalty costs, it was produced by the CRT in February 1950.

Royalties for plays were exorbitant in Canada at that time and often reached $200 or $300 a play; all theatres had to deal with the problem. Often they hoped to give a North American premiere of a particular play but found they could not afford it. In addition, most playwrights wanted the first production of their play to be done in a major theatre, preferably on Broadway, and not in a small, unknown theatre in Canada. The price of royalties on *The Heiress* was worth it for the CRT, though, because it attracted a large audience. Moreover, throughout the spring of 1950 public support for the CRT continued to grow; the operational loss dropped until it was only about $10 a show.

In June 1950 they staged their first Canadian play. *Days of Grace*, by Ottawa's William Doyle, involves a civil servant who resorts to lobbying and bribery to supplement his income. Unfortunately, it did poorly at the box office. That production notwithstanding, the thirty-three plays in the 1949–50 season were seen by 69,775 patrons. The theatre offered specials of three shows for as little as $1.80. Even though the financial upswing was not to last and never reached such heights again, advance subscription pledges for their second season were such that the CRT's actors were relatively secure about their theatre's future when they departed for the summer of 1950.

William Boyle (left), Sam Payne and Amelia Hall pore over the script for Boyle's play *Days of Grace*. It was one of only two Canadian plays staged by the CRT during Hall's reign there and did badly at the box office. (AMELIA HALL COLLECTION)

For most of the actors, that summer was once again a working one as they scattered to perform with groups such as Vancouver's TUTS, the Montreal Repertory Theatre and many summer theatre companies. As usual, one of the busiest actors was Amelia Hall. After performing with one of the summer theatres, she would dash to as many of the other theatres as possible to see their productions. And all of this at her own expense, for it was in this way that Hall searched out the talent and invited them to play with the CRT. Most considered it an honour.

"It was quite a feather in your cap to be invited to play at the CRT because of its uniqueness," William Hutt said. "Also, it was an organization that was capable of offering you a reasonably lengthy contract."

Her trips to all the summer theatres were tiring and required a careful allotment of her time, but then Amelia Hall had never been one to waste an hour. She was also a self-confessed "mother hen" to many of the CRT actors. She had a need for order in her surroundings and "hated" the building housing the theatre. Her overriding impression of it years later was that it was "dirty," and she worked hard to improve their physical surroundings. Her obsession with detail gave the CRT a top-rate reputation for performance. Although she was assisted through the years, the bulk of the responsibilities rested squarely on her shoulders. "I don't think anyone could have had a freer hand than I had," Hall recalled. "I say, 'I' because I was largely responsible for choosing the plays."

Working hard to bring professionalism to the CRT, Hall had many hopes for the young company. "We were in a unique position at the CRT," she said. "I had a kind of dream that whenever anyone that was good went away [for the summer], they would come back. Originally I had wanted us all to be Canadian. Then . . . I wanted to have it a sort of international theatre." It didn't quite work out that way, but it was still an incredible company. "The amazing thing is that we never had understudies and nobody ever missed a performance," she said. "I've seen people throw up in the washrooms and then go onstage."

Because repertory theatre involved such a gruelling schedule, mistakes, missed lines and other mishaps were inevitable—even with the utmost professionalism. One such faux pas happened in the winter of 1950 and could not have come on a more apt note. It was during a presentation of Oliver Goldsmith's *She Stoops to Conquer*. Silvio Narizzano as Tony Lumpkin and Sam Payne as Squire Hardcastle were in view on stage and Betty Leighton was hidden behind a bush. As with Totem Theatre out west, Sam Payne had acquired a reputation for his inability to remember lines.

"Sam came on," Leighton recalled, "on the blasted heath, and he was supposed to say, 'But I heard a voice here.' Sam didn't say the line so the prompter threw the line to him but he paid no attention, didn't hear it, I guess. So then Silvio whispered, 'I heard a voice.' Sam still didn't say a word. I'm behind a bush in a great feathered hat. Nothing was said again. Finally the prompter said again, 'I heard a voice,' and Sam turned to the prompter and said, 'Who heard a voice, oh I'm sorry, I did.' Well, the house went crazy, I knocked the bush over, my hat fell off, oh God, it was hilarious. Everybody adored Sam, he could do anything."

Plummer remembered the times when the lines came out jumbled. As he comments in his autobiography, ". . . our memories began to collapse—we were so damned mixed-up—how could you learn *Glass Menagerie* and *Private Lives* at one and the same time? It got to the point on stage . . . we fell about giggling."[13] In spite of this, Plummer had a reputation for an amazing memory and an ability to hold it all together, no matter what the circumstance. Actress Beatrice Whitfield recalled one night:

> I was in the wings waiting to go on when Chris Plummer dashed in the stage door, and lingered only long enough to ask "What play are we doing tonight?" I gave him the title and he made his entrance cool and letter perfect.[14]

The audience "never knew the difference," Whitfield said.

In its second year, the one Hall refers to as the "golden year," the CRT managed to survive financially with the help of Charles Southgate, who continued to stand behind the debt, which was increasing in spite of the fact that some eighty thousand people attended the thirty-five plays that year. Management had also introduced the "theatre party scheme," which was good for publicity and brought patrons into the theatre, but also took money out of the CRT's coffers. Under the plan, an organization took over the selling of tickets for a certain performance and then would share in the box office receipts. Unfortunately, the CRT's expenses stayed the same for the show but revenue was reduced. Still, the idea mushroomed quickly and thirty-seven theatre parties were organized in 1950–51.

During that season Eric House received a telegram asking him to join the CRT at $40 a week, a communication he said "changed my life." He was amazed to find how hard everyone worked, especially the backstage crew. "It was a great education," House said. "I couldn't do it now. I look back and wonder how on earth we ever did it then."

Among the plays that season was a revival of *The Glass Menagerie* starring Amelia Hall, Silvio Narizzano, Gerry Sarracini and Mary Sheppard. But the two plays which brought in the biggest crowds were Mary Chase's *Harvey* and *Born Yesterday* by Garson Kanin. Comedies were popular with Ottawa audiences, but unlike with summer crowds at straw hat theatres, mysteries were not. Another highlight of the second year was a production of Robertson Davies' *At My Heart's Core*, with the author's wife Brenda in the lead role of Frances Stewart, a part written especially for her. She was staggered at the speed of the group, that they could pull the production together in a week. The role of Catharine Parr Traill in *At My Heart's Core* was also written with a certain actress in mind—Amelia Hall.

The Canadian Repertory Theatre had its own censorship board of sorts—the Catholic Fathers who ran La Salle Academy. Any play the CRT wanted to stage had

Amelia Hall in one of her favourite roles, as Nora in Ibsen's *A Doll's House*, with the Canadian Repertory Theatre in 1951. Starring opposite her as Dr. Rank was Eric House. (AMELIA HALL COLLECTION)

to be first given approval. This was not the case with the group's predecessor, the Ottawa Stage Society, or even the first two years of the CRT, but one production changed everything and caused a censorship clause to be added to the rental agreement. In April 1951, the CRT presented *Separate Rooms* by Terence Rattigan, with Amelia Hall and Eric House in the cast and Sam Payne directing. Hall tells the story:

> It was a play we had thrown in at the last minute because the play we were going to do that week, the rights hadn't come through. I didn't know the play. It was chosen by the business manager and I got the script the night before we started rehearsing it. The next day I phoned him and said I thought it was rather dirty. He said, "Oh, if we do it fast it will be very funny." We played to "standing room only." I don't know if some of the people who attended it the first night complained to the Catholic bishop. Whatever happened, the theatre was immediately made out of bounds by the Bishop for that play. Someone who used to send word of what we were doing to *Variety* [magazine] in New York, sent in a report that we had been made out of bounds by the Bishop and played to "standing room only." This report made its way back to the Bishop himself and the CRT was in imminent danger of losing their home for the coming season. . . . It was only because Mr. [Charles] Southgate was very diplomatic [in a letter] that we got the theatre back.

In fact, Southgate wrote the letter to the Archbishop of Ottawa in which he pleaded their case and pointed to what the CRT brought to Ottawa and what they had overcome to bring theatre to the city. He also stated how much he believed in the CRT: "I can assure Your Excellency that, were it not our [he and H.S. Southam, publisher of the *Ottawa Citizen*] ardent belief that we are performing a public service within the framework of good Christian endeavour, we would not be associated with this venture."

He stressed that the operating committee looked over every play and censored any lines they thought unacceptable to the audience. "If, on occasions, we have given offence, it was a matter of misunderstanding rather than intent, for which we are indeed sorry," Southgate wrote. He managed to save the day but they were watched very closely after that. Hall recalled:

> The condition was that all the plays had to be read by Father John MacDonald. He was head of social services for the Catholic Church in Ottawa. He was a very charming man and I used to take all the plays to him. That was very difficult because it meant not only did I have the problem of reading plays all the time while I was acting and directing but I had to now take them to him. He didn't have much time and I had to wait while he read them. He sometimes took out odd lines and things. I quickly learned the thing to avoid was divorce. Affairs didn't seem to matter. He passed *Nina* without any alteration whatsoever although the wife in that was having an affair. I just took it [for fun]. I thought he would say, "Miss Hall, you know this isn't possible." Instead he picked up the script, started to chuckle and said, "This is very amusing but it will have to be awfully well done."

The biggest argument the two had was over a play called *The Beaux' Stratagem* from the early eighteenth century. "That's a Restoration play and the theme of divorce is stated in the poem at the end—'if you're not happy, break it up.' That was the only time I ever really argued with him," Hall said.

The censorship issue had an impact for the balance of the CRT's existence. "Every script we did we had to submit to the Fathers for censorship which immediately cut out a lot of plays we would like to have done," William Hutt said. The group had to eliminate the use of the words "hell" and "damn," Eric House added, "We had to watch ourselves very carefully. We couldn't say 'God' for instance."

While they were under strict controls, the CRT was very popular with the Fathers themselves. "The Saturday afternoons we never sold the balcony tickets," Hall said, "and the Brothers used to nip in and watch the play, I remember they particularly liked *Born Yesterday*."

Because of the censorship constraints, the group began looking for alternative locations but were unable to find one. They reopened back at the Academy in the fall of 1951 with Ted Follows and Bea Lennard joining the company for the season, which also saw appearances by Araby Lockhart, Donald Davis and Richard Easton. It was exhausting doing that many plays over the course of a season and it was virtually impossible for every play chosen to be a success. The type of play changed swiftly from farce or light comedy one week to heavy drama the next. The productions staged in 1951–52 were typical of a CRT season:

1951
- Sept. 18–22 / *The Taming of the Shrew*
- Sept. 25–29 / *Heaven Can Wait*
- Oct. 2–6 / *The Butter and Egg Man*
- Oct. 9–13 / *Two Blind Mice*
- Oct. 16–20 / *You Never Can Tell*
- Oct. 23–27 / *George Washington Slept Here*
- Oct. 30–Nov. 3 / *A Doll's House*
- Nov. 6–10 / *Clutterbuck*
- Nov. 13–17 / *Three Men on a Horse*
- Nov. 20–24 / *When We Are Married*
- Nov. 27–Dec. 1 / *Home of the Brave*
- Dec. 4–8 / *The Barretts of Wimpole Street*
- Dec. 11–15 / *On Monday Next*
- Dec. 26–29 / *Treasure Hunt*

1952
- Jan. 1–5 / *The Happy Family*
- Jan. 8–12 / *Jane Steps Out*
- Jan. 15–19 / *Chicken Every Sunday*
- Jan. 22–26 / *The Middle Watch*
- Jan. 29–Feb. 2 / *Years Ago*
- Feb. 5–9 / *Heartbreak House*
- Feb. 12–16 / *Hay Fever*
- Feb. 19–23 / *Home and Beauty*
- Feb. 26–Mar. 1 / *Nothing But the Truth*
- Mar. 4–8 / *Imaginary Invalid*
- Mar. 11–15 / *On Borrowed Time*
- Mar. 18–22 / *You Touched Me*
- Mar. 25–29 / *Noah*
- Apr. 1–5 / *Arms of the Man*
- Apr. 14–19 / *Hamlet*
- Apr. 22–26 / *Traveller's Joy*
- Apr. 29–May 3 / *Black Chiffon*
- May 6–10 / *Tonight at 8.30*
- May 13–17 / *The Petrified Forest*

The Canadian Repertory Theatre company in 1950 standing in front of La Salle Academy. Among the smiling crowd were Amelia Hall (third from left) and Christopher Plummer (fifth from left). (MCNICOLL COLLECTION)

It is impossible to imagine a contemporary company doing so many plays in one season today.

The group was now attracting widespread attention for its efforts to bring theatre to Canada's capital and for the quality of its shows. Reviews of the plays were appearing in Toronto and Montreal. *Variety* magazine in the United States was also beginning to take notice. Every year at least one play would break previous attendance records or bring some praise to the CRT for its production. *Hamlet*, staged near the end of the third year, did both, a combination rarely achieved. More than four thousand people saw *Hamlet* during the six days it was presented, yet high production costs meant it actually lost money. Critics raved over the show. The CRT had given itself two weeks to prepare for *Hamlet* instead of the usual one. In the demanding role of Hamlet was teenager Richard Easton who had joined them earlier in the season. All the performances were praised, as was Sam Payne's direction.

"As director, Sam Payne has done much more than stage *Hamlet*," the review in the *Ottawa Journal* said. "He has cut it with much skill, concentrating always on the main character in the play, and in so doing has arrived at the essentials. . . . This reviewer would like to give credit to the company for the difficulties it has met and overcome in reaching a point where, as Canada's only professional repertory company, it can in two short weeks rehearse, produce and stage one of the most difficult of plays."

The remainder of the cast included Donald Davis as the King, Gertrude Allen as the Queen, Amelia Hall as Ophelia, Ted Follows as Laertes and Peter Sturgess as one of the Gravediggers. Sturgess said the memory he carries of the production is that the grave he was in almost ended up being his own:

> There was a trap door [on stage] that went right down about twenty feet into the basement, just a hole. There was only one way to do the grave scene. They would put a table, one of those folding tables, with a long ladder on it so that one could stand on it and look as though one were in the grave. Of course it was pitch-black down below, otherwise the light would shine up through the grave. I suddenly found myself wobbling around wildly. I was standing on something which was going up and down. The brothers [who ran the Academy] had during the day, unbeknownst to anybody, decided they needed the ladder and had never returned it. And come the actual moment what they did was to balance three chairs on top of each other on the folding table. They had even put cushions on the top chair. I cut the scene very short, producing the skull at the quickest possible moment.

The near disaster obviously didn't happen on the night the reviewers were in attendance because the scene was singled out as a highlight of the production.

By the end of that season, the CRT had staged 630 performances of more than 100 plays. In their brief history, the theatre had played to a total of 210,531 patrons with a box office revenue of $152,268, amazing really because ticket prices ranged from only 60¢ to $1.20. However, expenses for the same period were $171,988. Something had to give. The CRT sharing scheme of "the theatre party" had put a much needed $12,000 in the pockets of various city organizations in that third season rather than into those of the CRT, and in spite of record-breaking plays like *Hamlet*, the season ended with a loss of $5,000. They had expected to put a dent in the existing deficit, so this news was very discouraging. Management of the CRT had no choice but to announce they could not set an opening date for the fall 1952 season until assured of sufficient patronage. They finally opened a month late in October, but it was not only the lack of financial support that caused the delay.

Hall had intended to stage *Private Lives* to open the season. She was going to use the staging and most of the cast from a production of the play that summer by the Straw Hat Players. Because it had been performed previously by the Ottawa Stage Society it never occurred to her there would be a problem, but the censor suddenly intervened and said they could not perform it. Hall argued that it had already been staged there, but Father MacDonald was adamant. He'd already had complaints about a play in the previous season: Noël Coward's *Ways and Means* in which a couple was in bed together. "I said, 'But they have a big breakfast tray between them and they are supposed to be married.' He said he thought it was rather foolish but people had complained."

The couples in *Private Lives* were divorced and that was taboo. The play was out. She had to scramble to find a new play and would have to direct it herself from scratch. She chose *Captain Carvallo* by Denis Cannan. It introduced William Hutt to CRT audiences for the first time.

The replacement of good actors continued to be one of the group's greatest accomplishments because, with the dispersal of actors every summer, many chose not to return to Ottawa but stayed in the more active cities. There were some stalwarts such as Peter Sturgess, Betty Leighton, Gertrude Allen (who had more than five hundred appearances with the CRT), Bea Whitfield and Reginald Malcolm. The company was still managed by Amelia Hall and Sam Payne, although the latter would move back to Vancouver in 1953. In addition to William Hutt, other actors appearing with the CRT in 1952–53 included Barbara Chilcott, George McCowan, Max Helpmann, Lynne Gorman and a man who is among the most-recognized of CRT alumni, Captain James T. Kirk of the starship Enterprise in *Star Trek*, alias William Shatner.

Shatner came to the CRT from Montreal where he had made quite a name for himself on radio as a juvenile. He also worked on stage in the Open Air Playhouse production of Shakespeare's *Cymbeline*. Shatner was acting with the Montreal Children's Theatre by the time he was nine years old. He joined the CRT for $31 a week. William Hutt recalled one significant talk he had with the young actor. "This was one of William Shatner's first times on stage," Hutt said. "I remember having a conversation with him one day and saying to him, 'Bill, I think some day you are going to be a movie star but I don't know about a stage star.'"

The two biggest productions of the CRT's fourth season were the first Canadian presentation of Christopher Fry's verse play *The Lady's Not for Burning* and *Victoria Regina*, a long historical play by Laurence Housman which was presented in honour of Queen Elizabeth's coronation year. Fry's play would run for a week immediately following the two-week Christmas break. Because of its success, this was eventually extended to four weeks, something that had never happened in Ottawa before. Amelia Hall starred in and directed the production that ended its final rehearsal late on Christmas Eve. The play required tremendous preparation and it all had to be done during the holiday break. Hall remembered:

> I went to a high school and found a lot of levels [risers] among their gym equipment which we borrowed so we would not have to build those different levels inside the

A Canadian Repertory Theatre 1952 production of a hit comedy of the day, *Castle in the Air*, starred William Hutt (left), William Shatner of later *Star Trek* fame and Barbara Chilcott. (MCNICOLL COLLECTION)

> castle. I had to find the music I wanted. I also went down to Montreal and chose the costumes while the actors were away. Then when they came back we rehearsed, there being no union rules, day and night. So the play had more rehearsal than it normally would have. I just knocked myself out but it was well worth it; it was a beautiful show.

Both Governor-General Vincent Massey and Ottawa's mayor, Charlotte Whitton, saw the highly praised show.

The season ended with a two-week run of *Victoria Regina* with more than three thousand patrons seeing the first six performances. It was a very costly production because of the elaborate costumes and the huge cast, which included William Hutt, Sam Payne, George McCowan and Reginald Malcolm. They did the play at the insistence of Charles Southgate who wanted to do something to celebrate the coronation of Queen Elizabeth II.

During that season, the CRT gave five plays their North American premiere and five others their Canadian ones. Every year brought its own adventures or changes, and the 1952–53 season was no exception. Two weeks prior to the Fry play they staged Chekhov's *Three Sisters*. They invited the senior members of Ottawa's Soviet Embassy and were surprised when they attended. Their guests praised the show and afterwards invited the cast back to the embassy where they were treated royally.

At the end of the fourth season, Amelia Hall and a number of others headed for Stratford's first summer. After Stratford's success, and in spite of an offer to join the Crest Theatre, which would open six months later in Toronto, Hall began her fifth and final season with the CRT in September 1953. She wanted to take one more stab at trying to reduce the massive debt. "There was always the worry about the bank debt," she said. "I went back with various ideas that had been given to me by Tyrone Guthrie, such as running all the plays for two weeks, raising the salaries [in her last year Hall made $60 a week, not the top salary] and raising the price of admittance."

With the departure of Sam Payne, Hall asked William Hutt to be her associate director. "Between the two of us we sank it right into the ground," Hutt said with humour.

In truth, the CRT did not do any worse financially during the 1953–54 season than it had done in previous years—but it did not do any better either. And there were other problems to contend with that did not make life any easier. "I also did something I think was a mistake," Hall recalled. "We originally had a board of only seven people, three of whom were people who worked at the theatre." One of those on the board suggested expanding it. Hall agreed, thinking it might solve some of her problems but instead it created more of them. She recalled:

> None of the new members were from the CRT. So we had the kind of board all kinds of artistic organizations have nowadays with no artists on them. That proved a big mistake as I was more busy going to meetings than I had ever been. They began to worry

> a lot about the artistic side of the theatre which made it even more difficult to choose plays than it had been before. When they came on the board they were full of praise about what I had done but once on the board they would say, "Why are you doing this play?" Then the play would be a success and they'd say, "Why can't you get another play like that play?" . . . They had no courage at all.

Despite the expanded board, the CRT had at least one major success in Hall's last season: Molière's *Tartuffe ou l'Imposteur*, starring William Hutt. Unfortunately, *Tartuffe* was the only highlight of an otherwise depressing season for both of the theatre's directors. "Bill and I had wanted to leave during the season, but we didn't want to cause a situation that would get into the papers," Hall said. "That was the only year at the CRT I did not enjoy at all. . . . I guess it was high time I left because I was very, very tired, so I just slipped quietly away."

When Amelia Hall left the Canadian Repertory Theatre in May 1954, the accrued debt was still some $19,000. After her departure the situation became worse. The theatre would limp on for another two years in one form or another but the soul of the CRT left with Hall. The fall 1954 season began with the group in the hands of actress Margaret Braidwood and her then-husband Harry Geldard. They had been given a completely free hand by the theatre's board of directors. They opened with the governor-general attending *The Fourposter* by Jan de Hartog, but after a good start things went rapidly downhill. The audiences began to grow irritated when the system changed and they no longer saw their favourite actors in a small part one week and the romantic lead the next.

"As the weeks went by and it began to dawn on them that the only person they ever saw in a good part was [Braidwood] herself, the opposition amongst the regulars began to build," recalled actor Peter Sturgess, who was also the CRT's business manager at that time. He took a lot of the brunt of the public's discontent and took even more of it during the period leading up to one of the highlights of the CRT's history, its royal performance of Mazo de la Roche's *Whiteoaks* on November 18, 1954. The Queen Mother attended the performance. What she must have thought of the slightly seedy school auditorium in which she witnessed Canadian theatre was not recorded, but she did give her verbal approval to the production itself. For the performance, the front row of seats in the auditorium were removed. In its place, a strip of expensive red carpet was laid down and five or six armchairs placed there. Later, Charles Southgate bought and took home the chair used by the Queen Mother. Sturgess said it became his most prized possession.

The events surrounding the performance offered as many twists and turns as the plot of the play. The original choice for the royal performance, made by Margaret Braidwood, was Jean Cocteau's *The Eagle Has Two Heads*. "However, [Braidwood] had not considered one thing," Sturgess said. "Because this was a royal performance, the script had to be passed by Government House and they turned it down flat." It was considered "unsuitable" and it was strongly suggested to the CRT that the play in question be by a Canadian. Hence *Whiteoaks*. It is ironic they chose a play that Amelia Hall had excelled in earlier, not only with the Mountain Playhouse in Montreal but also with the CRT itself. This time, however, the role of 101-year-old Adeline Whiteoaks was taken by Margaret Braidwood. Once the public was aware that a royal performance was in the works, Peter Sturgess had yet another problem. "About a week before the performance, the phone started to ring and never seemed to stop," Sturgess said. "Everyone who rang, it seemed, had supported the CRT for years, through thick and thin, and now was the time when that old debt was to be repaid by a couple of tickets to that much sought after royal performance."

In fact, those who had been consistently loyal, the subscribers, did get the first seats. The production was a joint benefit between the CRT and the Mothercraft Society, a favourite charity of the Queen Mother. Half the ticket revenue would go to each, although all the expenses would be absorbed by the CRT. With higher ticket prices ranging from $5 to $10, the theatre still made money, but it was the only glimmer of hope in the season.

As president of the Canadian Repertory Theatre Society Incorporated, Southgate was alarmed about the growing public discontent with the theatre but even more worried about what this meant at the box office—returns that were diminishing each week. For him the final blow came when actor Eric Christmas was brought in for the CRT's pantomime *Mother Goose* by Wayne and Shuster and was given a very high salary plus a percentage of the take. Southgate called a board meeting with Sturgess being brought in to "present them with the latest figures." The news was not good.

The average attendance over an eight-week period was 23 percent of the theatre's capacity. Adding to the huge accrued debt at the beginning of the season, was a current weekly operating deficit of more than $400. Without any argument, Margaret Braidwood and Harry Geldard quietly resigned, and the CRT shut down operations a few days after Christmas of 1954.

The theatre was not yet down for the count, however, and following another intense board meeting, a tentative ten-week season beginning in mid-January 1955 was planned. The public support for the group, now run by Peter Sturgess, Charles Jarrett and Ian Fellows, was so strong that there was no operating loss for any of the ten weeks. It was decided during the summer of 1955 that the CRT would not operate out of the La Salle Academy any longer; it would also stay closed until some of the previous debts could be paid off and a new location found.

At this critical point, however, a group of CRT subscribers and "friends," headed by Ian Fellows, formed a CRT Club on their own and decided to stage a series of plays at the La Salle Academy, commencing with a pantomime in December 1955. By this time Peter Sturgess was living and working in Toronto. While refusing to take over as business manager again, he agreed to go back and act in one or two shows. It was clear from the beginning, Sturgess said, that there was one thing lacking from this new venture—an audience. After two productions he returned to Toronto only to receive a late night phone call from Charles Southgate two weeks later. "He told me that as far as he could tell, the CRT Club was broke," Sturgess said. "He explained that Ian had been to see him and had asked him to come to his rescue. Mr. Southgate asked me, as a friend, to please come down to Ottawa at once and help him find out what the exact position of the theatre was, and decide between ourselves what was the best thing to do."

A "grim" situation is what Sturgess and Southgate found. No books had been kept covering the CRT Club's financial state so the first order of business was to reconstruct the books as best they could. The most sensible thing to do was close, but the CRT Club had already collected $5,000 in advance subscriptions for their ten planned plays. Because the money had already been spent, with five plays still to be presented, the two decided they simply could not add to the CRT's debt. They had no option really, except to finish the season so that the subscribers did not lose their $5,000 in subscriptions. This they accomplished with the help of the La Salle Academy management, which did not press for the rent. Sturgess, Reginald Malcolm and Ian Fellows worked the last few weeks without salary. The final play, the North American premiere of a Ben Travers' farce, *Wild Horses*, ended on March 3, 1956, and brought the curtain down on a venture that was the vehicle for so much Canadian talent. Included in that final cast were Sturgess, Bea Whitfield and Reginald Malcolm.

Hugh Parker later reflected in the *Ottawa Journal* on his early attempt to bring theatre to Ottawa:

> We were obviously years ahead of our time when one notes the lavish subsidies granted to the arts these days by government. . . . But many of the original group carried on and I am extremely proud of my alumni. Their reward, in some cases, has been international recognition. This they richly deserve, for their tenacity and their incredibly hard work in the toughest school of them all—repertory theatre.[15]

And what became of Charles Southgate?—"the ideal patron," as Eric House rightly called him. He died a year after the Canadian Repertory Theatre closed its doors for good.

CHAPTER EIGHT

# HART HOUSE & THE STRAW HAT PLAYERS

"We had this advantage—our audiences were almost as inexperienced as we were."

—DONALD DAVIS

Because there were hardly any professional training schools for actors before and after the Second World War, university theatre groups, amateur though they were, proved important breeding grounds for the growth of professional theatre. Actors were also attracted to university theatre groups because universities often hired the best drama teachers in the country and the actors could receive the top-notch directing they desired. Consequently the university theatres tended to produce many actors who went on to make names for themselves on a professional stage. None perhaps contributed more than Hart House Theatre.

The actual theatre itself was not in the original plans for the Hart House student union building, constructed and donated to the University of Toronto by the Massey family at a cost of more than a million dollars. Built into the basement, Hart House Theatre opened in 1919 as an experimental theatre for the use of not only the university but also the wider community it served. It was owned by the Massey family and operated as a separate entity from the university. Even though it seated fewer than five hundred people, it was considered to be one of the best-equipped theatres in

North America at the time. Initially it served more as a community theatre than one for the students and, as such, in 1919 it became home to Roy Mitchell's Players' Club, which he founded in 1913. Many professionals performed with Mitchell's group and others during the ensuing years, with Hart House under the watchful eye of the Massey family and run by the board of syndics. Between 1937 and 1946, however, it was largely non-operational because of the lack of a theatre manager.

The beginning of what could be called the modern era of Hart House was in 1945, when the Massey family donated the theatre itself to the University of Toronto for exclusive use by undergraduates as an amateur theatre, with the board of syndics responsible directly to the University Board of Governors.

In 1946, American Robert Gill was appointed director of the theatre. The Washington-born Gill, graduate and later teacher at the well-known Carnegie Institute of Technology, worked with both the Pittsburgh and Cleveland Playhouses before coming to Canada. He planned to stay only a year but he was still there at his death in 1974, having become a Canadian citizen in 1958 and receiving the Centennial Medal in 1967. He would nurture many aspiring actors in post-war Toronto.

The 1946–47 Hart House season included productions of George Bernard Shaw's *Saint Joan*, starring Charmion King and *The Infernal Machine* by Jean Cocteau. The list of talented actors who performed under Gill during those early years is staggering: Eric House, Charmion King, William Hutt, Araby Lockhart, Kate Reid, Ted Follows, David Gardner, Barbara Hamilton, Beth Gillanders, Anna Cameron, Henry Kaplan, Bea Lennard, George McCowan and Donald and Murray Davis.

"When I think back, it was sort of a curious group of people just at random," Donald Davis said. "Murray graduated in political science and economics, I graduated theoretically in English, David Gardner in archaeology and art, Ted Follows in psychology and Eric House in geography. We all then took those BAs and promptly went into the theatre! If you are going to ask me to explain it [the proliferation of talented actors coming out of Hart House], I don't think I can. I've puzzled over it."

Robert Gill was certainly a large part of it. His knowledge of theatre and his enthusiasm for it was instilled in his students, Davis remembered:

> He was a very, very skilled teacher and he came from what was considered then and still is, one of the best training programs in the United States—Carnegie Tech. He was enormously proficient at theatre craft and it wasn't just earnest discussions about acting. He understood stage design. He understood the technical necessity for things like voice and movement and so on.

The students were "schooled in professionalism by this earnest director," Herbert Whittaker wrote of Gill.[16] William Hutt said the quality of the productions was excellent "because Bob Gill was a marvellous combination of director-teacher. If I was to assess his place simply as a director in the history of theatre, I can't honestly say I think he was another Tyrone Guthrie or a Robin Phillips but he was absolutely suited for the job he had in directing students and teaching them some of the basics of stage performing."

Gill also offered another form of support, David Gardner said:

> First of all he was marvellously approachable. We were going to do four shows and he interviewed all of us, got to know us and became a great friend and for many of us became a father figure because our own fathers and mothers were not in the theatre so suddenly here was somebody who, if you had a theatre problem, you could talk to.

Gardner claimed that Gill gave confidence to the young actors: "The greatest thing he gently instilled in us was that we could have a career in this crazy thing that we loved, a professional career. 'Why not?' he said. 'You're good, all of you. You could earn your living by doing this.'"

There were, however, other reasons besides the professionalism of Bob Gill for the amount of talent that poured out of Hart House Theatre. Part of it had to do with the type of student going to university shortly after the war. The Department of Veteran Affairs (DVA) paid for many returning servicemen to attend university or other learning institution of their choice such as the Banff School of Fine Arts. Charmion King explained:

> When the war ended, a lot of people with DVA came into the university so that we had younger and older people there at that time. It made it very stimulating. . . . The people who did come back from the war, and even the young people who were there at the natural age level of the university, I think felt it was a new beginning as you always feel at the end of a war. You start again. I think that definitely had something to do with it. You were dealing with people who had a lot more experience in life. And determination.

It also required dedication because theatre was an extracurricular activity and the students were already holding down a full slate of classes. Gill himself was always concerned about the students' academic life; he would not allow any student to be in more than two productions in one year.

❧

Finally in the summer of 1947 Robert Gill took a step that helped towards the formation of a professional theatre company, the Straw Hat Players. It began when he took a job as the resident director of the Woodstock Playhouse in New York State. "The Woodstock Playhouse was considered then one of the first-string summer theatres in the Eastern States," Donald Davis said. "Gill invited a bunch of us from his students, undergraduates from U of T, to go with him to Woodstock that summer to serve as apprentices. This was a normal situation for those kind of theatres because it was a good way of getting some manpower to work for nothing because we were paid nothing."

Among those who went down with Gill were Donald and Murray Davis, Araby Lockhart, Henry Kaplan, Bea Lennard and Charmion King. "We were allowed to act in three of the productions over the [summer] season," Charmion King remembered. "So we gained experience. We did the lighting. . . . We also acted and we could sit in and watch rehearsals. They were really insignificant joe jobs but it was a very quick and good way to learn about the theatre."

Soon the day came when thoughts about their futures took a more concrete form: they decided that they wanted their own theatre. Donald Davis recalled how he discussed the idea of starting one with his brother, Murray:

> We all agreed that after this heady experience, just being an apprentice another summer wasn't going to be the answer. We talked about it and recognized the fact that at that moment in time, the summer of 1947, there were no summer stock companies operating in this general area of southern Ontario so we couldn't apply anywhere. So we literally said, "Let's make it Rooney and Garland, let's put on a show in Daddy's barn." We said, "Let's do our own company."

They decided to call it the Straw Hat Players, from the commonly used name to describe the summer touring shows: the straw hat circuit.

By the late 1940s and the early '50s these summer theatres had become very popular, especially in Ontario. They were different from their winter counterparts; audiences were on vacation and wanted to be entertained. Their tastes were for light comedies such as Noël Coward's *Hay Fever* or thrillers like Emlyn Williams' *Night Must Fall.* They did not want to think, just enjoy themselves.

For their venture in 1947, the Davis brothers decided on Muskoka because it was a large summer resort area north of Toronto and they felt this would ensure them an audience. It was also an area they knew well. Charmion King described how they chose the exact location. "We went up to the Davis summer cottage [in Muskoka]. We took a pin and figured which was the area in the summer residence, cottage area, that was the richest area. And Port Carling it was. Then we put in a radius of so far around it that we could handle from that spot and that's how the Straw Hat Players was formed."

Now they needed a director and the obvious choice was Bob Gill with all his experience at Hart House. Donald Davis explained how it happened:

> We finally convinced him to, in effect, direct the first season of the Straw Hat Players. Our first season was relatively modest. We were going to undertake to do four productions and we rehearsed in [Murray's] recreation room in Toronto. We blocked and

> rehearsed all four plays at once if you can imagine. . . . Bob Gill pretty well fully directed [the first two] and framed the other ones. Then Murray and I sort of put them into final shape, whatever that was!

In spite of all his input, a glance at the programs from the Straw Hat Players' first summer season in 1948 reveals no mention of Bob Gill. "There was a problem," Davis said. "Who were we going to credit for directing these because Bob had no idea how all this was going to work out, and he felt reluctant to allow his name as director of Hart House to appear publicly on the program. . . . Perhaps his caution was well advised. So we concocted a sort of pseudonym, David Leroy."

In keeping with other summer theatres, the four plays they chose to present were all comedies. The Straw Hat Players opened at Minet's Point near Barrie on July 12, 1948, with *The Drunkard*, which was written by the Reverend William Smith in the mid-1800s as a melodrama, but which post-war audiences found uproariously funny. The first-year company consisted of Donald and Murray Davis, Charmion King, Ted Follows, Eric House, Araby Lockhart, Barbara Hamilton, Beth Gillanders and Opal Miller, with Bruce Yorke as business manager. Opening night started amidst an electrical storm that blew off the villain's wig and a lightning bolt that struck a tree very close to where Beth Gillanders was standing. Despite the problems of opening night, they valiantly carried on, rounding out the season with Noël Coward's *Blithe Spirit*, Patterson Greene's *Papa Is All* and Norman Krasna's *Dear Ruth*.

In talking about their pay that summer, actor Eric House said: "[They] offered Ted and me . . . $30 a week and that was the first time anyone offered to pay me for something I would have almost paid them to do." Admission prices were set at $1.00 per play or $3.50 for all four plays. The group's finances were precarious at best. Both the Davis brothers invested their own money in the summer theatre, and entrepreneur Brian Doherty also contributed (he was later repaid). Their total capital was approximately $1,500.

Donald and Murray Davis were young, enthusiastic and not the least apprehensive about the future of the company. "We had very few doubts, I'm ashamed to say," Donald Davis remembered. "I shudder to think what those productions would look like to me today. . . . I guess one of the luxuries I had, we all had as performers, was the opportunity of learning and making our mistakes in front of a live audience." Like many of the other theatres of the time, the members of the Straw Hat Players were determined to find a place for themselves as professional Canadian actors and to show their audiences that drama had a real function in society.

After opening with *The Drunkard*, the Straw Hat Players barnstormed the Lake Simcoe and the Muskoka Lake resort area, performing in the community centres and dance halls of such towns as Jackson's Point, Huntsville, Port Carling, Camp Borden and Barrie, attracting some eleven thousand patrons. The Rotary Club in Gravenhurst helped secure their summer by offering them a minimum of $150 a performance for three shows a week in their town for a period of four weeks.

The actors all took on a variety of roles with the theatre. Donald Davis recalled that "Ted and Eric and I were the sort of stage crew and stage management . . . and travelled in the truck, put up the scenery. The girls did all the props and costumes." "There was a great kind of pioneer spirit," added Barbara Hamilton. "We would be playing the lead and we'd be sewing costumes in the afternoon and painting scenery and doing props . . . nothing was too small for us to do. You've got to build sets and scrounge props and rob your parents' home of their bed if need be. We did all those things in those days."

When the audiences began to build, the company's presence actually helped businesses in the resort area as more and more people came to watch them. Of the four plays produced that summer, *Papa Is All* by Patterson Greene won the award for proving that theatre could be a danger to your health, as Ted Follow's hand and Beth Gillander's face were both cut by flying crockery during a dish-smashing scene. The same play also gave the audience an unscheduled laugh. Davis recalled the scene:

> This is one of my favourite Straw Hat anecdotes. We were doing . . . a play about a Pennsylvania Dutch family called *Papa Is All*, which in that dialect means Papa is dead. He [the father whom Davis played] was a cantankerous old gentleman with a club foot. Beth played my wife and Araby Lockhart played a neighbour named Mrs. Yoder. There was a scene when I was grumping off on one side of the stage in an armchair, generally being disagreeable. The two ladies were sitting facing each other with a quilting frame, quilting. Araby was the garrulous neighbour, chattering away, making me more furious all the time. The scene ended, at which point Araby was supposed to get up, take the quilting frame and exit. But in her enthusiasm she had quilted her costume to the frame. There was this hysterical moment of Araby trying to negotiate herself and this quilting frame, which was firmly sewn to the front of her dress, out the door.

As with so many other humorous incidents in the theatre, there was nothing the actors on stage could do except laugh along with the audience.

The play that changed the acting fortunes of many members of the Straw Hat Players was the same one the theatre used to open with, *The Drunkard*, or *The Fallen Saved*, its alternate title. The play had a villain at whom the audience hissed, and a hero for whom it cheered. "It was an enormous success," Davis said, "so in a somewhat jazzed-up version, jazzed-up to the extent we added two 'star' comedians in the form of John Pratt and Murray Matheson, we toured the play from Vancouver to Montreal and back with a couple of side trips to the United States." Pratt and Matheson performed skits and songs, both before the show and interspersed between the many scenes of the melodrama.

It is worth pausing here to consider the tour and the experiences of the company as they took the show on the road, in Canada and the United States. One reason the touring company was established was to offer employment during the winter months to the Straw Hat Players actors. Davis explained:

> It's all very well if you are going to be an actor, to occupy yourself for ten weeks in the summer, but what on earth do you do with the other forty-two. So, touring was thought to be one idea, but the problem was we were playing towns all across the country where the last live theatre they had seen was the Army or Navy Show [in the Second World War] and, in some cases, the Dumbells from 1929. So you go in and create an interest in a live theatre production and try to get everybody all hyped up and then, of course, you wouldn't get back to that town until the next year. Then you had to go through it all over again.

While touring, the group was under Brian Doherty's umbrella and performed under the name the New World Theatre Company. The tour of *The Drunkard* was ultimately successful, largely due to his abilities as a producer.

"Brian Doherty had something of a reputation of being an entrepreneur by that time," Davis said. "He had, right after the war, brought over the John Gielgud Company and the Dublin Gate and all that kind of thing. However, I do know [the tour] was not a model of theatrical efficiency. . . . It was frequently a very hand-to-mouth operation." Throughout the tour, the financial situation was never without worry, for expenses were very high

Prior to the beginning of the tour, all the rehearsals took place in Doherty's house, which began to resemble a command post: musical numbers being thumped out on a piano; actors wandering through the halls reciting from their scripts; and the prop man, business manager and others ironing out remaining details.

The tour started in Ottawa in October 1948, and the company spent the following weeks travelling through Ontario towns. They played Toronto for the first time in November, to excellent reviews, and then continued the Ontario part of the trip, winding up with their second Toronto engagement, the Royal Alexandra Theatre, shortly before Christmas. In January they headed to Canada's West Coast, and by this time the actors were receiving a respectable salary of $65 a week. The show grossed $60,000 in its first three months. The touring cast included Charmion King, Barbara Hamilton, Murray Davis, William Drew, Beth Gillanders and Araby Lockhart. A couple of the Straw Hat Players in the cast, Eric House and Donald Davis, had to leave to finish their university education and were unable to join the tour.

They travelled almost exclusively by rail. "One of the problems was we were travelling by train, and for some peculiar reason we always seemed to book on a train that would leave at five in the morning and not arrive until just the same time as the train that left at 11 a.m.," Charmion King said laughing. "I don't know how that worked out. Maybe it was cheaper. That was the most difficult part of the tour, getting up at the crack of dawn. That and the cold weather [their train was once stuck for sixteen hours thanks to a snow slide]. . . . We were all young enough to tolerate it."

The cast generally stayed in second-class hotels with most doubling up to save on costs. The buildings they performed in were varied. "We played in everything from real theatres to movie houses which converted," King said. "I believe we played at the Ottawa Little Theatre, at the Royal Alexandra . . . in a stadium I think, in North Bay. In Brandon [Manitoba] we played in a school and when you had to make your exit—instead of going backstage, you had to go out through a window and around on the fire escape. And it was forty degrees below."

The reviews for *The Drunkard* were occasionally lukewarm, citing a lack of direction, but the audiences were always wild about the production. They frequently threw vegetables and coins at the villain on stage. The program even stated: "All fruits and vegetables thrown are property of the management." The set was minimalist in order to fit into the variety of locations they played in. *The Drunkard* was pure vaudeville anyway, so they were able to get away with a great deal. The "Beautiful Woodland Dell" described in the program was actually a flimsy piece of cotton background with some strange looking trees painted on it. When the drunk hero arrived and announced he had come for the crock hidden in the trunk of the tree, the audience had to wonder how this could be achieved with the piece of fabric wavering in the breeze. At that moment an arm came out through a slit in the cloth tree trunk and gave the vessel to the hero – amid tremendous laughter. It was just the type of show that could carry it off. The tour not only took *The Drunkard* from Ontario to the West Coast but also down to Minneapolis and Detroit, with a long run in Chicago, where they arrived in February 1949. They played in Chicago's Studebaker Theatre for two weeks and then Doherty moved his show to the Via Lago nightclub.

Events on opening day at the club were so outrageous that they could have been additional comic scenes for the show. The owner of the Via Lago was nowhere to be found when Doherty and his business manager, Bruce Yorke, arrived in the morning to find the phone ringing off the hook with customers wanting reservations. There was nobody to answer it so the men worked throughout the day, continually stopping work to answer the phone. The stage manager reported that the curtains had not come, and later when they did they were too heavy and were pulling the supports from the ceiling. Returning from coffee, the cast found the hired help had not yet appeared and were faced with having to take tickets, seat the customers and serve them refreshments. Eventually the help showed up, the customers were all seated and the show began. Halfway through the performance the absent owner finally appeared, a little the worse for wear from alcohol. In spite of all the first-day problems, the production had a long, healthy stay at the nightclub. More important for the cast, the club came under a different entertainment union than theatres in the United States. As a result, their salary rose dramatically although their hours increased as well.

"When we went to Chicago and had to join [the union], we ended up being paid something bizarre like a $115 a week," Charmion King said. "That was because on the weekends we did three performances a night and wouldn't get home until seven to seven-thirty in the morning."

*The Drunkard* tour was ultimately successful and provided many of the Straw Hat Players invaluable experience and an income throughout the winter months. It came to an end because most of the cast members were committed to another summer of the Straw Hat Players in the Muskokas.

During the months *The Drunkard* tour was taking place, plans for the Straw Hat Players were still moving forward. Donald Davis was back in Toronto attending university, working with Bob Gill at Hart House, and lining up the 1949 summer season for the theatre. Most of the actors from the previous summer were returning. They had also decided that they needed a permanent business manager, and Donald Davis had someone in mind. "Jimmie Hozack worked at Hart House before the war, during the thirties," Davis said. "I can remember when I was a kid, Josephine Barrington's Juveniles would perform at Hart House and I remember Jimmie Hozack being there. During the war he enlisted and travelled with the Army Show. When Hart House then reopened after the war, Jimmie came back and was indeed its business administrator." When the Davis brothers began preparing for the 1949 season they realized the importance of a person with Hozack's experience and hired him.

They made another change in 1949 by deciding to travel less. The group divided their performing time between Port Carling and Gravenhurst, but they both lived and rehearsed only in Gravenhurst. Donald Davis remembered:

> We all lived in one place and commuted to Port Carling, back and forth every night. The reason we chose Gravenhurst as I recall, was in those days the Port Carling Hall, which is still the same old hall but jazzed up, was also the town clerk's office and the library and wasn't very convenient to rehearse in. On the other hand, the Opera House in Gravenhurst, the actual auditorium part of it, was not used during the summer months so . . . [Gravenhurst] was obviously the logical place to rehearse."

They took over an unused airport at Gravenhurst (Muskoka Airport), with barracks and a swimming pool, for their living quarters. "It was just great," Barbara Hamilton said. "We were all very close and it was wonderful."

The 1949 season was five weeks long, with the theatre group appearing Monday,

Tuesday and Wednesday in Port Carling and Thursday, Friday and Saturday in Gravenhurst. The season got underway with a production of *The Barretts of Wimpole Street* by Rudolf Besier, starring Donald and Murray Davis and Beth Gillanders. The other productions included *The Late Christopher Bean* by John Gassner and Noël Coward's *Hay Fever*. The actors, who still handled backstage duties as well, included newcomers Kate Reid and David Gardner. Others who returned were Araby Lockhart, Ted Follows, Eric House and Charmion King.

Following the end of the 1949 season, Charmion King was involved in another winter tour, this time with a Canadian revue called *There Goes Yesterday*, produced by the Davis brothers. "Murray and I concocted a revue," Donald Davis said. "It was described as a cavalcade from 1900 to 1950 because we were going into the half-century. We used that as a very loose framework to hang a whole lot of material from, literally from 1900 right up to the present time [1950], ending up I remember with a sendup of what was beginning to be rock and roll." It was an all-Canadian song-and-dance revue, blending comedy and nostalgia. The tour started in Eastern Canada and was instantly popular with both critics and audiences. They played in eighteen cities from one end of Canada to the other, including an encouraging run at the Royal Alexandra Theatre in Toronto. They also had a successful stint in Detroit, finishing up their eight month tour in May 1950, not long before rehearsals began again for the next Straw Hat Players' summer.

For its third season, the Straw Hat Players was still under the sponsorship of the Rotary Club in Gravenhurst, which continued to be home base. Not content merely to sit back and play tried and true comedies to vacation audiences, they changed the format slightly to offer thrillers such as Daphne Du Maurier's *Rebecca* and *Kind Lady* by Edward Chodorov. They presented seven plays, one of which was Robertson Davies' *Fortune, My Foe*. Three newcomers, Marie Stein, Toby Robins and Kay Hawtrey, joined the returning faithful—Eric House, Araby Lockhart, Ted Follows, David Gardner, Donald Davis and Beth Gillanders.

The theatre had a problem-plagued production that summer with the staging of Emlyn Williams' popular *Night Must Fall*. In fact, the performers began to wonder if night was falling on the show. The problems began long before the opening curtain when, during the dress rehearsal, Kay Hawtrey dropped the coat she was to wear on stage that night into a pot of paint and someone broke a $25 mirror needed as a prop. A car transporting actors from afternoon rehearsal in Gravenhurst to the performance in Port Carling broke down with a flat tire. They were late for the show, which had to be delayed, but the evening's adventures were only just beginning.

The next incident Eric House recalled was "when the stage manager hit the needle with his arm and 'God Save the King' skipped to the end of the record." Then the old curtain in Port Carling wouldn't close unless it was pinned together. "No one had removed the pin so someone had to go on stage and remove it," House said. "He finally gets [the curtain] open and there on stage is the loudspeaker, which he had forgotten to take off in the confusion." The loudspeaker was again accidentally left on stage for the beginning of the second act, and by the time the curtain opened to reveal it there at the beginning of the third act, the audience thought it was a running gag and laughed hysterically.

At one point Gillanders had the key to the secret box—an important part of the plot. She had it around her neck on a necklace and hidden next to her breast. When the time came to reach down and give it to someone, it had slipped around back and she couldn't reach it. In another scene, she was wearing thin ballet slippers and had to rise dramatically out of her wheelchair. As Gillanders walked across the stage, she stepped firmly on a tack, causing her to limp for the rest of the play. The upsets continued when a scheduled knock on the door occurred after the actor had uttered the line "come in." The actors were glad to see the end of the performance, but the gremlins were not through with them yet.

Eric House recalled what happened after the performance: "That night Ted and Don and I struck the set and went across the street to get a cup of coffee, leaving the truck parked, before we drove from Port Carling to Gravenhurst. It was a big truck and Port Carling is hilly. We hear this crash and we thought, 'Oh no, it couldn't be.' It was. The truck had slipped its brakes, gone backwards and smashed into a car." And not just any car either. It happened to be the town's only police car! Thankfully the remainder of the summer was less eventful."

The 1951 summer season began June 28 with a popular comedy of the day, Terence Rattigan's *While the Sun Shines*. The cast included the Davis brothers, their sister Barbara Chilcott, Eric House, Ted Follows, Beth Robinson and David Gardner. Business manager Jimmie Hozack even made a rare appearance on stage that season in Arthur Macrae's *Traveller's Joy*. Shaw's *Candida* and *At My Heart's Core* by Robertson Davies were also performed.

While the actors were devoted to the theatre and to putting on the best show possible, it was also true that audiences were caught up in the pioneering spirit of early post-war theatre. This was never more evident than on a day in 1951 during the run of the aptly titled *While the Sun Shines*, when the hydropower in Port Carling shut down. The management of the Straw Hat Players was sure this would keep the public away but they came in droves anyway. There was still considerable light when the performance began, so the actors started the show hoping the power would come back on before sunset. It did not, and it was not long before total darkness set in. At this point the two actors on stage at the time, Eric House and Ted Follows, ad libbed invitations for cigarettes and continued to use their lighters as much as possible. At one point Follows even called offstage to the butler, "Horton, check the fuses!" Eventually their spontaneous ideas for light fizzled out, and Jimmie Hozack offered the audience their money back. But no one took him up. Then he had an idea and drove his car around to the front of the theatre and ran it up to the door on a couple of planks. It was just small enough that it could pass a little way through the double doors and shine its headlights on the stage. In this way the show was able to continue until the power was restored. The audience applauded.

As mentioned earlier, the theatre had a positive effect on tourism in the Muskoka Lakes region. The populations of Gravenhurst (three thousand) and Port Carling (three hundred) were not enough to support the theatre, but with the additional summer vacationers, the theatre did a good trade. Hotels in the area encouraged their guests to attend the shows; one even listed the current play on its menu. The interest generated by the theatre resulted in Gravenhurst residents staging a mini drama festival, presenting nine one-act plays during the 1951–52 winter.

Local residents were very supportive of the Straw Hat Players and its actors, and sometimes they struck back at criticism directed at the theatre. A retired clergyman who had seen most of the plays and often invited the actors home for meals, took exception on two separate occasions in 1951 and 1952 to Herbert Whittaker's criticism of certain productions. Writing to the local newspaper, the clergyman called Whittaker's review "pettifogging chicanery."

In 1952 the actors' salaries reached $40 a week, and the company of actors, stage crew, directors and business manager swelled to twenty-two. At this point, Murray Davis was in England working in repertory theatres, leaving his brother Donald largely in control of the theatre. Two directors were brought in for the summer: Peter Potter, director of the Glasgow Citizens' Theatre in Scotland, and Russell Graves from Florida State University.

The biggest change in 1952 came with the decision to operate two different plays simultaneously in Gravenhurst and Port Carling, in effect running the equivalent of two full companies. They all still lived in Gravenhurst, which allowed them to rehearse upcoming plays together. Productions were interchanged. They opened the season with Benn Levy's *Clutterbuck* in Gravenhurst and a double bill of Terence Rattigan's *The Browning Version* and *Overlaid* by Robertson Davies playing in Port Carling. The productions played for six nights and then switched towns for the second week. Not only did this give each play a run of two weeks; more importantly, it gave the actors two weeks to rehearse the next duo of plays. They presented eleven plays in ten weeks, attracting thirty thousand theatregoers at $1.25 admission. Management thought the switch to operating in both towns simultaneously might result in financial losses, but

Amelia Hall and Ted Follows in the Straw Hat Players' 1952 production of *The Glass Menagerie* by Tennessee Williams. It was the most popular of his plays and performed by many of the early post-WWII theatres. (MCNICOLL COLLECTION)

the season actually ended profitably. Productions included Noël Coward's *Private Lives*, T.S. Eliot's *The Cocktail Party*, *Harvey* by Mary Chase and Tennessee Williams' *The Glass Menagerie* starring Amelia Hall as Amanda. Donald Davis, Barbara Chilcott and her then-husband Max Helpmann, Ted Follows, Araby Lockhart and Eric House were among those appearing that season.

*The Cocktail Party* was particularly successful. So much so, the Straw Hat Players later transferred it to Toronto. Donald Davis remembered:

> I can tell you precisely the only time the Straw Hat Players came to Toronto as a company. We did a very proud-making production of T.S. Eliot's play *The Cocktail Party*. It was sufficiently good that, through Jimmie Hozack, we booked Hart House Theatre for a week in September and played it very successfully there.

Two years prior to this sortie to the big city, the Davis brothers had begun examining the possibilities of starting their own year-round theatre in Toronto, but they concluded that they needed experience in repertory theatre that would run for an entire year, something that the Straw Hat Players could not provide. "Great Britain was full of repertory theatres operating great guns," Donald Davis said. "Murray and I decided to get ourselves to England and just learn as much as we possibly could about the business of starting a repertory." While they spent as much of the next three years as possible in England, one of the brothers still returned to Canada every summer to run the Straw Hat Players, which was still extremely important to them.

Murray and Donald were both back in Canada for the 1953 summer during which the Straw Hat Players had another successful ten-week season. Productions included the North American premiere of *Unhallowed* by Gerard McLarnon, Shaw's *Pygmalion* and *Come Back, Little Sheba* written by William Inge and starring Ruth Springford. Two directors, Pierre Lefevre and John Blatchley, were brought over from England. During Stratford's inaugural season that year, the Davis brothers decided to close the season with Shakespeare's *A Midsummer Night's Dream*. In addition to performing the play at Gravenhurst and Port Carling, they did one more performance of the play outdoors. Davis said that he remembered it vividly:

> It was in 1953 and by that time we were getting grand enough to presume, in the first year of Stratford, to do a production of *A Midsummer Night's Dream*. This was over and above the regular schedule. In those days the Gravenhurst Sanatorium was still a TB hospital. Over the years we had gotten to know a lot of the people from the san and the director dropped in. In a discussion we conceived the idea and we did one special performance. . . . There was a corner made by two wings of the building, a right-angled corner, and then lovely, rolling green and beyond that Muskoka trees and rocks. We put up some very primitive flood lighting. It was magical, it was really extraordinary. I will never forget that performance. And the patients who were ambulatory came and sat on top of this rise looking down on the play. The patients who weren't ambulatory, they wheeled to the windows so we had these windows full of people watching. It was a spectacular night fortunately. That was the only outdoor performance we ever gave.

Staging Shakespeare with the Straw Hat Players and competing successfully with Stratford gave the Davis brothers the push they needed to fulfill their dream of starting a permanent professional theatre. The Crest opened in January of 1954 in a rented movie house on Mt. Pleasant Road in Toronto.

The 1954 season for the Straw Hat Players was wholly under Murray's management because Donald had become involved with the Stratford Festival. However, because of the Crest's expanded season, the 1954 summer theatre's season was cut from ten to eight weeks. Many of those involved with the Crest, such as directors John Blatchley and Pierre Lefevre, spent the summer of 1954 with the Straw Hat Players, along with actors Charmion King, Murray Davis, George McCowan, Araby Lockhart, Max Helpmann and Jack Medhurst. The summer season opened with Molière's *Amphitryon 38*, which had been the closing show of the Crest's first season.

Despite its continuing success, the 1955 season of the Straw Hat Players would turn out to be the last one managed by the Davis brothers. Because Donald was once again at Stratford, the running of the theatre continued to fall on Murray's shoulders. "The reason we gave it up was that by that time it was just too much," Donald Davis said. "We were working fifty-two weeks a year and it was backbreaking."

At that point, it seemed the Straw Hat Players was over. For the next two summers the Port Carling Summer Theatre kept dramatic interests in the area alive. Then in 1958, Karl Jaffary and William Davis, a cousin of Murray and Donald, resurrected the name of the Straw Hat Players. Both Murray and Donald returned to guest direct, but 1958 was their last connection with the Straw Hat Players. Their work with their new venture, the Crest Theatre, was only just beginning, however, and it is safe to say that without the knowledge and experience the Davis brothers gained in their youthful and enthusiastic summer company in the Muskokas, they would not have gone on to run the Crest so successfully for fourteen years. But that is a story for another time.

CHAPTER NINE

# THE INTERNATIONAL PLAYERS, THE PETERBOROUGH SUMMER THEATRE & THE NIAGARA FALLS SUMMER THEATRE

"I remember bursting into tears once because it all got too much for me at two o'clock in the morning. Drew [Thompson] and I were playing the leads in a two-hander the next week, and I was trying to learn that, and I was directing as well, and here we were painting the set."

—JOY COGHILL

The Straw Hat Players was a shining example of a successful summer theatre but it was not the only one. Some summer theatres survived for a number of years but only by changing location and ownership. There were two Ontario groups, however, who deserve to be singled out for surviving seven and nine years respectively, with only minor changes in management or home base. The International Players of Kingston, which eventually expanded beyond a summer theatre, and the Peterborough Summer Theatre were both unique contributions to Canadian theatre history. Michael Sadlier, who began the Peterborough Summer Theatre, also started another group worthy of mention, and that is the Niagara Falls Summer Theatre.

It was 1948, the same year the Straw Hat Players began, when Arthur Sutherland decided to take a giant step and start his own theatre company, the International Players, in Kingston, Ontario. Still a young man in his thirties, he nevertheless had a great deal of stage experience. A native of Kingston, Sutherland first became involved with theatre at Queen's University. His graduation from the American Academy of Dramatic Arts in New York a few years later led to Broadway and film work. Following a war stint with the U.S. Army overseas (he appeared in Army shows with such stars as Bob Hope, Jack Benny and Ingrid Bergman), he worked for some time with the Imperial Players in the New York area before returning to his hometown to establish his theatre.

The International Players performed in the La Salle Hotel in Kingston, opening an eleven-week season on June 29, 1948, with *Apron Strings* by Dorrance Davis. The ballroom of the hotel seated three hundred and fifty and became their home base. Their stage, nothing more than a platform where an orchestra usually sat, was forty feet wide and twenty feet deep. Joy Coghill said, "It had very limited wing space but just enough to store one set of flats while you used one other set."

That first season saw a number of Americans appear with the theatre, far more than in subsequent years, when the emphasis was on Canadian actors. Among the Canadians in 1948 were Pegi Brown, Josephine Barrington and Drew Thompson, who was Sutherland's co-producer. Born in Ottawa, Thompson followed his graduation from the University of Toronto with a season of stock in Vancouver and the first Everyman Theatre tour. He would go on to perform in more than half of the International Players' productions. The group appeared nightly Tuesday through Saturday, at 8:45 in the evening, which was a late start. Among the earliest shows were *Yes, My Darling Daughter* by Mark Reed, Lawrence Riley's *Personal Appearance* and *Kempy* by J.C. and Elliott Nugent. Paid attendance for the summer was almost twelve thousand, a more than respectable number for an opening season.

The most noteworthy play presented came as summer drew to a close. On August 31, 1948, the International Players presented the world premiere of Robertson Davies' *Fortune, My Foe*. Arthur Sutherland had asked Davies, editor of the nearby *Peterborough Examiner*, to write a Canadian-based play, and the author obliged. Davies had never written a full-length play before, only one-acts, and in the beginning he had no great expectations for any of his plays. "It never occurred to me when I began writing plays that I was contributing to the growth of a Canadian drama; my self-esteem did not extend so far," Davies said.[16]

The action of the play was set in Kingston and the central character was a legendary city figure of prohibition days. The theme centred on the lot of artists and intellectuals in Canada and those artists that left for money, an important issue at the time and one which still resonates in the 21st century. One of the characters in the play says: "So let the geniuses of easy virtue go southward; I know what they feel too well to blame them. But for some of us there is no choice; let Canada do what she will with us, we must stay."[17] There was also a side discussion in the play of the Canadian view of England as a sentimental dream of a country that never really existed.

Davies directed the production with William Needles, Glen Burns, Josephine Barrington and the group's two producers in the cast. The highly praised set, which included an exquisite spiderweb across one of the artificial entrances at the back of the scene, was designed by Grant Macdonald. *Fortune, My Foe* turned out to be the hit of the summer and was held over for a second week. During the next two years, it was staged by many theatre groups, including the Straw Hat Players, University of Toronto's Hart House, the Kitchener-Waterloo Little Theatre, the Ottawa Drama League (which presented it at the Dominion Drama Festival) and the Peterborough Summer Theatre.

With a successful first season under their belt, the International Players planned a longer, more ambitious one for 1949. Sutherland brought in more Canadian talent including Margaret Shortliffe, Bea Lennard and Rod Coneybeare. Also a prolific writer, Coneybeare became best-known in Canada as the puppeteer and voices for Jerome the Giraffe and his barnyard friend Rusty on *The Friendly Giant*, a long running children's show on television. First-year stars Josephine Barrington and Drew Thompson returned in 1949, and Arthur Sutherland occasionally appeared in productions himself. After opening with George Kelly's *The Fatal Weakness*, the group staged *The Family Upstairs* by Harry Delf. At that point well-known actress Barbara Hamilton joined the theatre for the summer, playing a twelve-year-old in the production. *The Family Upstairs* was the second production to be successful enough to be held over for another week.

One of the reasons for the longevity of the International Players, was the ability of its two producers to find ways to attract audiences. They both learned that vacationing patrons wanted to see farce and light comedy. However, Sutherland still found that this did not guarantee success, as the crowds were not coming out in great numbers during the early weeks of the 1949 season. In fact they had decreased from the previous year. Drastic measures were needed. Sutherland came up with an original idea that began to pull people back to the La Salle Hotel ballroom. Under his plan, audiences were allowed into the theatre for free. They watched the first two acts, and between the second and third acts a collection plate was passed around and patrons contributed what they wished.

In the beginning the pay-what-you-like policy, which became the theatre's trademark, sometimes brought in as little as a couple of dimes in total, but it did not take long before the strategy paid off. Farces and other plays were frequently chosen with this new policy in mind. "*Personal Appearance* had a very good second act ending," said Joy Coghill, who directed and acted with the group in 1950. "At Kingston you had to have a good second act ending because . . . if you didn't you'd be ruined." They deviated from the pay-what-you-like policy during their later winter seasons in Toronto when they were often sponsored by a Rotary or Kiwanis club and charged 60¢ and $1.20 a ticket.

Other 1949 productions included *The Male Animal* by James Thurber and Elliott

CANADA'S FIRST AND ONLY

**PAY - WHAT - YOU - LIKE - THEATRE**

**HOTEL LA SALLE, KINGSTON, ONTARIO**

**THIRD SEASON**

ARTHUR SUTHERLAND and DREW THOMPSON

PRESENT

THE INTERNATIONAL PLAYERS

(Direct from Four Months In Toronto)

IN

**"See How They Run"**

**A Farce Comedy in Three Acts**

**BY PHILIP KING**

STAGED BY JOY COGHILL

**ACKNOWLEDGEMENTS**

*Modern furniture courtesy of Imperial Furniture Company.*
*Antique furniture courtesy of Cramer's Antique Shop.*
*Stage properties courtesy of Spearn's Gift Shop.*

**—NEXT ATTRACTION—**

**Week Beginning Monday June 26th at 8.45 Nightly**

**THE LAUGH-A-MINUTE BROADWAY COMEDY HIT**

**"THREE CORNERED MOON"**

"A guaranteed laugh from start to finish"—*New York Sun.*

"Three Cornered Moon is one of the best of the 'screwball' family comedies."
—*New York Times.*

A 1950 playbill by the International Players for *See How They Run* shows how their pay-what-you-like-policy was prominently displayed. (MCNICOLL COLLECTION)

Nugent, *Baby Mine* by Margaret Mayo, and J. Hartley Manners' *Peg O' My Heart*. The most popular offering that summer was a thriller, not a comedy. Emlyn Williams' *Night Must Fall*, was, without doubt, the most produced, and popular, play in any summer circuit during the post-war years, and it ran for more than two weeks with the International Players, longer than the Davies play of the previous summer.

Never standing still, Sutherland and Thompson continued to look for ways to expand and improve the group. Kingston would always be their home base and summer stage, but it was decided to undertake a winter season in Toronto each year, where home was to be the new auditorium in Leaside High School. They planned to have a series of productions, finishing up in March. In the first winter, however, they were successful enough to continue through to May.

They opened their first Toronto season at the end of December 1949 with *The Male Animal*. If a production had been a hit in the hot summer months you could be sure it would show up in the group's winter season, and vice versa. Other plays in the winter series were *Dear Ruth* by Norman Krasna, *While the Sun Shines* by Terence Rattigan, *Personal Appearance* by Lawrence Riley and Sidney Howard's *The Silver Cord*, which was directed by William Hutt. One young actor in the company that winter went on to become one of Canada's pre-eminent authors, Timothy Findley. Many other Toronto actors starred with the theatre during their Toronto run, including Charmion King, Dorothy Fowler, Fred Mallett, Murray Westgate and Cosy Lee, who received excellent reviews for her performance in Lynn Starling's farce *Meet the Wife*.

Starling's farce also opened the group's third summer in Kingston in June 1950 and started a successful season with many standing-room-only nights. Among those joining Cosy Lee were Josephine Barrington, Rod Coneybeare, William Needles, Kathleen Roberts and Joy Coghill, who was hired as the resident director for the summer. Coghill, who had met Drew Thompson at the 1948 Dominion Drama Festival, was on summer hiatus from the highly regarded Goodman Theatre in Chicago. As she recalls, her time at Goodman gave Drew Thompson unrealistic expectations as to her abilities as a director:

> Drew was a talented comedian. He had dreams [for] the International Players, he wanted to learn everything about theatre. I came up and had this terrible shock of doing thirteen plays in thirteen weeks, directing and acting in them. It was no wonder I couldn't bring the standard of his company up: a different play every week and six days of rehearsals and playing. Then the actors got a day off but nobody else did because that was when you pulled the set down and put the other up and you just kept going flat out.

The quality of the work was often "dreadful but it was entertaining," Coghill added.

Patrons had their favourites amongst the group and would come each week to see what "their" actor was doing. Coghill said they chose to do mostly farces, thrillers, and plays with smaller casts. "If you could put in two two-handers and get away with it, then you could afford to get an extra actor for the next week and do something a little more. . . . You didn't always know what the play was going to be the following week. You would plan a play but sometimes they didn't get the actor or something so they changed to something else."

Another winter season playing to large crowds in Toronto followed for the International Players. The sets for the winter productions were always simple but adequate, and the list of quality actors now starring with the theatre underlines the status it had

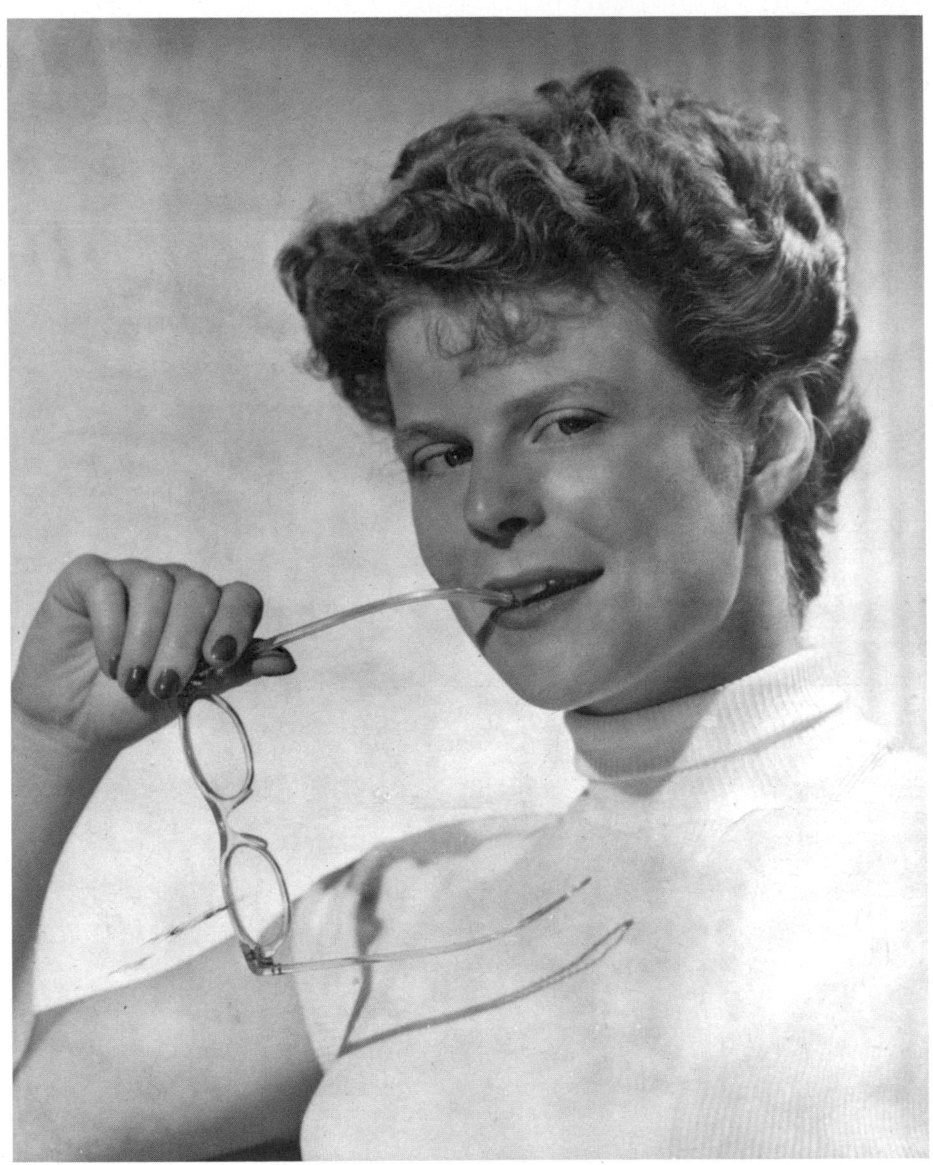

Joy Coghill said she barely survived directing and acting in thirteen plays in thirteen weeks for the International Players in Kingston in the summer of 1950, c. 1953. (COGHILL COLLECTION)

attained within the acting community. A production of S.N. Behrman's *Biography*, staged in February 1951, had an impressive cast: Donald Davis, Jean Cruchet, Toby Robins, Josephine Barrington, David Gardner, Murray Westgate and John Atkinson, with Robert Christie directing. Other well-known performers on the Leaside auditorium stage that winter included Ted Follows, Eric House, William Hutt, Charmion King, Kay Hawtrey and Bernard Slade. The winters were going well, and each year the Kingston summer season expanded, becoming a twenty-week affair at the La Salle Hotel in 1951. For their summers, the International Players continued the pay-what-you-like policy. More than three hundred were turned away from the opening night of their first 1951 production as they continued to offer up comedies with performers such as Pegi Brown, Hugh Webster, Timothy Findley, Vernon Chapman (who was the resident director) and Cosy Lee. Lee appeared more than two hundred times with the International Players, exceeding any other performer except the two producers.

In the autumn of 1951, Sutherland and Thompson made the decision to stay in Kingston until mid-December, prompted in part by an offer made to them by the city fathers to use the Memorial Hall of the Kingston City Buildings, which seated about six hundred and fifty, an impressive size. They opened there in October with J.B. Priestley's *Dangerous Corner*, running Monday through Saturday. By the end of 1951 the International Players were staging plays forty weeks of the year during runs in both Toronto and Kingston. In addition to their plays at Leaside Collegiate, the annual trip to Toronto in the spring of 1952 included presentations as a part of the Forest Hill concert and theatre series. *Charley's Aunt* by Brandon Thomas, starring Eric Christmas, and Noël Coward's *Blithe Spirit* were among the productions. The latter received excellent reviews, but the most popular play that spring was Oscar Wilde's *The Importance of Being Earnest* with Jane Mallett as Lady Bracknell. The winter sojourn was only half completed when the summer season opened back in Kingston with *Out of the Frying Pan* by Francis Swan.

The International Players also took its first steps to appear outside Kingston during the summer theatre season. For twenty weeks ending in September 1952, the group appeared at the Gananoque High School on Monday and Tuesday nights before taking the show back to home base for Wednesday through Saturday. They were immensely popular in Gananoque, approximately thirty kilometres east of Kingston, with an estimated quarter of the town's population turning out to see them each week. The most successful plays in the summer of 1952 were Patterson Greene's *Papa Is All*, *Kempy* and *Tobacco Road* by Jack Kirkland, and at the other end of the scale was G.B. Shaw's *Arms and the Man*. *Tobacco Road*, which was involved the following January in the prominent censorship case in Vancouver, was the biggest hit ever for the International Players in Kingston to that point, surpassing their all-time attendance records. By the summer of 1952 the group had staged more than eighty-five plays, and in

August Vernon Chapman directed his fiftieth production. "Those years were good for me because from 1949 to 1952 I worked for the New Play Society in the winter," Chapman said. "Then I would go down to the International Players and be the director and got another $40 a week. So I was working for fifty-two weeks of the year, which most people in the profession were not, unless they could make it on radio."

During the fall of 1952, the International Players presented the musical revue *Look What's Dolin'* by Clifford Braggins, who had written numerous skits for the New Play Society's famous *Spring Thaw*. Following only three Toronto productions in the spring of 1953, the International Players returned to Kingston and back to their original home, the La Salle Hotel. In what would be their most ambitious summer, the actors split into two groups. While one group remained at home base for the first week with one production, the other spent two nights each in Prescott, Gananoque and Napanee with a different play. In the second week the two companies would switch locations. This schedule was followed for twelve weeks and included productions of *The Man Who Came to Dinner* by George S. Kaufman, André Roussin's *Nina*, and *The Glass Menagerie* by Tennessee Williams.

The International Players reached a major milestone for post-war theatres in the fall of 1953 when they celebrated their one thousandth performance. But they were also dealt a disastrous blow when they lost their tireless leader. Only in his early forties, Arthur Sutherland died suddenly from a heart attack at the end of September. Drew Thompson decided to rename the group Arthur Sutherland's International Players and carry on.

Thompson began 1954 early with a short trip to Toronto where the theatre staged *The Glass Menagerie* at Leaside High School and Western Technical Commerce School. For the summer season, Thompson dropped the pay-what-you-like policy adopted by Sutherland, but the Kingston season remained successful proving that the theatre had acquired loyal patrons.

An actress who had been with the group when it opened in 1948 returned to star in one of the shows. Josephine Barrington's lead in S.N. Behrman's *Jane* during August brought the number of her appearances with the International Players to more than 160. The group also staged *Uncle Tom's Cabin* by Harriet Beecher Stowe; it was so successful that it was held over for a second week. The theatre supplied tissue with each program, said to be needed for Russ Waller's moving portrayal of Uncle Tom. Drew Thompson appropriately played the lead in *The Moon Is Blue* by F. Hugh Herbert, which ran for two weeks in September 1954.

It was, however, the last production for Sutherland's International Players. Managing the theatre and taking a leading role had simply proved too much for Thompson. As has been seen with a number of early post-war theatres, success was easier when more than one person was involved. Without Arthur Sutherland, Drew Thompson found he could not carry on alone, and he reluctantly shuttered the theatre. The Kingston audience would have to find their theatre elsewhere, and, in addition to the newly formed Stratford, there were now a number of other Ontario summer theatre start-ups from which to choose.

On a hot, sticky night in June 1949, an overflow crowd in formal wear saw a new theatre company, the Peterborough Summer Theatre, open with hometown playwright Robertson Davies' *Fortune, My Foe*, the play that the International Players had used to close their 1948 season. The man behind the venture was Michael Sadlier, an Irish-born Canadian who served with the RCAF during the Second World War and was well known on both American and British stages. He helped establish a summer theatre at Cornell University in the United States and wanted to start one in Canada but was having problems finding a suitable location. Attending a Kitchener Little Theatre production of *Fortune, My Foe* one evening, he discussed his dilemma with the play's author, Robertson Davies, who told him about the new Queen Mary elementary school which had just been completed in Peterborough. Its auditorium had a good stage, a seating capacity of four hundred, as well as air conditioning, a rare commodity in those days,.

It took Sadlier only a week to sign a contract with the Peterborough Board of Education, permitting his theatre to operate out of the school for eleven weeks each summer. The Peterborough Summer Theatre was established as a non-profit organization in order to keep admission prices at an absolute minimum and thus provide affordable theatre for everyone. A number of local women became patrons of the theatre and Sadlier and co-producer Graham Ferguson did two months of speechmaking in the city to drum up other support. Their efforts paid off with some outside financial backers and a large enthusiastic crowd in attendance for *Fortune, My Foe*. In one of the lead roles was British actor Michael Lynd. A few days prior to opening, a good luck telegram arrived from Sir Laurence Olivier and his wife, actress Vivien Leigh, the former having worked with Lynd.

Joining Lynd in *Fortune, My Foe* were Robert Christie, William Needles, Anna Cameron, Frank Perry and Gerry Sarracini, all of whom made up the core of the company for that summer. Brenda Davies was also in the cast, as she usually was for productions of her husband's plays. Other plays included *Arsenic and Old Lace* by Joseph O. Kesselring, Daphne du Maurier's *Rebecca*, *The Importance of Being Earnest*, and *Angel Street* by Patrick Hamilton. The company played Monday to Saturday with two performances on Fridays and Saturdays. One interesting promotional move was "Industrial Night," when every Wednesday, a local industry bought out the entire auditorium at a reduced price. Specials for out-of-town buses were also organized.

One of management's goals when they started the summer theatre was to extend it into a winter tour, presenting one or more of the successful summer plays. Their first attempt at this was early in 1950, in between their first and second summer seasons, when Sadlier and Ferguson teamed up with Brian Doherty to take *Arsenic and Old Lace* on the road. Under the name of Doherty's New World Theatre Company and directed by Ferguson, the actors presented the play throughout Ontario. The parts of the two aunts were played by Catherine Proctor and Barbara Hamilton. The rest of the cast included Gerry Sarracini, Kate Reid, Floyd Caza and William Drew, with William Hutt playing the lead role of the old ladies' nephew, Mortimer. "I had completed my Bachelor of Arts degree at Trinity College," William Hutt said, "and was going on for a fourth year to get a masters degree in English. . . . Sometime towards December, Brian Doherty offered me a short tour of *Arsenic and Old Lace*. I think the [financial] arrangements were that they paid for the hotel room and obviously for transporting us from place to place. Then they would give us a salary that they expected would cover the rest of our expenses throughout the course of the tour. Everybody had to act and put up the set as well."

The tour was not a long one, lasting not more than eight weeks beginning in January 1950. It covered most of southern and eastern Ontario with a side trip to His Majesty's Theatre in Montreal. Catherine Proctor was an excellent choice to play one of the elderly ladies, for she had played the same role for two years in the Boris Karloff Company in the United States. She had also starred in a production done at the Peterborough Summer Theatre the previous summer. Born in Toronto in 1879, Proctor left Canada for New York at the age of sixteen and achieved great success in American theatre. "I remember her," said William Hutt, "as being a lady I considered, of considerable talent and courage and a sense of humour. And really quite a beautiful woman she was, for her age. A fine actress."

A number of well-known, up-and-coming stars appeared in Peterborough's 1950 summer season, which coincided with the city's centennial. The actors included Kate Reid (who married Michael Sadlier in 1952), Charmion King, Barbara Hamilton, William Needles, Catherine Proctor and William Hutt. Henry Kaplan directed many of the productions and Australian Bruce Yorke became co-producer. The group continued to perform six days a week, with seats selling at $1.50, $1.00, and 50¢. Buses came in weekly from Lindsay, Port Hope and Coburg as the theatre's popularity spread. The hits of that summer were *Harvey* by Mary Chase, *Night Must Fall*, and a play written primarily to celebrate the city's centennial, *At My Heart's Core*. Penned by Robertson Davies, who also directed the theatre's production of it, the play takes place in 1837 Peterborough and concerns itself with the city's early settlers, who included two of Canada's successful authors, Catherine Parr Traill and her sister Susanna Moodie. The Peterborough production starred Kate Reid and Clarine Jackman as

Traill and Moodie, as well as Frank Perry, Donald Glen and Brenda Davies.

Events in the months between the 1950 and 1951 summers kept Michael Sadlier and Bruce Yorke busy. The group had once again agreed to rent the Queen Mary school auditorium from the board of education for 1951. However, neighbours living near the school complained about the parked cars of theatre patrons and the noise and commotion on Sundays when the group prepared for the following week's opening. Because of this, the board was slow to approve the rental agreement for 1951 and tried to offer a substitute building totally unacceptable to the producers. The public, however, rallied behind the group with petitions and public meetings. The end result was that after opening the season with *Charley's Aunt* at the Collegiate Auditorium, the Peterborough Summer Theatre presented the remainder of its third season, on schedule, at the Queen Mary auditorium.

In fall 1950 and spring 1951, under the banner Theatre Series, Michael Sadlier organized a tour to twenty-five Ontario towns with two plays, *The Wind and the Rain* by Merton Hodge and *See How They Run* by Philip King. One of the actors with the group was David Gardner and he remembered the tour as largely a series of obstacles:

> Donald Davis, Kay Hawtrey, Kate Reid, myself and many other performers were all with this funny little company that toured essentially through southern Ontario. It was a bus-truck tour with a bus and a couple of little cars—really broken-down cars. I remember vividly an auditorium on the second floor. We had to carry all this stuff up a slippery fire escape to the second floor. It was February and all the flats would blow in the breeze. The auditorium had a raised platform at one end of the hall. There were two or three little footlight troughs that opened up into red, white and blue bulbs. Then the curtain was just a wire stretched across as taut as they could make it but it still drooped in the middle and it had to be hand pulled open. You had to walk it open. I think our show was set for eight o'clock. At seventy-thirty we heard "In an English Country Garden" played by the local orchestra, a collegiate orchestra all dressed in red; they had learned the one piece. They were all squashed right up against this so-called stage and they played [the song] over and over and over as the audience came in.

In this same "theatre," Gardner recalled how the stage had a hardwood floor, which meant stage screws could not be put into it. Although the flats had right-angled pieces of wood to hold them up, they still moved easily if they could not be secured to the floor. He said that every time a cast member made an entrance or exit someone had to hold on to the flat to make sure it did not come crashing down.

It was the transportation that would provide the group with its most hair-raising incidents, Gardner said. "One of the cars was . . . a kind of Rover roadster, which was so falling apart that you started the motor with a string up in the ceiling and you pulled on a cord to start it. There was a hole in the floorboards and snow would come up . . . by the time you had reached your destination you were covered in snow." There

.was one night, however, when they wished for that snow. They had to improvise, Gardner said, laughing at the memory:

> We were returning from Niagara-on-the-Lake. This antiquated car, suddenly steam is erupting out of the engine. This is February and the water or antifreeze in the radiator had evaporated. And there's clouds of steam and its liable to blow and all the rest. We get out and sneak up and open the bonnet. Suddenly somebody got the thing undone and whoosh, steam came up. There we are on the highway at two in the morning. We've done a show, we are all freezing. No moisture is available to pour into this radiator, so we all look at each other. We say to Kay Hawtrey, "You go down the road and watch for cars," and [the men] all stood up on the fender and peed into this radiator. Then Kay would say, "Here comes a car, here comes a car," and we would get down and look nonchalant and then get back up on the fender until we filled this thing.

Gardner recalled how they "drove back to Toronto with the smell of urine as the motor heated up."

While those on the tour were battling less than ideal conditions, Michael Sadlier, who never seemed content to sit still, was becoming involved in yet another theatre venture, this time on the island of Bermuda. Because so many Canadian actors from the Peterborough Summer Theatre participated, it is worth pausing at this point in the Peterborough story to consider Sadlier's newest theatre. "He had a tremendous amount of energy and charm," Christopher Plummer said of the enterprising Sadlier. "Immense Irish charm. He also knew where to find money [for his ventures]."

In April 1951, Sadlier and Bruce Yorke contracted, with some help from local Bermudans, to present a nine-month series of plays in the newly completed 465-seat theatre at the Bermudiana Hotel in Hamilton, Bermuda. For the core of their plays, the producers rounded up actors who had appeared with them in the Peterborough Summer Theatre back in Canada: Charmion King, Toby Robins, Kay Hawtrey, Henry Kaplan (who directed) and John Colicos. The first-year highlight was the world premiere of *Finale*, a new play. *Variety* magazine, the actor's bible in the United States, had particularly good things to say about two of the Canadians in its review. "Standout performances are given by Charmion King as Pat Leeds and John Colicos as Chuck, the stage manager," the review said in part. "Their scene together, in which Chuck, in a drunken stupor, goes to Pat's apartment and attacks her, is particularly effective."

The majority of actors drifted home to Canada after the year, and a new crop of performers replaced them for each of the next two seasons. Sadlier directed the second Bermuda season, and among the Canadians who took a busman's holiday in the sun were Kate Reid, Eric House, Kay Hawtrey, Peter Mews, Derek Ralston, Gerry Sarracini, Betty Leighton and Barbara Hamilton. "They already had a season before I went down . . . with the idea of doing one or two shows," Barbara Hamilton said. "I thought, 'Well, that sounds like a nice little holiday.' And I loved it so much I stayed for six months, did all the shows."

One day Barbara Hamilton limped into the dressing room exclaiming that she had been shot. Kate Reid, who heard the story, almost fell down laughing. It took Hamilton a few indignant minutes to convince her friend that the hole in her dress and the bruise on her thigh were real. While rehearsing *The Petrified Forest* by Robert E. Sherwood, in which she appeared with Franchot Tone, Hamilton walked on stage during a volley of blank cartridges and a wad from Tone's gun struck her in the thigh.

For the most part, however, life in Bermuda was much less dangerous and much more idyllic for the actors. They had a salary choice of £12 a week or £8 plus free room and board, with most opting for the latter. The contract called for ordinary clothes and modern dress for productions to be the responsibility of the actor, with period costumes supplied by the management. "It didn't always work out that way," Eric House remembered, but "it was the real English repertory kind of contract."

In the second year of the Bermuda venture, a new star-studded policy was adopted and well-known actors from the United States were imported to act alongside the Canadians. Fay Bainter, Franchot Tone, Burgess Meredith and Edward Everett Horton were among the stars who not only added impetus to the venture but gave the young Canadian actors more experience and exposure. One such actor benefited even more than others. Christopher Plummer, who received critical acclaim and fan adulation in Bermuda, had accepted the invitation from Michael Sadlier because he felt the need to move on. "I could have stayed [in Canada] and done more Andrew Allan [radio], some great work with Andrew actually, but I was already playing leads," Plummer said. "Now I had to play with international people because there was nowhere further to go than where I had gone. So I went, not knowing what the hell was going to happen but what did happen, of course, was that I made marvellous contacts." One of those was Edward Everett Horton, who was so impressed with the young actor in Bermuda that he signed Plummer to tour the United States with him in *Nina*. Plummer also met Ruth Chatterton, who he said championed his cause when he finally made the move to New York.

Even though the Bermudian theatre was going full steam, the rotating system of actors still meant good entertainment for the Peterborough Summer Theatre's eleven-week 1951 summer, their third in business, with such up-to-date hits as Tennessee Williams' *A Streetcar Named Desire*, Garson Kanin's *Born Yesterday*, starring Murray Westgate and William Needles, and the North American premiere of London's 1950 hit, *Castle in the Air* by Alan Melville. In *Streetcar*, Gerry Sarracini played Stanley with Betty Leighton as Blanche, Kate Reid as her sister and Peter Mews as Mitch. The biggest box office success was *The Man Who Came to Dinner*. It broke all previous attendance records, which the theatre did every year with a different play. The season drew to a close with *Claudia* by Rose Franken, starring most of the company regulars with special mention going to Peter Mews for his set design, a function he undertook in addition to acting for many of the shows.

The 1952 season of the Peterborough Summer Theatre opened with *The Silver Whistle* by Robert E. McEnroe, directed by Robertson Davies and starring William Needles. Barbara Hamilton, Kate Reid, William Hutt, Betty Leighton, Gerry Sarracini, Peter Mews and Frank Perry all appeared on the Queen Mary auditorium stage that summer. One of the plays staged was picked as a result of an audience poll taken at the close of the previous season. *Life with Father* by Howard Lindsay and Russel Crouse was the play that audiences chose. It was a successful but uneventful summer which saw the group extend the season by a week.

The summer of 1953 presented the same dilemma for the Peterborough company as it did for many other theatres. The opening of Stratford took many of the country's finest actors and left the summer theatres scrambling to pick up the pieces. There were still many good performers to be had but not as many as Sadlier would have liked, so he imported talent directly from England and from his Bermuda theatre. His involvement with the latter caused him to turn over many of his duties at the Peterborough Summer Theatre. Robert Gill from Hart House at the University of Toronto was hired as the resident director, with Robertson Davies directing the occasional production. The first imported star to appear was Edward Everett Horton in *Nina*.

The Peterborough theatre staged many top-notch and popular plays that summer including *The Male Animal*. Perhaps the most interesting production was Shaw's *Pygmalion*, which gave audiences the rare chance to see Robert Gill on stage, as he played Higgins. Also in the cast were Harry Geldard and his wife Margaret Braidwood, imported from England where she had won acclaim in the role of Eliza. Audiences even saw Michael Sadlier himself when he stepped onto the stage with a small role in the group's final 1953 production, *The Moon Is Blue*. The play also starred Peter Mews, who arrived directly from the end of Stratford's first season.

The highlight of the 1954 season was *Come Back, Little Sheba*, starring Lorne Greene, fresh from his Broadway appearance in *The Prescott Proposals* by Howard Lindsay and Russel Crouse. Once again the Peterborough production set an all-time attendance record after drawing rave reviews, filling the Queen Mary auditorium every night. In fact they had to turn patrons away. By continually setting new attendance records, the Peterborough theatre showed that Canadians were becoming more interested in theatre, that Stratford was not the only theatre able to bring in the crowds. This boded well for the future. Another 1954 production showed the theatre had spread its wings beyond the usual light summer fare, Somerset Maugham's *Rain*.

While he remained the producer, Michael Sadlier relinquished most of his responsibilities for the group during the 1955 and 1956 seasons. Harry Geldard directed the first of those summers, which saw the premiere Canadian stage presentation of Samuel Taylor's *Sabrina Fair*, which was already a movie starring Audrey Hepburn and Humphrey Bogart. Also staged successfully were Oscar Wilde's *Lady Windermere's Fan* and *The Country Girl* by Clifford Odets. Among the better-known actors to appear were Betty Leighton, Kay Hawtrey, Hugh Webster, Stuart Baker (from Totem Theatre fame), Ronald Bailey and Eric Christmas. The latter took over as the director-producer for Michael Sadlier in the 1956 season.

In 1957 Michael Sadlier once again took control of the group that had now become the oldest surviving professional summer theatre in Ontario history. After a three-year absence, Peter Mews, fresh from his Toronto triumphs in the New Play Society's *Spring Thaw*, returned to star with the theatre, directed by Englishman Henry Comor. The artistically successful 1957 season opened in June with the first Canadian presentation of *The Teahouse of the August Moon* by John Patrick.

Unfortunately, money problems had begun to surface, and the end was in sight for the Peterborough Summer Theatre. Citing losses for 1955, 1956 and 1957 of $400, $1,000 and $1,500 consecutively, Sadlier felt that his main mistake had been not raising admission prices over those years. When 1957 ended, the cost of a ticket was still only $1.25. He hoped to be able to reopen the theatre in 1958 but it was not to be. There were later sporadic attempts by others to present summer theatre in Peterborough, but none at the level of Michael Sadlier's theatre.

Michael Sadlier was also responsible for the formation of yet another Ontario theatre that would remain on the scene for a number of years. In 1950 he decided a large pool of talent alternating at two theatres in two cities might be the best of all possible worlds for both actors and audiences. Already operating in Peterborough, Sadlier looked to Niagara Falls as his second city where he had found the brand-new and wonderfully equipped Collegiate Auditorium in Epworth Circle. It had more than a thousand seats, box office facilities, lounges, a huge stage and perfect acoustics. Sadlier chose *Harvey* by Mary Chase as the opening production for the 1950 Niagara Falls Summer Theatre, with William Needles in the role of Elwood P. Dowd. Needles' performance won good reviews from critics and audiences.

The Niagara group was completely intertwined with the Peterborough Summer

Theatre, with the lineup of plays the same for both companies. A production opened in Niagara on a Tuesday with reserved ticket prices of $1.50 and $1.00, and general admission 50¢. They played through Saturday and then the same show and cast would open the following Monday in Peterborough while a new play opened back in Niagara. Because the productions appeared first at Niagara, the world premiere of Davies' *At My Heart's Core*, written specifically for the town of Peterborough, actually happened in Niagara. By performing the same play for two weeks the theatres enjoyed a longer rehearsal period and had a larger pool of actors to choose from when handing out parts. Kate Reid, Gerry Sarracini, William Hutt, Barbara Hamilton, Catherine Proctor and Charmion King all appeared at Niagara and Peterborough. Because it was a hard task to fill a thousand seats every night in Niagara, the results were discouraging at first but business picked up as the season progressed and the theatre ended up extending its run by two weeks.

Changes were in store for the Niagara theatre in the second year when the two theatres began operating as separate entities, with Sadlier as the only link left between the two. It was at this time that Bruce Yorke and Michael Sadlier went into partnership with American Maude Franchot to run the Niagara Falls Summer Theatre. She was the aunt of stage and screen star Franchot Tone. Unlike at the Peterborough theatre, they decided to bring in well-known stars as often as they could to Niagara and use Canadians in the company mainly as supporting players only. This was never the case in Peterborough, however.

While there were some complaints at the time about Canadians not starring more often with the Niagara theatre, the policy did give the still-inexperienced homegrown actors a chance to act alongside established talent. They opened the 1951 season with Sam Behrman's *The Second Man* and snagged Franchot Tone himself to star. The others in the short cast list were Canadian Anna Cameron and Americans Jackson Young and Barbara Payton, the latter having starred opposite James Cagney in the movie *Kiss Tomorrow Goodbye*. Most of the productions, which included *French Without Tears* by Terence Rattigan and *Rebecca*, were directed by Edward Thommen.

The theatre also presented a pre-Broadway tryout of Jan de Hartog's *The Fourposter*, with Canada's own Hume Cronyn and his wife Jessica Tandy. It was well received but, as far as audiences were concerned, the biggest hit of the twelve-week season was a play that had already proven itself both on Broadway and across the summer circuit in the United States—*Gramercy Ghost* by John Cecil Holm. Advanced seat sales for the production were so high that the company added both Wednesday and Saturday matinees. The crowds wanted to see Sarah Churchill (Sir Winston Churchill's daughter), who had starred in the play on Broadway and who brought co-star Richard Waring with her to the Niagara theatre. Canadians in *Gramercy Ghost* included Lew Davidson and William Hutt. The applause on opening night lasted so long the actress was forced to make an impromptu speech to the audience, which included many drama critics from around Ontario and New York State.

In 1952 Michael Sadlier, who had spread himself too thin with his involvement in three theatre operations, dropped out of the Niagara operation completely, leaving it solely in the hands of Maude Franchot. She went all out to bring in popular productions with big name stars, charging ticket prices of 75¢ to $2.50. Although there was no union yet in Canada, she insisted on paying American Equity wages to all her actors. She also put into place a very effective publicity department, something most of the early theatres had neither the time nor money to do.

The Niagara Falls Summer Theatre featured a number of successful hits, often bringing in the actors who had appeared in the originals on Broadway. One such play, Tennessee Williams' *The Rose Tattoo*, gave audiences the opportunity to see Maureen Stapleton and Eli Wallach, with Toby Robins, Josephine Barrington and William Hutt as the Canadian contingent. The play had a complicated set which in New York cost about $25,000 while the Niagara theatre was able to produce an excellent replica for a mere $250. Other imported stars in 1952 were Franchot Tone, Lawrence Tierney, Arthur Treacher and Edward Everett Horton.

The theatre presented its first musical, *A Tree Grows in Brooklyn*, for which Maude Franchot brought the complete cast en masse from the United States. Most of the time, however, the practice of having the major stars arrive and fitting them into the pre-rehearsed secondary parts taken by Canadian players was one that was continued for as long as Maude Franchot was at the helm. John Van Druten's *I Remember Mama*, *Death of a Salesman* by Arthur Miller, and *Nina* were among the most popular plays. Niagara was the only Canadian stop on the tour of *Nina*, starring Edward Everett Horton and Christopher Plummer.

The most interesting feature of the 1952 summer had nothing to do with productions or casts. It involved the temperature. Struggling through a heat wave, the Niagara theatre found that its attendance suffered badly, which prompted Franchot to present a gift of air conditioning to the school that housed the theatre. An instant hit, the cool auditorium attracted record crowds to the remainder of the season's productions.

The 1953 summer would be the most profitable in the short history of the Niagara Falls Summer Theatre. With Franchot still at the helm, they continued to import big names, often with complete casts, with one major change from previous years. Management began to see that musicals scored bigger audiences than straight comedy or drama, so almost 75 percent of their shows were now musicals. With eight performances a week in the thousand-seat auditorium and ticket prices from $1.00 to $3.00, the group became more financially secure than in past years. Prior to the last production of the season, the biggest box office hit had been *Carousel*. Others pulling in full houses were *Finian's Rainbow* and *Gentlemen Prefer Blondes*. *John Loves Mary* starring

Farley Granger of movie fame, was second only to *Carousel* in attendance. The season ended with the theatre's own (as opposed to Broadway's) staging of *Brigadoon*. David Brooks, star of the original Broadway production, was invited to direct and star in it. The first week's take was so good that for the first time Franchot held a show over for a second week, declaring the season a complete success. If she could have foreseen the problems of the coming year she might have been less optimistic.

Because the theatre operated out of a school, it had to deal with the local school board, which began to put numerous obstacles in its way. First, it withdrew permission to use the gymnasium which had been utilized to build and paint the sets. This meant Franchot would have to rent other premises at additional costs and transport the completed sets to the school. Then the school board, in contravention of the agreement between it and the theatre, rented out the auditorium for a dance on a night during the scheduled first week of the summer season. There was no guarantee as the season grew closer that this would not happen again. More disastrous than the first two factors, however, was that censorship raised its head. As a result of a couple of shows in the 1953 season with which the school board had been unhappy, it now wanted to approve all productions. It was the final straw, and a condition Maude Franchot was not prepared to accept. In January 1954 she walked away from the theatre.

For a time it looked as though the Niagara theatre might remain dark in 1954, but then it was taken over in March by Charles Michael Turner, an English actor and producer. He brought in Leslie Yeo and Oliver Gordon's London Theatre Company. Yeo's company had already been operating in Newfoundland for a number of years, and it is worth pausing for a moment to consider the company, for although it was not really Canadian, it played an important role in Atlantic Canada and then in Niagara.

Leslie Yeo's first visit to Canada (or an area that officially became part of Canada in 1949) was in 1947 when a wealthy Newfoundlander set up a British company to perform a season of plays in St. John's, Newfoundland. Also in the company was Alec McCowen who went on to become a mainstay of the British stage. Although the 1947 venture was a financial disaster, Yeo believed that the seeds for a company were there and returned to England determined to come back with his own company. It took him three years to raise the needed capital; in 1950 he landed back in Newfoundland with a fourteen-member company made up of only British actors. In their first winter, the London Theatre Company (London, England, and not London, Ontario) staged twenty-six plays in twenty-six weeks in St. John's. The following season they branched out to Halifax, Sydney, Moncton and Saint John. When this proved too costly, they eliminated all but Halifax and St. John's. There was very little theatre to speak of in the post-war Maritimes and what did exist was amateur, so while the company was solely British with nothing to offer Canadian actors, it did provide a service by establishing an audience for professional theatre in the Maritimes. The London Theatre Company wintered in St. John's for seven years and ventured into Ontario for two summers, but still used only British actors. Yeo himself directed seventy-four of the one hundred and fifty-six plays produced by the London Theatre Company.

They decided on an Ontario tour in early 1954, but by the time they ended up at the Grand Theatre in London, Ontario, they had unfortunately already lost $14,000, and the future looked dismal. Then they met Charles Turner of the Niagara Summer Theatre and they joined forces with him. Subsequently, the London Theatre Company presented a twelve-week season at the invitation of the Niagara Falls Summer Theatre location. They were successful enough to recoup some of their earlier losses. The group was largely the same as their winter one, consisting of imported English actors, including Yeo's wife Hilary Vernon.

Leslie Yeo and his London Theatre Company returned without Turner in 1955 as guests of the Niagara Falls Summer Theatre, although under their own company name, and staged a series of plays including *The Moon Is Blue*, *Dial "M" for Murder* by Frederick Knott and *The Importance of Being Earnest*. It was the last year a summer theatre operated out of the Collegiate auditorium in Epworth Circle, and although there were subsequent attempts to stage summer plays elsewhere in the city, it was the end of the remnants from the Niagara Falls Summer Theatre that began in 1950. Yeo would remain and work in Canada for the balance of his life, contributing greatly to professional theatre in Canada.

The International Players, the Peterborough Summer Theatre, the Niagara Falls Summer Theatre and of course the Straw Hat Players, when taken together, offer conclusive proof that summer theatre could succeed in Ontario with some level of longevity. Moreover, when the International Players and the Peterborough Summer Theatre expanded into winter operations they showed that Canada was ready for theatres that ran throughout the year.

CHAPTER TEN

# ONTARIO SUMMER THEATRES INCLUDING THE RED BARN THEATRE, THE MIDLAND PLAYERS & MELODY FAIR

"I got paid $5.00 a week and all I could steal. . . . Management also supplied us with accommodation and two meals a day so that we had $5.00 a week to spend on rather fragile lunches, the odd cigarette, a bit of laundry and perhaps an occasional drink."

—WILLIAM HUTT, BRACEBRIDGE PLAYERS

Summer theatre in the post-war period was especially prolific in Ontario. As has been seen, the four main theatres—the Straw Hat Players, the International Players, the Peterborough Summer Theatre and the Niagara Falls Summer Theatre—all enjoyed periods of solid success, and two of them moved on to winter productions. They are not, however, the only summer theatres of the early post-war period worthy of mention.

Many of these summer theatres lasted for only one or two years but some survived longer, albeit by changing their location or management with regularity. One of the most interesting of all the Ontario theatres on the straw hat circuit was the Red Barn Theatre, not only because it was one of the few actually operating out of a barn, but because the building itself stood for decades and performances were still being staged there until it burned to the ground in 2009.

In 1949, Alfred Mulock, twenty-three years old at the time, spent more than $20,000 to renovate an old barn in Jackson's Point, forty-four miles north of Toronto in cottage country. Jack Sibbald, the Reeve of the town of Georgina, agreed to lease Mulock a barn on a property owned by his family. He also gave his permission for it to be converted into a theatre. Mulock turned a cowshed into dressing rooms and a storage area for scenery. They bought 120 seats for $2.00 each from a movie house in Guelph that was closing down, and a large number of others were donated, giving them a capacity of 250, with the space to add fifty more temporary seats if the need arose. It often did. Yet the capacity was still small, and it may have been this small capacity that kept the Red Barn's existence constantly in jeopardy, although its out-of-the-way location did not help either.

The Toronto-born Mulock already had five years of theatrical experience in the United States when he decided to start the theatre in Jackson's Point. He brought with him another young Canadian, his wife Steffi Lock. Wanting to establish a summer theatre first, and then a year-round one, Mulock felt the only way to achieve this was to have a permanent stable of experienced actors from Broadway and supplement them with young Canadians learning their trade. He hoped that the latter would then take over in the coming years. To this end he brought in Isabel Bonner, whose Broadway appearances included *The Front Page* by Ben Hecht and Charles MacArthur, and leading man Stewart Nedd who not only performed on Broadway but also in movies. By setting the theatre up as an Equity company, Mulock hoped to encourage professionalism from the start.

He raced to open the theatre on schedule and succeeded, although the curtain rose two hours late. Making the most of a bad situation, management invited the audience to sit in their seats during that time and watch the stage crew get the set ready. Also adding to the ambience was the occasional bat that swooped down from the rafters.

The crowd that night loved both the extra pre-show and the opening production, *The Little Foxes* by Lillian Hellman. In addition to the two stars, the cast included Clarice Blackburn, Larry Gates and Canadian Sydney Banks, who was also the group's manager. Later in the season, John Wayne and Frank Shuster made an appearance in the Broadway farce *Boy Meets Girl* by Bella and Sam Spewack.

Other plays staged during the Red Barn's first summer were John Van Druten's *The Voice of the Turtle*, the ever-popular *Night Must Fall* by Emlyn Williams, and *Room Service* by Allen Boretz and John Murray. They also staged an interesting production of Tennessee Williams' *The Glass Menagerie*, using an innovative set. Designed by Mulock, the curtainless stage was scattered with platforms and only the suggestion of walls. Behind the stage on the barn's walls was a large screen on which slides appropriate to the action were projected. The backstage crew operated in partial view, and the closing of a scene was indicated by the blackening of the spotlights attached to a beam above the stage.

By the end of their first summer, the Mulocks had amassed a number of liens on the property, which then had to be covered by Jack Sibbald. Although the lease initially remained in Mulock's name, new interests took over the theatre in 1950. This was to be the pattern over the ensuing years. During the decade 1949–59 only one producer ever returned to the theatre a second year, although the Red Barn continued to turn out an interesting and often entertaining product.

The first to take over the theatre were Brian Doherty and Roy Wolvin in 1950. Noting the success of revues such as the New Play Society's *Spring Thaw* and the Davis brothers' *There Goes Yesterday*, the two men jumped on the bandwagon. The casts were almost entirely homegrown, and the revue skits were all written by Canadians, for Canadians and, notably, about Canadians. Sponsored by the Sutton Kinsmen, Doherty planned to present four musical revues, the first three being original and the fourth a compilation of the most popular skits from the first three. Doherty and Wolvin rented a cottage near the Red Barn and the rest of the company stayed at the Grandview Hotel. Calling themselves The Barnstormers, the group performed nightly at 8:45 except on Saturdays when they did two evening shows at 8:00 and 10:00. Each revue lasted two weeks. The producers spruced up the Red Barn and helped make the name more recognizable by actually painting the building red.

They opened with the revue *Crazy with the Heat*, and were an instant success. John Pratt was hired as the star, and others with the company at the opening were Barbara Field, Dick Nelson, Jack Merigold, Gladys Forrester (also the choreographer), Jack Northmore and Olive de Wilton, who was the business manager and one-time wife of actor Boris Karloff. The group had two pianists, Rusty (Morris) Davis of Montreal and Paul Chabot of Toronto. The sketches and musical numbers were directed by Roy Wolvin, who was also a prolific writer and composer, with twenty-eight of his songs or sketches in the first three revues. One of his ballads, "On & On & On," was eventually published. Robertson Davies, Brian Doherty and Dick Nelson were among the others who wrote sketches.

The Barn was overflowing on opening night and people had to be turned away. Most of the sketches revolved around the joys of summer, with praise in the press going to a sketch in which John Pratt attempts to cook following directions given out on the radio, and another skit called *The Charm of the Farm*.

During the run, Doherty and Wolvin held a children's Wednesday matinee (admission 50¢) which was so popular that they continued them throughout the summer. They wanted children to be involved with the theatre and encouraged younger people to come to rehearsals, which they did in droves, often collecting autographs from the actors.

The second revue, *Fair And Warmer*, opened July 17, and its sketches were aimed at making fun of Canadians abroad, using the International Trade Fair as its theme. For the third revue they brought in an actress who had, in a short time, become one of Canada's veteran young performers. Barbara Hamilton joined the theatre in time for *Rollin' the Hay*, as did new assistant director Henry Kaplan, who had learned his trade under Bob Gill at Hart House and continued on with many of the post-war theatres. Kaplan later became a successful director in London, on Broadway and in television.

Prior to the opening of the fourth revue, *One for the Road*, the producers announced they were extending the season by a week and adding a fifth original revue, *Here and There*. Brian Doherty and the other members of his company spent September 1950, preparing *One for the Road* for a Canadian tour which included Montreal, Ottawa, London, Hamilton, St. Catharines, Kitchener, and a stay at the Royal Alexandra Theatre in Toronto. One member of the fall tour was the actress who had joined them part way through the summer, Barbara Hamilton.

At the close of the summer of 1950, Doherty announced his intentions to return to the Red Barn in 1951 with a series of new revues. As a result of his increasing commitments, however, he was unable to do this, so he subleased the theatre to Amelia Hall, Bruce Raymond and Silvio Narizzano, all from the Canadian Repertory Theatre in Ottawa. "It was in the Spring of 1951," Amelia Hall said. "The business manager, Bruce Raymond, and I decided to go away for a few days to the Dominion Drama Festival in London [Ontario]. One morning I got a telegram from Brian Doherty. . . . He asked me if I would care to rent the Barn for the summer. A telegram I always wish I had never received because it caught my imagination. I forget what the rent was but the only person who made any money out of it that summer was Brian Doherty."

From day one there were numerous problems to overcome. Hall remembered wondering what she had gotten herself into:

> By the time we got going it was very late and hard to get actors, and we had very little money. It was a lovely theatre but it was backbreaking work. We had Robert Barclay who did Trojan work there helping build sets and whatnot. We did some plays with a lot of people in them. We rented the annex to a hotel and we had no one to clean the place and look after it, and I took on the job of being a kind of house mother there and seeing that people once a week produced their laundry. There was no one to look after the laundry from the theatre either so I took that on as well. I was so ill before the season had ended that I had to move myself into a hotel, and I lay in bed for a week with no visitors. I thought I was going to die, I was so tired. If there is a watershed in my life, that is it. I must have been out of my mind.

Out of her mind or not, the product in front of the footlights belied what was going on backstage.

The Red Barn's productions that summer were praised from the start. Even before the opening play, Russel Crouse and Howard Lindsay's *Life with Father*, onlookers had been coming to the rehearsals and enjoying them. The twenty-member cast included Derek Ralston, Peter Sturgess, John Frid, Robert Barclay and Barbara Field, who was in charge of props and was the only carry-over member from the musical revues of the previous summer. Other shows in the eight-week season included Garson Kanin's *Born Yesterday*, *Arsenic and Old Lace* by Joseph Kesselring and *Charley's Aunt* by Brandon Thomas, as the theatre followed the traditional summer, light comedy route. Directing duties were shared by Hall and Silvio Narizzano. Narizzano's younger brother Dino was recruited to play the juvenile lead in the group's closing play of the theatre's encouraging summer, *The Man Who Came to Dinner* by Moss Hart and George S. Kaufman.

Brian Doherty took over the Barn again in 1952 but the performances were limited to two a week, Wednesday and Saturday nights, and were more entertainment than theatre. They were mostly vaudeville-revue nights with performers such as Harold Barry, Billy Meek and Gordon Tapp, a young man who would go on to become better known to Canadians as Gordie Tapp in the television show *Hee Haw*. The highlight of the summer was the reunion of the two stars John Pratt and Murray Matheson, who returned for two revue performances that incorporated many of the sketches from *The Drunkard*, *There Goes Yesterday* and *One for the Road* (see Chapter Eight). With Jesse MacDonald backing them up on the piano, the show was such a success that two more performances were held the following weekend.

After the 1952 season, however, the Red Barn Theatre remained dark for three years. Doherty had gone to CHCH TV in Hamilton to become program director and no one stepped in to pick up the slack. It was reopened in 1955 with a series of light comedies. The following year another manager took over, and this pattern continued until 1959 when Marigold Charlesworth and two partners took over the operation. They, in turn, threw in the towel after three years (they went on to run the National Arts Centre in Ottawa), and from then on the Red Barn's survival was always precarious in spite of many talented theatre people passing through its doors.

In the 1970s it fell on even worse times and was within two weeks of demolition in 1972 when a "Save the Barn" campaign was launched by a committee of twelve residents of Georgian Township. They formed The Lake Simcoe Arts Foundation, headed by John Sibbald, whose family originally owned the land on which the Barn stood. They succeeded and, under the foundation, the Red Barn continued to stage plays and bring in well-known performers. It was a large tourist attraction for Jackson's Point.

The theatre was getting ready to celebrate its sixtieth anniversary (although some years had remained dark) in 2009 when tragedy struck. On April 18, 2009, at 10:30 p.m., a mysterious fire broke out and quickly engulfed the barn in flames. Two hours later when the fire was finally under control, there were only two partial walls left. The company used a temporary location, the Stephen Leacock Theatre in Keswick, for 2009 but this was not financially successful. A Red Barn Festival with performances at a number of locations was planned for 2010, but unfortunately it did not take place, and any final remnants of the theatre started by Alfred Mulock in 1949 were gone.

---

There was another theatre that spent part of its history in a barn which actually started in a curling rink. The Midland Players had the distinction of being the first professional summer stock company set up initially by a municipality itself. The city fathers in Midland, Ontario, had wanted to start a theatre for a number of years and the plans finally came together when they hired a drama teacher from Forest Hill Collegiate in Toronto, Jack Blacklock, to become their director. A large redbrick arena in the town park, normally used for curling, was converted into a theatre with more than five hundred seats. A floor was laid over the former ice arena and a stage was erected with a temporary proscenium extending to the walls on either side. The stage was also bordered by new dressing rooms, makeup tables and a space big enough behind it for rehearsals of the following week's play.

The Midland Players opened July 1, 1948, with *Meet the Wife* by Lynn Starling, the first of a nine-play season, performing Wednesday through Saturday nights. Sold-out signs were often posted in that first season, which included plays such as *Blithe Spirit* by Noël Coward, *Night Must Fall* and Patrick Hamilton's *Angel Street*. Among the actors appearing were Toby Robins, Marjorie Douglas and Elwy Yost, who years later would become well known in Ontario for hosting TVO's immensely popular *Saturday Night at the Movies*.

Not content with being only a summer theatre, the Midland Players invaded Toronto in the 1948–49 winter season and presented a series of plays, including *Angel Street* and *Ramshackle Inn* by George Batson. They performed two nights a week at the Royal Ontario Museum theatre during a season ending in April. Bigger plans emerged for the summer of 1949 as the theatre continued to operate in Midland but now added an excursion every week. On Mondays and Tuesdays they appeared at the Brant Inn in Burlington where they presented the play they had staged the previous week in Midland.

Audiences at the Brant Inn increased steadily until, by mid-August, they were reporting capacity houses on a regular basis. Productions included *Arsenic and Old Lace*, Norman Krasna's *Dear Ruth*, *Mr. Pim Passes By* by A.A. Milne and the Canadian premiere of *Madame Ada*, a 1900s comedy. Among those returning from the previous summer were Elwy Yost and Marjorie Douglas, with Jack Blacklock still at the helm.

Following another winter season in Toronto, the theatre gave up their two-year home at the curling arena. Moving to a rustic barn on a property in Allanburg, near St. Catharines, the Midland Players also changed its name and now became known as The Niagara Barn Theatre. The rough-hewn benches seated approximately three hundred and fifty, and, as if the atmosphere was not rustic enough, the barn's walls were decorated with cut-outs of pigs, cows, scarecrows and other rural symbols. Marjorie Douglas, Jill Foster and Bernard Slade (who later became a successful Broadway playwright) all starred in the successful seventeen-week season.

In 1951, the Niagara Barn Theatre returned to Allanburg, their fourth year together under Jack Blacklock. They opened their twenty-four-week season early in May with *Apple of His Eye* by Kenyon Nicholson and Charles Robinson, with Blacklock himself starring. The fourth production was *Haywire Holiday* by Canadian S.G. Bett, a music teacher in St. Catharines. He set the location for his farce in a Muskoka summer lodge and his play ran to full houses, being held over a second week.

As capacity houses happened more often, extra seats were added to the barn. The theatre also operated a school on Saturdays, with classes in acting, movement, makeup and other theatrical techniques. Other plays for the 1951 summer included Jack Kirkland's *Tobacco Road* (which ran without incident for a record three weeks), *For Love or Money* by F. Hugh Herbert and *Uncle Tom's Cabin* by Harriet Beecher Stowe. The latter, played in its original form and style, was staged for the 100th anniversary of the first production of the play. Doreen Engle starred as Eliza, Jack Blacklock as Simon Legree and the lead role of Uncle Tom was played by Bernard Slade.

Slade returned to the Niagara Barn Theatre for the 1952 season. While still retaining its name, the theatre did, however, move once again prior to that summer. The new location was in Vineland, a few miles west of St. Catharines where they rented, and then renovated, a building. A press release described the construction in great detail:

> Exterior will be white with brown trim boards, and a bright red roof. Interior will be rustic Barn decor with natural pine finish. A balcony will be installed, raising total seating capacity to 450. Basement will have a large coke bar, and rehearsal room. Stage will be well equipped, including light dimmers. It is large, with a set studio at its back. Wing at back also includes dressing-rooms and managers' office. Barn will be heated and air-cooled.

With Mark Saunders as his coproducer, Jack Blacklock was still running the theatre and continuing to direct. The group performed six nights a week and repeated a practice they experimented with the previous summer, that of having two performances on Saturday nights. In spite of that, it was not uncommon to turn patrons away from the second showing.

The most popular plays were Jean-Paul Sartre's *The Respectful Prostitute*, *Tobacco Road* (again without incident) and *Come Back, Little Sheba* by William Inge, with the thirty-four week schedule pulling in more than sixty thousand theatre goers. They had another busy thirty-week season in 1953, opening April 10 with *Angel on the*

*Loose*. The biggest hit of the season was *Natalie Needs a Nightie*, a farce by Neil and Caroline Schaffner, which was given its Canadian premiere and ran for three weeks with a cast including Charles McBride, Anne Roberge and Elwy Yost.

In spite of the change in name and the constant moves, Jack Blacklock was managing to run a financially successful operation, a true rarity in those days. Vernon Chapman noted that Blacklock was earning a solid reputation: "He was the most successful theatre entrepreneur probably in Canada at that time, financially. [In 1953] he made, cleared, over $60,000. It wasn't an Equity company because there was no Equity at that time and you were paid peanuts."

In December 1953, the two producers announced they were moving yet again, this time to Stoney Creek, Ontario, near Hamilton, where they built their own theatre rather than renting a space as they had always done. They constructed it to look like a barn on the outside but with modern amenities of oil heating (to make winter use possible) and air conditioning. The theatre had 420 seats plus a lounge, a snack bar, dressing rooms and offices. They opened their thirty-week season in April 1954, with *Charley's Aunt* by Brandon Thomas. Other plays included *The Male Animal* by James Thurber and Elliott Nugent, George Kelly's *The Show-Off* and *Stalag 17* by Donald Bevan and Edmund Trzcinski. One 1954 hit ran for four weeks, *Lullaby* by Don Appell, and they also had great success with a revival of *Natalie Needs a Nightie*.

In February 1955, the Niagara Barn Theatre, still under Jack Blacklock and Mark Saunders' management, opened for its second year in Stoney Creek, a planned ten-month season, the only major change in policy being a two-week run for each production. The theatre closed down some time prior to the scheduled end, however, and it was the last year the two producers ran it because Blacklock, reportedly due to ill health, dropped out of the theatre scene permanently. The theatre continued for one more summer in 1956 under producer Donald Ewer. Then it went dark.

The most financially structured of the summer theatres was Toronto's Melody Fair. Leighton Brill was looking for a financial supporter to back his plans for a theatre-in-the-round venture; he found one in R. Stuart Lampard, a Toronto stockbroker. The two met in New York in the fall of 1950, and Brill, who had been executive production assistant to Oscar Hammerstein for twenty-five years, quickly sold Lampard on the idea. With five other men, Lampard formed a syndicate under the name of Music Circus of Canada Limited. In 1951, they invested close to $75,000 in the company, a large portion of which went to the construction of an arena theatre on the Dufferin Park Racetrack grounds in Toronto. A circus-style tent was erected, the name Melody Fair chosen, and the group was ready to go to work.

In the centre of the tent was the stage with 1,640 armchair seats placed around it in rows edging upwards on a sloping concrete floor. Even though it was two hundred yards away from the tent, the cast's dressing rooms were in a building used for betting during race times, with parimutuel windows substituting for makeup tables. Minimal scenery and props were used in the productions so the audience could easily view the show from every angle. The performers made their exits and entrances via the aisles.

The executive producer was Leighton Brill himself, and he brought in Ben Kamsler as general manager. The syndicate hired the two of them for five years. Their aims were straightforward, as seen in the following excerpt from a first-year program:

> Early this year MUSIC CIRCUS OF CANADA LIMITED was formed by a group of public spirited Toronto business men for the purpose of bringing the best in musicals to the people of Toronto under the name of MELODY FAIR. It is our intention to bring to the citizens of Toronto top-ranking Broadway and Metropolitan Opera stars in the finest of musical comedies and operettas. One of the main aims of this company also is to find and develop young Canadian talent. To this end, I believe, a real start has been made. Our brilliant young singers and dancers in the ensembles are all Canadian, mostly from the city of Toronto.

Except for one or two Canadians in minor roles, such as Alex McKee and Josephine Barrington, all the players except the Canadian singers and dancers mentioned in the program above were imported. Brill and Kamsler hired top choreographers and persuaded director Bertram Yarborough to stage the musicals. The whole venture was professional, on stage and off. It operated under American Equity rules, with members of the ensembles receiving $55 a week and musicians $75. Some of the imported stars received as much as $1,000 a week plus percentages, and by the second year the total weekly payroll was approximately $8,500. In total, there were more than sixty people on staff and only half of those were performers.

This brings us to one of Melody Fair's greatest strengths, its administrative staff. Kamsler spent at least $1,000 a week on publicity, as he used newspapers, radio spots, car and window cards, hotel publications, high school papers and even television in Buffalo to bring the message to the people. Melody Fair also employed two full-time publicity men who worked on getting free promotion in newspapers and on radio. As far as the latter went, they had a great deal of help from disc jockeys who would play the songs featured in the current show. Kamsler and Brill spoke at a number of service clubs and often took a member of the cast with them to provide a preview of the upcoming musical. This paid off handsomely as the service clubs began to buy blocks of seats to resell to their members.

The publicity Melody Fair generated did not stop with local promotion. In addition to Buffalo television, *Variety* magazine in the United States wrote about them nearly every week, listing the grosses for each show. The only other theatre in those years to employ such an effective publicity department was Maude Franchot's Niagara Falls Summer Theatre in Ontario.

It did, however, take a few weeks that first summer to propel Melody Fair financially into high gear. Chosen for the first musical was *Song of Norway* starring Irra Petina of the New York Metropolitan Opera and Lawrence Brooks, co-stars of the original Broadway production. Natasha Carr was the season's choreographer; she recruited dancers from the local ballet schools, while the Royal Conservatory Opera School supplied the singers. In spite of all the advance publicity, attendance for the opening show was only 40 percent, with 60 percent being the break-even point.

Word of mouth spread, however, and the second show, *Brigadoon*, broke even, and attendance increased as the season progressed. The final musical, *Show Boat*, was held over a second week and had an attendance figure in the 90 percent range. Other shows the first summer included *Rosalinda* and *The Chocolate Soldier*. When income and expenses were tallied at the end of the eleven-week 1951 season, Melody Fair had broken even, a remarkable feat for a theatre with such large costs. They had attracted almost one hundred thousand patrons. Audiences liked the intimacy of theatre-in-the-round, and felt very much a part of the proceedings. On one evening, when the lighter held by one of the leading men went dead at a crucial moment, from the audience a foot away, a man lit the actor's cigarette and the scene continued.

In 1952 Brill and Kamsler introduced more innovations aimed at bringing crowds into the tent. They kept ticket prices low, ranging from 75¢ to $3.40, and instituted the relatively new practice of telephone reservations. Patrons needed only to pick up their tickets twenty-four hours before the performance. Perhaps the most important change regarding tickets was that management decided to print up the seat tickets for the entire season before it even began. It was a great deal of work as more than 120,000 tickets had to be printed, but it paid off. Instead of having to come in each week to buy tickets, a patron could, at the beginning of the year, pick and choose which shows they wanted to see and purchase all the seats at once for the twelve-week season. This was highly unusual for the early 1950s and explained why advance sales for 1952 were at $30,000—up from approximately $3,000 the previous year.

For the most part, Melody Fair stuck to the same method it had in year one—that of bringing in name stars. However, some of those in dancing and singing ensembles the first year were elevated to bigger roles. One of these was Kathryn Albertson of Winnipeg, who in the off-season had gone on to appear on Broadway and to tour in two musicals before returning to Melody Fair for its second season.

The most popular show of 1952 was the final one, *Annie Get Your Gun*, starring Marilyn Day and Earl Covert, which pulled in grosses of $25,000. Other favourites were *Carousel*, *Finian's Rainbow* and *Kiss Me, Kate*. Performers included Irra Petina, Alex McKee, Iggie Wolfington and Gil Lamb (who with salary and percentage of the take received almost $2,500 for the week). In the group's first year, Wolfington became such a crowd favourite that they often called out his name, "Iggie, Iggie," in much the same fashion sports fans do for their favourite athlete. Melody Fair grossed $250,000 in 1952 with attendance up 40 percent. With $180,000 representing 60 percent capacity, or the break-even point, the investors made a profit of $70,000 which covered most of their original investment in 1951.

Considering the success at the current location, it was a surprise to many that between the second and third seasons Melody Fair moved from Dufferin Park to the Canadian National Exhibition grounds. They put on shows Monday through Saturday at eight every evening, and during the Exhibition itself they added a matinee at two o'clock. The price of tickets remained the same but the number of seats increased to 1,800. The weekly grosses published in *Variety* made it obvious Melody Fair was having an excellent 1953 season, or at least it seemed that way.

By season's end, some 115,000 theatregoers had shelled out $250,000 at the box office. The productions were still staged by Bertram Yarborough, with choreography done by Bettina Rosay, who was also prima ballerina with the company. They began 1953 with $13,000 in advance sales for the opening production of *Call Me Madam*, starring Gene Raymond, who was married to Jeanette MacDonald. She flew in for the opening, which added a great deal of excitement and Hollywood atmosphere to the occasion. *Paint Your Wagon* was a July hit with Ontario-born Gene Lockhart in the lead. At the audience's request he was asked to sing *The World Is Waiting for the Sunrise* at the close of each performance.

In August they staged a musical which had not done well in its previous production by them, but what a difference two years made, as *Song of Norway* pulled in huge crowds this time around. Irra Petina was back as the star and, on the Thursday performance, a record one-day take of $4,558 was established. The Saturday matinee of slightly more than one thousand patrons, was also the largest attendance of the season. The subsequent production of *Brigadoon* was not to be outdone, however. With good weather and even better reviews, it set a gross record of $27,800, with three hundred people being turned away each night and more than one thousand people paying the minimum of $1.50 in order to stand and watch the performance. The year closed out with *Carousel*, starring Walter Cassel and Gail Manners of the New York City Opera Company.

Although it appeared to be a phenomenal summer, their payroll and other costs at their new Exhibition Grounds home exceeded the income. The books showed that Melody Fair had a deficit of $70,000 for the fourteen-week season. The Exhibition had charged Melody Fair $10,000 in rent, and they were stuck with a lease that covered the next four years. According to the March 24th edition of *Billboard* magazine, which is currently only devoted to music but then was the leading news weekly for the entertainment industry, 1953 was not an easy summer for anyone: "At the CNE it faced nightly noise of stock car races, excessive heat and the attempt to operate during the exhibition."

There were other signs of trouble as well. Ben Kamsler left his position as general manager at the end of the 1953 season, being replaced by Larry McCance. In spite of their contract with the CNE, Melody Fair began looking for a new home following the 1953 season and found one indoors at the Arena Gardens on Mutual Street. "This acoustically perfect setting for your favourite musical comedies will be gayly decorated to create the illusion of a tent theatre but will eliminate all the hazards of noise and bad weather and provide a cool and comfortable home for the talents of the best Broadway Musical Comedy and Operatic Stars," an announcement read.

Advance bookings were high for the 1954 summer, their fourth and what would be their final, season. The new theatre seated more than five thousand people and the ten-week season saw an attendance increase of some thirty-five thousand over 1953. Among the shows were *Oklahoma* (breaking all previous records), *Kiss Me, Kate*, *Pal Joey* and *Brigadoon*, with casts that included Barbara Hamilton, Robert Goulet, Babs Hitchman, Kathryn Albertson, Pegi Brown and Iggi Wolfington. Problems, however, were growing. Halfway through the 1954 summer, R. Stuart Lampard resigned. In addition, the cost of moving indoors, the previous contract commitment to the CNE, which they were still required to honour, and incorrect calculations when figuring ticket prices, all had a drastic effect on the net return. Melody Fair never reopened in 1955.

There were a few smaller groups in Ontario that did not survive long but still deserve mention, not only for their attempts to bring professional theatre to Canadian audiences, but for the experience they gave to actors who went on to make a name for themselves.

A ten-week summer season in 1948 was run in Bracebridge by Mark and Sylvia Shawn. One member of The Mark Shawn Players was a University of Toronto student who went on to become one of Canada's premiere stage actors, William Hutt. "[Sylvia] was one of the first people who gave me a professional opportunity," Hutt said. They played "in an auditorium, I think over the fire hall. It was the local community hall," Hutt continued, "and the clanging fire engines temporarily stopped more than one performance in midstream." Opening with *Claudia* by Rose Franken, the company then followed with plays that included Noël Coward's *Blithe Spirit*, *Night Must Fall* and *Theatre* by Guy Bolton and W. Somerset Maugham. In the cast of the latter was an actor recently arrived from England who had been in Canada during the war while serving in the Royal Air Force. John Atkinson went on to perform with almost every major early post-war theatre in Ontario.

Directed by Henry Kaplan, the Bracebridge casts included Anna Cameron and Bea Lennard with lead roles usually taken by William Hutt and Sylvia Shawn, who was also in charge of running the company. The Ottawa-born Shawn studied at The Neighborhood Playhouse in New York. In the early 1960s she established the first cabaret-style theatre in Toronto, Theatre in the Dell, which would be much more successful than her 1948 Bracebridge venture. The Mark Shawn Players did, however, give some valuable experience to William Hutt. "If memory serves me right" Hutt recalled, "we actually closed one show shorter than we intended to because it wasn't a highly successful season. I think we made a mistake of opening with a play called *Claudia* which is a story of a pregnant lover. To do that in 1948 in Bracebridge was risky." So risky in fact that the Shawns did in fact close the Bracebridge season early and did not return the following year.

Also worth a brief mention is the Holloway Bay Players, who operated in Crystal Beach (Port Colborne-Fort Erie) for a couple of years in the late 1940s. Plays staged by them included *The Philadelphia Story* by Philip Barry, *Night Must Fall* and Lawrence Riley's *Personal Appearance*. The most famous alumna of the theatre was Cosy Lee but others who starred were Russ Waller, Mac Inglis and Florence Wittington.

Closer to Toronto was another theatre with a place in the history books—in spite of its short existence. It showed that even with stellar casts and critical acclaim, success was precarious and doubtful in those post-war years. The Scarboro Summer Theatre survived less than one season (1952), and it is difficult to understand why, as it presented top-notch productions with some of the best-known stars of the day, and yet the expected audiences never materialized. Organized by Donald Glen, the group performed in the auditorium of the Scarborough Collegiate. They opened June 30, 1952, with Garson Kanin's *Born Yesterday* and had no less a star than Lorne Greene playing the lead, backed up by Richard Easton and Bea Lennard. As he did with most of the other plays, Robert Christie directed the inaugural production. *Just Married* was their second offering, with Bud Knapp taking the lead. Adelaide Matthews and Anne Nichols wrote *Show-Off*, the theatre's third production, with the well-known radio and revue actress Jane Mallett starring. She was paid $100 for a week's rehearsal and a week's run. Also in the cast were Donald Glen, Bea Lennard and Montrealer Marion Dennis.

The season progressed and the good reviews kept coming in but the audiences did not, so it was decided during the run of George Dibdin-Pitt's *Sweeney Todd*, to close down the season at the end of the production, two weeks earlier than expected. That last show starred Eric Christmas, with Bea Lennard, Richard Easton, Cal Whitehead and Robert and Margot Christie. As summer groups usually did in those days when they folded, Donald Glen announced they were trying to formulate a plan for a second summer in 1953. It never happened.

West of Toronto another summer theatre was also getting underway in 1952. The Carousel Players of Oakville was started by Hugh Webster and Alex Naszadi, with Toronto actor George Hislop as president of the group. Some members of the theatre were young actors fresh from schools, such as that run by Sterndale Bennett, and the remainder were experienced actors. Realizing the necessity of promotion, they worked hard at pre-opening publicity, showing up with announcement handbills at all the important spring theatrical functions in Toronto. They also erected road signs and delivered notices door-to-door. The group had no backers or sponsors, but pooled their own funds, hoped they would break even, and set up shop in the Pine Room of the Oakville-Trafalgar Memorial Arena.

The Carousel Players did not open with a light, frothy comedy as most other summer theatres did; instead, it chose the old romantic classic *Camille* by Alexandre Dumas Jr. It starred Hugh Webster, Stan Dalton and Robert MacLeod, with Jan Campbell in the pivotal Camille role. Other plays were *Angel Street*, J.M. Synge's *The Playboy of the Western World*, and *You Touched Me* by Tennessee Williams and Donald Windham.

Unlike the Scarborough theatre, Carousel survived to return for a second year to the same location but under new administration and the name of the Oakville Summer Theatre. Management at the Oakville Arena had offered their theatre to Vernon Chapman to run a ten-week season there for the 1953 summer and he accepted. This time around, the theatre stuck with comedies like *Hay Fever* by Noël Coward and *Life with Father*, with Drew Thompson, Pegi Brown, Sandra Scott and Margaret Griffin appearing. No one took over in 1954 and another summer theatre closed its doors.

Among other theatres that appeared during the early post-war years were a number of U.S. stock companies that came to Canada, but few gave any opportunities or experience to Canadian actors, except occasionally in bit parts. One of the best known of these stock companies was the Shelton-Amos Players who appeared for a few summers at the Grand Theatre in London, Ontario.

There were also numerous one-shot productions staged by individual entrepreneurs, both American and Canadian, which quickly faded from the scene. One was the Kool-Vent Theatre; it was based in Montreal but toured through Eastern Canada in the fall of 1952. Another was started by two young actors, one English-born and the other born in Canada but raised in England, who had appeared with companies from the United States in 1947 at the Royal Alexandra Theatre in Toronto. Stanley Bell and Peter Boyne made good contacts and liked the city, so in 1948 they returned and presented a series of summer plays at the Royal Ontario Museum. Unlike the American companies, they did use Canadian talent in plays such as George Bernard Shaw's *Candida*, *Laburnum Grove* by J.B. Priestley and their opening show, Terence Rattigan's *O Mistress Mine*. That talent included Don Harron, Betty Leighton, Jack Ammon, and Joanna Baker. In spite of what Don Harron called "a fairly successful season," Stanley Bell's company did not return in 1949.

In conclusion, one can see that many of Ontario's summer theatres were successful with audiences and critics alike, and yet were unable to sustain that success beyond a couple of summers. Even though the business side of the theatres was often handled well, permanent success was elusive. In the case of most theatres, it required not only intense dedication on the part of the one or two people running them but often their money as well. These types of individuals were scarce. Some knew theatre and some business but few knew both. And they were all faced with the same problem as the winter groups, a lack of suitable theatres to perform in.

Yet in spite of their difficulties, Ontario's summer theatres were successful, and the historical record needs to record that success. Not only did they consistently draw large audiences; they gave people a taste for theatre. Just as important, however, is the fact that they also gave actors the chance to perform, helping to develop professional theatre in Canada.

CHAPTER ELEVEN

# ENGLISH QUEBEC THEATRE

"That was a marvellous youth [to have]
and it was a marvellous time, a perfect
time to grow up in Montreal."
—CHRISTOPHER PLUMMER

Throughout the post-war years, the theatre scene was thriving in Quebec, both on the French and the English stages. It was on the English side—even more so than in Ontario and the other provinces—that the amateur and professional theatres were so entwined they were almost indistinguishable from one another. Actors slipped easily from theatre to theatre, sometimes getting paid, other times receiving only an honorarium or nothing at all. It was also in English Quebec at this time that two of the longest surviving theatres in Canada operated. The Montreal Repertory and Brae Manor Theatres were both professional in intent and, for the most part, presentation. They both began prior to the Second World War and continued throughout while most other theatres fell by the wayside after only a short time.

The Montreal Repertory Theatre (almost always referred to as the MRT) was formed following a November meeting in 1929. The spark plug was Marguerite (Martha) Allan, daughter of Sir Montagu Allan who, among other things, contributed the Allan Cup to amateur hockey. Born in 1895, her only brother died in the First World War and both her sisters drowned in the 1915 sinking of the *Luisitania*. Martha Allan was involved in amateur theatre from an early age. At the outbreak of the First World War she was studying in Paris and resumed those studies after a stint as an ambulance driver in the war, during which she acquired a shrapnel wound that bothered her for the rest of her life, although she was able to work through it on stage. On returning to Montreal, she acted with the amateur Community Players. Their demise in the early 1920s led Allan to travel to the United States, where she worked with a high calibre little theatre in Pasadena, California. Three years later, much wiser, Allan came home and began exploring the feasibility of starting her own theatre in Montreal. Being bilingual, Allan took it upon herself to use theatre to mend some of the rifts between the French and English in Montreal, putting on plays in both languages.

Allan found a location in Moyse Hall at McGill University and, in the late 1920s, six productions were performed, three in French and three in English. In November 1929 Allan persuaded Sir Barry Jackson, who had founded the Birmingham Repertory Theatre in England, to address a meeting of those interested in forming a theatre. It was a somewhat unusual group to launch a theatre because it also included drama critics. Herbert Whittaker, one of Canada's best future theatre critics, told the story:

> [The critics of the day] were grateful in the sense they felt they were part of the movement. The Montreal Repertory had two critics on its platform when it had its opening meeting. On the platform also was a great theatre man from England, Sir Barry Jackson. These were people of note gathering to launch a theatre. They recognized the importance of theatre in the country and supported it. They were also, though, watchdogs, so that they couldn't allow bad theatre to give theatre a bad name. They had to say "this won't do." But there was always a sense not of charity so much but of support of something that was believed in.

In fact, most of the theatre critics of the early post-Second World War era felt much the same way as Whittaker did about the situation back in 1929: that they were as much a part of the theatre as critics of it.

The result of the November 1929 meeting was a committee to organize a nonprofit, bilingual theatre devoted to the encouragement and performance of theatre, dance and music. When the MRT staged its first production in March 1930, *The Perfect Alibi* by A.A. Milne, it was actually under the name The Theatre Guild of Montreal. The Guild's objective was to ascertain the extent of public interest and to secure plays suitable for production, preferably Canadian ones, although that would not happen immediately. They quickly ran into problems trying to obtain rights to George Bernard Shaw's *Candida* as these North American rights belonged to the New York Theatre Guild, whose constitution did not allow their granting production rights to any group having the words "Theatre Guild" in their official name. The Montreal group quickly solved the problem by changing its name. They staged *Candida* and, by the time of their third show, *The Constant Wife* by Somerset Maugham, they were formally called the Montreal Repertory Theatre.

With the purchase of a membership, subscribers could buy a theatre ticket for $1.50, or they could pay $2.00 without one. That first year there were two hundred members; ten years later this had swelled to about fifteen hundred. Presentations of *The Constant Wife* and John Galsworthy's *The Roof* by the MRT were both Canadian premieres. In keeping with their bilingual goals, the theatre's French division, known as Le Mont-Royal Theatre Français, staged *La Souriante Madame Beudet* by Denys Amiel. Although by the time the MRT folded in 1961 the French division had long since been disbanded, the group was unique in its pre-war years for its promotion of both French and English theatre simultaneously.

Martha Allan appeared in most of the MRT's productions and shared directional duties with Rupert Caplan, better known for his later work in radio drama. In the beginning, rehearsals took place in the coach house at Ravenscrag, the home of Allan's parents, and then later in a building on Union Street. Plays were first staged in Moyse Hall at McGill University and then in the Ritz-Carlton ballroom and Victoria Hall. One especially interesting MRT production was a 1932 production of *Hamlet* at Moyse Hall. In the title role was Viscount Duncannon, the son of the governor-general, the Earl of Bessborough, who himself designed the stage settings for the show and was also influential in the formation of the Dominion Drama Festival.

In addition to major productions at their main theatre, the MRT also set up the Studio in 1932. Housed in a building on Union, the Studio was begun partly to showcase new talent, but mainly to produce experimental or non-commercial plays. Over the years these included many original ones, as well as Canadian contributions such as Robertson Davies' *Eros at Breakfast*.

In an effort to encourage indigenous playwrights, Allan held a one-act play contest in 1931. The result was a workshop evening the following year of six Canadian one-act plays, two of them in French. *Summer Solstice*, a one-act play written by Allan herself, was staged by the MRT in 1935. They also started a school in 1933, offering courses in acting, directing, stagecraft and makeup.

By 1939 the MRT had aspirations to build its own theatre. Unfortunately the Second World War put an end to those plans, and indeed almost to the theatre itself. Many theatres were forced to cease operations completely at this time. Allan decided to continue, however, and made the Montreal Repertory Theatre a branch of the Red Cross. In turn, she became chairwoman of the organization's entertainment for the province. It was decided a revue would be the best form for this entertainment, and after numerous auditions and rehearsals, the Tin Hats were born.

Formed in December 1939, the Tin Hats continued to perform to thousands of troops in Eastern Canada until March 1946. Although the forty members were not paid, fundraising was still needed to cover the many other expenses. Unlike the soldiers who watched free of charge, civilians had to pay, and this revenue helped with the costs. The technical section of the Montreal Repertory Theatre designed and built a completely equipped portable stage, twelve feet deep and thirty-two feet wide with a sixteen-foot proscenium arch. It was made in sections for easy transport and erected whenever the Tin Hats played in a location without a suitable hall or stage. The group also carried a unique padded case filled with thousand-watt lights, a portable switchboard and a complete public address system.

Many of the camps the Tin Hats visited were filled with French-Canadian soldiers and, in keeping with MRT's spirit, the leading performers were bilingual. Thus they were able to switch their speech and gags to suit the audience. The Tin Hats gave hundreds of performances throughout the war years, gaining a reputation similar to that of the Army and Navy shows of the same period and that of the Dumbells during the First World War.

Two other events happened to the Montreal Repertory Theatre during the war that would change its course forever. In 1942 they acquired the use of a building at 1550 Guy Street, which became their permanent headquarters. In the beginning it housed only the Studio presentations but in 1943 it became their main stage. Before the group had even moved into its new quarters, however, a catastrophe of major proportions occurred, which became a very real threat to their existence. This was the death of Martha Allan in April 1942. Any time an organization loses its driving force, the danger exists that it will not recover, and Allan, to this point, had been the MRT.

She had, however, set a strong foundation under her, and many people picked up the slack, with Filmore Sadler at the forefront. Both he and his wife Marjorie had long been associated with the MRT and its school. Under Sadler the group moved into the Guy Street building. Although the space was unbelievably cramped, they had to move because their previous location in Victoria Hall was no longer easily reachable by the public due to wartime rationing of gasoline. The MRT had also not been the sole organization to use Victoria Hall, and the noise of other activities could often be heard during the performances. The major drawback of the new building was a seating capacity of only 200, compared with 700 at Victoria Hall. To compensate, the theatre increased the number of performances of each play from three to seven.

During the difficult years following Allan's death in 1942, the school and the Studio both ceased to function for a time. When the war finally ended and other theatres began springing up and creating a larger local pool of talent, the MRT started up again, with many actors joining for only one or two productions. Mildred Mitchell was now running the theatre, succeeded by Doreen Lewis.

One part of the MRT that continued throughout the war was their magazine *Cue*. It had been founded early on by Martha Allan, in December 1930, to "give the theatregoer the cue to the Montreal Repertory Theatre" and also "to the plays that the Repertory company places before him." It was a remarkable piece of Canadian theatrical history, for it also contained information on the other theatres in Quebec and occasionally elsewhere in Canada. The first issue stated that the MRT's "aim is to discover talent, to encourage and foster its growth." *Cue* would later issue pleas for funds when the MRT ran into financial trouble a few years down the road.

During the post-war years, the MRT's most prolific, *Cue* was under the editorship of Charles Rittenhouse, one of the many unsung heroes of Canada's post-war theatre, one of the true nurturers. Rittenhouse not only edited *Cue* magazine but taught in MRT's school and also starred in one of their productions. When the theatre staged a translation of François Mauriac's *Asmodée* (*The Intruder*) in December 1946, Rittenhouse played the lead role of the tutor. It was directed by Pierre Dagenais, a young man who was making a name locally with his own French theatre, L'Équipe. Rittenhouse, Edward Wilson, Christopher Plummer (only sixteen years old at the time) and Betty Wilson were all singled out by critics for their performances.

The plot of *Asmodée* revolves around the arrival of a visitor, a young English boy, to a household. His effect on the young widow in residence and her seventeen-year-old daughter is noticed by the tutor and his resulting jealousy propels the play onwards. The critics thought the production good and a sign of the theatre's continuing maturity, but many in the audience disliked it. Also staged and applauded that season was Jean Giraudoux's *Amphitryon 38* and *The Barretts of Wimpole Street* by Rudolf Bessier, with the latter breaking all MRT box office records to that time and forcing them to add extra performances. The crucial role of Elizabeth Barrett was taken by Eleanor Stuart with George Alexander as her unpleasant father.

It was, however, *Amphitryon 38* that brought the most recognition to the MRT in that 1946–47 season. It was directed by Roberta Beatty and starred Eleanor Stuart, Richard Gilbert, Leo Ciceri and Virginia Watt. Watt was making a rare stage appearance because her usual role with the theatre, a role for which she received many accolades through the years, was as costume designer. Indeed, her costumes for *Amphitryon 38* received special praise, as did the set by Hans Berends, who built many sets for the theatre. This was all the more remarkable considering the tiny space he had to work with on Guy Street, where the stage was only nineteen feet wide by fifteen feet deep and the proscenium arch, nineteen feet high. *Amphitryon 38* was the MRT's entry in the Dominion Drama Festival in 1947 where it won for the best English-speaking production and was later presented at the Royal Ontario Museum in Toronto under the sponsorship of Dora Mavor Moore and her New Play Society.

When the MRT school reopened following the war, the two most popular classes were drama technique and radio announcing. The Studio also began operating again and the Montreal Repertory Theatre came into its own once more when revenues in the spring of 1947 showed a surplus over expenses. It was at this time that they began to pay honoraria to some actors appearing with them, although the payments were scanty and discretionary. Herbert Whittaker, who directed more than one production with the MRT and occasionally designed the sets as well, noted:

> If some actors were paid more than others it was a matter of politeness and honour not to divulge that, to make other people feel badly. . . . I know that in the beginning MRT money was handed out surreptitiously to the people who needed it, who were giving up other to work for the MRT. Lots of people were doing it out of sheer love. I think they felt they could afford it. If they had a good job and could spend their evening at something they so much wanted to do, they didn't resent the fact that some of the actors were paid.

He also noted that some of the company contributed "if they happened to be very well off."

Whittaker co-directed one of the 1949 productions, *The Glass Menagerie* by Tennessee Williams, with Roberta Beatty, and designed the sets as well. Amelia Hall was invited by Whittaker to play the demanding role of the mother. "I was paid an honorarium, $50, to go to Montreal and play Amanda," Hall said. "I think you could say that then I began to think of myself as a professional actress."

In 1949 the Montreal Repertory Theatre was also preparing to stage a twentieth-anniversary production; it chose *The Constant Wife* by Somerset Maugham, which had been the group's first play under the official name of the Montreal Repertory Theatre back in 1930. The production opened November 23, 1949, with one member of the original 1930 cast in it, although this was not planned. Doris Hedges had turned down the request to recreate her original role in the anniversary version but an accident left actress Roberta Beatty with a broken leg and Hedges came in to fill the void. Others included Nancy Graham and Rosanna Seaborn, the latter well known for her Open Air Playhouse atop Montreal's Mount Royal. Among those attending the performance was Vincent Massey, who at that time was heading up a Royal Commission on the arts situation in Canada.

The MRT was now presenting five major plays and three Studio productions in a season that stretched from fall through to spring. The school was going strong and the theatre had assembled a large collection of scenery, properties and costumes, which it gladly lent out to many other local groups for their productions. A major asset was their Community Theatre Library, which had more than five thousand volumes, some of them irreplaceable. A subscriber could join and take out books for only $1.00 a year. The building constantly bustled with activity and had truly become a theatre, albeit a cramped one.

The benefits of having their own home, however, far outweighed their confining quarters. It was something most other theatres could only dream about. "I can still smell it actually," Christopher Plummer remembered of the Guy Street building. "It was very exciting to me because it was the first theatre I ever knew, that I had ever been inside. It always smelled of theatre. . . . It was kind of heady and attractive to me. It was always a smell of size [glue] and paint. I was fond of those people. I loved Eleanor Stuart and I was very fond of Doreen [Lewis], who was very loyal to me."

The theatre went all out for their twenty-first anniversary party in 1950 when they staged an English translation of Jean Cocteau's *La Machine infernale*, a version of the Greek tragedy *Oedipus Rex* by Sophocles, starring Christopher Plummer as Oedipus. It was praised by the critics, who said the play was a difficult one to stage and gave the MRT credit for not only attempting but succeeding at it. In addition to Plummer, who received plaudits for the quality of his voice, the play starred Gwyn Williams, Virginia Watt and, in supporting roles, two young actors well known to Montreal audiences, Richard Easton and Richard Gilbert. There were only six unsold seats for the entire nine-performance run, with requests for tickets still coming in when *The Infernal Machine* closed.

The MRT had a profitable period in 1945–50, definitely its pinnacle, but as the decade ended, cracks were beginning to appear. Other professional theatres had started up, and not as many good actors were available anymore who were willing to work for next to nothing. The group would show an increased operating loss for the 1949–50 season.

| | 1947–1948 | 1949–1950 |
|---|---|---|
| Total Income: | $15,357 | $17,445 |
| Total Operating Cost: | $15,802 | $20,179 |
| Yearly Loss: | ($445) | ($2,734) |

Their main expense was the rent on Guy Street, which had gone from $1,368 to $3,000 for the season. The theatre had also tried to make ends meet by repeating their major shows at a school auditorium in Mount Royal but it had not helped. Not wanting to raise ticket prices, they began looking at possible subsidies and a way to set up a permanent fund from donations, but these were slow in coming. Buying the Guy Street Playhouse was also explored as a viable alternative, and an announcement was made in *Cue* magazine that a decision had been made to go ahead with this plan. Fate would say otherwise.

On March 5, 1952, fire engulfed the premises and, with alarming speed, the work of twenty-three years was almost completely erased. Following the blaze, the Montreal Repertory Theatre regrouped but their losses had been tremendous. For Canadian theatre, the biggest losses were the destruction of the Community Theatre Library and the theatre museum collection. The library had been founded in 1939 with the remaining funds of the Community Players theatre group, which had been placed in a trust fund after the theatre's dissolution in 1924. The library was really one of a kind: it was devoted to the dramatic arts and dealt with both French and English languages. Even if other copies could be found, the cost made many of the books impossible to replace, including the four volumes of Auguste Racinet's work on theatrical costuming. The museum contained Canadiana memorabilia dating back a hundred years. Costumes, programs from the early 1800s, autographed portraits and many heirlooms from Martha Allan's home Ravenscrag were all gone forever.

Although it seemed to rally from this misfortune, the Montreal Repertory Theatre never really recovered. While it managed to break-even financially during the 1951–52 season, this was the result of fire insurance money and public donations following the blaze. The ongoing deficit was still $5,000.

The main dilemma facing the group was finding a location in which to perform. The majority of future productions were staged at either the Mount Royal High School Auditorium or Victoria Hall, their old stomping ground. The directors set up an office in a local hotel, and with cooperation from other organizations, the MRT was able to go ahead with their scheduled opening of the play *Harvey* only fifteen days after the 1952 fire. One of the highlights of the post-fire period was a staging of Shaw's *Saint Joan* performed for the Montreal Festivals in 1953, starring French actress Denise Pelletier. Directed by Charles Rittenhouse, who also stepped in at the last minute to play the Bishop of Beauvais, the production was well received by both critics and audiences.

While there had been an outpouring of public support for the theatre following the fire, this faded rapidly and by 1953 the first of never-ending overhauls of the MRT took place. It found some stability in 1957 when they moved into their first permanent home since the fire—the Navy Building at 1429 Closse Street in Montreal. Nevertheless, the theatre battled continuing financial problems throughout the 1950s. The situation was made even worse when they were not given any funding from the newly formed Canada Council in spite the fact they officially became a professional theatre in 1956.

The final blow came in 1961, when the Navy Building housing them was sold. They would never find another home. In spite of all the problems, the MRT still presented some credible productions in their waning years, with one of their mainstays being the actor Leo Ciceri. The final production of the Montreal Repertory Theatre came in March 1961, with Ciceri starring in Luigi Pirandello's *Henry IV*. It was a bravura performance, but when the curtain came down, the MRT was no more.

∞

The other long-running group in English Quebec, Brae Manor Playhouse, began primarily as an acting school. Set up by Marjorie (Madge) and Filmore Sadler, who had worked closely with the Montreal Repertory Theatre during its formative years, Brae

Manor quickly evolved into a highly respectable summer "barn" theatre. The couple met at Leland Powers School of the Theatre in Boston and became engaged, appropriately enough, while playing the leads in *Romeo and Juliet*. Work in New England repertory companies led to an invitation from Martha Allan and the couple's close association with the MRT.

The Sadlers wanted to use their extensive teaching skills by opening up their own summer school. The question was, where? Madge had inherited a large house, Brae Manor, near the centre of Knowlton on Brome Lake in the Eastern Townships, about sixty-eight miles from Montreal. The property surrounding the house was substantial and proved useful for the theatre a few years down the road. Brae Manor was one of the few places in Canada where aspiring actors could go to obtain theatre training, while actually performing in front of an audience. They started with four students, whom they called the Brae Manor Players. Performances began in 1936 with one weekly show in the nearby Lakeview Hotel. Students in the productions were supported by some leading actors from Montreal, including Martha Allan, who starred in their opening production. The Brae Manor Playhouse caught on quickly with local residents, who turned out in large numbers. A few years later, Filmore Sadler's thoughts turned to building his own theatre. Residents of Knowlton got wind of his dream and, in 1940, a group of them offered an interest-free loan to build a theatre on the property beside the Sadlers' house. This loan was completely repaid—a tribute to both the theatre and the Sadlers.

Built in the true tradition of "barn" theatre, the building looked the part from the outside; the inside was also rustic, with beams and unpainted boards. The floor was sloped for easier visibility and the seats were wooden. Where there was no rusticity or simplicity was in the building of the actual stage which, at forty-five feet wide and twenty-six feet deep, was amazingly large for so tiny a theatre. There were also good dressing rooms and sufficient space backstage for actors to move around.

The 1940 season in their new theatre was an unqualified success and the Sadlers continued in the same vein during the war years. For eight weeks every summer, students attended the school and performed Thursday through Saturday, a different play each week. Their achievements throughout the early 1940s were all the more remarkable considering the gasoline and manpower shortages brought about by the war. Brae Manor was some distance away from any large populace, and yet they still attracted crowds substantial enough to survive during a time when, in the United States, 75 percent of summer theatres closed down.

With the end of the war and the blossoming theatre scene in Canada, Brae Manor would experience its most productive period from 1946 to 1950. Students vied to be among those selected to attend the school, and Filmore Sadler began to invite actors who had experience. One of those who attended in 1945 and again in 1947 was Ottawa's

Amelia Hall, who commented, "I don't think anyone was paid much except perhaps the stage manager. We paid to go to Brae Manor. We paid for the pleasure. After all, we had a lovely house to stay in with lots of gorgeous people and our meals. And we were doing what we wanted to do."

Most of the others felt the same way. By 1948 they were paying $35 to $38 a week for the privilege of combining "valuable dramatic studies with the joys of a delightful summer holiday," as the Brae Manor program stated.

The only thing you did not do was drink on the property. Amelia Hall explained, "As the Sadlers were Christian Scientists, there was no drinking in the house. But who needed it? We had buns and cocoa or coffee at night; we sang around the piano, and the conversation was always stimulating. Sunday suppers we ate out under the trees. Outside too we would have a reading of the next play."[19]

With cast and crew, there were often thirty people under the same roof, which made for lively discussions about theatre. On Sunday mornings the cast met and dismantled the set from the previous week. Then chairs would be placed on stage, representing the furniture for the new show. There was a rehearsal Sunday night and by the following evening all lines for the current play had to be memorized. Rehearsals continued morning and evening. From Monday to Friday many students also attended classes in "voice training, diction, technique of acting, body movement, dancing and makeup." By Tuesday the costumes were chosen from the theatre's large inventory, and Wednesday was the dress rehearsal. Somewhere in the mix, sets had to be built and painted. It was hard work, and the Sadlers toiled just as hard as the students they were trying to inspire. The actors ate, drank and slept all aspects of the theatre.

When they were not busy readying a play, the actors were often out on prop-hunting tours with Filmore. Any student who showed ability eventually landed a small role in a production, although the leads went to the advanced students and actors brought in from Montreal. When not appearing in front of the footlights, the apprentices were involved in the backstage undertakings of running a theatre.

The theatre began to receive widespread attention following the war as more Montrealers made the drive and Americans began coming up to see the productions. Among the first well-known actors to appear post-war were Anna Cameron, Leo Ciceri, Betty Wilson and Pierre Dagenais. For Dagenais, who was known in French theatre circles in Montreal, his appearance in Shaw's *Candida* was his first experience performing in English.

Most of the plays were produced, and sometimes directed, by Filmore Sadler while Madge took on the mammoth task of running the rambling house with its numerous occupants, with most actors receiving free room and board. Filmore also appeared in some of the productions and even Madge took a part in the occasional play. When the school was running, they both taught most of the classes and also came up with a unique way to bring in more money by operating a shop selling antiques and gifts on their property. When the theatre closed down in the winters, the Sadlers worked in Montreal, teaching and acting.

By 1947 Brae Manor had a core of talented actors, many of whom appeared frequently during the next three or four years. They included Amelia Hall, Leo Ciceri, Silvio Narizzano, Richard Easton, John Colicos, Betty Wilson and Maud Whitmore. David Haber spent many summers as the production manager, becoming an important part of Brae Manor Playhouse, while Herbert Whittaker frequently directed and designed the sets. The Sadlers put a great deal of thought into the type of play presented. As most patrons of summer theatres liked comedies and thrillers, they were given a steady diet of these, although sometimes Brae Manor threw in a more serious play and hoped to be forgiven. They also allowed themselves licence when categorizing a play, such as the time they advertised *The Silver Cord* by Sidney Howard as a comedy, something it definitely is not.

The rundown of plays in 1948 illustrates an average year. Still performing Thursday through Saturday, the theatre opened July 8 with the first Canadian presentation of *Pink String and Sealing Wax* by Roland Pertwee. To star in it, Sadler brought in a couple well known in Montreal's theatrical circles: Bea Whitfield and Maud Aston. The theatre followed with their "heavy" production of the season, *A Bill of Divorcement*. Clemence Dane's play had already been made into a movie with Katherine Hepburn and John Barrymore, while Brae Manor's version starred Dorothy Walter, Filmore Sadler, Kay Fowler and John Colicos. This drama was followed by the immensely popular murder farce of the day, Joseph Kesselring's *Arsenic and Old Lace*, and *Yes, My Darling Daughter* by Mark Reed. Still yet another comedy, Norman Krasna's *John Loves Mary*, was followed by a mystery-drama, *Nine Pine Street* by Carlton Miles and John Colton, which took its story from the famous Lizzie Borden case about a young woman who killed both her parents with an axe. George S. Kaufman's *The Royal Family of Broadway*, about the Barrymore family, was next, and Brae Manor closed out the 1948 season with the classic eighteenth-century British comedy *The Rivals* by Richard Brinsley Sheridan. The latter starred John Colicos, Filmore Sadler, Richard Gilbert, Richard Easton, Christopher Plummer and Maud Whitmore.

As Brae Manor's reputation grew, and it became one of the few financially independent projects of its kind in North America, it moved further away from the school concept. By 1948 it had become largely a resident company augmented by six or so apprentices each season. These apprentices were the only ones still paying to be a part of the theatre; the balance of the members were paid.

Following a 1949 expansion, the barn had some two hundred and fifty regular seats with room for fifty more rush seats to be added when needed, which thankfully was often. Under the stage there were new dressing rooms, a costume room and a workshop. These renovations also facilitated an increase in the number of subscribers, and Brae Manor continued to thrive in their unique setup. In 1950 Brae Manor set new attendance records two weeks running with the popular Garson Kanin's *Born Yesterday* and *Life with Father* by Howard Lindsay and Russel Crouse. By this time full houses were normal, and they had extended their shows from three to four nights a week. Brae Manor drew 6,940 patrons in 1950, up from 2,725 in 1945. 1950 also saw new dimmers, spots and other lighting fixtures, given from a patron as gifts to the theatre.

The opening play for the 1951 summer was the Brae Manor Playhouse's 100th production. To celebrate, the Sadlers chose a Canadian play, *At My Heart's Core* by Robertson Davies, which had already been presented by the Peterborough Summer Theatre and earlier that year by the Canadian Repertory Theatre. As with the previous presentations, Brenda Davies starred in the play directed by her husband.

There continued to be improvements to the theatre almost every season. In 1952 there was a new canteen and a roof over the front of the playhouse which covered the terrace. It seemed Brae Manor would go on indefinitely, but in December 1953 Filmore Sadler died suddenly and things would never be quite the same again.

In January of the following year, his wife announced that the theatre would continue, and everyone rallied around her, making the 1954 summer the most successful in the theatre's history. David Haber obtained a leave of absence from the National Ballet of Canada to return and help out as production manager. Amelia Hall both directed and acted during the 1954 summer, which was highlighted by a staging of Christopher Fry's *The Lady's Not for Burning*, directed by Herbert Whittaker. The presentation starred Betty Wilson and John Colicos, fresh from his theatre experience in England. Others in the production, which drew raves from the critics, were Edward Wilson, Pierre Dagenais and David Gardner.

They all continued to live at the house. Gardner, the company's leading man for the summer, recalled:

> It was a very happy setup. My greatest experience there was meeting a Montreal director, Roberta Beatty, and just becoming enamoured with her. She had been a real New York actress in many plays at the turn of the century and so on. Statuesque, Jewish . . . she was older but striking. She had bangles up her arms and would say things like "come on darling, entertain me, entertain me" and jingle, jingles [with the bangles]. She directed with sex appeal and nobody had ever done that in Canada. She'd say, "come on, this is a romantic comedy and I don't believe the two of you have ever been in bed together." A very maturing kind of person.

The following summer of 1955 was a hard one for Madge Sadler. George Palmer took over from David Haber as production manager, but he left halfway through the season.

In August 1955, Madge put the theatre up for sale, saying the task of running it was too much for one person. Brae Manor Playhouse was still under her management, however, when it opened for the 1956 season, which included *The Rainmaker* by N. Richard Nash, *Anastasia* by Marcel Maurette and George Kaufman and Moss Hart's *You Can't Take It with You*. It was the last hurrah. When the barn theatre closed its doors after the 1956 summer, Brae Manor, one of the most innovative theatre operations in Canadian theatre history, disappeared forever.

Although not as durable as either the Montreal Repertory Theatre or the Brae Manor Playhouse, the Mountain Playhouse also played an important part in English theatre in Quebec. Its evolution, however, was entwined with two other theatres—the Canadian Art Theatre and the Open Air Playhouse—and their histories are by no means easy to separate.

Joy Thomson began the Canadian Art Theatre in 1944. It was essentially a touring company until she found a permanent home in 1950 on Mount Royal. At that time it became known locally as the Mountain Playhouse in spite of still performing under the name Canadian Art Theatre for the first few years. In 1947 Rosanna Seaborn began the Open Air Playhouse, an outdoor theatre also operating atop Mount Royal. Norma Springford joined Seaborn that first year and stayed with her until Seaborn disbanded the group in 1950. Following the 1951 summer, Joy Thomson left Canada and Norma Springford took the reins of the Mountain Playhouse and ran it for the next ten years.

When Joy Thomson began the Canadian Art Theatre in Montreal, in late 1944, its main objective was running a school of theatre arts and a children's theatre. Thomson was bitten by the theatre bug while at Montreal's McGill University and then went to the United States to learn the technical end of the business. After studying at Erwin Piscator's school in New York, where Marlon Brando and Elaine Stritch were two of her classmates, Thomson spent a couple of seasons on the United States' summer circuit before returning home to Canada.

For the first production by the Canadian Art Theatre in 1945, she chose *Kings in Nomania* by Percival Wilde, a children's play. Although known largely as an amateur theatre for children, the Canadian Art Theatre also staged adult plays, including Ibsen's *Ghosts* and *The Imaginary Invalid* by Molière. Among the actors appearing early on with the theatre were Mary Sheppard and John Colicos. Thomson's fledgling Canadian Art Theatre really geared up into a major force in 1948, when she set up a professional company of touring players. Not everyone was paid in the beginning, Amelia Hall said. "I got nothing in 1948 but I played most of the senior leading roles and I helped with advertising and changing the scenes. There were only about four people in the company who were paid and they got about $20 a week. In 1949 I got $35 a week."

In 1948 the Canadian Art Theatre performed eight plays in eight weeks. They followed an exhausting schedule, playing in Rock Island on Saturday and Monday, North Hatley on Wednesday and Magog on Thursday and Friday. The theatre made a large contribution to the development of theatre by touring the Eastern Townships and bringing theatre to people who would not otherwise see it. While in Rock Island they rehearsed and played at the Haskell Opera House, which had the distinction of being built on the Canada/US border with its stage in Quebec and its auditorium in Vermont. The Canadian Art Theatre opened with Emlyn William's *Night Must Fall*, starring Silvio Narizzano in the pivotal role of Danny, the baby-faced killer. Other plays included Ben Travers' *Rookery Nook* and *Ladies in Retirement* by Edward Percy and Reginald Denham. The theatre closed its first professional summer season with the always popular *Arsenic and Old Lace*. The actors included Amelia Hall, Silvio Narizzano, Bruce Raymond, Maud Whitmore and Mary Sheppard. Joy Thomson not only ran the theatre but was also set designer and occasional actress. The success of the Canadian Art Theatre was entirely owing to her unflagging energy.

In 1949, their second summer as a professional theatre, the Canadian Art Theatre expanded even further. Each play ran two weeks and for the second of those, the theatre followed much the same route in the Eastern Townships as it had in 1948. The first week, however, was spent travelling and presenting the current production in a number of Quebec towns, including Hudson, Point-Claire, Lennoxville, Laval and Montebello. The distance from one end of their travels to the other was almost two hundred miles. For $5.00 a subscriber could buy season tickets to all five plays while individual tickets sold for $1.50, $1.00 and 60¢. They opened with the thriller *Angel Street* by Patrick Hamilton, better known to audiences as the movie *Gaslight* starring Ingrid Bergman and Charles Boyer. The Canadian Art Theatre's version starred Bruce Raymond in the Boyer role and Amelia Hall as the wife he tries to drive insane.

Other plays in 1949 included *Squaring the Circle* by Valentin Katayev, *Laura* by George Sklar and Vera Caspary, with Noël Coward's *Hay Fever* as the closing production. They averaged only about seven rehearsals for each show, many of these taking place in their vehicle en route from one town to another. In addition to Hall and Raymond, Silvio Narizzano and Maud Whitmore were part of the company. The theatre gave sixty-six performances in ten different towns and villages. They travelled by car and trailer, both usually overloaded and temperamental. One time the trailer broke away from the car, overturned and caused considerable damage to the scenery.

In fact, touring caused so many problems that Joy Thomson began looking for a permanent home. In 1950 she found a building owned by the bankrupt Park Toboggan and Ski Club atop Mount Royal, and, as was mentioned earlier, began a theatre, which was known as the Mountain Playhouse. The building itself was far from ideal as it seated only two hundred people and the stage was only twenty-six by twelve feet.

The worst aspect was that any actor wanting to go from stage right to left, without actually crossing the stage itself, had to undertake an obstacle course. Descending the stairs at the side of the stage, the actor exited the building and ran along a pathway behind the building, which was often muddy from the rain. Entering up the stairs on the other side, the actor passed through French doors, up yet more stairs and through the accumulations of the prop room to arrive at the other side of the stage.

Not only was the building inadequate as a theatre, but Joy Thomson made a serious mistake with her ticket sales, one that almost destroyed her project at the beginning. While she offered six productions in her first year, an acceptable number, for some strange reason she decided to allow only season ticket holders to come to the plays—something that did not sit well with the public.

What helped save the theatre that first summer on the mountain was the booze, or more accurately the lounge. A club license, held by the Mountain Playhouse through a loophole in the liquor laws, was one of a kind in Canada at that time. It allowed the selling of liquor and beer to patrons before the show and at intermission, an attraction that pulled in people who might have otherwise stayed away. They opened with Garson Kanin's *Born Yesterday*, but the hit of the season was *Whiteoaks* by Canadian Mazo de la Roche. The production was the group's contribution to the Montreal Festivals, a city-wide yearly tribute to every aspect of the arts, which began in 1936.

Amelia Hall was chosen to portray Adeline Whiteoaks, the domineering matriarch of the family, with the equally demanding part of her grandson Finch going to Christopher Plummer. An incident following a *Whiteoaks* rehearsal caused Amelia Hall to be late to another play in which she was presently starring—"for the only time in my life," she said. "We were chatting after a [*Whiteoaks*] rehearsal and I had to go to the Mountain Playhouse because I was playing the lead [in another production], Chris [Plummer] was playing a leading role in the current Open Air Playhouse production [of *Cymbeline*], also on the mountain, directed by the famous Komisarjevsky. Joy invited the two of us to go to a restaurant for dinner. She kept us talking and I was getting frantic and it was getting to be after 8:30 p.m. Finally she . . . drove us up the mountain. I don't know what happened to Chris because he was supposed to be hiding behind some great stone before his production opened. The only time I have ever been late to a theatre in my life and it was the fault of the producer."

Joy Thomson had been one of Christopher Plummer's earliest supporters. He called her "a marvellous egg," and recounted how "Joy was one of the greatest drinking companions of my life, of anybody's life. It is not difficult to be bad with Joy. She actually pulled me out of the police station several times. . . . There I would come out with a bloody lip because [the police] roughed me up a bit. Those were good days."

The successful *Whiteoaks* production also included John Colicos, Winifred Dennis and John Pratt's eleven-year-old son Robin as the youngest member of the Whiteoaks clan. Because of the season-ticket-only idea, however, Mountain Playhouse was not a financial triumph in 1950.

To increase revenues, the following summer Joy Thomson threw the theatre open to patrons who wanted to pay for one play at a time, while still offering a season membership. For $6.00 plus 80¢ a play, members were guaranteed six plays while individual reserved seats were $2.00, which still represented a slight savings to the theatregoer and attracted many subscribers. What Thomson did not count on, though, was that two of the productions would be tremendously popular. When they ran into longer runs than expected, the number of plays in the season had to be reduced, forcing Thomson to return some money to subscribers who had been promised the six plays. In spite of this, the 1951 summer still turned a profit.

They opened the 1951 season with Noël Coward's *Present Laughter*, which ran for four weeks because of the high ticket demand. Starring in the play were Barry Morse and his wife Sydney Sturgess who had recently arrived in Canada. Building on the success of that first play was *The Male Animal*, written by Elliott Nugent and James Thurber, and starring Christopher Plummer, Kay Ryan, Henry Gamer and Jack Creley. *The Voice of the Turtle* by John Van Druten followed and was considered the artistic triumph of the 1951 season, which closed with a double-bill of *Harlequinade/The Browning Version* by Terence Rattigan.

Except for a brief later period, Joy Thomson dropped out of the Montreal theatre scene following the 1951 season to teach in New York. The Mountain Playhouse might have folded with Thomson's departure, but the reins were taken up by Norma Springford, who was not a stranger to Joy Thomson or to Montreal audiences. Springford certainly had more than enough experience to take over, and her willingness to do so prevented the Mountain Playhouse from closing.

Her choice of Coward's *Private Lives* as the first offering in 1952 was an excellent one to begin her long tenure at the reins of the theatre which was now known solely as the Mountain Playhouse, having dropped the use of the Canadian Art Theatre name.

In order to attract audiences, most summer theatres were forced to stage at least six to eight plays during the season, but in 1952 Mountain Playhouse needed only three as they closed out the season with a long run of Rose Franken's *Claudia*. Besides Morse and Sturgess, among those appearing during the season were Jack Creley, William Shatner, Richard Gilbert, Corinne Conley and Maud Whitmore. At the close of the summer, general manager Bruce Raymond announced financial success, no easy feat for a theatre with only two hundred seats.

As television appeared on the scene, it became more difficult for Norma Springford to find actors, as most English-speaking actors migrated to Toronto, the centre of English television work in the East. Stratford, in its opening year, was also beginning to take the cream of the crop. The winter months also presented problems as Mountain Playhouse's unprotected location was often broken into and vandalized. In spite of all this, Mountain Playhouse survived by continuing to offer light comedies, which remained popular with audiences. For twelve weeks each summer they followed a gruelling schedule as they performed Monday through Saturday.

In 1954, extensive alterations were made and a fifth anniversary party was held. Four plays were presented but the one attracting the record-breaking crowds—*Gigi* by Anita Loos—closed out the season. One actor who worked with the theatre around this time was Thor Arngrim of Totem Theatre (see Chapter Three). He explained how, at least on one occasion, Mountain Playhouse moved to a different location, and an outdoors one at that: "I performed a couple of times outdoors and I would never do that again. . . . We went to the Laurentians and we did outdoor theatre. . . . I ate so many insects doing Noël Coward, I can't tell you. Ever tried eating a lot of insects on a summer evening in a tuxedo? It's just totally gross."

There were many highlights during the remainder of the 1950s including *Harvey* and *Off Limits*, a 1958 revue written by nine Canadian television writers, Dave Broadfoot and Jack Creley among them. *Off Limits* broke all their attendance records with 14,120 patrons, which was 90 percent capacity for the ten-week run. Among others performing with the group in the late '50s were Betty Leighton, Catherine Proctor and Charmion King.

In the 1961 season, which turned out to be its last, the Mountain Playhouse opened early in May with *Breath of Spring*, but also closed earlier than planned. The theatre had rented the site for a token dollar-a-year, but when a dispute arose between the landlord and the city, Montreal's mayor at the time, Jean Drapeau, forced the theatre to close. That signalled the end of Mountain Playhouse.

Before taking up the reins of the Mountain Playhouse, Norma Springford had previously worked for another summer theatre up on Mount Royal, the Open Air Playhouse. Also an outdoor theatre, as its name indicates, the Open Air Playhouse was on a much smaller scale than Mountain Playhouse in terms of the number of productions it would present, but it became known especially for its innovative Shakespearian productions. The theatre had been started in 1947 by Rosanna Seaborn and a few other enthusiasts (including Herbert Whittaker and Malcolm Morley). They had begun talks about forming an outdoor theatre and, on the spur of the moment one day, they went up the mountain searching for locations.

They found one adjacent to Beaver Lake. The natural stage was eighty-four by fifty feet, banked with evergreens but unraised, and the backdrop was a small rocky hill (about fifty feet high) over which actors appeared, sometimes to great effect.

Thor Arngrim, who appeared with Mountain Playhouse, is shown here opposite his future wife Norma Macmillan in Totem Theatre's production of *No Time for Comedy*, c. 1953. (ARNGRIM COLLECTION)

Wings were formed by eight-foot high cedar hedges planted fresh each year. The actors dressed in tents set up at the sides of the stage. The audience sat on folding chairs or on the grass of the hillside facing the stage. At the top of this hill was a marquee, which not only provided patrons with an entrance, but shelter when it rained. The whole area was roped off from the general public and patrolled by security to ensure no one sneaked in for free. The patrons, four hundred or more, depending on the elements, were even protected from mosquitoes as management had the area sprayed with DDT prior to each performance.

The sparkplug for the Open Air Playhouse was Rosanna Seaborn, who contributed financially in a large way to the project. The Montreal-born Seaborn, daughter of McGill professor John Todd, trained in England at the Royal Academy of Dramatic Arts. After graduation she played for a year with the Festival Theatre in Cambridge and then with the London Mask Theatre, operated by playwright J.B. Priestley. She then toured the United States for six months in *Ladies in Retirement*, starring Flora Robson, before returning to Montreal where she worked with a number of local groups.

With beautiful eyes and dark features, courtesy of some First Nations heritage, Seaborn wanted to put all her training to use and prove herself at the same time. "[Open Air Playhouse] was partly a showcase for herself," said Christopher Plummer, who not only starred alongside her but was a close friend, as their family homes were next to each other in Senneville, Quebec. "To be quite honest she had never been taken seriously enough as an actress, she felt. Certainly not only by her family but by her friends in Montreal."

Only one play was presented by the Open Air Playhouse each summer, and in 1947 the group chose Shakespeare's *A Midsummer Night's Dream* as its inaugural production, which seemed made for the sylvan setting. Malcolm Morley directed and, although no salaries were paid, the cast included many fine actors. Among them were Christopher Plummer as Lysander, Amelia Hall as Peaseblossom, Silvio Narizzano as Starveling and Rosanna Seaborn as Hermia. Christopher Plummer appeared in three of the four productions in Open Air Playhouse's history and was thankful for Seaborn's support. He said of her: "I was extremely grateful to her because she did encourage and push in those early years. My own family were quite doubtful, and quite rightly, about whether I was good enough. I attached myself to Rosie and she was always so colourful and terribly theatrical. She was always championing me. She was terrific."

The choreography for *A Midsummer Night's Dream* was handled by Ruth Sorel, a Polish refugee who had been a prima ballerina in her homeland. During Open Air's first three years, Sorel used many of her own students to create a number of dance sequences that enhanced the woodland setting. Although in the beginning it was never intended for all the productions to be by Shakespeare, the theatre found his plays lent themselves to the outdoors, as many of the playwright's comedies, such as *As You Like It*, are set in a forest. No scenery was used and the lighting was planned and executed by Norma Springford's husband William, who also set up the sound system. The loudspeakers he erected were important, for they had to pick up the voices and carry them to the audience across the open-air space.

Outdoor settings were beautiful visually but not all actors liked performing in them. Christopher Plummer said of performing out among the trees in the night air:

> It was strange. I was never totally married to it. It was a very pretty sight and the audience came and all sat on that little bank. I'd heard about Regent's Park but I hadn't been to London yet so I didn't know much about it, but even then I didn't like the idea of not being heard if the wind blew. I was critical of the outdoors. I mean, Shakespeare supplies his own nature.

The settings were key to the productions, however, in spite of the rain occasionally disrupting the proceedings. On one night in the first year when the skies opened up prior to a performance, a member of the theatre told the audience their tickets would be honoured for another night. They would have none of it. Rain or no rain they wanted the show to go on. The cast obliged. Although both cast and audience were dripping wet at the conclusion, they both applauded each other. *A Midsummer Night's Dream* was scheduled to run only one week but, due to popular demand, was held over a second week with ticket prices ranging from 75¢ to $2.50. All proceeds went to the Canadian Cancer Society.

For its second season in 1948, Seaborn chose *As You Like It*. Production management was placed totally in the hands of Norma Springford and a permanent backstage crew for the Open Air Playhouse was organized. Actors now received a small honorarium. The City of Montreal, at its own expense, lighted the pathway from the road to the theatre, as they were well aware that the theatre was now a tourist attraction. The production comprised sixty-five actors (including Leo Ciceri, Christopher Plummer and Rosanna Seaborn) and thirty backstage workers. Including committees, ushers and a publicity department, more than one hundred and fifty people worked voluntarily for the Open Air Playhouse that summer.

The cast also included a few non-human members in the form of two sheep and a pony, who were forever trying to steal the show. The pony also caused further difficulties when, in the middle of the two-week run, it was suddenly sold by its owner, and the crew had to scramble to find a replacement.

Harry Norris composed some music in the Elizabethan vein for the production, Ruth Sorel continued her innovative choreography and Malcolm Morley once again directed. Each summer the theatre took ever more advantage of its natural surroundings, and in *As You Like It* they used the backdrop hill effectively on more than one occasion. One of these was near the play's closing when Rosalind (Seaborn) and Celia (Mary Douglas), attired in bridal dresses, appeared over the crest of the hill between two foresters carrying blazing torches. Led by the goddess Hymen who is singing, Rosalind walked down the hill to join friends gathered for the wedding. Then the crowd turned upstage to watch Celia descend towards them in a blue dress with wreath and veil, almost floating down the hill. The torches continued to blow in the wind adding an almost mythical tone to the setting.

In the fall of 1948 the City graded a section of the mountainside, increasing the seating capacity. The stage was raised, levelled and covered with sod but the natural shrubbery, bushes, trees and backdrop hill were all preserved. In 1949 the Montreal Festivals (of Music, Ballet and Drama) were staged at various auditoriums and outdoor sites around the city and the Open Air production of *Much Ado about Nothing* was a preview show for the two-week festival.

Ruth Sorel had fitted ballet sequences in between dramatic scenes in earlier Open Air productions, and in 1949 she incorporated three ballets with Elizabethan and Italian folk music into *Much Ado about Nothing*. Herbert Whittaker, who was also closely involved in the first two years' productions, designed the outfits worn by Rosanna Seaborn as Beatrice. It was perhaps a harder play to produce than the previous two, which had outdoor settings as part of the action, while *Much Ado about Nothing*, for the most part, did not. This did not seem to bother audiences; they continued to come out in large numbers, twelve hundred on beautiful nights and even four hundred in the rain.

In 1950 the Open Air Playhouse became incorporated as a non-profit cultural organization. Seaborn, who was still the production manager, decided she wanted something different for the season so she and Norma Springford travelled to the Connecticut home of famed Russian director Theodore Komisarjevsky to ask him if he would be interested in staging *Cymbeline* for them. Seaborn and Springford knew of the director because he had staged Verdi's opera *Aida* for the Montreal Festivals the previous summer.

When Komisarjevsky agreed to direct Shakespeare's *Cymbeline*, Montreal became abuzz with talk of the production, especially when it was learned the director intended to present the play in modern dress. England had been exposed to some Shakespeare in modern costume, but Canadians up to this point had seen only traditional presentations. An excellent cast included Ronald Kinsmen, Robert Goodier, Christopher Plummer, William Shatner, Eleanor Stuart and Rosanna Seaborn.

Komisarjevsky had emigrated to Britain in 1919 where he was a theatre designer. While most of his acclaim came for productions of Russian plays, he also worked at the Shakespeare Memorial Theatre where his controversial *Macbeth*, for which he designed aluminum scenery, was staged in 1933. He felt that Shakespeare should be presented in a contemporary way, and he certainly stirred things up with his *Cymbeline*, which brought mixed reviews from critics. Herbert Whittaker wrote of the production that "the Montreal audience who climbed up Shakespeare Road was startled to find Shakespeare, even unfamiliar Shakespeare, in garden-party frocks and Fascist uniforms, and to hear snatches of American popular tunes among the couplets. The result was ahead of its time, but pleasant enough and well acted for the most part."[20]

Komisarjevsky added Gershwin tunes as background to the opening scenes. He had a guitar and saxophone accompany the famous "Hark, Hark the Lark" lyric, and two actors exited a scene singing "We're off to see the Wizard, the wonderful Wizard of Oz." But, as Christopher Plummer commented, "Don't forget that Komisarjevsky was getting on. I think he was sort of slap happy actually." Plummer, nevertheless, liked Komisarjevsky and found the modern interpretation a refreshing change of pace. "Yeh, I thought it was kind of interesting. I had grown up with such conventional productions. *A Midsummer Night's Dream* was pretty conventional, in those awful Malabar costumes. So was *As You Like It*, but somehow right for Open Air in a funny way. [*Cymbeline*] was a relief."

In spite of audiences totalling 8,500 annually, the Open Air Playhouse never staged a play after *Cymbeline*.

The business sides of the early post-war theatres were often well thought through but success was still elusive. In the case of most theatres, it required an intense dedication on the part of the one or two people running them, and often their own money as well. That was certainly the case in the Montreal area as people such as Martha Allan, Joy Thomson, Rosanna Seaborn and Norma Springford gave everything they had to bring professional theatre to Canada.

CHAPTER TWELVE

# FRENCH QUEBEC THEATRE

"There were three farces of Molière staged by Théâtre du Nouveau Monde. They toured and showed the world that Montreal and this theatre in particular had developed its own style of playing Molière."
—HERBERT WHITTAKER

While the English-speaking Canadian theatre was flourishing during the post-war years, the French contingent was having a renaissance of its own. In some ways its successes were all the more remarkable because they took place in the stifling atmosphere of the Duplessis era in Quebec. In the late 1940s and early '50s, the church in Quebec exerted a repressive influence, which went hand in hand with the rampant anti-communism of the period. In 1937, Premier Maurice Duplessis passed The Act Respecting Communistic Propaganda, commonly called the Padlock Law (because the doors of buildings suspected of having propaganda meetings could be "padlocked"). The legislation gave the government broad powers in acting against any left-wing group and, while ostensibly aimed at communism, it effectively worked against all freedom of expression, and hence all artistic activities.

In fact, the situation for the arts became so critical in 1948, that a group of artists, led by painter Paul-Émile Borduas, and members of Les Automatistes, began meetings to discuss the necessity of furthering intellectual and artistic freedom in Quebec. They signed a manifesto called *Refus global* (Total refusal), essentially an anti-establishment and anti-religious document. The group wrote it to challenge Quebec's traditional values (largely controlled by the church) and to refuse any ideology which stifled experimental and creative endeavours, including those in theatre. Because Duplessis' influence was extensive, they were widely condemned in the press.

In spite of the clampdown on artistic freedom, French theatre in Quebec did manage to find its way through, ironically as a result of church patronage. Most French theatre in Canada ended with the Depression during the 1930s, but it was not completely dead, as Jean-Louis Roux explained:

> It started again with Les Compagnons de Saint-Laurent. If you think of the Collège Sainte-Marie putting such importance in the extracurricular activity of theatre, I think that you can say the Church had a pretty important influence on theatre here. Outside of that you have Gratien Gélinas who was on his own, and everything else came either from Sainte-Marie or Les Compagnons de Saint-Laurent.

Les Compagnons de Saint-Laurent (generally known as Les Compagnons) emerged from the Church environment when Father Émile Legault began the theatre as an amateur group, later guiding it into professional status. Its seeds began tentatively in 1937 with student productions at the Collège de Saint-Laurent. Recognizing his great love of theatre, Legault's superiors in the Order of the Holy Cross sent him to France to study the latest stage techniques. While there, he was influenced by the plays of Henri Ghéon and others, but particularly by the theatrical style of French director and manager of the world-renowned Théâtre du Vieux-Colombier in Paris, Jacques Copeau.

On his return to Canada a year later, Legault began Les Compagnons in earnest, putting much of what he had learned into practice on a 150-acre estate at Vaudreuil-Dorion, twenty-five miles outside Montreal. Here, many members of the group lived together. There were small cottages on the grounds for the married actors, and the bachelors lived in a community house. Everything needed for a production, from sets and costumes to the music and choreography, was organized on the estate, which also housed rehearsal halls.

Because he wanted his actors to be free in their approach to performing, Legault focused on improvisation, which was unusual in those years. He also wanted his protegés to know all aspects of the theatre, so he organized classes in stage design, makeup, costumes, dance, music and theatre history.

With the exception of an occasional star, such as Ludmilla Pitoëff, all actors appeared anonymously throughout the early years of Les Compagnons. Because Legault stressed teamwork over personal stardom, the audiences were not told in the programs who was playing each role. Two of those early, anonymous actors were Jean Gascon and Jean-Louis Roux. "Father Legault came to see a performance [in 1939] at Le Collège Sainte-Marie where Jean Gascon and myself were involved," Jean-Louis Roux said. "It was Racine's *Mithridate*. He came backstage and asked me if I would be interested in playing with Les Compagnons de Saint-Laurent. At that time I felt as though God himself had asked me to join him, and I accepted . . . and that is how I started playing semi-professionally."

In the first five or six years, the group focused mostly, as might be expected, on Christian drama, in particular that of Léon Chancerel, Henri Brochet and Henri Ghéon. Ghéon went to see Les Compagnons the year after they began, bringing with him an original play for them to produce. "Ghéon was a very prolific author," Jean-Louis Roux said. "The man was charming and I think was a better novelist than a playwright. He wrote a couple of fairly good novels, which are completely forgotten. His theatre wasn't as strong. . . . Well-fabricated, if I may use that word, but not very interesting. There was another author also, Chancerel, who had started using mime in theatre in France so we began that too."

By the early 1940s, Les Compagnons began doing plays which moved away from religion, and, finally, were completely secular. Molière and Racine were the two playwrights whose works were done most often, and Legault continued to be the driving force behind the theatre. "Father Legault was an animator [leader]," Roux said. He had "the ability to inspire people, attracting people around him, using them, but he really wasn't much of a theatre man."

In 1942 Legault decided the group needed to be performing within Montreal itself, and Les Compagnons settled into Théâtre de L'Ermitage, an eight-hundred-seat theatre. By this time they had developed a loyal following, partly because their productions became more polished, but also because theatrical competition in Montreal at that time was practically non-existent. In 1945 they moved again, renting the Gesù Theatre on Rue de Bleury, which would later be used by both Théâtre du Rideau Vert and Théâtre du Nouveau Monde. It was during the years at the Gesù that Les Compagnons reached the height of its popularity. At the first post-war Dominion Drama Festival in 1947, the theatre won the Bessborough Trophy (they won again in 1951) with Molière's *Le Médecin malgré lui* (The Doctor in Spite of Himself). In the same year they staged their first, and only, Canadian play—*Maluron* by Félix Leclerc.

Audiences for Les Compagnons averaged three thousand for a single play, frequently going much higher when the theatre toured small towns in Ontario and Quebec and later in Boston and New York. By the late 1940s the actors were being paid for their work and the anonymity of the early years was abandoned. They staged five or six plays a year, giving more than 150 performances. Ticket prices were on par with other theatres at the time, from $1.00 to $1.50 each.

In 1947, Les Compagnons launched a financial campaign aimed at buying their own theatre in downtown Montreal. They succeeded and used those funds to buy St.

Thomas Church at the corner of Sherbrooke and de Lorimier Streets. As a result, the estate at Vaudreuil-Dorion had to be sold and the base of operations moved into the city. The communal life that Les Compagnons had known for so long all but ceased to exist. The church itself was renovated into a 450-seat theatre and the nearby presbytery was used to house any actors appearing with them who came from outside Montreal. They christened the new theatre in October 1948 with a French adaptation of Tennessee Williams' *The Glass Menagerie*.

Before the new building even opened, however, Father Legault had his first hint of the problems he might face with his own church about the choice of plays. In the spring of 1948, Les Compagnons staged André Obey's *Le Viol de Lucrèce* (The Rape of Lucrece), which Legault retitled simply *Lucrèce*. As a precaution against controversy, afternoon student showings of the play at the Gesù Theatre were discontinued for the run of the play in Montreal, and there seemed to be no problems with the production. Following a trouble-free presentation in Quebec City, Les Compagnons took their show to Ottawa, where the bishop promptly banned it.

The controversy eventually died down, but from that moment on the Jesuit Fathers began to keep a closer eye on the plays chosen by Father Legault. In the spring of 1948, their own self-censorship created a different sort of problem for Les Compagnons when they presented a play at the Dominion Drama Festival. Adjudicator Robert Speaight was extremely upset with the cutting job done on Jean Anouilh's *Antigone* in the name of religion. A Roman Catholic himself, Speaight nevertheless stated he had no patience with those who tampered with masterpieces. He also deplored all "imbecile" censorship, which he said had no place at the Dominion Drama Festival.

In 1949, Les Compagnons staged Pierre Corneille's *L'Illusion comique* for the Montreal Music and Drama Festival, and at the following year's Festival presented *La Passion de notre Seigneur*, which was written by Legault's brother, Father André Legault. For four years following the opening of their own theatre, Les Compagnons continued to present a wide variety of plays. Productions, however, were becoming more expensive, and the Jesuit Fathers were still picking up the tab, more reluctantly each year. "Les Compagnons were costing money to St. Croix Fathers," Jean-Louis Roux said, "and at one point they said 'that's enough. We're not giving you a cent more.'"

Les Compagnons had always survived because they had secure financial backing from the church. Without that support, it was simply no longer financially feasible for the group to continue. With a production of *L'Honneur de Dieu* (The Honour of God)—also known as *Becket*—by Jean Anouilh, in April 1952, Les Compagnons closed down. In the next year Legault backed another venture called Théâtre Marist, operating out of the Les Compagnons theatre, and in 1953 was responsible for an entertaining and successful production of *Le Bourgeois gentilhomme* for the Montreal Festivals. Following that production, Father Émile Legault returned to his teaching duties within the church and severed all ties with the theatre.

For well over a decade, however, Les Compagnons played an important part in Quebec theatre, staging more than 100 plays and functioning as a springboard for many important French-Canadian actors such as Jean Gascon, Jean-Louis Roux, Georges Groulx, Guy Hoffman, Jean Coutu and Denise and Gilles Pelletier.

⁂

There was another major factor in the end of Les Compagnons and that was the emergence of competing French theatres, with performers such as Gratien Gélinas and groups such as Théâtre du Rideau Vert, L'Équipe and Théâtre du Nouveau Monde. It was the success of the latter's opening that really gave Les Compagnons competition for the French theatregoer's dollar. Théâtre du Nouveau Monde is one of the longest surviving professional theatres in Canadian history and, on the French side, it brought more international recognition to Canada in its first ten years than any other French theatre of any era could hope to. The seeds for it were sown in Les Compagnons de Saint-Laurent and two of its early players, Jean Gascon and Jean-Louis Roux.

Because of the important role they played in post-war French theatre in Quebec, and specifically with Théâtre du Nouveau Monde, it is worth pausing to consider the two men: how they came to the stage and finally joined together to form a power house theatre. Gascon and Roux met at a young age but were not close friends initially because of a two-year age difference. During their adolescence, both attended Le Collège Sainte-Marie where, Roux said, "theatre was a very important extracurricular exercise." They joined Les Compagnons while still attending school and, while with the theatre, met Ludmilla Pitoëff, the French-Russian actress who was invited to Montreal by Father Legault to appear in Paul Claudel's *L'Echange*. "She accepted work with Les Compagnons even though we were only semi-professionals," Roux said. "She was not only a charming lady but she was very simple, and really loved to work with people who loved working in theatre, even if they were not professionals." Pitoëff would have a profound effect in the theatre on both men. "She taught me, she was my school," Roux said. "She taught me how to breathe, how to act, etc. And she taught me how to work, to be more disciplined on the stage."

Because of the war and a daughter living in the United States, Pitoëff stayed in North America for some years before returning to Paris in 1947. While in North America, she set up a theatre company, and Roux appeared with her in Jean Racine's *Phèdre* and *Le Pain dur* by Paul Claudel, both in Montreal.

During the war years both Gascon and Roux were enrolled in medicine at university but still pursued theatre. They entered into a pact. "It started as a joke, in fact," said Roux. "We decided that if one quit university [for the theatre] one day, the other had to follow. One day Jean said, 'That's it, I told my father today that I am quitting medicine.' The war was over at the time so I said, 'Well, now I have to do the same.'"

Jean Gascon had been helped in his decision by Pitoëff, in whose Montreal company he had also performed. Soon after she persuaded him to give the stage his full attention, he received a French government scholarship to study in France and left for Paris in 1946. Gascon's family was supportive of his decision to enter the theatre, as was Roux's. Although Roux had been afraid to tell his father, once he did, his father told him, "You're old enough to know what you are doing." With his family's moral support, Roux then had to find the money to join Gascon in Paris. "My father was a doctor, he had six children that he raised and fed so he wasn't rich enough to send me to Europe. Then a miracle happened. I had an aunt who had a little money and I wrote her that I needed $1,000 and . . . the next Wednesday she was in Montreal and handed me a cheque for $1,000."

Roux and Gascon were in fact part of a wave of French actors in Quebec who went to France for their training. It was an accepted move, and there was no resentment on the part of the acting community who stayed behind, or in the minds of the press. "In those days it would never have entered their minds, as it did enter the English [side's] press minds, that anybody was a traitor by going, it was a necessary step," said Christopher Plummer, who spent some years as part of the early post-war Montreal theatrical scene. "They didn't feel the same way as our English folk did about us going away. Not in the least."

That view would change in the French press by the 1960s but in the early post-war years it was understood that going to France was a natural evolution for an actor. Although many returned, they did not necessarily see that eventuality in their plans when they left Canada. Roux recalled:

> I should explain it a little. All the people of my age who got educated in the classical course were very European-minded, French-minded. During the war we were completely cut off from France and from writers we used to cherish and respect a lot, like André Gide. So immediately when the war ended our first idea, I say "our" because many of us were like that, including Pierre Trudeau, was to go to Europe. My idea when I left Montreal was to go to France and stay there for good. We [Gascon and Roux] were, both of us, very anxious to stay there and to work there.

Roux worked a little with Ludmilla Pitoëff and other groups while in France, but mostly he had his "mind broadened" by attending concerts and plays. Gascon was luckier, appearing with Pitoëff, Compagnie Grenier-Hussenot and Centre Dramatique de l'Ouest. He also studied at l'Ecole du Vieux-Colombier in Paris. The two Montreal friends occasionally worked together and "talked a lot about theatre, and very often discussed the founding of a company." Roux was the first one to return to Canada, although only temporarily. "I came back because I had no money left and it was very difficult to make a living over there," Roux said. "There are many, many talented actors in France."

On his return to Canada in 1949, Roux founded his own group, Le Théâtre d'Essai and directed *Un Fils à tuer* (A Son for the Killing) by Canadian playwright Éloi de Grandmont. The storyline had political overtones Quebecers could understand. The hero, Jean, is born to French parents in New France, but from a young age wants to leave his father's farm for a more exciting life. His father will have no part of it and at the end, when no one can persuade Jean to remain on the land, his father calls him a deserter and, rather than let him go, shoots him. The father is portrayed as stifling the young man's freedom and dreams and so came to represent Duplessis to many Quebecers, just as Jean epitomized those trying to break out of the oppressive atmosphere in the province. Presented at the Gesù Theatre, the cast of *Un Fils à tuer* included Jean Coutu, Robert Gadouas and Jean Duceppe. They were all paid to appear with the company and, added to the other operational costs, this resulted in Roux coming out of the experience "something like $2,500 in debt."

However, "I felt so sad and lonely [in Montreal] that a few months later, having made a little money working for radio, I decided to go back to Paris," Roux said. But when he still had trouble finding work in Paris, he returned home to Canada for good four or five months later. "I said to myself," Roux recalled, "that I would definitely do more important things here [in Canada] than I would ever be able to do in France or in Europe." His Théâtre d'Essai presented its second, and last, production in the spring of 1951. Roux chose to present his own play, *Rose Latulippe*, with a cast of forty-two. Once again, the young actor ended up heavily in debt. It was at this time his old friend Jean Gascon returned to Canada, and the two resumed their lifelong friendship that ended only with the latter's death in 1988. In fact, Gascon's last stage appearance was shortly before his death, starring opposite Roux in Anton Chekhov's *Uncle Vanya*.

They were the perfect pair to undertake the formation of a theatre because they complemented each other so well. Gascon was flamboyant and absent-minded while Roux was intense and meticulous. Roux arrived at meetings ahead of schedule and phoned Gascon to make sure he arrived at all.

Christopher Plummer, who appeared with Gascon and Roux in the 1956 *Henry V* at Stratford, remembered Gascon as "hilarious in the farces, playing all those old men. As a character actor he was extraordinary. Even in later years, as Doctor Caius in *Merry Wives* he was wonderful. He was the most definitive Doctor Caius I'll ever see."

As good an actor as he was, it was really as a director that Gascon made a name for himself. "As a director," Roux said, "he was very good, again probably more brilliant in comedies than in dramas. He knew how to direct an actor. He had authority, a good sense of timing in dramatic situations and he was inspiring, definitely."

Roux was slightly more hot-tempered and sharp-witted but no less passionate about the theatre than Gascon. "Jean-Louis was much more the organizer on the administrative end than Jean, who was sort of the personality of the company," Christopher Plummer said. "Roux was much more introspective than Jean was as a person. There was also a sort of sibling rivalry between the two, they were so close. Like Olivier and Richardson. Great affection but at the same time, trying to juggle for position."

Shortly after both Roux and Gascon returned to Canada in 1951, they met up to discuss their options. Roux remembered:

> When he came back, he was offered by Father Legault to take over the direction of Les Compagnons de Saint-Laurent. But we met with Father Legault and [he didn't want] to retire completely. Since he insisted on having a part in the direction of Les Compagnons, Jean and I decided no, it wasn't what we were looking for. We were looking for a company of our own where we could do what we liked to do. So we decided to found our own company.

The name of the new company, Théâtre du Nouveau Monde (New World Theatre), was chosen for them by playwright Éloi de Grandmont. "There was a newspaper here at one point named Le Nouveau Monde," Roux said. "A very, very backward, rightist, religious paper. But the name was beautiful. It sounded good." The formation of the theatre was announced in July 1951, although their first production was not until October. Those involved included Roux, Jean Gascon and his older brother André, Guy Hoffman, Éloi de Grandmont, Robert Gadouas, Georges Groulx, and the future speaker of the senate during John Diefenbaker's reign as prime minister, Mark Drouin, who would be the pivotal financial resource for the theatre's inception. "Mark Drouin was at that time a very influential Quebec lawyer," Roux said, "very close to Maurice Duplessis but it never had anything to do with our friendship with him. He knew very well, in fact, that we were not on his political side. He became president of our group and he managed to have ten of his friends backing us up at the bank for $500 each."

Five thousand dollars was a substantial sum in 1951. Money also began coming in from subscribers and, in August 1951, the company received official notice of the registration of their name. The phenomenal saga of Le Théâtre du Nouveau Monde had begun. "When we started Nouveau Monde we really didn't have any theories," Roux said. "We were simply aiming to do what we loved to do." Their only two goals were, first, to have a theatre building of their own, and second, to develop their own permanent company of about fifteen players who would work exclusively with them, as

Jean Gascon and Denise Pelletier in a scene from *L'Avare* by Molière, Théâtre du Nouveau Monde's inaugural production in October 1951. (THÉÂTRE DU NOUVEAU MONDE COLLECTION)

most actors in those days moved from theatre to theatre. It took them twenty-one years to acquire the building. While there was a core of actors who continually appeared with the theatre, they were never able to develop a permanent company.

As secretary-general of the company, Roux handled the correspondence, publicity, meeting schedules, etc. He also shared directing duties with Gascon, who focused mainly on the creative side of the theatre. Their inaugural production was *L'Avare* by Molière. The choice to use a work from the famed French playwright was not an accident, Roux explained:

> It was a deliberate move. He [Gascon] had played Harpagon while he was in Rennes with Centre Dramatique de l'Ouest. So that is probably one of the reasons he suggested it as the opening play for Théâtre du Nouveau Monde. Molière also meant something to us. What we know of him, he definitely wasn't on the left side of, he was very close to the king. You know, Molière is a little to us French-speaking people what Shakespeare is to the English-speaking people. What I mean is that what we know of them both . . . enables us to imagine people like us who were playing, directing, working with their hands in the theatre. You know, very, very human people. We can't imagine the same with Ben Jonson for example or Racine. Racine was a despicable character but what we

> know of Molière makes him so generous, so human. It was a conscious move. Later [Molière] became what we called our mascot so it wasn't for nothing that we started with Molière.

Available theatre buildings were almost non-existent in 1951 and Théâtre du Nouveau Monde spent the first six years operating out of the Gesù Theatre, situated underneath a church connected with Collège Sainte-Marie. The theatre had a seating capacity of twelve hundred but the side seats were so poor that they removed them, ending up with a quite functional nine-hundred-seat theatre. "It was a strange stage," Roux said. "It was about thirty feet wide and it was deep enough, another thirty feet, but it was very, very low. Something like twelve to fifteen feet high. We used to say we were doing theatre scope. It was all on the width. It was a living stage though, and something happened there that very seldom happens elsewhere. The communication with the public was very good. It was living, it was warm, very, very warm."

As was the case with the English theatre in Quebec, the French actors supplemented their income with radio, and later television. This extra income may have given the actors financial support to appear in theatre, but it also meant most rehearsals were difficult to schedule. "Because we were not paid during rehearsals, it forced us to stretch the rehearsal time over many weeks," Roux said. "For the first production of *L'Avare* we rehearsed for something like eight weeks but with people being busy with radio, we actually had to rehearse at night. Sometimes we started at midnight. So that was a main, main difficulty."

*L'Avare* opened in October 1951, with Jean Gascon, Robert Gadouas, Guy Hoffman, Georges Groulx, Ginette Letondal, Gabriel Gascon, Janine Sutto, Jean-Louis Roux and Denise Pelletier in the cast. The critics went wild with praise for the group's first effort. The theatre did nineteen performances of the play at the Gesù in Montreal and then did what they continued to do for many years: they took their show on the road with two showings in Quebec City and three at Ottawa's Little Theatre.

In addition to the quality of their productions, Théâtre du Nouveau Monde developed a reputation for thoroughness and attention to detail. Their set designs were often intricate, with Robert Provost's work in this area being frequently acclaimed. The other three plays that first season were *Un Inspecteur vous demande* (a French version of J.B. Priestley's *An Inspector Calls*), Eugene Labiche's comedy-farce, *Célimare le bienaimé*, and *Maître après Dieu* by Jan de Hartog. More than thirty-three thousand theatre goers saw sixty-six performances of the four plays.

The season was a critical and, even more unbelievably, a financial success for Théâtre du Nouveau Monde. The budget for the four plays had been set at $45,000. "At the end of our first season we had a profit of about $5,000, I think," Roux said. "We sent back all the notes to the people who had signed. One of them returned it to us. All the others took them back." The reason for the profit was that the players took very little out of the company. "We insisted that since we were a professional group, everyone would be paid," Roux said. "But the conditions were very, very poor. I think the general payments were something like $15 a performance, at the top. The director had to act in the play as well, and he used to have a double fee for directing. A designer would be paid a few hundred dollars only. . . . That is why we succeeded in managing with so little money."

In their early years of struggle with Théâtre du Nouveau Monde, Gascon and Roux had a great deal of help from Gascon's older brother, André, who managed the company and kept firm control of the purse strings. He could also be ingenious with his financial management, proving this in court one day. When a theatre gave a performance on a Sunday in Montreal, it was more often than not prosecuted and fined $20 for giving a performance for profit on the Lord's Day. Usually Théâtre du Nouveau Monde would plead guilty and pay the fine, but one day André Gascon startled the judge with a "not guilty" plea. When the judge asked for the reason behind the plea, Gascon told him that on that particular occasion the group had not made a profit. The judge was amused and reduced the fine to $15. André Gascon was obviously good at his job, for only once in its first nine years did the theatre show a loss.

The biggest hit of Nouveau Monde's second season was another Molière play, *Le Tartuffe ou l'Imposteur*, which not only pulled in large audiences (more than twenty thousand) but was also filmed for television. The theatre also produced a radio broadcast of their first-season hit, *L'Avare*. The number of performances of each play varied greatly in the early years and this was due to an unusual, but effective, policy. A play's run was generally decided by the audience. As soon as they began to thin out, Théâtre du Nouveau Monde took the production on a short road tour and, simultaneously, began rehearsals for the next play.

For the first two years of their existence they also operated a theatre school. "It's because we felt that the actors and actresses we were working with lacked training," Roux said, "that we had to teach them practically everything on stage. We decided to open a school, which was well attended. Many people came out of it, like Marc Favreau, Jacques Godin and Monique Miller. . . . Finally we had to close it because it cost money to the theatre. I think we were asking something like $10 a month but many of the young actors and actresses couldn't pay even that and, of course, we were saying, 'stay.' And we were paying our teachers and renting a place, which at the same time was our rehearsal hall." It cost more than $2,000 a year to operate the school and it was an expense the theatre could not absorb in those pre-grant days. After the close of the school, many students continued on with private lessons from Jean Gascon, Jean Dalmain and Georges Groulx.

The 1953–54 season was notable for two productions. The by-now-traditional yearly Molière play was the curiously named *Dom Juan* and it drew more than half the total season's attendance. With Jean Gascon in the lead, the comedy was a tremendous hit and even provided an unscheduled laugh one night. During the action a servant enters on stage and announces to Dom Juan (Gascon) that a veiled woman is outside. A slip of the tongue caused the actor to say violée (violated) instead of voilée (veiled). It was an appropriate remark to make to Dom Juan, however, and it brought the house down.

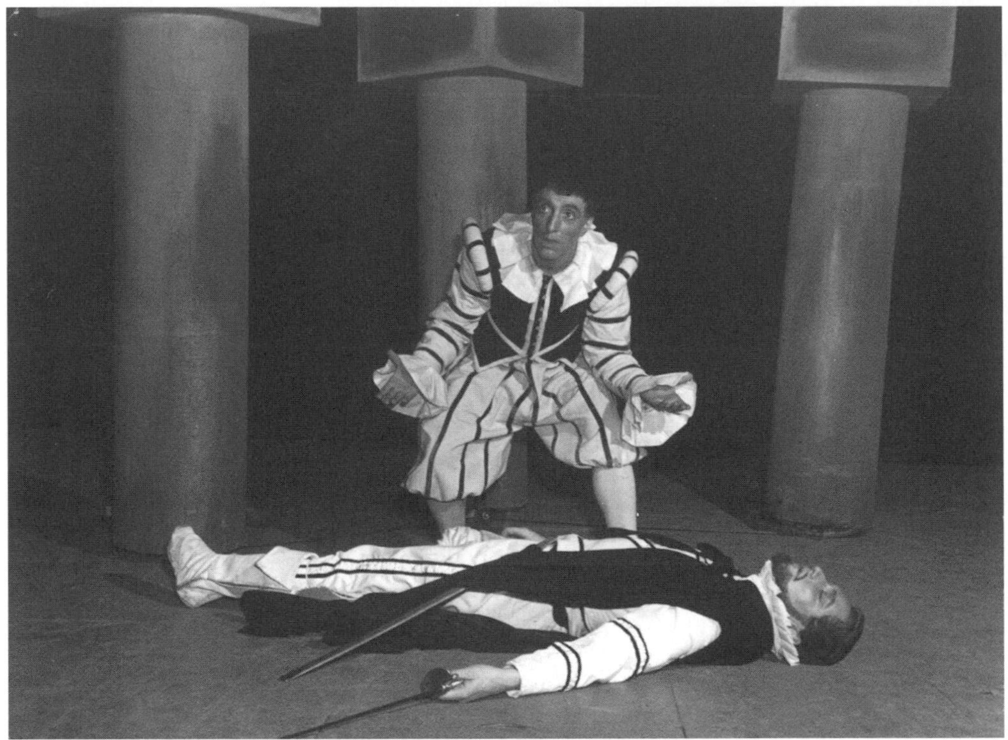

Jean Dalmain, as Sganarelle, and Jean Gascon (lying on the ground) as the lead characters in Molière's curiously named *Dom Juan*. The 1953 production by Théâtre du Nouveau Monde was also directed by Jean Gascon. (THÉÂTRE DU NOUVEAU MONDE COLLECTION)

The second production of note in the fall of 1953 was Théâtre du Nouveau Monde's first foray into English. During the next few years they presented other plays in English, such as Eugene O'Neill's *Long Day's Journey into Night* and *The Trial*, a theatre adaptation of the novel by Franz Kafka, but for their first attempt, they chose *Come Back, Little Sheba* by William Inge. More accurately, it was chosen for them. "Rupert Caplan, who was a radio producer in the English CBC here, was the one who suggested that we should put on English productions," Roux said. "You know at that time the Parti Québécois did not exist and we thought it was a good thing to give such a service to the English community."

Caplan, who directed the production, had approached Jean Gascon with the idea of doing a play in English using a mostly bilingual cast. He saw it as a possible forerunner to having plays at the Théâtre du Nouveau Monde in English and French on alternate nights. The idea never materialized, but *Come Back, Little Sheba* did. The lead role was taken by Lorne Greene; the other major English performer was radio actress Eileen Clifford. The French side was represented by Ginette Letondal and Gilles Pelletier. The 1953–54 season also saw the first Canadian plays to be produced by the theatre—*La Fontaine de Paris* by Éloi de Grandmont and André Langevin's *Une Nuit d'amour*. In addition to Gascon and Roux, the actors who appeared with the group in its third season were Jean Dalmain, Georges Groulx, Monique Miller, Guy Hoffman, Jean-Louis Paris, Denise Pelletier and Jean Duceppe.

Although this history of Canadian theatre generally stops with Stratford's first summer in 1953, it is worth following Nouveau Monde a little further, for over the next few years it brought both the theatre and Canada international acclaim.

The fourth season began with Théâtre du Nouveau Monde's first presentation of the three Molière farces that became the group's trademark. In August 1954, the theatre appeared at the Montreal Festivals with four presentations of *Le Mariage forcé*, *Sganarelle* and *La Jalousie du barbouillé*. The central actor in all three farces was Guy Hoffman. Théâtre du Nouveau Monde repeated the Molière farces for a long run later in the fourth season at the Gesù Theatre and their success was astonishing. So much so that the theatre decided it was time for a bold move and asked to be invited to the Second International Festival of Dramatic Art of the City of Paris in June 1955.

"The reason why we asked is obvious, I think," Roux said. "We needed a little flamboyance and it was a real challenge also. We were very excited about it. We succeeded in being invited." They had the courage to take Molière directly to the French and the results were instant. "It was incredibly successful, in the newspapers at least," Roux continued. "'Molière dépuceler' [Molière deflowered], it was almost a scandal. We were very, very nervous but with the kind of reviews we got, it was so enthusiastic." France had felt that they owned Molière, and here was this upstart French company from Canada having incredible success. Théâtre du Nouveau Monde had set out to conquer Paris and they accomplished their goal. "They were doing things before anybody else was doing them in Canada," Christopher Plummer said. "They weren't ashamed to go to Europe and show the world what Canadians can do."

They had an uphill financial battle to reach Paris. Jean Gascon had been turned down at all government levels for support to take the theatre to Europe. In the end, it was private donations from individuals and businesses, pulled together by Montreal's mayor Jean Drapeau, which permitted the overseas venture to take place. Nevertheless, the theatre still absorbed a net loss of $3,000 as a result of the trip.

Now that Théâtre du Nouveau Monde had international recognition, the next step was to gain further respect at home. This came swiftly the following summer at Stratford, where they not only presented their three Molière farces but some of the group appeared with Christopher Plummer in the main production, *Henry V*. That 1956 summer was extraordinary in the annals of Canadian theatre because it brought together the French and English on the same stage for the first time, in a way that really has not been duplicated in the years since.

When it was decided *Henry V* would be one of the plays performed, the Stratford Festival brain trust came up with the idea of having the French court played by French-speaking actors (speaking English but with their French accents, of course). It was a risk. The words and rhythms of Shakespearean English are hard enough to master even for English-speaking actors; for the French ones it would be enormously difficult. Although all the Nouveau Monde actors, as well as Gratien Gélinas, had accepted in principle, it was not long before doubts began to set in. They met and decided to back out of the deal. However, when they told artistic director Michael Langham their decision, Roux said, "He looked so disappointed that after many discussions we finally made an offer."

They would accept the Festival's invitation to appear in *Henry V*, if they could stage a play in French at some time during the Festival. The result was four showings of the theatre's trademark, the three Molière farces that the theatre had staged in Paris the previous summer. In order to house the Molière presentations, the Avon Theatre, which had been a movie house for thirty years, was put back into use as a theatre. Although it was a cinema, "it was arranged as a theatre," Roux said. "I remember our dressing rooms were exactly where the boxes are now and it was not very well equipped, electrically speaking."

They took the critics and audiences—large sections of whom did not understand French—by storm. Le Théâtre du Nouveau Monde had moulded the farces into a style that was unique and all their own. "Not Comédie-Française style but Théâtre du Nouveau Monde style," said former *Globe and Mail* drama critic Herbert Whittaker. "It was bold and rough and it was funny."

"Their own style . . . was actually closer to Molière's than that of the Comédie-Française," said Christopher Plummer. "They were doing it in the real high farce tradition of that kind of acting, which the Comédie-Française had kind of genteelized to the point of dullness in my opinion. I think they were the best group doing Molière around that time." Plummer not only went to see them at Stratford, but in the fourth presentation of the farces at the Avon Theatre, he actually ended up performing on stage with them. "Jean Gascon and Jean-Louis Roux said, 'Come on, Chris, we have to get you in there as a surprise,'" Plummer remembered. "So I played the old man at the end of the second act, a tiny part. I had the speech which brings down the curtain. The gag worked. Everybody wondered who it was. It was very scary because

Molière is taken at such speed. Even though I do understand French, I had to be pushed on when my cue came because I didn't recognize it." Plummer's impromptu appearance "was very, very funny," Roux remembered.

The entire Stratford company that summer got on well, in spite of the fact that a number of the "stars" of previous years were relegated to bit parts due to the introduction of the French actors. But there were no hurt egos. "Not at all," Roux said. "When Dougie Campbell and Guy Hoffman came face to face, that was something to see, oh boy. One of Stratford's newspapers titled the review 'Hoffman out-Campbells Campbell.' I think we took a lot, one from the other. Generally speaking I think that it would be true to say the French took some discipline and the English some fantasy." Christopher Plummer carried wonderful memories of that summer:

> That [play] was I think the most fun, and the closest I've ever seen or been a part of at least, of Canada really unifying itself and getting together with both the French and English on the same stage. It was wonderful and it should have been much more praised because it was history making. They did really bring on another world you know, and that is what that play was all about. [It was] the French boys getting together [with us] and doing a Canadian play as it should be done. It became a Canadian play, it wasn't Shakespeare any longer. The French in *Henry V* isn't French anyway. It's Shakespeare's, he made that language up. So what the French actors tried to do was improve it a little bit, get it closer to the real thing.

The biggest problem the French actors faced occurred when they left the theatre and were confronted with an anglophone lifestyle. With highly developed palates for food and wine, the actors were horrified at the lack of restaurant fare. Finally they found a solution. Guy Hoffman and Jean-Louis Roux went in together and rented a house, while Jean Gascon and his family moved into another. Food and wine were rushed in from Montreal, and the problem was eliminated, with both houses having large groups for meals every day, often hosting the English contingent.

"[Gascon] really took over the company in a way," Plummer said. "He was a great host, cooked so well. [Their house] was full of people and they were always cooking for the entire company. It was a wonderful French summer we had. Well fed, good booze. We were great pals. It was a perfect sort of marriage of English-Canadian and French-Canadian. One wondered why there had ever been any problems in that department." In fact, they never really discussed the French-English dilemma. "[Gascon] was much too big for that," Plummer continued. "He didn't feel it, neither did I. I never had anyway, even growing up in Montreal. I had so many French friends; it never entered our minds."

The critics were overwhelmingly impressed, not only with Plummer's portrayal of Henry V, but with the artistry of the Quebec actors. "The French-Canadians score on mannered and graceful finesse, the others on their blunt and aggressive approach to Shakespearean English and action," commented the review in *Variety* magazine. Brooks Atkinson of the *New York Times* referred to the "witty, incisive characterizations in the French scenes." Among the French singled out in reviews were Gratien Gélinas, Jean Gascon, Guy Hoffman, Jean-Louis Roux, Georges Groulx and Ginette Letondal, who went on to do well as an actress in France. Perhaps the only dissenting note came when the group, at the end of the summer, took *Henry V* to represent Canada at the Edinburgh Festival. While most of the critics applauded the effort that "put Canada on the cultural map in big block letters," one member of the Scottish press lambasted the actors for their phoney French accents!

Expectations for the future were high all around as a result of that summer. Jean-Louis Roux said they really hoped it would unite the French and English theatres. Gascon was quoted at the time saying he would not be surprised to see French actors appearing in other theatres across Canada. This was a wish that sadly never really came to fruition although Roux firmly believes that without that *Henry V* production, the National Theatre School of Canada would never have been founded in Montreal (1960) with the same amount of enthusiasm and, indeed, might not have been located in Montreal at all.

Prior to the 1957 season, Théâtre du Nouveau Monde moved from the Gesù theatre and rented the Orpheum, a former stock theatre that had been converted into a movie house. Censorship was the main cause for the move. The Gesù Theatre was run by the same religious order that Father Émile Legault belonged to, and they had to approve all the chosen plays, which Roux agreed they had the right to do. The theatre pulled all offensive references out before submitting them but sometimes the Fathers still refused a play. One such play was *The Power and the Glory* by Graham Greene. A few years later the Fathers turned down *The Threepenny Opera* by Bertolt Brecht. They wouldn't give their reasons. At that time, Roux said, "we decided we'd had enough."

Although not ideal, the Orpheum on St. Catherine Street remained their central home for a number of years. They opened the season in their new home with a production of *L'Oeil du peuple* by André Langevin, which was the winner in a playwriting contest inaugurated by Théâtre du Nouveau Monde to encourage French playwrights.

Théâtre du Nouveau Monde had the busiest and most hectic year of its existence in 1958 as it undertook a lengthy tour of two full-length plays and their trademark Molière farces. They stormed New York, Paris, the World's Fair in Brussels and cities all across Canada. They left only successes in their wake as even the most influential critics in New York afforded them high praise. In addition to Roux and Denise and Gilles Pelletier, the casts included many of Canada's finest actors: Guy Hoffman, Jean and Gabriel Gascon, Huguette Oligny, Georges Groulx, Denyse Saint-Pierre, Victor Désy and Jean-Louis Paris. In total, they staged ninety-four performances in twenty cities.

During its early years, Théâtre du Nouveau Monde was very much a male-centered theatre and, while actresses such as Denise Pelletier, Janine Sutto, Huguette Oligny, Ginette Letondal and Denyse Saint-Pierre all appeared in supporting roles, the theatre's management rarely chose plays that spotlighted women. The men who dominated this group more than any of the others were the two old friends, Jean Gascon and Jean-Louis Roux. From Gascon at the beginning of the theatre in 1951 until Roux relinquished the post in 1982, Théâtre du Nouveau Monde knew only two artistic directors—quite an achievement in the changing world of theatre.

The story of Théâtre du Nouveau Monde's later years would fill another book: they survived a fire in 1960; a number of location changes; other tours; a major financial crisis which darkened the theatre for a time in the 1980s; and internal struggles that threatened their very existence. Through it all they continued to be a theatre for the people and celebrated their sixtieth anniversary in 2011.

If Théâtre du Nouveau Monde was largely the domain of the male actor, the female side of French Canadian theatre was admirably represented by Yvette Brind'Amour and her Théâtre du Rideau Vert. While Théâtre du Nouveau Monde garnered much of the publicity through the years, Rideau Vert quietly went about its business, avoiding many of the problems that plagued their counterpart's later years. Much of this was due to Brind'Amour's administrative assistant and friend, Mercedes Palomino, who was by her side from the beginning of the theatre in 1948.

Montreal-born, Brind'Amour was a restless teenager who, at eighteen years of age, "had no idea what [she] wanted to do." In 1936 she answered an ad for the Montreal Repertory Theatre's French section (see Chapter Eleven). In spite of having had no experience, Brind'Amour said she was accepted "because they took everyone, they needed people." She worked with them for four or five years, playing in François Mauriaç's *Asmodée* and Edmond Rostand's *Cyrano de Bergerac* and *L'Aiglon*. She also appeared with the Montreal Repertory Theatre's English division. It was during those years she "caught the bug" and realized how much she loved acting.

In 1940, Brind'Amour began doing radio. She quickly became one of the queens of French radio soap operas, which helped support her theatre work with a new group, L'Équipe, which was run by Pierre Dagenais. It was after this theatre essentially went bankrupt in 1947, that Yvette Brind'Amour followed many of her peers and left for Paris because "the war was over and [I] wanted to experience France."

On the boat going over she met a young Spanish actress-journalist, Mercedes Palomino. Although born in Spain, Palomino was raised in Argentina and was involved with the theatre from the age of five. She studied at the Conservatory of Dramatic Art of Argentina and began a career in journalism and radio, while also keeping up with her acting. Palomino's chance meeting with Brind'Amour as the two headed to Europe proved to be advantageous. In 1948 after Brind'Amour returned to Canada, Palomino, who spoke almost no French, paid a visit to Montreal to write a series of articles on Canada. She never left, becoming the producer of Spanish services for Radio-Canada International.

Meanwhile, Brind'Amour had returned to her lucrative radio career where she starred once again on soaps, some of which lasted twenty years. "I loved working in radio," she once said. With some security in her radio career, Brind'Amour and Palomino started talks in 1948 about staging a play. "We decided to put on a play, just one play," Brind'Amour recalled. They had no clear-cut goals and certainly no great aspirations of starting a permanent theatre. They picked the name "Rideau" (curtain) "because of its association to the theatre" and "Vert" (green) because "it's the colour of spring, of rebirth," Brind'Amour explained.

On November 30, 1948, Théâtre du Rideau Vert was formally organized by the two women who were the guiding lights of the theatre until Brind'Amour's death in 1992. Even after that, Palomino continued to work for many years with Théâtre du Rideau Vert. Once the legalities were completed, the two women needed a play and financial backing. The play they chose was *Les Innocentes*, a French translation of Lillian Hellman's *The Children's Hour*. Written in 1934, it is the story of a neurotic schoolgirl's defamation of two of her teachers with a rumour of lesbianism, and how this accusation affects their community. Brind'Amour said they picked this play "because it had a lot of parts for women. There were only two parts for men." This was done partly to promote the cause of women in the theatre but also because so many of the top male actors from Montreal were in France at this time and there were many talented actresses languishing in the city without any work. This pattern of choosing plays spotlighting women continued through the years. "It was not conscious, but unconsciously I did pick plays that had good parts for women," Brind'Amour said.

Brind'Amour and Palomino approached a group of friends for the money they needed to proceed. The deal was that the theatre would stage an act of *Les Innocentes* for them and if the assembled friends liked it, they would give Théâtre du Rideau Vert the needed money. "They liked it," and gave "about $400." The production was directed by Brind'Amour, with the business and administrative end of the theatre handled by Palomino. They were a good team and this arrangement became permanent. Théâtre du Rideau Vert opened February 17, 1949, at Les Compagnons theatre, which required them to have their plays approved by the Fathers. This never proved to be a problem, in spite of the fact some of their choices were somewhat controversial.

That first production of *Les Innocentes* ran only two nights. In addition to Brind'Amour, the cast included Denise Proulx, Rene Verne, Yvette Thuot and Gaétane Laniel. The play was a hit with the public, and the two women decided this justified a second production. They chose *K.M.X. Labrador* by Jacques Deval. When this also proved a success, the fate of their theatre seemed relatively secure and thoughts of a permanent company more reasonable.

Between 1949 and 1952, the theatre staged eight plays with casts that included Denyse Saint-Pierre, Roger Garceau, Ginette Letondal, Rolland D'Amour, Jean-Louis Paris, Jean Duceppe and Gilles Pelletier. Pelletier, the younger brother of Denise, worked with most of the post-war theatres, from L'Équipe and Les Compagnons, to Théâtre du Nouveau Monde and Théâtre du Rideau Vert. He became one of the stalwarts of Quebec theatre. Jean Duceppe also went on to become a mainstay in Quebec theatre, appearing with most French groups, even starting his own company years down the road.

Brind'Amour herself directed and starred in most of the theatre's productions. Two of the plays, however, were directed by author Loïc Le Gouriadec (also writing under the name of Paul Gury), whom Brind'Amour married in 1950. In fact, the first Canadian play staged by Théâtre du Rideau Vert (in 1950) was *Maire et martyr*, a comedy about municipal life, and it was written by Loïc Le Gouriadec. He was, and continued to be, a large source of support throughout the years. Brind'Amour added that he often gave her suggestions on how to approach a play. Years later, in 1958, he would come to their rescue on stage as well, during their tenth anniversary production of *La Reine morte* by Henry de Montherlant. "The actor playing one of the larger roles became sick and my husband had to learn the role and step in by the next day and he did this," Brind'Amour said, adding that the production of this play was one of her favourites in the history of Rideau Vert.

From the time they opened in 1949 until Théâtre du Nouveau Monde was launched in 1951, Théâtre du Rideau Vert was the only competition Les Compagnons had on the Quebec French theatre scene. The first era of Théâtre du Rideau Vert ended in 1952 with a staging of Jean Anouilh's *Antigone*. "We closed because I just did not have any more money," Brind'Amour said. She had put much of her radio earnings into the theatre and even though they operated on a miniscule budget, with actors often being paid only $3.00 or $4.00 a night, it was still difficult to survive.

It looked like another good theatre was lost, but there was one person who refused to throw in the towel. "Mercedes did not close the doors on the group," Brind'Amour said. They always intended to do another play at some point. That time occurred in 1955 when they decided to stage *Sonnez les matines* by Canadian Félix Leclerc. "He was much loved and we thought a play of his might attract the audiences," Brind'Amour said. They had not planned to do a Canadian play but picked Leclerc because he was so well-loved. The two women were right, as *Sonnez les matines*, directed by Leclerc himself, was their "first financial success." It gave them the confidence to keep going with the theatre.

During the next five years, Théâtre du Rideau Vert staged the majority of their plays at the Anjou, a tiny theatre located above a restaurant. As was the case with Théâtre du Nouveau Monde, Brind'Amour said that in the early years the run of a play was determined by how successful it was with audiences. One production in 1957, *La Magicienne en pantoufles* (a French adaptation of John Van Druten's *Bell, Book and Candle*), played for almost three months. Later plays had a set one-month run.

Once settled in the Anjou, Rideau Vert presented a diet of mostly boulevard plays, a general term for a certain type of French drama from the middle of the 1800s on, which embraced both fast-moving farce and domestic drama. They were strictly for entertainment and not meant to be experimental or too serious. Brind'Amour was criticized for relying too much on this genre, something she was quite defensive about. They did not deliberately set out to pick boulevard plays, she pointed out, only plays with audience appeal, ones that would attract crowds, and these plays did the trick. The validation of their decision was the theatre's success. They did what they had to do in order to survive. The experimental and more serious plays would come later when the foundations were stronger.

In spite of good audiences, the theatre definitely had its struggles in the late 1950s, and at one point Brind'Amour and Palomino considered shutting the theatre down permanently. Their fortunes took a major upswing in 1960, however, when, at the suggestion of Montreal mayor Jean Drapeau, they moved into the Théâtre Stella on St. Denis Street. The four-hundred-seat converted movie house had a private dressing room for Brind'Amour, and six other well-equipped rooms downstairs for the other actors. Rideau Vert purchased the building in 1968.

As with Théâtre du Nouveau Monde, the future exploits of Théâtre du Rideau Vert would fill a book but some highlights must be singled out. The 1960s proved to be profitable for the theatre as it expanded its repertoire to include the classics, and also made an effort to create and present Québécois theatre. In the 1967–68 season they gave the world premiere of Michel Tremblay's subsequently famous play *Les Belles-Soeurs*, an event which did a great deal to cement Théâtre du Rideau Vert's history in Canadian theatre. International acclaim also came in the 1960s when the company travelled to Paris and Italy and went on to become the first Canadian theatre to be seen in Russia. They were greeted warmly and generously in Russia, where Brind'Amour said audiences "were very much trained to go to the theatre" and where the theatres themselves "were large and very beautiful."

Throughout the 1960s the competition between the theatres of Rideau Vert and Nouveau Monde was strong, as it had been throughout the fifties. Brind'Amour felt things were easier for the other theatre because they were men, and they had a number of political connections—the proverbial old boys' network. Years later, Rideau Vert was cited by Arts Councils as having a management that should be a model for all theatre groups, but when Canada Council grants first came into being, Brind'Amour said the powers to be were reluctant to give money to a theatre run by women. "They wondered if we would spend the money shopping," she said.

During the 1950s and '60s, Rideau Vert and Nouveau Monde gave Quebec theatre a solid foundation, although Brind'Amour said she "was much too busy" to realize she was in on the birth of theatre in Montreal. She would have been very proud of the stamp Canada Post issued in 1999 celebrating the Rideau Vert's fiftieth anniversary. The stamp featured the traditional masks of tragedy and comedy, but overtop of them were outlines of the faces of Brind'Amour and Mercedes Palomino. The latter remained the company's administrative director until her death in 2006.

A third French theatre in Quebec, and one that Yvette Brind'Amour had spent many years working with, was L'Équipe, the brainchild of Pierre Dagenais, often referred to in those years as "l'enfant terrible." He was unorthodox, was willing to take risks on the stage, and did not have a high regard for the financial side of theatre. He formed L'Équipe in 1943, but it did not have much structure or financial backing, nor did it have a permanent home. The theatre was loosely composed of leading Québécois actors who played in the productions on mostly a one-shot basis. From the age of eight, Dagenais was interested in acting, appearing early with Father Legault's Les Compagnons de Saint-Laurent. Later he was forced to leave university when the authorities discovered that he was spending most of his time working with radio stations rather than attending classes.

From the time he started L'Équipe, Dagenais was hard to dismiss as an artistic force in Quebec. L'Équipe opened at the Monument-National in Montreal with *Altitude 3200* by Françoise Loranger, and starring Dagenais, Yvette Brind'Amour, Marc Audet and Micheline Loranger (sister of the playwright). Other early productions included *L'Homme qui se donnait la comédie* (a French translation of Emlyn William's *Night Must Fall*) and *Marius* by Marcel Pagnol. In 1945 Dagenais directed an outdoor production of *A Midsummer Night's Dream* in French, presented in the garden behind L'Hermitage building in Montreal. It enhanced the young man's reputation, both on and off stage. Audiences and critics praised all aspects of the show, but rain two nights in a row severely cut into the profits for the show. Dagenais paid his actors with funds earmarked for the outrageous government entertainment taxes of the time, and then calmly went to jail until friends bailed him out.

In the summer of 1946, Dagenais appeared in George Bernard Shaw's *Candida* at Brae Manor Playhouse, and earlier in the year had directed *King Lear* for the Montreal Shakespeare Society, both in English. In December 1946, he directed, in English again, a translation of *Asmodée* for the Montreal Repertory Theatre.

It was, however, the L'Équipe production of Jean-Paul Sartre's *Huis clos* that would bring him the most personal satisfaction. The play had been performed in London, England, as *Vicious Circle*, and in New York as *No Exit*, but for his production, Dagenais stuck with the original French version of the play. It was highly praised by the critics, including Herbert Whittaker who called it "brilliant," and who would later direct a L'Équipe production himself. When a lecture tour brought Jean-Paul Sartre to Montreal later in the year, Dagenais took his cast down to give a private performance for the playwright. It so impressed Sartre that the young French-Canadian was offered a directing assignment in New York, which only a previous commitment to a *King Lear* production prevented him from accepting.

However artistically successful his productions were, Dagenais seemed incapable of showing a box office profit; each year found him further in debt. In 1947 Dagenais staged one of his own plays, *Le Temps de vivre* (Time to Live), organizing a lavish premiere which befitted Broadway. In spite of an opening night which included limousines, fur coats, photographers and a reception, it failed miserably. If L'Équipe had any form or structure before, it now disappeared completely and the group essentially went bankrupt. Nevertheless, Dagenais chose to continue on.

Undaunted by the failure of his first play, he wrote and produced his second, *Le Diable s'en mêle* (The Devil Gets Involved). This time Dagenais was at least cautious enough to take the play on a tryout to Baie-Saint-Paul, Quebec, the actual setting for the play's action. It was based on a Quebec legend about an unlucky sailor who makes a deal with the devil to win a girl away from another man. If, in three days, the angelus bell fails to ring he will know that the girl is his but his soul belongs to the devil. In the end, the bell does ring, so he loses the girl but saves his soul.

The tryout was successful and launched Dagenais into a full-scale production in Montreal with a cast of thirty, including a ballet sequence called the Seven Deadly Sins. Dagenais played the devil, with Mimi Durand and Jean Lajeunesse as the young lovers and Jean Coutu as the rival willing to sell his soul. It was produced as an outdoor production at L'Hermitage. Dagenais built a sixty by forty foot stage, brought in some lighting equipment, and planned a month's run. It succeeded artistically and critically but crowds stayed away in droves and the play closed after twelve performances. Dagenais lost $6,700.

With theatre debts now totalling $17,000, Dagenais turned to the financially lucrative world of radio to bail him out. It was a nightly show called *Faubourg à m'lasse*. Focusing on a poor district in Montreal's East End, the show was written and directed by Dagenais, who also starred in it. Although the nightly radio show solved Dagenais's immediate financial problems, he never again returned to his theatre, L'Équipe.

No discussion of French Canadian theatre in the 1940s and '50s would be complete without considering the role of Gratien Gélinas. For a few years he practically *was* French theatre. At five feet, two inches in height, Gélinas was a small man in stature only. The 1951 Royal Commission on National Development in the Arts, Letters and Sciences stated that Gélinas was "a man of the theatre who with rare vigour combines with equal distinction the qualities of the playwright, the producer and the actor." His efforts in all these areas laid much of the foundation for contemporary theatre in Quebec. In the street urchin Fridolin, Gélinas created one of the most beloved characters of the Canadian stage, and in his first play *Tit-Coq*, he wrote one of Canadian theatre's earliest big hits.

In the mid-1930s the diminutive actor began to do amusing monologues for friends. Then in 1936 at the cabaret *Mon Paris* the seeds of the character Fridolin began germinating in a series of monologues Gélinas created and performed about Le Bon Petit Garçon and Le Mauvais Petit Garçon. That same year, Gélinas had his first chance to present some of these monologues on stage. They were an instant hit.

By all accounts, the character of the irrepressible gamin Fridolin came easily to Gélinas, as did his introduction to radio, where he quickly garnered a following in the French-language soap opera *Le Curé de village* (The Village Priest). After working on the character for more than a year, Gélinas made his radio debut as Fridolin in September 1937, and the actor never looked back. Now that he was successful, artistically and financially, Gélinas had a decision to make. With the encouragement of his wife (former amateur and radio actress Simone Lalonde), he quit his steady job at an insurance company, and in 1938 *Les Fridolinades*, the stage revue, was born.

His Fridolin radio show, *Le Carrousel de la gaîté* (later called *Le Train de plaisir*), continued to increase in popularity, so much so, that the radio station issued statements warning the public about the other fake Fridolins being heard on the airwaves. Sponsored by brewery companies, the show was very lucrative for Gélinas, who was paid $400 a week. By 1941 the actor was so busy doing both radio and the Fridolin revues that something had to give. Radio lost as Gélinas gave himself completely to the theatre.

He chose the Monument-National as the venue for the revues. Built in 1893–94, it was a huge theatre with more than a thousand seats, yet it had good acoustics and was able to create a feeling of intimacy in spite of its size. It hosted many important performances through the years and was eventually taken over by the National Theatre School. Gélinas first opened at the Monument-National on March 8, 1938. The revues were a mixture of mime, song, dance, musical comedy, romantic vignettes and scenes of everyday habits and trends, with a heavy dose of satire thrown in. They offered comments on all aspects of the contemporary scene.

The revues always revolved around Fridolin, who aged from fourteen upwards. Culled from the European meaning of the word—"a little underdog type of man"—

Gratien Gélinas on stage as his famous character, Fridolin, the street urchin. He developed the character on radio and then performed it successfully on stage for many years. (BIBLIOTHÈQUE ET ARCHIVES CANADA / E000001332)

Fridolin was a phenomenon easy to understand. Much as the New Play Society's *Spring Thaw* would do a decade later in Toronto, the character gave French Quebecers a chance to look at, and laugh at, themselves. Gélinas, now using Fridolin as his stage name, dressed in short pants held up by suspenders, with a slingshot sticking out of his back pocket. He also wore a mended Les Canadiens hockey team sweater, a cloth cap, and frequently a mischievous grin, as he pulled up a chair, sat down and talked to the audience in a dialect that was distinctly their own. He would talk of the events that had transpired since he last appeared before them, one moment sending them into hysterics of laughter and the next tugging on their heartstrings.

The boy Fridolin would peep over the wall into the convent garden, accidentally break a storekeeper's window or suffer through his own birthday everyone had forgotten. An older Fridolin announced that he was sending Ottawa his own design for a Canadian flag and produced a model of it for the audience. It showed a cat and a dog standing on their hind legs, paws in the air.

Although he stayed away from an affiliation with any political party (he felt this was necessary in order to show the absurdities of all sides), politics still provided Gélinas with endless fodder for the monologues. In one show, the fourteen-year-old Fridolin wrapped his legs around his chair, took a bite from the often-present apple, and announced he had formed a new party: the Flop Populaire. This was a direct hit against The Bloc Populaire, a federal and Quebec provincial movement set up in 1942 (it dissolved in 1949) as a reaction to the removal of the ban on conscription for military services overseas. The joke travelled like wildfire through the city of Montreal.

The war brought endless new material for Fridolin, who said that in wartime "you have to laugh or die." His was a world of propaganda, censorship, chocolate bars without any chocolate and matches you could buy only if you returned the old ones! No subject escaped the barbs of Fridolin who was not, even in the highly religious environment of Montreal, above attacking the weaknesses in the way people practised their religion.

Gélinas' revues also contained skits, in which Gélinas played other roles. These were fast-paced and, like the monologues, ranged from the humorous to the poignant. One told of the life of a poet whose writing was stifled by the Quebec environment and, so, became a notary. The climax showed Gélinas portraying the dried-up old notary facing his God, who was decidedly unhappy with the man's choice. Some of the vignettes were slightly risqué with double entendres that sent the audience into convulsions of laughter. Many were centred on the effects of war in the workplace and at home. One wartime woman, married a year and already with a small baby, will not let her husband touch her until he buys her a washing machine. He tries to explain they are not making them at the moment, to which his wife responds: "Well, if their factories are closed, so is mine." A sign in a manufacturing plant populated with females, proclaimed "Young women, lose anything you want but not the war."

In yet another wartime skit, Gélinas played the part of a man who manages miraculously to flag down a taxi, rarely available in wartime, but the driver feels like going north rather than in the direction the man wanted, so the client has to go north too—and be grateful for it. Frequently the skits involved the little man battling the rest of the world. Who could not identify with the characters always on the losing side, never quite realizing their ambitions, and resigned in life to being easily dismissed by others?

Although Fridolin's monologues (and hence Gélinas') were the focal point, he brought in many talented French actors to share the skits with him. A nucleus of performers stayed with him year after year. Fred Barry helped direct, and the actors included Yvette Brind'Amour, Juliette Béliveau, Juliette Huot, Olivette Thibault and Amanda Alarie.

During the summers Gélinas closed down the revues and retreated with his wife and six children to Oka, Quebec, where he regenerated and prepared for the following year. The number of revues grew each year. In 1938 there were only eleven shows but by 1946 there were performances for at least eight months of the year. More than one hundred and fifty thousand people saw them each year, while they grossed $125,000. When attendance fell below 90 percent, Gélinas closed down the revue for that year, usually sometime in June during the later years.

In 1946 Gélinas felt it was time for graduation from the revues, worrying that staleness would creep into the material if he continued with them. He had also been involved in a venture the previous year, which may have influenced his decision. A New York producer, Eddie Dowling, wanted to translate a Hungarian play he owned into a French-Canadian setting. A scout sent to Montreal looking for actors with a true accent found Gélinas.

He needed persuading. Broadway seemed a long way off to Gélinas, who felt a strong sense of loyalty to both Quebec and Canada. Dowling was persistent, though, and when the Broadway-bound *St. Lazare's Pharmacy* had its premiere in Montreal, Gélinas was co-starring in it with Miriam Hopkins. Not many were happy with Hopkins or the play in general, but Gélinas garnered rave notices for his double portrayal of a father and son. The production went on to Chicago with the same poor result and never made it to New York.

He returned to Montreal and staged the 1946 revue, his last. One of the skits, *Le Retour du conscrit*, served as the inspiration for a project that consumed many of the coming years for Gélinas—*Tit-Coq*. In the skit, the gamin Fridolin is a bewildered conscript returning from war to find he has lost his girl to the munitions worker who stayed home and made money while he was off fighting. Gélinas took the bare bones of this and spent a year and a half fashioning a full-length play, *Tit-Coq (The Little Rooster)*, out of it.

The title character, Tit-Coq, is illegitimate and has grown up lonely and in institutions. By the time the play opens, Tit-Coq is a bitter and angry soldier in the Canadian Army. His illegitimacy runs as a theme throughout the play, although it seems to mean more to Tit-Coq that he is a bastard than it does to the other characters. In the plot, an army buddy takes him home for Christmas where Tit-Coq sees the warmth and love in family life for the first time, and falls in love with his friend's sister, Marie-Ange. He goes overseas for two years and returns to find his love has been pressured into marriage with a man she does not love.

If the play had an inherent weakness it is that the audience was only shown briefly the pressures which caused Marie-Ange to forsake a man she genuinely loved. After re-declaring her love for the returning Tit-Coq, she tentatively agrees to leave her husband. However, the priest steps in to point out that in Catholic Canada, where divorce is not allowed, if they do run away together, then the children would be bastards. In effect, Tit-Coq would be condemning them to the same uncertainty and demons that he has had to fight his whole life. This is too much for him to bear, so he leaves, and Marie-Ange returns to her loveless marriage and empty life.

The play had fifteen scenes in three acts and opened May 22, 1948, at the Monument-National. The stage settings were done by Jacques Pelletier and costumes by Laure Cabana. Co-directed and starred in by Gélinas and Fred Barry, the play's cast also included Clement Latour, Christopher Ellis, Armande Alarie, Juliette Huot, Juliette Béliveau, and Muriel Guilbaut as MarieAnge. Following a summer break, *Tit-Coq* moved into the Gesù Theatre where its two-hundredth performance took place May 22, 1949. More than two hundred thousand people saw the production, which grossed $400,000.

Not satisfied, Gélinas decided to translate the play into English, with a large portion of the French cast remaining. Christopher Ellis, who portrayed the priest, died suddenly and was replaced by experienced stage and radio actor Jacques Auger. There were two other major cast changes, the first being Denise Pelletier, who took over the role of Germaine, the cousin of Marie-Ange. The second change Gélinas made was adding Huguette Oligny in the pivotal role of Marie-Ange. Oligny had worked with many of the French theatres in Montreal and during the Second World War did dubbing for New York and Hollywood film companies. A number of years after his wife's 1967 death, Gélinas married Oligny.

For the English version of *Tit-Coq*, the title was changed to *Ti-Coq*, so there would be no embarrassing mispronunciations of *Tit-Coq* in English circles. Gélinas opened *Ti-Coq* in Montreal, and the play was just as warmly greeted in English as it had been in French. As a result, the author found himself being pressured to take it to Broadway. Still unsure, Gélinas decided on a tryout in Toronto to see if an audience outside Quebec would appreciate the play. Toronto audiences went wild at the play's opening in January 1951. All eight performances at the Royal Alexandra Theatre were sold out in advance, and on opening night the cast had more than ten curtain calls. The word had spread that *Ti-Coq* was a hit, something Canadians could take much pride in. That fact is important as it set the stage for the production's trip to Chicago, where it was not completely successful, and to Broadway where it was an unmitigated disaster. *Ti-Coq* closed there after three performances.

There were many possible reasons why it failed in New York, but the most probable was the play's ending. With the usual scenario of the 1950s being boy meets girl, boy loses girl and boy wins girl back, the fact that *Ti-Coq* walks away from Marie-Ange at the end, in spite of their love for each other, did not sit well with American audiences. Before heading to the United States, Gélinas said that acceptance or rejection of *Ti-Coq* would rest squarely on people's personal attitudes towards the ending. He also realized that it was necessary to view the play in the Catholic-Quebec environment in which it was set. The moment American audiences tried to relate it to their own lives, *Ti-Coq* was doomed.

One interesting aspect of the whole venture was the reaction of Canadians as *Ti-Coq* limped home. People in Canada exploded with deep indignation. They were furious at the treatment *Ti-Coq* had received in Chicago and New York. Angry editorials were written, and many supporters threatened to boycott every American production appearing in Canada. The significance of *Ti-Coq* cannot be overstated as it achieved a success in Canada unequalled before. Even after its trip to Broadway, the play still continued to sell out in Canada and broke every existing box office record with 480 performances. *Tit-Coq* was also made into a movie in 1952.

Gélinas could have retired at this point and still been assured of his place in Canadian theatre history, but his career was just moving into second gear. He went on to write three more plays and form his own theatre, La Comèdie-Canadienne in 1957.

For many people, the modern era of professional theatre in Quebec really began with Gratien Gélinas and his *Tit-Coq* in 1948, but in fact it had evolved from an amateur tradition that was as polished as any professional one. That tradition began with Les Compagnons de Saint-Laurent, which straddled the amateur and professional ranks by paying its actors in the later years, even if the amounts were small. L'Équipe, Théâtre du Rideau Vert, Théâtre du Nouveau Monde all contributed to create a solid and unbroken chain of professional theatre in Quebec.

CHAPTER THIRTEEN

# THE EARLE GREY PLAYERS & STRATFORD

"I think Stratford was not only a good thing for this country, I think it was absolutely essential for this country. Absolutely essential."

—WILLIAM HUTT

It may have seemed to many of those inside the magnificent Stratford tent on that humid July 13 in 1953 that, as Alec Guinness playing Richard III spoke of "the winter of our discontent," theatre had finally been born in Canada. The truth was it was much more a coming of age than a birth. Without all the post-war struggles to bring professionalism to Canadian theatre, there would have been no Stratford, no cast of Canadian actors to make up the bulk of the company that trod the boards so tentatively that first summer. Of the sixty-five players, only four were not Canadian by birth, upbringing or training. The other sixty-one had all struggled by for many years on little money and under theatre conditions that simply would not be accepted decades later. They did it for love of the theatre, because most were compelled to do it, and because some dreamed that it would one day bring them to a place in time such as Stratford.

While the arrival of Stratford was a momentous occasion in the history of theatre in Canada, and while it certainly went on to become the theatre most synonymous with the playwright, it is sometimes forgotten that there were other earlier successful post-war Canadian theatres that focused solely on Shakespeare's plays. In fact, it was these theatres that showed Stratford there was an audience for Shakespeare in Canada.

There are four Shakespeare theatres in particular that deserve mention. The first was the Shakespeare Society of Montreal, a highly thought of amateur theatre connected with the Montreal Repertory theatre. Among those that worked there were Herbert Whittaker, Christopher Plummer, Leo Ciceri, John Colicos and Pierre Dagenais. The second company has already been considered (see Chapter Eleven): Rosanna Seaborn's Open Air Playhouse, which treated Montrealers to out-of-doors Shakespeare productions for four summers.

The third effort was also in Montreal and is worthy of inclusion if only for the fact it chose to present a Shakespeare play at the same time theatre-goers were filing into Stratford's tent for the first summer. The Montreal Festivals, which celebrated all areas of the arts with art showings and musical and dramatic presentations around the city, had expanded from a couple of concerts in 1936 to a month-long extravaganza in 1953. The Festival committee that year chose *King Lear* and was lucky enough to secure John Colicos, who had recently made quite a name for himself playing Lear for the Old Vic Company in England.

Herbert Whittaker designed the sets. He commented, "I think the peak of my salaries as a designer in Montreal was $1,000 to design a one-night production of *King Lear*." The production took place on a stage built on the terrace at the Chalet on the mountain. Almost 5,000 attended that one-night presentation of *King Lear*.

The last and the most impressive of the pre-Stratford Shakespeare efforts was the Earle Grey Players. They began many years prior to Stratford and continued on simultaneously for many more years alongside its more famous relative. The Earle Grey Players began tentatively in 1946 with two performances of one play, and within a few years the theatre was presenting a summer Shakespearean Festival of three plays.

Earle Grey and his wife, actress Mary Godwin, came to Canada in 1939 as members of a touring British company and decided to stay in North America. Godwin remained in Canada while her husband, who had worked with many major theatres in England, toured the United States before they settled in Toronto. While strolling one evening, the couple came across the Trinity College buildings at the University of Toronto and decided the outdoor quadrangle made a perfect location to perform Shakespeare. At the end of the Second World War, Grey began a search for available actors. He also obtained the ongoing support of Dr. R. Seeley, provost of Trinity College.

The two performances of their opening play, *Twelfth Night*, took place in the quadrangle on June 4 and 5, 1946. Tickets were $1.00 and the cast included Earle Grey, Mary Godwin, Marjorie Leete, Vernon Chapman, Vincent Tovell, Dorothy Jane Goulding and Robert Christie. Original music in the Elizabethan genre was written for the production. The show was such a hit that two repeat performances were given in September.

"It was lovely," Vernon Chapman said of playing outdoors. "That quadrangle has now been completed on the north side but at that time it was open. There was a raised grass area where people sat . . . summer students were looking out the windows. It was kind of fun. I don't think the calibre of production was all that great but it was the only real Shakespeare game in town."

The following year, 1947, saw the group give five performances of *A Midsummer Night's Dream*, which was also staged twice in October at the Art Gallery of Ontario, a schedule that would be followed with other plays in the future. They also began the high school presentations for which Earle Grey became well known, as he tried to stimulate a love of Shakespeare in the minds of the young. In 1948 they ran six nights with *The Taming of the Shrew*, starring Robert Christie as Petruchio. "I think we had one rehearsal," said Don Harron who had a small role in the production. "I played it like Danny Kaye. I had no other alternative with no rehearsals."

The theatre continued to perform in the outdoor quadrangle. If it rained, productions moved into the adjacent Strachan Hall, although this was done reluctantly, for the hall was not conducive to Shakespeare. Playing in the quadrangle was often a challenge, especially on nights when the symphony orchestra was playing not far away. "It was fine except we had to fight the orchestra," actor Peter Sturgess said. "It was a very funny experience in some ways. Everyone seemed to accept this blast coming 350 yards away and it echoed there naturally anyway. The audience accepted it. They knew it was there but wanted to see some Shakespeare."

In the 1948–49 winter season the group continued to perform scenes from Shakespeare in various schools around Toronto and also appeared for the first time at Queen's University, in their first non-Shakespeare play. With a cast including Sam Payne, they presented Sophocles' *Antigone*. The play had been reworked for radio by Lister Sinclair. When Earle Grey heard the Lister production, he decided to re-adapt it for the stage.

By 1949 Grey felt confident about the company and wanted to start something with a "permanent" status. To this end, the First Open Air Toronto Shakespearean Festival was set up under the sponsorship of Grey and Godwin. Because they wanted to establish an aura of professionalism for the company, the theatre's objectives were drafted and brought to the attention of city council and tourist associations. The Festival survived entirely on ticket sales and the founder's money.

From June 27 to July 16, 1949, the Players presented *As You Like It*, *A Midsummer*

*Night's Dream* and *Twelfth Night* in the first Festival, opened by the lieutenant governor of Ontario, Ray Lawson. The public was really beginning to take notice of the theatre, as were admiring critics, and the calibre of the acting improved each year as well-known actors began to fill the ranks. The casts in the Festival's first year included John Drainie, Margot Christie, William Hutt, Jonathon White and Dorothy Jane Goulding.

One of the Festival's most interesting innovations, and certainly the most popular, was the free Elizabethan concerts. On three Sunday nights during the Festival, sixteenth-century cadences were heard as the strains of the treble viol, harpsichord and viola-da-gamba drifted through the candle-lit hall at Trinity College. In keeping with the Festival's spirit, the musicians tried as often as possible to use authentic Elizabethan instruments. The songs Shakespeare knew, the music he loved, lived again. Accompanying the concerts, lectures on Elizabethan music and social background were given by experts such as Northrop Frye.

In 1950, increasing interest extended the second year of the Festival to four weeks as more and more visitors, many from the United States, ventured into the quadrangle to see the productions. *The Tempest*, *The Taming of the Shrew*, *A Midsummer Night's Dream* and *Twelfth Night* were the plays in what would be the only four-play season in the Earle Grey Players' history. Tickets were still a reasonable $1.25 each and the concerts free to those who had a ticket to one of the plays. The casts were also the most illustrious in the group's history, with Lorne Greene coming in to star as Petruchio in *The Taming of the Shrew* opposite Mary Godwin as Kate. Others appearing were John Drainie, Jonathon White, Alice Mather, Jo Hutchings and Paul Kligman.

In spite of those impressive actors, the Players lost at least one fan. In his own publication, *The Critic*, Nathan Cohen complained that "Mr. Grey's productions were a distinct disappointment. Having come to expect important things from him, I was not prepared for the motley, discordant, sometimes-vulgarized representations he sponsored on this occasion. Unsatisfactory casting was the main problem."

Cohen's views notwithstanding, the crowds enjoyed the productions and the actors were grateful for the classical experience, even if remunerations were small. "We did *The Tempest* and I played Stephano, the drunken butler, with John Drainie playing Caliban," Paul Kligman said. "I think we got $25 apiece for doing that. It was a big joke, let's put it that way."

For each of the next two summers, the Earle Grey Players staged three Shakespeare plays. The high reputation the Festival had achieved was shown in 1951 when they received a gift of a cutting from the mulberry tree that grew in Shakespeare's garden in Stratford-on-Avon, England. It was given by trustees of the playwright's birthplace and planted in the Trinity College quadrangle by the High Commissioner for the United Kingdom as "a symbol of the growth in Canada of a new awareness of the value of Shakespeare."

Grey was delighted when Stratford opened with a flourish in 1953. It was too far away from Toronto to be competition for his players, and he felt it fostered a wider interest in Shakespeare. There were some unforeseen drawbacks, however. More than once a Toronto visitor would ask a taxi driver to be taken to the Festival (meaning Grey's) only to be told by some helpful but uninformed individual that it was a couple of hours away in a town called Stratford. Earle Grey's five-week-long 1953 Festival in Toronto staged *Much Ado about Nothing*, *The Winter's Tale* and *As You Like It*. Perhaps inspired by Stratford, Earle Grey built a new stage in 1954, set up against one wall of Trinity College. Using the surrounding architecture as an extension of it, the stage had a large trap door and ten entrances on three levels. The Players continued to stage the Festival every year, presenting three plays in the quadrangle.

By 1957, with bills now totalling more than $20,000 a year, Earle Grey realized something had to be done, and so the Festival Company became a foundation, incorporated under Ontario's laws as an educational and non-profit organization. They received grants from the Metropolitan Council of Toronto ($5,000), the Atkinson Foundation ($5,000) and the Ontario Department of Education ($2,000) with Canada Council matching those amounts. It is with more than a little irony that, after finally becoming a foundation and obtaining financial support for the first time in their history, the Earle Grey Players would fold at the end of the 1958 season—for reasons not related to money. With the death of their staunch supporter, the provost at Trinity College, the theatre lost its home. Additions to Trinity College, and the loss of rentals to summer students because of the noise from the Festival, led the University of Toronto to stop making the quadrangle available to Earle Grey.

In spite of an intense search, Grey was not able to find an alternative theatre space, and the oldest Shakespeare Festival on the North American continent came to an end. In total, the Earle Grey Players provided entertainment for thirteen seasons with *Macbeth*, *Twelfth Night*, *The Merchant of Venice* and *As You Like It* proving the most popular with audiences. Earle Grey was disappointed with the way things turned out but was certainly not bitter. Both he and his wife left the country in 1960 but, while they had lived in Canada, Grey had spent seven years as President of the Association of Radio Artists and, as a legacy, ACTRA (Alliance of Canadian Cinema, Television and Radio Artists) set up an award in his name, given for lifetime achievement.

While Grey's theatre may have been the first in Canada to mount an entire festival devoted to Shakespeare, Stratford created a permanent home for one. The conception for such a festival had begun as an idealistic glimmer in the mind of a young boy lying on the grass in the park that would one day house the Festival Theatre in Stratford, Ontario. Listening to music coming from the band shell, he envisaged Shakespeare

As a young man, Tom Patterson dreamed of bringing a professional theatre to his hometown of Stratford. Many thought the idea foolish; he had the last laugh. (STRATFORD SHAKESPEARE FESTIVAL ARCHIVES)

being played there, outdoors, surrounded by crowds of people. As Tom Patterson matured, the vision never quite left him. The town of Stratford had been hit hard by the Depression, and Patterson hoped to find a way to help his town survive. His dream never wavered, not even through his five years of overseas service in the Second World War. On his return to Stratford in 1945 he continued to think about the idea even as he went off to the University of Toronto. After graduating in 1948, he went on to work for Maclean-Hunter's *Civic Administration* magazine.

In the spring of 1951 the seemingly impossible idea really began to take shape while Patterson was covering a convention in Winnipeg and found himself talking over old times with Stratford's mayor. He brought up his Shakespeare idea, and the mayor was enthusiastic enough to make Patterson believe that his idea might take off.

The slight, balding and spectacled man was gregarious but other than that certainly did not look the part of the person who was going to bring Canadian theatre full blast into international prominence. Patterson looked more comfortable in a library than a theatre. Vernon Chapman recalled the man:

> Tom Patterson's fear at that time was that other people would get hold of the idea and steal it from him. [He] knew absolutely nothing about theatre. His great asset, outside of the fact that he was a very charming person, is that he had a tremendous ability to make people want to help him. Absolutely incredible. You thought, "This guy is genuine, he's got an idea that's worth encouraging," so all sorts of people would help and give him information.

Patterson had more than sincerity going for him. He was now in the publishing business with Maclean-Hunter. He not only had many contacts; he knew how to use them. After receiving tentative verbal support from as many important names as possible, he began phoning people in January 1952 and finally had his first official meeting with Stratford's City Council. Having told them he was sure Sir Laurence Olivier would be interested in coming, he then asked them for $100 to go down to New York City and approach Olivier in person. One member of the council decided it was not enough and voted to give him $125.

The New York trip was a complete disaster. Although he tried hard to see Olivier, Patterson was unable to get any further than his secretary, who gave him only a formal expression of interest from the actor. Olivier was unbelievably busy appearing in both *Antony and Cleopatra* and *Caesar and Cleopatra* while directing a third play at the same time. It is doubtful he even knew of the existence of Patterson, much less cared.

Stratford's saviour would have to be someone else, and that someone else turned out to be the man who really gave Olivier his beginnings in Shakespeare, Tyrone Guthrie. In the mid-1930s when Olivier joined the Old Vic under the directorship of Guthrie, the only Shakespeare he had done was a much talked about John Gielgud production of *Romeo and Juliet* in which he and Gielgud had alternated the parts of Romeo and Mercutio. Under Guthrie, Olivier would come into prominence as a Shakespearean actor of the highest rank, but it was Guthrie who came to Canada's aid years later, not Olivier.

Patterson could not have foreseen this on that New York trip when, in desperation, he took his meagre press-clipping scrapbook to both the Carnegie and Rockefeller Foundations. The former turned him down flat, but he was able to get a vague promise to "consider it" from the Rockefeller Foundation, although it was obvious they really had no interest in the idea. Deciding that no one needed to know this fact, Patterson made sure that this vague promise appeared as news in the local Stratford paper. It was picked up by Canadian Press and went nationwide where it generated much publicity. The City Council was satisfied its money had been well spent, and a committee was set up to organize a Shakespeare Festival in Stratford.

It was at this point that one of the most important catalysts for the Festival arrived on the scene. On the recommendation of her son Mavor, Tom Patterson went to see Dora Mavor Moore to tell her of his dream. It would be Moore who was to change his focus from obtaining a "name" star to first finding a quality director. Moore knew just the person, she said, and his name was Tyrone (Tony) Guthrie. She then got the ball rolling by contacting John Coulter, a Canadian playwright living in England, and he told Guthrie of the Stratford proposal. When the message was relayed back that the world-renowned director was indeed interested, Moore called Patterson to her office and they phoned Guthrie, who was in Ireland. A long letter followed from Patterson to Guthrie and a return one from him.

One of Guthrie's main motives for taking an interest, it seemed, was that he wanted to influence the design of the stage, which was, of course, neither designed nor built yet. Guthrie was hoping for a return to the more intimate stage that Shakespeare intended. He agreed to come out for a visit and mentioned the question of remuneration for such a trip. Another call to Ireland was made by Patterson to solidify the visit. The question of Guthrie's fee arose again and in spite of the fact he had been given no authority, Patterson offered him $500. For a minute or two there was silence on the line and then Guthrie said it would be fine. It was not until the director arrived that Patterson discovered that the telephone line had gone dead at the moment he uttered the amount and Guthrie never knew what he was to be paid. It says a great deal for the man that he came anyway.

Guthrie's visit was to be in July 1952 and this precipitated another crisis: money to pay the man had to be raised immediately. Fortunately, Patterson discovered that he was no longer alone in this venture. While the Festival was his brainchild, the burden for its success no longer rested solely on his shoulders. Dr. Harry Showalter, chairman of the committee, called people on the phone and quickly had the $500 in cash.

The day after Guthrie's arrival in Toronto he was driven to Stratford to meet with the committee. He was surprised by the group's youth, but impressed with their honesty about their lack of theatre knowledge. He made it clear to them that he would not be involved with anything designed solely to bring money and tourists into Stratford. They would, he cautioned them, have to find a lot of money that first year with little hope of recouping it. But he also assured them that if they wanted to produce the finest Shakespeare in the world and give Canada something to be proud of, then he was with them all the way.

When the committee decided to back him completely, the Festival took another giant step towards reality. The two biggest decisions to be made during that initial visit were the type of theatre to be built and its location. Guthrie saw the park that would eventually hold the theatre, and although he had never advocated outdoor Shakespeare, he was almost swayed by the beautiful setting around him. He decided, however, he did not want to compete in the open air with noisy birds, playing children and distant train whistles, and so opted for an indoor structure. Little did he realize that the company would deal with all these problems anyway. Moreover, with the unbearable heat the group endured inside the tent that summer, Guthrie probably wished for the open air.

Following the visit to Stratford, the committee went back to Toronto, and now Guthrie's interest turned to tents. Melody Fair operated out of the Dufferin Park Racetrack grounds in West Toronto so he was taken to a performance, which, reportedly, did not impress him. The tent did, however, and after examining it from all angles, Guthrie declared it was just what was needed. He also made a visit to the Straw Hat Players in Muskoka and another visit to Peterborough to see his friend Robertson Davies, where he took in a production by the summer theatre there.

Both these excursions were valuable the following spring when Guthrie began to assemble a company of Canadian actors. He had further talks in Toronto with Dora and her son Mavor Moore. The location and type of theatre having now been chosen, Guthrie turned his attention to the next crucial step. He told Patterson the design of the stage was critical and recommended Tanya Moiseiwitsch. Patterson had not given this aspect of the venture even a brief thought and gratefully accepted Guthrie's suggestion.

At a last meeting with the committee before returning to England, Guthrie laid out all the decisions that had been made and finished by urging them to send someone to England to sign up a "star." He proposed Alec Guinness, adding that someone would have to sign him up, and that they could not count on him to do it for them. Although Guthrie made it clear that he wanted the Stratford Festival to be totally Canadian, he knew that at first the public needed a big name to attract them to the remote location. It was important to return to the idea that had first sent Patterson to New York in search of Olivier, and would now take him to London.

Before he embarked on his search in late summer 1952, Patterson discussed for the first time with Dora Mavor Moore the subject of financing. Initially they settled on $15,000, but in their discussions it became clear they needed advice. They went to the agent for J. Arthur Rank in Canada, not only for that guidance but also because Alec Guinness was under contract to Rank in London. Told they had grossly underestimated and should be thinking more in the region of $75,000, they were eventually guaranteed the last $15,000 of this from the Rank company itself. It was also suggested that if Patterson wanted Guinness, he should go to England and speak to the actor in person.

While on his way to see Guinness, Patterson stopped off in Scotland to visit with

Guthrie who, true to his earlier statement, stayed out of the initial negotiation with Guinness, which he felt was the business end of the Festival and not his responsibility. The meeting with Guinness was not an easy one, but the actor listened politely to the plan for two plays, with six weeks rehearsal and four weeks playing time. He did not quibble over the salary of $3,500 but was still not convinced he should accept.

Patterson then suggested he talk to Guthrie, and this is when Guthrie did step in and push Guinness in favour of the Festival. At this point there was a disagreement between the director and Guinness over the choice of plays, a disagreement so serious that Guinness temporarily backed out of the deal. Patterson, however, was able to soothe ruffled feathers and restore calm to the proceedings. At the core of the fight was the fact that Guinness did not agree with Guthrie's choice of *Hamlet* as the "star" vehicle. Guinness felt he had nothing new to give to the interpretation of the role he had played on the British stage in a trouble-plagued, modern dress production, directed by Guthrie himself. They finally settled on *Richard III* as the right play for Guinness.

Next in line for persuasion was Tanya Moiseiwitsch. This took a scant few minutes. She would plan and design a stage for Shakespeare to be played on as the playwright intended and she would have much input from Guthrie. Moiseiwitsch, who became designer of not only the stage but also most of the costumes for that first season and many after, was one of the leading designers of English theatre. Her father was well-known pianist Benno Moiseiwitsch.

After graduation from art school she had begun work as a scene-painting student at the Old Vic Theatre in London and then spent a year as an apprentice to a scene designer. This was followed by three years as a designer with the Abbey Theatre in Dublin. Back in England she moved around until hired by Guthrie at the Liverpool Old Vic and subsequently the Old Vic in London. The last play Moiseiwitsch worked on just prior to Canada's Stratford was the Old Vic's coronation production of *Henry VIII*, directed by Guthrie. Queen Elizabeth and her husband attended the opening night performance of this production, and the new monarch remarked on the beautiful costumes.

Now that Moiseiwitsch was signed up, Patterson (with Guthrie's help once again) was able to attract one more crucial person to the Stratford venture. Cecil Clarke was well known to Guthrie and became the assistant director and production manager. He had spent seven years in the latter capacity at the Old Vic and was known in theatrical circles as a top lighting expert. Clarke was a key acquisition, for he was the one who arrived in Canada first to do the advance work. Most of the responsibility during the first year of production fell on his shoulders, and Patterson has acknowledged that the Festival could not have been put together without him.

Another event took place during Patterson's trip to Britain, but it was one he was mostly oblivious to at the time. It involved the Stratford Council and the issue of payment for Patterson's trip. Vernon Chapman recalls what happened:

> Patterson was given a grant by either the Chamber of Commerce of Stratford or the City Council, to investigate this [Festival] further. He went to England and through Rank was introduced to Alec Guinness. While he was over there, I was in the office at the time, Mrs. Moore got a phone call from Mr. Showalter in Stratford saying "disaster, they've changed their minds, they are not going to come up with the money after all." And here was Tom Patterson in England talking to these people. Mrs. Moore got on the phone and said, "If necessary we'll . . . find the money for him, we'll pay for the cost of the trip at any rate." She sent Patterson a wire saying "all rumours to the contrary, go ahead."

Once the trip was over and Patterson was back in Stratford having signed up an incredible package of talent from the British theatre, the skeptics began to disappear, although the money problems were far from over.

Guthrie's next visit to Canada, which took place at the beginning of December 1952, was mainly for the recruitment of the Canadian actors. By this time word had begun to filter through the acting community that Stratford was not just a rumour with no substance. "I never dreamed of anything like Stratford really happening," said Amelia Hall, who appeared in both plays that first season. "Even in 1952 when I read about this man Tom Patterson, I thought he must be crazy. Rich and crazy I thought—going to lose his shirt."

She was not alone in her thoughts. William Hutt at first did not believe the whole venture was real. "I must confess," Hutt said, "at that time I didn't even know where Stratford was except that it was in Ontario. The rumour was that it was in Western Ontario. That's how vague it all was and I must say a lot of us simply giggled up our sleeves and said, 'who is this idiot Tom Patterson who wants to start a Shakespearean Festival in Stratford, Ontario — wherever the hell that is.'"

Hutt went on through the years to become the actor most associated with Stratford; he missed appearing there only a few times from that initial 1953 season until his death in 2007. Hutt had been planning a return to Stratford in that year but had to turn it down because of his health. It was a performance with the Canadian Repertory Theatre that led to an invitation from Tony Guthrie to join the company, Hutt recalled, although he added that he sensed Guthrie was not "overwhelmed" with his performance:

> One afternoon we were doing the *Three Sisters*. I wasn't very happy with my performance because I didn't understand Chekhov then. Millie Hall said that Tyrone Guthrie was coming to see the show that afternoon, and anyone who wanted to talk to him about going to the Stratford Festival, he would meet with them. I walked into the room afterwards and to my astonishment there was Tom Patterson, this little man who I remembered being at university the same time I was there. Some of the people [at university] were elected to sort of take us new boys around. The chap who took me around was Tom Patterson. . . . He was pleasant, affable, showed me everything and was a good conversationalist.

Amelia Hall and Tony Guthrie sitting amidst the tent's construction at Stratford in 1953. Hall and Judith Guthrie (right) were dressed up for a reception to promote the season. (AMELIA HALL COLLECTION)

In fact, Hutt was so surprised to see Patterson that he virtually ignored Guthrie, who did, however, briefly ask him if he was interested in Stratford. "I said yes without a moment's hesitation," Hutt said. "I had heard rumours about Guthrie possibly being involved, and now that the man was asking me, I knew I'd be a bloody fool to say no, not to get involved with a man of that stature."

In addition to Hutt, Guthrie saw and talked with more than three hundred actors. An invitation to Stratford was greatly coveted by members of the acting community and some came to Toronto from far away to obtain an interview with Guthrie. The director attended as many productions as possible to assess available talent. He had a good memory for performances and names, and recalled his visits to theatres the previous summer. One actor chosen because of such a visit was Peter Mews. "We [Peterborough Summer Theatre] were playing *The Ghost Train* and Tony came to stay with Robertson Davies, and he actually came and saw part of the production," Mews said. "A year later when I called Guthrie to see about the possibility of going to Stratford, he remembered me. Name and all. It was remarkable."

There were no actual auditions because Guthrie did not believe they were an accurate measure of anyone's ability. He chose actors mostly from performances he saw and then followed that up with a meeting. Most of these were brief and to the point.

"I went upstairs and walked in," Eric House recalled of his meeting with the director. "Guthrie stood up and kept going up and up. He was reputedly 6'4" but I think he was taller than that. He said, 'How nice to see you. Do sit down. Saw you in *The Importance of Being Earnest*, thought you were wonderful. Would you like to join us?' I said yes and he said, 'Fine. Will you go and see Cecil Clarke and he will arrange the financial side. Thank you. So pleased you are going to be with us.' That was the entire meeting."

All the Toronto interviews took place at the New Play Society offices, courtesy of Dora Mavor Moore. Vernon Chapman remembered listening in on many of those interviews:

> [Stratford] didn't have much money so they shared our office for a while. When Guthrie came up to interview people I was there to welcome him. We put him in the studio in the back. He didn't like it back there after the first couple of interviews because it overlooked the railroad, so we had another little reception area outside our offices and gave Guthrie that.

Chapman added, "I could hear everything that was said and boy, oh boy, it was a revelation to hear what people said they had done when they hadn't."

The financial arrangement for the actors varied, ranging from $1,000 to $2,000 for the members of the Canadian contingent. Eric House received $1,000 for the season (which turned out to be twelve weeks), Amelia Hall $90 a week, and Peter Mews $100. The Equity minimum in New York City at that time was $75 a week.

Betty Leighton remembered being paid very well. "I can tell you exactly how much I was paid," she said. "It was $50 more than Don Harron. He was very cross. What happened was that I had a contract and they had made a mistake. They had written $1,800 in one place and $50 more in another. So I called Cecil Clarke and said, 'which one of these am I to take?' He said, 'well as we've made the mistake, make it the larger.' Well, some time later Don and I were talking about it and it transpired we both had contracts for $1,800 but I got the fifty extra. Anyway I was quite pleased with it. I would have gone there for nothing. I would have lived on air pie." Peter Mews concurred. "I think most of us would have gone for half the price."

The main reason for all this enthusiasm was Tyrone Guthrie. The great-grandson of Irish actor Tyrone Power, Guthrie was born in Ireland in 1900, and by 1924 he had made his first stage appearance in England. "He tried to be an actor," Peter Mews said. "He said himself that he wasn't a terribly good one. He could figure things out mentally but he couldn't actually project them himself and that is why he turned to directing. He was also so tall that in a play he just stood out like the proverbial sore thumb. But it was wonderful that all that energy he had went into his ideas of how to do a production."

It would not take long for Guthrie to move from acting to directing; from 1926 on he worked with companies in Scotland, Cambridge and London until he became the resident producer-director of London's Old Vic and Sadler's Wells companies (1933–47). Guthrie was not a stranger to Canada when he visited in 1952. He had come in 1931 to direct a series of radio plays, *The Romance of Canada*, and at that time met Dora Mavor Moore and Rupert Caplan. Guthrie would rely on those two people for advice on which actors to hire all those years later when he began the paring down process looking for actors—although it was rumoured he and Moore had quite a falling out when he refused to accept an actor she particularly wanted to see in the Festival.

There was no doubt that Guthrie was the decision maker. He was also the person who made the whole venture real. "Suddenly the theatrical community in this country had a leader in Tony Guthrie and it had a focus," William Hutt said. "Of all the theatrical activities that have ever taken place since I can remember, Stratford certainly created, even before it opened, the greatest amount of interest, if for no other reason than it seemed like such a bizarre scheme." Bizarre or not, Guthrie now had his long list of actors to work with, some already signed up. Tom Patterson was named the first full-time employee of the newly established Stratford Shakespearean Festival of Canada Foundation.

There was another aspect of the Festival that was now coming into the spotlight: the stage. Working with Guthrie, Tanya Moiseiwitsch was able to design and build a scale model of the stage just in time for the director to bring it with him on the December visit. The structure of the stage generated a great deal of interest and was one of the unique parts of the Festival. Its seeds came from a Guthrie production of *Ane Pleasant Satyre of the Thrie Estaitis*, done for the Edinburgh Festival (1948). The play was to be staged in the Assembly Hall and, because Guthrie was not allowed to remove the moderator's chair, he built a platform right over it, creating many steep stairs and forcing the actors to climb up and down them. It also required the actors to make their entrances down the aisles. He loved the results, and when it came time for Stratford's stage to be designed Guthrie turned the idea over to Moiseiwitsch. The stage also originated from Guthrie's desire to recapture the functional aspects of the Elizabethan stage itself and to foster intimacy between actors and audience.

The Stratford stage was an adaptation of the thrust stage of Shakespeare's time. At the back, a small balcony jutted out over the stage and was supported by five pillars. The entrances were through aisles coming from under the audience, from the back of the stage and directly out onto the balcony, all making for swift action and fast scene changes. The audience was on circular tiers of seats around three sides of the stage, the furthest seat being only slightly more than fifty feet away. It was a totally open stage. Gone were the obstacles of an orchestra pit and footlights. And, of course, there was no curtain.

Architect Robert Fairfield also played a large role, as he drew up the plans for the

A clear view of the Stratford stage with the tent poised above it and surrounded by the auditorium. It shows the intimacy of the thrust stage with the seats close to the stage.
(STRATFORD SHAKESPEARE FESTIVAL ARCHIVES)

construction of Moiseiwitsch's stage and also the auditorium. Moiseiwitsch called Fairfield a saint. "Everything that Guthrie and I asked for, Robert Fairfield interpreted and brought to life."[21]

While Guthrie was in Canada displaying Moiseiwitsch's scale model of the stage, she was back in England designing the costumes for both Stratford's first season and Guthrie's Old Vic production of *Henry VIII*. When January 1953 arrived it was decided the play to accompany *Richard III* would be *All's Well That Ends Well*. The comedy was rarely performed anywhere at this time and was chosen partly because it would not only be new to audiences but to Guthrie himself. It also provided a contrast to the bleak *Richard III* and enabled Guinness to melt more into the background and let other members of the company share the season's spotlight. "We [the actors] knew the shows were going to be good," Amelia Hall said. "We were a little bit doubtful about the choice of *All's Well That Ends Well*. We thought that was a poor choice. It turned out to be the smash hit."

In February it was announced that Irene Worth had been signed in England as the female "star" of the Festival. The other two non-Canadians were also named, Douglas

Campbell and Michael Bates. Slowly the names of Canadians chosen for the Festival began to filter out. The majority of those picked had performed in one or more of the Canadian post-war theatres. The final Festival cast lists for the two productions, containing sixty-five actors in total, were as follows:

RICHARD III

Richard, Duke of Gloucester, afterwards King Richard III — Alec Guinness
George, Duke of Clarence — Lloyd Bochner
Sir Robert Brackenbury — William Hutt
Lord Hastings — Douglas Campbell
Lady Anne, Widow of Edward of Lancaster, afterward married to Richard — Amelia Hall
Tressel — Bruce Scott
Berkeley — Neil Carson
Earl Rivers — Norman Roland
Sir Thomas Vaughan — Richard Easton
Lord Grey — Alex Smith
Marquis of Dorset — Douglas Rain
Elizabeth, Queen to King Edward IV — Betty Leighton
Duke of Buckingham — Robert Christie
Earl of Derby — George Alexander
Margaret, Widow of Henry VI — Irene Worth
Catesby — Timothy Findley
1st Murderer — William Needles
2nd Murderer — Eric House
King Edward IV — Edward Holmes
The Bishop of Ely — Eric Atkinson
Duchess of York, Mother to King Edward IV, Clarence and Richard — Eleanor Stuart
Richard, Duke of York, son to King Edward IV — Tony Rotherham
Edward, Prince of Wales, son to King Edward IV — Garrick Hagon
Lord Mayor of London — Michael Bates
Cardinal Bourchier, Archbishop of Canterbury — Peter Mews
A Messenger — Roland Bull
Ratcliffe — Robert Robinson
Lovell — Donald Harron
A Scrivener — Eric House
A Page — Jim Colbeck
Tyrrell — Douglas Rain
1st Messenger — Roland Bull
2nd Messenger — Jonathon White
3rd Messenger — Harold Burke
4th Messenger — Neil Carson
Sir Christopher Urswick, A Priest — Eric House
Henry, Earl of Richmond, afterwards King Henry VII — Robert Goodier
Sir Walter Herbert — Bruce Swerdfager
Earl of Oxford — Peter Mews
Captain Blunt — William Hutt
Duke of Norfolk — William Needles
George Stanley, son of Earl of Derby — Neil Vipond
Aldermen, Men at Arms, Monks and Priests — Roland Bull, Harold Burke, Neil Carson, Vincent Edward, Morris Fine, William Glenn, Don Gollan, Peter Harcourt, John Hayward, John Jeffery, Alex Jeffories, Jim Jorgensen, Eugene Jousse, Ron Knowles, Drew Lennox, Jim Manser, Newman O'Leary, Kenneth Pauli, Bruce Scott, Dan Slote, Graham Stratford, Neil Vipond, Jonathon White, Beverley Wilson.

ALL'S WELL THAT ENDS WELL

The King of France — Alec Guinness
The Countess of Rossillion — Eleanor Stuart
Bertram, her son — Donald Harron
Helena, her ward — Irene Worth
Parolles, Attendant on Bertram — Douglas Campbell
Lafeu, an old Courtier — Michael Bates
Ministers of State at the Court of France — Robert Christie, Eric Atkinson, William Hutt, Bruce Swerdfager
The Duke of Florence — George Alexander
Longaville — Lloyd Bochner
Dumain — Robert Goodier
Two Officers — Timothy Findley, Robert Robinson
Rinaldo, Butler to the Countess — William Needles
Morgan, A Soldier in the Florentine Army — Eric House
Another Soldier — Peter Mews
A Widow, resident in Florence — Amelia Hall
Diana, her daughter — Beatrice Lennard
Neighbours of the Widow — Betty Leighton, Leone Kastner, Jo Hutchings, Marionne Johnston, Ann Corke
A Gentleman, encountered by Helena in Marseilles — Norman Roland
Ladies, Officers, Gentlemen and Footmen at the Court of France — Wendy Aitken, Ann Corke, Dawn Greenhalgh, Jo Hutchings, Marionne Johnston, Shirley Jordan, Leone Kastner, Rosamund Merivale, Kathleen Roland, Norma Turner, Joan Watts, Lynn Wilson, Roland Bull, Neil Carson, Richard Easton, Vincent Edward, John Hayward, Edward Holmes, John Jeffery, Eugene Jousse, Douglas Rain, Bruce Scott, Dan Slote, Alex Smith, Graham Stratford and Neil Vipond.

The one Canadian actor most conspicuous by his absence was Christopher Plummer, who had spent the previous six or seven years making a name for himself in Canada, Bermuda and in a U.S. tour of *Nina* with Edward Everett Horton. Along the way, however, he had ruffled a few feathers, and Rupert Caplan, one of those advising Guthrie, was definitely not a fan of Plummer. In addition, as Plummer freely admits, "I wasn't particularly disciplined in those days. I was leading a rather wild life."

If he needed vindication, Plummer received it in Stratford's 1956 season, which he said was "the turning point in my career." It was the first year the Festival had not brought in a star from England and a lot rested on his shoulders. The *Henry V* production that summer was a massive success, and Plummer's lead role in it brought numerous glowing reviews. Brooks Atkinson of the *New York Times* exclaimed: "Christopher Plummer emerges as a Shakespearean actor of first rank [who] has stepped over the threshold of a career that can turn out to be as gratifying for us as for him." Back in 1953, however, future laurels could not be seen by Plummer when the young actor was not among those invited to Stratford. "I was [disappointed]," recalled Plummer. "I was also quite angry. I tried to ask Don [Harron] if he would put in a good word for me—because I had not been asked." All pleas fell on deaf ears.

As spring 1953 came into bloom, Cecil Clarke arrived to begin the final push. He brought with him Tanya Moiseiwitsch's costume designs for both plays. *Richard III* would be more traditional while *All's Well That Ends Well* would be more modern, closer to the turn of the twentieth century. As a designer, Moiseiwitsch had always been known for her effective use of colour. In *Richard III*, bright hues stood out against a background of black and greys. When Richard ascended the throne, for example, Moiseiwitsch had him enter in a gigantic robe of crimson.

Cecil Clarke also brought along another valuable member of the team, his wife Jacqueline Cundall. She was the principal property designer for the Old Vic Theatre in London from 1949 to 1952. At Stratford, Cundall was responsible for finding or making all properties needed for both productions. She had seven assistants to help her construct the armour, jewellery, weapons, and even a corpse. Ingenuity was called for on more than one occasion. Discarded electrical cord was twisted and painted to make necklaces. When a toilet in the building housing the property department broke down, the float in it was retrieved and worked on until it was appropriately turned into Richard III's orb of office. The only props not actually made from scratch were the swords that came from England, and the giant bell whose ringing began the performance each night.

With Dora Mavor Moore's assistance, a wardrobe department was set up in the New Play Society's rehearsal premises and Ray Diffen was hired as the head costume cutter. The main concern about costumes was the question of footwear. Some boots were coming from England but sandals were desperately needed. Cecil Clarke's habit of walking the streets in search of any stores that could supply needed goods paid off when he found a craftsman at the Snugfit Shoe Store who agreed to take on the challenge of making footwear fit to walk a Shakespeare stage.

On the management side, The Stratford Shakespearean Festival of Canada Foundation and its president Harry Showalter were beginning to have serious cash flow problems. By this time they had set their budget at a more reasonable $150,000. A local campaign to raise capital had gone well but efforts outside Stratford had been nothing short of a disaster. The City of Stratford itself also contributed $5,000 and another $500 came from Ontario's Department of Education. Ticket prices were set from $1.00 to $6.00, which equalled the highest ticket prices in New York at the time; advance sales at the box office were brisk but the problem was immediate, available cash. The tent, being made in Chicago, would cost $15,000, and they were told it had to be paid for prior to delivery.

In the midst of all this apprehension, Harry Showalter took up a shovel on April 15, 1953, and broke the first sod for the new theatre, which would stand on two acres of land provided jointly by the province of Ontario and the Parks Board of Stratford. Notwithstanding the sod-turning, the financial crisis was building, and in May a chilling call was put in to Guthrie overseas. It was suggested to the director that perhaps the Festival should be delayed a year. Guthrie's response was swift. He felt a postponement would be absolutely fatal, that it would be better to abandon the plan entirely. He asked that the decision be made quickly because Alec Guinness was due to sail shortly from England.

The company in Chicago had stopped work on the tent until payment in advance was made in full, and this escalated the financial urgency of the situation. Cecil Clarke and another board member flew to Chicago on a Friday where they were told to have the money by Monday if they wanted work on the tent to continue. Back in Ontario, Clarke went to Ottawa to talk about the Festival and lay out the seriousness of the financial situation. He received an anonymous gift while there that would carry them past the tent crisis.

Unknown to most at the time, the gift actually came from none other than the governor-general of Canada and the man responsible for the report that would ultimately lead to the formation of the Canada Council, Vincent Massey. In addition to having the money kept strictly confidential, which at the time it was, he had one more condition. "We just made it by the skin of our teeth," said Peter Mews, "and with the help of Vincent Massey who donated from his own pocket with the agreement that we perform at least one night of each play because they still weren't sure about opening at all."

But the financial stranglehold was not over yet as the number of outstanding bills kept growing. Miraculously a bank manager (without authorization) came through with a loan, as did a local insurance company. Finally, Cecil Clarke was able to assure Guthrie it was full steam ahead.

When Guthrie arrived he found the concrete structure and stage almost complete although the tent to provide the covering was still nowhere to be seen. One of the most reassuring acts of faith during the time of financial strife was that Oliver Gaffney of the Gaffney Construction Company kept on building the theatre even though payments to him were in arrears by $14,000. He was one of the many unsung heroes in Stratford's story, those people without whose faith the Festival never would have opened on time, if at all.

Advance ticket sales had extended the length of the Festival; it was now due to run from July 13 to August 15, with the two plays to run on alternate nights and both being performed on Saturdays so patrons could watch one in the afternoon and come back for the other in the evening. Rehearsals were due to start for *Richard III* on June 1st and the following day for *All's Well That Ends Well*, but since there was still no tent, a makeshift stage was set up in a long wooden barn with a corrugated iron roof.

One actor still had his doubts about what was to come. "As we dumped our bikes into the dust outside the barn up there in the fairgrounds," Timothy Findley wrote, "we couldn't help wondering just what would happen when we actually started to perform Shakespeare's plays in Stratford, Ontario, in a tent that did not yet exist. Was it to be a circus? Who could tell?"[22] At that moment the "circus" included a flock of birds nesting in the roof of the barn, with their eggs and other treasures repeatedly dropping on the actors and their scripts. "The swallows used to dive-bomb us all the time," remembered Betty Leighton.

Nevertheless, the actors were finally coming together, getting to know each other and renewing old friendships. More than 80 percent of the post-war theatres were represented among the actors appearing in that first year and they became a very close-knit group. "We shared things," Leighton recalled. "We ate together a lot and we had birthday parties for people, and it was one great big family. The chemistry was right. And the time was right."

Everyone helped everyone else. One actress who gave a great deal to the younger actors was Eleanor Stuart, and she was rewarded in a very warm way. Twenty-five of her cast members joined together to buy Stuart the elegant corded silk gown which she wore as the Countess of Rousillon in *All's Well That Ends Well* and which had been designed by Tanya Moiseiwitsch. It was their way of thanking her for the help she gave them in voice production and dramatic coaching during the summer.

Although his reputation preceded him, the opening rehearsals were the first glimpse most of the actors had of Tony Guthrie at work, and they were in awe of him. "Do you know that Guthrie knew everybody by their first name at the first rehearsal," Betty Leighton said. "He made it his business to do that. He was a great man. Not only a great director but a great man."

Peter Mews was most affected by Guthrie's enthusiasm and "press-on-regardless" attitude, while Eric House said the man "was like a God to me. He was just the person I was looking for at that point in my career." William Hutt explained why he loved working with Guthrie:

> He had a marvellous way of freeing one on stage, and he had a huge personality. Extraordinarily inventive, impetuous and I don't mean foolhardy but he was very fond of improvisation, particularly if it came from the artists themselves. He was very open to suggestions. It is ultimately why Tony's productions began to, after running for three quarters of the season, slightly to fall apart at the seams. I don't mean to fall apart completely but they got a little looser simply because they were conceived with a lot of improvisation and freedom but nonetheless he knew how to handle actors. It's been said, and I think with a certain amount of justification, that actually Tony preferred working with inexperienced young people, if not in fact, gross amateurs, because he could make them look good. It has also been said, on the other side of the coin, he didn't really like working with major stars because they were, as it were, competition.

As Hutt indicates, Guthrie was not without flaws as a director, and he generally had a scapegoat or two among the actors. He once told Don Harron that he did not know how he had come so far with so little. He was also well-known for his eccentricity. Even on especially hot rehearsal days he wore woollen bathing trunks that invariably kept falling down in spite of having a white belt, so he was constantly hoisting them up. "Over them, he wore a transparent plastic raincoat and blue running shoes with the laces undone. He was a spectacle indeed."[23]

Whatever eccentricities Guthrie might have had, most of the actors did not dispute his genius. He taught them a great deal as he helped them believe in themselves and make Shakespeare their own. As Robert Christie explained: "We were fascinated because we thought that we might be able to achieve, and Guthrie said as much, a kind of attitude about classic theatre that would be intensely our own. . . . Guthrie gave us a feeling of nationalism. He gave us self-respect, which was a remarkable thing."[24] As stated earlier by William Hutt, Guthrie liked to work with less-experienced actors but he also learned a great deal himself from the young Canadians' raw and fresh approach to Shakespeare. And they certainly learned from him.

"He was a giant in every way," said Amelia Hall, "and he had a great gift of making you feel you were his equal, that you were just as intelligent as he was. He never talked down. Mind you, he could pick on somebody. That first year it was Bob Christie, he always seemed to be in trouble, but I found him marvellous to work with. You wanted to go to rehearsals just to hear what he would say. He always rehearsed at the top of his voice. Whatever he said you could hear it throughout the theatre. He had such wit and such rhythm, he never wasted time."

Hall was also impressed with everyone else connected with Stratford, from the top down. It was the most wonderful summer, she recalled:

> I seemed to walk without my feet touching the ground the whole time. I was enormously impressed by the discipline because that is what I had been going on about to the young actors. The way they ran the fittings for instance. If you were having a fitting for your costume or your wig, nobody else was allowed in that room or near except the designer and the cutter and the person making the costume. There was no rude interrupting. I mean there was a great English sense of what was right, what was proper. You were treated as if you were somebody. The courtesy and charm of everybody that came over from England. And Cecil Clarke was so quiet and efficient.

The rehearsals continued in the shed where the acoustics were terrible and the heat even worse. The tent had still not appeared, and before it did, the worst rainfall and flooding Stratford had seen in thirty years descended on the town, setting up panic in Festival organizers, but the hot sun soon came and dried out the site.

An aerial view of the tent, constructed in 1953 as the showcase for the Stratford Festival. More than 66,000 sat under it to watch *Richard III* and *All's Well That Ends Well.* (STRATFORD SHAKESPEARE FESTIVAL ARCHIVES)

It was just prior to the tent's arrival that one of the Festival's more colourful characters showed up. Skip Manley was a tent master from Chicago with thirty years of experience. Once the Festival began he frequently slept in the tent, which he referred to as "she," and was known to use ants to predict the weather. Wearing his ever-present panama hat tied with a pink and gold ribbon, this eccentric quickly became a local favourite. He could be seen scrambling over the canvas with his needle and twine, repairing tears caused by the weather.

Manley was there and waiting on June 28 when the gigantic fireproof tent was ready to go up. It weighed more than three tons and needed four eighty-foot poles moored into position with steel wire to hold it. Except for the Ringling Brothers' circus big top, it was the largest theatrical tent in the West. The interior walls were maroon with gold entrance drapes and the ceiling inside was a smoky deep blue. It took most of the day for the canvas to be erected, with almost half the town watching.

This was a positive sign because not all the townspeople had been in favour of the Festival. Realizing that the Stratford populace was uncertain about the effects of the Festival on their town, the organizers had earlier that month, in a wise public relations move, invited the residents to a large reception to meet the cast, a meeting that did much to allay local fears.

With the tent up finally, the town behind them and only two weeks to opening night, rehearsals moved into the theatre proper, and the company faced a whole new set of nightmares, not the least of which was that no one could be heard. "Guthrie nearly went mad," Peter Mews said. "He was running around saying, even to Alec Guinness, 'I cannot hear you when your back's to me.'"

In addition, most of the company had never played on a thrust stage before and were accustomed only to the forward projection needed on a proscenium stage. Even accepting that premise, however, the acoustics were quite simply a disaster. After considerable debate, and with only a few days left until the opening, Guthrie decided the problem was the concrete and that it needed to be covered. Contractor Oliver Gaffney rounded up as many tarpaulins as he could and these were laid over the concrete. This brought about an immediate improvement, but something had to be found to replace the tarps, which were not a permanent solution. This turned out to be coconut matting. A large supply was rounded up and the concrete covered with it. When all the seats were installed on top of this, the result was a phenomenal improvement although there continued to be some acoustic problems until the new permanent theatre was finished in 1957. The tent was expected to hold approximately 1,800 patrons. By opening day half the seats for the five-week season were already sold so more seats were fitted into the theatre, which eventually held closer to 2,000.

Opening night was fast approaching as the actors prepared to make history. Some prepared more elaborately than others. "The whole week before we opened I had a breakfast which consisted, to the alarm of my lovely landlady, of only coffee and a raw egg beaten up in lemon juice because I was afraid of putting on weight," Amelia Hall said.

"I think we knew before we opened that it was very obviously going to be successful," William Hutt said of the anticipation as the day drew closer. "That is to say, people were going to be admiring of the productions, admiring of the performances and admiring of the idea. I don't think we were quite prepared for the explosion it made in the theatrical picture of this entire continent, and it did."

Finally July 13, 1953, the night Herbert Whittaker called "the most exciting night in the history of Canadian theatre" had arrived. It was unbelievably hot as the cars rolled up to the theatre. The distinguished audience included the Stratford Festival's number one patron, Governor-General Vincent Massey. Church bells peeled, a cannon went off and the theatre bell rang to announce the beginning of *Richard III*. Betty Leighton said the night was "magic, my whole body was tingling."

"I remember opening night," Amelia Hall said, "because Betty Leighton and I, who shared a dressing room, were so excited because we got so many telegrams and

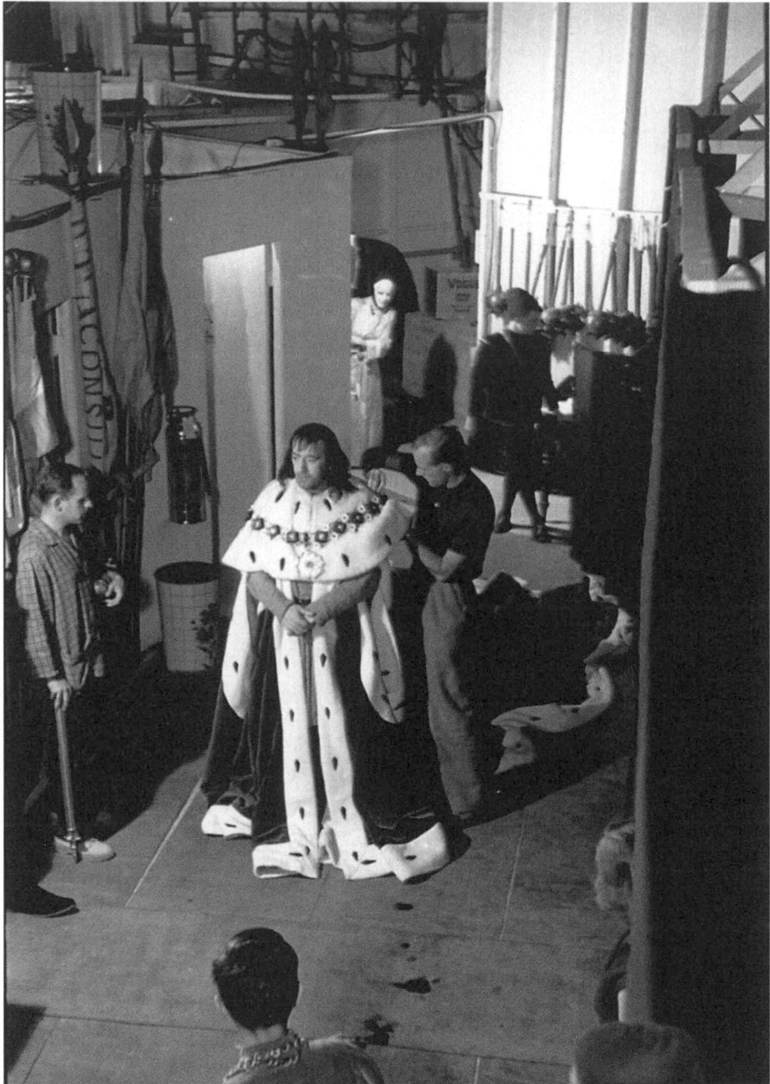

Alec Guinness shown backstage, having last minute adjustments done to the magnificent and elaborate robe designed for him by Tanya Moiseiwitsch. (NATIONAL ARCHIVES OF CANADA PA-142699, ID #21002)

flowers that suddenly one of us said, 'Good grief, we've got to go on.' We'd forgotten. It was more like a party. And then I was absolutely petrified when I got on because I thought that nobody could hear me. There was a funny noise, it turned out to be an airplane that was saluting the theatre and it was there all the time I was in my first scene."

The plane notwithstanding, Hall went down in history as the first actress to speak on the Stratford stage. When the last words of *Richard III* were heard that night the crowd went wild. They clapped, stood up en masse and began cheering and yelling. They would not let the actors go and kept calling them back again and again. The following night's *All's Well That Ends Well* was given a similar reception. Although the drawing card was Alec Guinness in *Richard III*, most of the critical acclaim went to *All's Well That Ends Well*, starring Irene Worth. Among Canadians singled out for worthy performances in the two productions were Amelia Hall, Betty Leighton, Eleanor Stuart, Donald Harron, Robert Christie and Eric House. Also highly praised were the costumes and decor of Tanya Moiseiwitsch and the music of Louis Applebaum.

The newspaper critics were more than encouraging. "Mr. Guthrie's production of *All's Well That Ends Well*, and the acting of Mr. Guinness and the rest of the company," wrote Brooks Atkinson of the *New York Times*, "have resulted in the composition of a little gem of imaginative theatre." Toronto's two pre-eminent critics, Herbert Whittaker and Nathan Cohen, were also wildly ecstatic.

Prior to the opening it was suggested that people would not make the long trek from Toronto to see Shakespeare in some remote town. In the end they came not just from Toronto but from New York and other states, South America, Europe and right across Canada. After only a couple of weeks, ticket sales were so brisk that another week was added to the season. This could not have happened without the co-operation of the lead actors. For Guinness it meant foregoing a planned vacation.

The heat inside the tent, which had been so noticeable on opening night, continued to be a dilemma even after they made a hole in the canvas behind the stage and set up a large fan with buckets of ice in front of it. Some of the actors found other ways to cool down. "We used to sit out at the back of the tent, on very hot evenings when we weren't on stage, chatting to Irene," recalled Betty Leighton. "All with our great costumes on pulled way up our legs, getting the air as best we could."

Jean-Louis Roux, who performed in the 1956 season, the tent's last, recalled that "the heat was one of the great difficulties of the tent because of those costumes. When we played matinee and then evening, the second time we would put our costumes on, they would still be damp [from sweat]. But [the tent] had a lot of charm of course, a lot of charm."

Then there were the problems of noisy children, whistling trains and the worst of all—rain. Not just the kind falling on the roof but the kind falling through the roof. Eric House recalled that people in the audience used to bring umbrellas because the tent would sometimes leak. William Hutt remembered the rain and all the other problems vividly:

> If it rained, particularly if it rained heavily, the noise of the rain falling on the tent was deafening and there were a couple of times where we just had to simply stop the performance and wait until the rain died down because nobody could hear anything. We

> couldn't even hear each other on stage. There was also the question of baseball games right outside the theatre, kids screaming, which is terrific. And CNR trains whooping it up as they went through town. All of those noises penetrated deeply inside the tent. Eventually we did convince the Canadian National Railway that when they went past at that particular time and place in Stratford would they please not toot their horns if it were between 8:30 and 11:00 at night. We also persuaded the local baseball teams to have their games over by 8:30 and they agreed to do that.

Hutt, concluded, "We could do nothing about rain because nobody had a direct contact with God, except possibly Tony Guthrie, and I don't think even he presumed."

There were, of course, the usual onstage mishaps that are often not noticed by the audience but are a source of horror for the actor. Betty Leighton recalled one in particular:

> You know we had this very exaggerated makeup, this sort of medieval makeup. And we had to get very long eyelashes . . . and in the tent we used to get an awful lot of flies. One Saturday matinee Guinness was in one of his long speeches and I was standing on one of the steps on the side, and this bloody fly flew right into my eyelash. It looked like an elephant and drove me crazy buzzing, caught in there trying to get free. I didn't dare move because in Guinness' long speeches you don't move. I then had a line so I made the biggest gesture you ever saw. I not only knocked the fly off but also knocked my eyelash off.

She said that she played "the rest of the scene with one eye."

That first year ended with a total of forty-two performances over six weeks with an extra matinee show added in order to have the money to set up a scholarship in Guthrie's name. More than 66,000 attended the two plays with a box office total of $206,942. The Festival operated with a deficit of a little more than $4,000.

Most of those early actors saw Stratford as a positive experience, for themselves and Canadian theatre. "It was marvellous, wonderful," Amelia Hall said. "I think it has been different every year but it was wonderful that first summer." Her words were echoed by Peter Mews who said, "It was the biggest and best thing done in Canada for years and years."

In retrospect, however, not all actors felt that Stratford was entirely good for home-grown theatre. Eric House expressed mixed feelings about the Festival:

> Of course it was good for theatre in Canada but it was a mixed blessing. There was a little flower growing in Canadian theatre. That is what you were working on. This little flower. What was it? Was there anything there before [Stratford]? Of course I think there was but with Stratford it really put an end to anything that had grown, almost anything, and set it back—how many years? It delayed the growth of real indigenous Canadian theatre by ten, fifteen years. It took the focus away. All the interested energy of everyone went towards this [Stratford], including mine.

Nathan Cohen, who had applauded so strongly when the Festival opened, also deplored the damage it did to other Canadian theatres by the amount of energy and focus that would ultimately go to Stratford. The Festival's success may also have slowed the development of Canadian-authored drama. Paul Kligman felt the promise of Stratford was never completely fulfilled. "I was disappointed when it wasn't the breakthrough I thought it might be," he said.

But good or bad, Stratford was finally a reality and it continued to survive and grow. The tent, imported stars, Guthrie, they all left. The one tent transformed into four theatre buildings, until by the end of the century, ten thousand people often filled the theatres during one weekend alone. Yet all of this could never compare with the excitement and hope of that first summer in 1953 when all the post-war drama groups culminated in a theatre that has become recognized around the world.

"I think it's a great pity," Betty Leighton lamented. "I know it's inevitable that things get bigger and grow, with business managers and accountants and stores worried about the cost of everything, but there was a time when we knew everybody. Oh, that loving, wonderful care we all had at the beginning. The beginnings in Ottawa, the beginnings in Montreal and the beginnings in Stratford. That opening night was—I don't care how long I live—nothing will ever compare to it."

# THEATRE VIGNETTES

The following brief accounts of the actors and directors of the period are not intended as biographies but as additional insights into the lives of those who helped create Canada's professional theatre. Regrettably, many names have been omitted, the result of space constraints.

## ANDREW ALLAN

Born in Scotland in 1907, Andrew Allan came to Canada as a teenager. While attending the University of Toronto he acted at Hart House Theatre and became drama editor for *Varsity*, the university paper in which his reputation for being outspoken was cemented for life. In February 1931, Allan read in the *Globe & Mail* that a Toronto minister had preached a sermon about godlessness being taught at the university, and he responded to it the next day in *Varsity* with an editorial meant to be full of irony. When most of the humour was lost on those in power, a major controversy ensued. *Varsity* was suspended by the University, and Allan became front page news in all the regular newspapers.

Following a year in England, Allan was returning to Canada in 1939 aboard the ship *Athenia* when it was torpedoed. He was with his then-fiancée, actress Judith Evelyn, and his father. The three made it safely into a lifeboat but it was subsequently crushed by the propellers of another ship. While Allan and Evans survived, his father was lost at sea. In order to forget, he plunged back into his work, and from 1939 to 1943 was regional supervisor for the Canadian Broadcasting Corporation in Vancouver. Shortly afterwards, Allan became supervisor of drama at the CBC in Toronto where he produced the famous *Stage Series* from its birth in 1944 until 1955, when Winnipeg's Esse Ljungh took over. After retiring from the CBC in 1962 and spending two years as the first artistic director at the Shaw Festival in Niagara-on-the-Lake, Allan fell into a self-confessed period of depression and heavy drinking. He emerged in 1967 to become a popular radio essayist—writing essays and then reading them on air—and the author of his autobiography, *Andrew Allan: A Self Portrait*.

## THOR ARNGRIM, STUART BAKER AND NORMA MACMILLAN

When Totem Theatre folded in 1954, neither Thor Arngrim nor Stuart Baker gave up the business. Stuart Baker went on to work for the National Film Board of Canada and later the Manitoba Theatre School. He also appeared for two seasons at the Shaw Festival, under the name Stuart Kent. Thor Arngrim decided the best part of Totem Theatre was the leading lady, Norma Macmillan. They were married three days after the last curtain came down and were quickly on their way to Toronto. From there the couple went on to success in New York and California. Arngrim appeared on Broadway in Christopher Marlowe's *Tamburlaine the Great*, directed by Tyrone Guthrie, and followed that by starring opposite Albert Finney in the Tony-award-winning play *Luther* by John Osborne. In California he became a personal manager of stars such as Liberace and Debbie Reynolds. Norma Macmillan's voice became much better known than her face

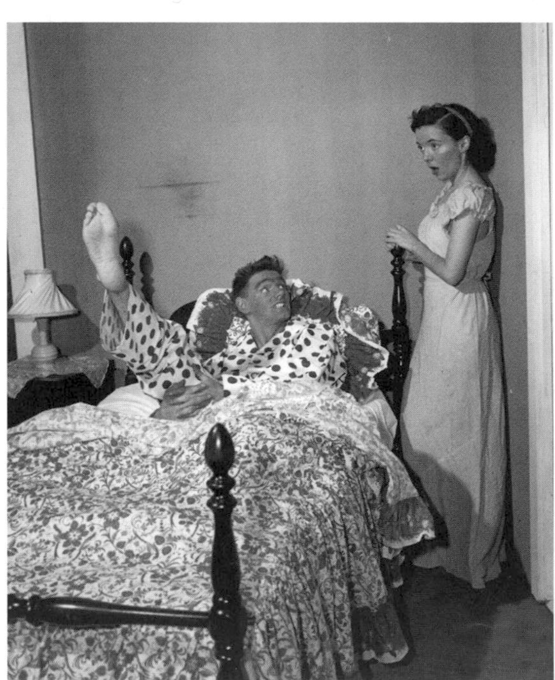

Thor Arngrim and Norma Macmillan playing up a scene from *Jane Steps Out* in the summer of 1952. (ARNGRIM COLLECTION)

when she appeared on television as the voice of Casper in *Casper the Friendly Ghost*, and Goo, the flying blue mermaid in *Gumby*, about a bendable green clay animation figure. Eventually she took over the voice of Gumby as well. Arngrim and Macmillan returned to Vancouver to live in their later years.

Their children followed in their footsteps. Stefan Arngrim was in a number of movies as well as the television series *Land of the Giants*. Their daughter, Alison, became more instantly recognized than either her brother or her parents by playing the role of Nellie Oleson in television's *Little House on the Prairie*.

### JOSEPHINE BARRINGTON

Born in Toronto in 1910, Josephine Barrington worked in stage, radio, film and television, first appearing at Hart House in the 1920s. Following studies at England's Central School of Speech and Drama, Barrington returned to Canada where she first appeared professionally with the John Holden Players in Bala, Ontario. In addition to radio work she ran a studio, teaching theatre to many aspiring actors who performed under the name of Josephine Barrington's Juveniles. Among them were Lloyd Bochner, Donald Davis, Frank Perry and William Needles. Barrington herself appeared with many of the prominent post-war theatres across Canada, including Theatre Under the Stars, Niagara Falls Summer Theatre, Jupiter Theatre, Mountain Playhouse and later the Crest. She also was seen on television in such shows as Stephen Leacock's *Sunshine Sketches*, *Quentin Durgen, M.P.* and *Whiteoaks of Jalna*.

### YVETTE BRIND'AMOUR

Away from the stage, Yvette Brind'Amour appeared with Jean-Louis Roux in the 1973 movie *The Pyx* starring Christopher Plummer and Karen Black, filmed in Montreal. When she received the Molson Prize in 1987, Brind'Amour was honoured and grateful for the $50,000, but she also felt that it "was about time" as the men had won it a number of years earlier (Jean Gascon in 1966 and Jean-Louis Roux in 1977). Through their competitive years, Brind'Amour and Roux, the leaders of the two major French theatres in Quebec, never appeared on stage together. It was, therefore, a special treat for Montreal audiences in 1989 when the two powerhouses of Montreal theatre starred opposite each other in Théâtre du Rideau Vert's fortieth-anniversary production, *Le Lion en hiver*, a French translation of *The Lion in Winter* by James Goldman. Brind'Amour recreated the role she had played in 1976 and the set was a replica of the one the late Robert Prévost had designed for the earlier production. The performances of Roux and Brind'Amour were highly praised, and the show was a hit. Brind'Amour was made a Companion of the Order of Canada in 1982 and three years later an officer of l'Ordre National du Québec.

## VERNON CHAPMAN

Vernon Chapman began his career as a child actor with amateur groups and was active in radio from the age of twelve. His first professional work was with Dora Mavor Moore's New Play Society, but even then he wanted to go to England. "Outside of radio," Chapman said, "there was no chance of making a living in Canada then. When I started at the New Play Society, I got $15 every two weeks. Even back in 1946 that wasn't very much. So we all had daytime jobs on the side. I was the business manager for the fisheries department in Algonquin Park. . . . That way I earned enough money to go to England because I wanted to get experience in a repertory company." Following his return to Canada, Chapman worked in the 1960s and '70s with the New Play Society, the Red Barn Theatre and many regional theatres. He was also a regular on the *Wayne and Shuster* television show for many years.

## LEO CICERI

A very talented actor whose life was cut short by a 1970 car accident, Leo Ciceri was born and raised in Montreal. After war-time service with the Air Force, he attended McGill University and worked with the Montreal Repertory Theatre, Brae Manor, the Shakespeare Society, the Open Air Playhouse and others. In 1948, still only twenty-four, Ciceri auditioned for and was accepted at England's famous Old Vic Theatre School. After triumphs overseas, including performances in Shakespeare's *Henry IV* and *Richard II*, Ciceri moved to Broadway and took over Christopher Plummer's role in Jean Anouilh's *The Lark*, opposite Julie Harris. Ciceri returned to Canada where, in 1957, he appeared in a French play at Comédie Canadienne, Gratien Gélinas' company in Montreal. This performance led to an invitation to Stratford in 1960, where he stayed until his death. One of his greatest contributions was the classes he held during the Stratford Festival for the younger members of the company to help prepare them for classical roles. To honour this work, the Festival established a scholarship in his name, offered annually by the National Theatre School.

## JOY COGHILL

Joy Coghill was born in Canada, raised in Scotland, and returned home as a teenager. Without realizing it she worked towards the theatre from an early age. "I took elocution lessons as a child," Coghill said. "It was a kind of mixture of speech and drama. You took your degree with examiners who came out from London. I also played with imaginary children because I was an only child."

Her lessons paid off years later when she acquired students of her own and worked her way through the University of British Columbia. In 1948, Coghill won rave reviews when, at age twenty-one, she portrayed the mother in Sidney Howard's *The Silver Cord* at the Dominion Drama Festival finals in Ottawa. Receiving a scholarship, Coghill attended UBC's Summer School of the Theatre and also worked with the university's amateur group, the Players' Club. "It was in my last year at UBC that I discovered you could go on and take a degree in theatre [outside Canada]," she said. "You had to choose between England and the States." Coghill enrolled at the Art Institute of Chicago's Goodman Theatre because "it was the only place I could find where they actually had a professional theatre where the students ran the company." At Goodman, she came under the influence of Charlotte Chorpenning, the head of Goodman's Children's Theatre, and this stimulus shaped Coghill's interests for many years to come.

Back in Canada, Coghill worked for Sydney Risk, heading up Everyman's children's theatre, one of the few theatres, albeit an amateur one, with adults performing in plays aimed at young audiences. She then returned to Goodman as a teacher and likely would have remained there if not for a request from an earlier mentor. "Dorothy [Somerset] asked me to come back and start Holiday Theatre," Coghill said. "[She] always kept an eye on the whole children's movement."

That movement really began in 1931 with the formation of the Toronto Children's Players. It proved there was a large audience for children's theatre in Canada. In fact, their popularity under director Dorothy Goulding forced them to keep moving into larger venues until by 1942 they were filling the 1,100-seat Eaton Auditorium. Numerous children's theatres were scattered throughout the country but most had young people as the performers. Somerset saw the need for a professional children's theatre with adults performing the roles, hence her encouragement of Coghill and Holiday Theatre, the first professional children's theatre in Canada.

Joy Coghill in Holiday Theatre's *Flibberty-Gibbet* of 1953. (COGHILL COLLECTION)

Somerset, still with UBC's Extension Department, offered the use of the Frederic Wood Theatre to Coghill. Six people contributed $25, and with this $150 investment, Holiday Theatre began. Among those with Coghill at the beginning were Myra Benson, Jessie Richardson, Peter Mannering and her future husband John Thorne. It became the prototype for many future children's theatres. The actors received salaries although Coghill did not pay herself anything extra as the permanent artistic director.

"For years it was my sort of contribution to theatre in British Columbia," Coghill said. "We started out at $35 a week [for actors] but we also paid board and bills."

According to Coghill, fiscal management was the key to their success, and they had a "tough business manager"—Myra Benson: "The reason Holiday Theatre survived financially was entirely Myra's doing."

Holiday Theatre also gave classes. "Actually, teaching classes made more money than doing plays, but doing plays was our mandate to ourselves," Coghill said. Almost all the plays were originals, many of them adaptations of fairy tales. The greatest influence Holiday Theatre would have on other children's theatres was in the area of raising money. "It was possible to get grants for children's work where you couldn't get it for adult work," Coghill said. "So it became quite common for theatres to put children's classes in and finally a children's tour of schools because it helped them get higher subsidies from the cities and province as this was their educational contribution to the community. That pattern was taken from Holiday Theatre."

Coghill went on to become artistic director of the Vancouver Playhouse, spent three years heading the English division of the National Theatre School in Montreal, and took on roles with theatres from coast to coast, including Sarah Bernhardt in *Memoir* by John Murrell and an award-winning performance in *The Road to Mecca* by Athol Fugard. Her television credits include *Street Justice*, *21 Jump Street*, *The Beachcombers*, *Da Vinci's Inquest* and *Ma!*, which focuses on newspaper editor "Ma Murray." She is also the author of a play about Emily Carr, *Song of This Place*.

## NATHAN COHEN

Samuel Nathan Cohen was born in 1923 in Nova Scotia into a Jewish immigrant family. He loved going to the movies, and early in his career he felt he knew and understood film better than the stage.

Cohen attended Mount Allison University in New Brunswick where, among other things, he edited the school publication, *The Argosy*, and helped run the yearbook. He was frequently involved in controversy due to his outspoken views. During this time he was also badly burned in a dormitory fire in which a number of students died. After recovering, and still only nineteen years old, Cohen ended up editing the *Glace Bay Gazette*.

Following a move to Toronto, Cohen's communist leanings came to the fore and he began to write book reviews for the *Canadian Jewish Weekly (Vochenblatt)*, a communist-leaning newspaper. At the suggestion of his future wife, Cohen wrote a theatre review of a New Play Society production they attended. It was 1946, and a theatre critic was born. On the basis of Cohen's theatre reviews for *Vochenblatt*, Mavor Moore recommended him for a new CBC radio show, *Across the Footlights*, where his reputation as a critic of Canadian theatre became legendary. Cohen ended up on CJBC's *Views the Shows*, where his biting reviews alienated him from vast sections of the artistic community. In fact, Cohen actually praised almost as many productions as he condemned, and he was unusual for taking the time to see amateur university productions. In fact, he saw a great deal of theatre he never actually reviewed. "He looked around for whatever theatre he could find in Toronto, so we'd see him quite often at the university," remembered Eric House. "He was a striking figure, but fat and kind of dishevelled. He'd turn up to watch one-acts by the students. He'd come up on visits to Gravenhurst to see the Straw Hat Players, stay overnight, bum cigarettes and drinks and never pay you back."

Cohen hosted the highly acclaimed *Fighting Words* on television. It was during this time that a past association with the Communist Party came into question and *Fighting Words* was taken off the air. After a stay in England, Cohen was reinstated by the CBC and returned to Canada. He wrote a theatre column for the *Toronto Telegram* before becoming the entertainment editor for the *Toronto Star* where he remained for the last twelve years of his life. Cohen died at the early age of forty-seven.

## JOHN COLICOS

John Colicos was born in Montreal and gained his early acting experience with the Montreal Repertory Theatre and a two-season stint with Brae Manor Theatre in Knowlton, Quebec. The man Thor Arngrim called "a good actor" and "terribly underrated" had a rich voice that made him a natural for radio, and Colicos took on leading roles in a number of radio shows. Following a season with the largely Canadian theatre in Hamilton, Bermuda, Colicos moved to England. In 1952 when the lead actor in *King Lear* fell ill, Colicos was asked to step in, becoming the youngest professional actor (at twenty-three-years old) ever to play the role of Lear.

On returning to Canada in 1953, while Stratford's first summer was underway, Colicos repeated his King Lear role at the Montreal Festivals. He would play it yet again, on the Stratford stage in 1964. In 1957 he appeared in New York as Edmund, the bastard son, to Orson Welles' King Lear. He also appeared on Broadway in *The Devils* by John Whiting and *Soldiers* (in which he portrayed Winston Churchill). Colicos moved to Hollywood and did well financially in television with many "villain" guest appearances and his Top-Gun commercials for Midas Muffler. His best-known television roles were Micos Cassadine on the soap opera *General Hospital* and the first Klingon commander in the original *Star Trek* series in 1966.

## DOROTHY DAVIES

Lilian Dorothy Davies' family moved from the United States to Victoria, British Columbia, when she was very young, and there was hardly a time in her life when Davies was not connected to the theatre. "My father was a preacher in Victoria and he had friends who were interested in the theatre," she said. "Sometimes he . . . would put on a play that had a moral, and occasionally there were roles for young people and I used to play those." Some years later she joined a summer group at Qualicum on Vancouver Island that included Phoebe Smith and Yvonne Firkins and other well-known theatre people. When the female lead in their major production dropped out, they asked Davies to take the part. Afterwards, she moved to Vancouver and quickly became seriously involved with theatre and radio. Her biggest radio role was Mary in *The Carsons*, which Davies played for more than twenty years. Davies was the first recipient of the Jessie Richardson Award for lifetime achievement, and it was well earned.

## DONALD AND MURRAY DAVIS, BARBARA CHILCOTT

It was inevitable that the Davis siblings would found their own theatre, the Crest, for they had been heading towards it almost from the day they were born. Their mother encouraged them all to be interested in the arts, and three of the four children remained with the theatre into adulthood. "My father, who was a very patient man, must have been mildly alarmed when he realized three of his four children were going into the theatre," Donald Davis said. "He lived, I'm happy to say, to be quite proud." At one stage in his final year at university, his father "had a chat" with Donald about his future. Donald refused his father's offer to pay his way through law school. "I said rather grandly that I would give myself five years [to make it in theatre] and if I hadn't justified this decision, that I hoped I had his blessing to come back and ask him if the offer was still open."

His sister Barbara (performing under the name Barbara Chilcott) studied in New York and then went to England. She appeared with Meet the Navy during the Second World War, returned to Canada in 1951 and worked extensively in the theatre from then on. Their brother Murray was co-founder with Donald of the Straw Hat Players, and with both his acting siblings he incorporated the Crest Theatre in 1953. The theatre presented its first play in January 1954, and Murray remained an artistic director with the Crest during its twelve-year operation, the first six with Donald and the following years by himself as Donald had left Canada for the United States. At one point during the run of the Crest, the three siblings met playwright J. B. Priestley, who wrote *The Glass Cage* specifically for them. It was performed at both the Crest and later in London, England, in 1957.

## JOHN DRAINIE

At the age of fourteen, John Drainie dislocated his hip in a car accident, and this left him with a slight but permanent limp, which made him feel uncomfortable on stage and television, but not on radio. "He was lame and he felt it very acutely. Perhaps more than he should have," Lister Sinclair said. Unable to involve himself in any sports activities, Drainie channelled his energies into the theatre. While performing on radio in Vancouver, Drainie met Andrew Allan who, he once said, helped him more with his acting technique than anyone else. He began appearing in radio drama, including a popular show called *The Carsons*, and was transferred to Toronto by the CBC shortly before he resigned in 1943 to become a freelance actor. Allan moved east in the same year, and when he launched his *Stage Series* in January 1944, he chose Drainie to play in the first two productions: Fletcher Markle's *29:40* and *Home Is Where You Hang Your Heart*.

His place in the annals of radio history is such that there are two major Canadian Awards honouring him. In 1968, ACTRA (Alliance of Canadian Cinema, Television & Radio Artists) established the John Drainie Award "for distinguished contribution in broadcasting," and the Writer's Trust of Canada presents the Drainie-Taylor Prize for best biography.

## TED FOLLOWS

Excelling in school, Ted Follows skipped grades from a young age. Because his classmates were much older, Follows felt left out in his early years, but his life changed when he drifted into the theatre. While finishing two years at the University of Manitoba, he won an acting award which led to a summer at the Banff School of Fine Arts. It was at this time that Sydney Risk was on the lookout for young actors for his new theatre. "I thought for five minutes and then quit school," Follows said of Risk's invitation to join Everyman Theatre. While his tour with Everyman was "exciting and hard," it also brought home financial realities, and sent Follows back to university in Toronto. But he could not escape the pull of the theatre, and quickly hooked up with Bob Gill and Hart House.

In the ensuing years he worked with the Straw Hat Players in the summers while finishing his degree. After graduating he appeared with many of Ontario's theatres. In 1952 Peter Potter of the Glasgow Repertory Theatre was directing Follows in a Straw Hat Players' production and asked him to go with him back to Glasgow along with Donald Davis and Eric House. "I was always kind of directed towards theatre because it was my main interest, not movies," Follows said. "The whole idea was to get a classical education in theatre which meant, really, going to England, so I think that was a kind of dream I had." Follows and Davis accepted Potter's invitation and Follows spent the next three years slowly making a name for himself in Scotland and England.

In 1955 Tyrone Guthrie invited him to Stratford, Ontario, for the summer and he returned home. Without that invitation, Follows says he likely would not have returned permanently to Canada. Five seasons with Stratford and four with the Canadian Players followed, during which time he married fellow thespian Dawn Greenhalgh. Years later, acting took hold of the couple's offspring: their daughter Megan Follows was best-known for her role as Anne from *Anne of Green Gables*.

From the 1970s on, Ted Follows performed in and directed many productions across Canada. He believed the theatre of the early post-war period was "absolutely" the foundation for the later regional movement and said he "would much rather have been an actor back then" than starting out decades later. Follows said he had "a great time [with] a great group of people. There was a sense of camaraderie . . . with people who were serious about being in the business. . . . We worked hard."

## JEAN GASCON

After establishing himself as a director with Théâtre du Nouveau Monde, Jean Gascon began to branch out. In 1958 he co-directed a production of *Othello* at Stratford, and in 1963 he went solo there, directing Shakespeare's *The Comedy of Errors*. In 1964 he became associate director at Stratford and then the sole artistic director from 1969 until 1974, becoming the first Canadian-born to hold the post. Gascon then spent several years as the head of the French theatre section at the National Arts Centre in Ottawa until budget cutbacks in 1984 all but eliminated his job. He won the Canada Council's Molson Prize in 1966 and the $50,000 Royal Bank Award in 1973, the first person in an artistic profession to receive it. Gascon was a founder and first director of the National Theatre School in Montreal, and became a Companion of the Order of Canada in 1975.

All his life Gascon worked to break down the French-English barriers in the arts. He believed passionately that music, dance and theatre were universal languages of communication and was surprised in later years to be thought of in some circles as selling out to English Canada. To him there was just the theatre, period. He was very outspoken about the way the Canadian government treated the arts in general and actors in particular, the people who had given their lives to the theatre and had nothing to show for it. Away from the theatre he had a well-known zest for life. "Everyone I know, particularly on the English side loved him. He was so Gallic," Jean-Louis Roux said.

"As a person," Christopher Plummer said, "he was adorable, one of the sweetest and one of the funniest friends I've ever known. Lots of guts and lots of courage and would do crazy things quite naturally. He had such an extraordinary life force and personality, he really wanted to be forever young . . . had a wonderful innocence and naiveté that he always kept."

The years of fast living and drinking finally caught up with Gascon, affecting his career and contributing to his first heart attack in 1983. At the time he died, however, he had stopped drinking and was directing a 1988 Stratford production of *My Fair Lady*. "When Jean died he hadn't drunk a drop for two years," Jean-Louis Roux said. "It was good timing for his death. He was working again. He was in relatively good shape and he was back in Stratford. That was very important to him, very important."

## GRATIEN GÉLINAS

Gratien Gélinas was born in 1909, in Saint-Tite, Quebec, and spent most of his youth in Montreal. His parents were divorced during the 1920s, and in his biography Gélinas said that this left him with a sense of orphanhood which permeated many of his later works. In 1929 he worked for an insurance company during the week and on Saturdays he toiled in a fast-paced department store, a job he credited for much of the physical adeptness of his later character, Fridolin. Although he worked hard at night courses to improve his position at the insurance company, performing was never far from his mind. He appeared frequently with amateur theatres, notably the French and English divisions of the Montreal Repertory Theatre. One of his roles in English was as Dr. Caius in Shakespeare's *The Merry Wives of Windsor*, which Gélinas re-created at the Stratford Festival in 1956.

After writing *Tit-Coq* with its sensational success, he wrote two more plays, *Bousille et les justes* in 1959 and *Hier, les enfants dansaient* (Yesterday the Children Were Dancing) in 1966. Both were praised and subsequently translated into English. The action in the latter play revolved around the tumultuous Quebec politics of the time. In 1957 Gélinas founded La Comèdie-Canadienne, whose main purpose, he said at the time, was to promote and encourage Canadian plays and playwrights. He directed the theatre until its dissolution in 1972. Gélinas was a Companion of the Order of Canada and was also awarded the Victor Morin Prize by la Société Saint-Jean-Baptiste de Montréal.

## LORNE GREENE

The man who later became known to millions as Ben Cartwright on television's *Bonanza* was born in Ottawa in 1915. It was at Queen's University in Kingston, Ontario, that Lorne Greene first became fascinated with theatre. After attending the Neighbourhood Playhouse School of the Theatre in New York on a fellowship, Greene returned to Canada and joined the CBC. It took only a couple of months before his booming voice was heard reading the national news and narrating the National Film Board shorts shown in movie theatres before the feature film. After the Second World War, Greene appeared on stage with a number of groups, including the New Play Society and the Earle Grey Players. His first professional dramatic role was on radio in 1945 when he asked Andrew Allan if he could be in one of his plays. Allan cast him as

Captain Ahab in *Moby Dick*. One of his oddest radio roles was in *Phantasmagoria* in which the central character is a radio announcer named Lorne Greene who goes stark raving mad on the air. There was no difficulty casting the lead.

An unusual invention by Greene was responsible for changing the direction of his life. He developed a stopwatch for newscasters that showed the announcer how much time he had left rather than how much had elapsed. On a New York trip to promote the watch in 1953, a chance meeting with a fellow Canadian, writer/director Fletcher Markle, led to his first Broadway appearance, opposite Katharine Cornell in *The Prescott Proposals* by Howard Lindsay and Russel Crouse. Back in Canada, he starred in Shakespeare's *The Merchant of Venice* and as Brutus in *Julius Caesar* for Stratford's 1955 season before returning to the United States. It was a guest appearance on television's *Wagon Train* that propelled Greene into his fourteen-year run in *Bonanza*.

### AMELIA HALL

After playing Amanda in *The Glass Menagerie* for the Montreal Repertory Theatre in 1949, it was only a few months before Amelia Hall played the part again in London, England. The catalyst for the invitation was in fact a production of a Canadian play. Officials of the annual Edinburgh Festival (formed in 1947) had written to the chairman of the Dominion Drama Festival asking that a Canadian one-act play be sent over to Scotland to be included in the 1949 Festival. It was decided that *Eros at Breakfast* by Robertson Davies was the best choice and that the Ottawa Drama League, for which Amelia Hall was a tireless worker, should produce it. The theatre had been involved with the play from the beginning when it was submitted by Davies in 1947 to a playwriting competition sponsored by the group. It won and was subsequently staged by them.

After acting in and directing *Eros at Breakfast* in Edinburgh, she was invited to London to play for a week in *The Glass Menagerie* at the Q Theatre. Because Hall felt "homesick and cold," she did not stay long in England in spite of many opportunities to do so. After she returned to Canada, the call came from the Canadian Repertory Theatre (see Chapter Seven) in November 1949 and Hall left Montreal for the theatre which took so much of her heart and soul for the next five years.

### BARBARA HAMILTON

Toronto-born Barbara Hamilton did not grow up dreaming of stardom on stage. As a young girl she was "interested in something in the medical profession." That all changed when she went away to a boarding school, and an orientation ritual found her performing a song in front of the whole school. "Unknowingly I was doing a take-off on the headmistress which made the entire school hysterical. . . . I think that is what made everybody think, 'God, she's a real clown, that girl.'" Actually she had never thought of herself that way: "I was shy and retiring sort of, and all of a sudden to get these waves of laughter over the footlights. I think it just gave me a kind of acceptance and I thought, 'I think that's what I want to do.' ... I fantasized, thinking movie star as opposed to stage, until I studied and realized the tradition of the stage and how important it was. And from there I was lucky."

Hamilton joined the talented group of young actors under Bob Gill at the University of Toronto. She then became a member of the Straw Hat Players, performed with a number of the other summer theatres around Ontario, and toured with Joseph Kesselring's *Arsenic and Old Lace* as well as the two revues: *The Drunkard* and *One for the Road*. It was after the latter revue that Hamilton found herself suddenly on Broadway. "I went down, auditioned, started rehearsal that afternoon and opened two nights later.... I thought, 'This isn't so tough.'" The show, *Razzle Dazzle* by Mike Stewart, lasted only a month, however, and although Hamilton herself was well received by the critics, the quick closing was a shock. "Here [in Canada] we knew we were going to be doing summer stock for six weeks ... doing this tour for three months, it was all set. It didn't occur to me that the show would close under me, and it came as a great blow."

While studying in New York, Hamilton planned to support herself as an airline reservations clerk, but almost immediately an offer came from Michael Sadlier's group in Bermuda. "So I reserved my flight [under another name so her employers would not know] and that's the only money I ever made from the job," she laughed. Following a year with Sadlier's theatre, she returned to Canada to become a star in both television and theatre. She spent three years on television's *Howdy Doody* show and many successful years as one of the stars in the New Play Society's *Spring Thaw*. Straightforward and unpretentious, Hamilton had a reputation for toughness that was garnered mostly from a combination of speaking her mind and her sense of indignation whenever she saw injustice of any kind take place. In 1963 Mavor Moore dropped her from his cast of *Spring Thaw*, reputedly for this "toughness." Hurt and angry, Hamilton retaliated by renting Toronto's Crest Theatre and presenting her own revue, *That Hamilton Woman*. Financially backed by her friends, the show ran for six and a half weeks instead of the scheduled three and returned a $30,000 profit to her investors. She was soon back with *Spring Thaw*.

Her biggest professional triumph came in the role of Marilla Cuthbert in the musical version of *Anne of Green Gables*, a role she had to fight for and won only after threatening to pull out of the producer's other show, *Spring Thaw*. As Marilla, Hamilton toured Canada, Japan and London, England, where, in 1970, she won the drama critics' award for best actress of the year. She was honest about her disappointment over losing the part of Marilla in the television series of the same name, a part that eventually went to Colleen Dewhurst.

## ⁂ DON HARRON

A radio stint for Don Harron before he was even a teenager lasted less than a year, and he said he was happy when it ended because it interfered with football practice. In high school he performed in amateur theatre but did not become interested in it as a profession until 1945. Over the years, he became one of Canada's best-known and successful personalities, both as himself and as his alter ego, Parry Sound farmer Charlie Farquharson.

Throughout his post-war university years in the late 1940s, Harron performed with the New Play Society and worked on radio. Between radio and stage work, both of which were done in addition to his studies, Harron became a Canadian oddity—a young actor making a living at his profession.

In 1950 he and his first wife went to England for "a holiday," but within twenty-four hours Harron had landed a job with Canadian Bernard Braden. While there, one of his performances was seen by playwright Christopher Fry who then recommended the actor for a part in the American premiere of his play *A Sleep of Prisoners*. Harron made his Broadway debut in this play in a New York church in 1951. Following this he appeared in Stratford's first three seasons. For eleven years in the late 1950s and '60s, Harron worked outside Canada, performing on both stage and television in England and the United States.

In Canada, his most frequent television appearances were on the *Red Green Show* and as Charlie Farquharson on the series *Hee Haw*. From 1977 to 1982 Harron was the successful radio host of CBC's *Morningside* for which he won an ACTRA award as best host. He and Norman Campbell wrote a musical adaptation of *Anne of Green Gables*, which became the mainstay of the Charlottetown Festival and toured across Canada. Harron also wrote a number of books using his Charlie Farquharson character, including *Charlie's Farquharson's Histry of Canada*, *K-O-R-N Filled Allmynack* and perhaps his most adventurous, a version of the Bible, *Olde Charlie Farquharson's Testament: From Jennysez to Jobe and After Words*.

## ⁂ ARTHUR HILL AND PEGGY HASSARD

A chance remark from Lister Sinclair was the catalyst for a change in Arthur Hill and his wife Peggy Hassard's careers. When a fellow actor in England suggested they come over, "Lister said, 'Why don't we do that, why don't we just go, what the hell?'" Hill related. Once in England, they were both performing on radio and television, but while Hassard continued, Arthur Hill turned to his first love, the stage. His earliest triumph was in James Thurber and Elliot Nugent's *The Male Animal*, in which he starred with Barbara Kelly, another transplanted Canadian, whose career had started in Vancouver with Theatre Under the Stars. (Kelly was an accomplished radio actress in both Vancouver and Toronto, while her husband Bernard Braden was also a popular and well-known Canadian radio personality. They were members of a large Canadian contingent present in England during the ten years following the Second World War.)

Arthur Hill appeared in many other London productions before the life-changing role of Cornelius Hackl, the love-struck clerk, in *The Matchmaker* by Thornton Wilder came along. The play was first staged in London and then, in 1955, the same production took Hill and Hassard to New York and Broadway where Hill starred in *The Matchmaker* for more than one thousand performances. In 1962 Hill starred in a play that not only brought public success but the 1963 Tony Award for best actor. He played George in Edward Albee's *Who's Afraid Of Virginia Woolf?* for eight months and then turned from the stage to the screen—both large and small—and had success in both.

## JOHN HOLDEN

When the Straw Hat Players began their summer theatre in Muskoka in 1948, they were not the first theatre to perform in the region. There was a pre-war professional group that spent summers in the Muskokas and a string of winters in Winnipeg (as well as one unsuccessful winter season in Toronto). This was the Actors Colony Theatre (the name was chosen because the first letters spelled out ACT), which opened in the summer of 1934 in the Muskoka town of Bala. The sparkplug and leader of the group was John Holden, an American raised in Canada. The summer venture was a success, so in the 1934–35 winter they played in Toronto. When this proved too costly, it was not repeated. The summer runs in Bala continued, and then a chance connection gave them an opportunity to spend their winters in Winnipeg, appearing as the John Holden Players at the Dominion Theatre.

This workable system of wintering in Winnipeg while summering in Muskoka lasted until 1941 when the war made the obtaining of actors difficult. Then in 1942 John Holden enlisted in the American Armed Forces and the theatre folded. In eight seasons at Bala and four in Winnipeg, however, Holden's group had presented theatre of the highest quality, with its alumni including Jane Mallett, Bud Knapp, Peter Mews, Mavor Moore, Babs Hitchman, Robert Christie, Alice Hill, Catherine Proctor and Alex McKee.

## WILLIAM HUTT

Toronto-born and raised, William Hutt "did the usual number of high-school plays, operettas and things like that." He also took longer to graduate from high school than most and had to repeat more than one year because he found something he enjoyed more than school. "I think my greatest interest came from skipping a lot of school and going to see motion pictures," said Hutt, who was often joined on these high school truancy jaunts by Eric House. They both later appeared in Stratford's opening season. Because Hutt was older than most of his classmates on graduation, he went directly from school into the Second World War. "I was in the European battle quite a bit of the time," Hutt said, "but when I was in England I would get leaves and go to London. I would see a lot of theatre, and it was during that time I think the idea of pursuing a theatrical career began to form itself."

On returning to Canada, Hutt enrolled at the University of Toronto and performed with Robert Gill's students at Hart House. "It was under him," Hutt said, "that it became quite a concrete aim or goal in my mind that I wanted to go into the profession. It was rather cavalier of me to make that decision at that time. Like most innocents in those days, I didn't realize that there wasn't much legitimate theatre to go into in Canada." In the fall of 1949 Hutt was offered a part in Brian Doherty's tour of *Arsenic and Old Lace*, and he decided to take the plunge. Before that he had done summer stock with theatres in Bracebridge, Niagara Falls and Peterborough. Hutt also appeared with Kingston's International Players and the Canadian Repertory Theatre before being asked to join Stratford in 1953.

William Hutt became synonymous with Stratford, one of the mainstays of the Festival. In 1954 he was one of the first two recipients (along with Bruce Swerdfager) of the Tyrone Guthrie Award at Stratford, given towards further study. He was so busy with work that Hutt was unable to make use of the $1,500 award until 1958 when he finally left for England where he spent three years before returning to Stratford. He appeared many times with the Canadian Players, the winter touring group that was formed from Stratford actors following its first summer. He also appeared in New York and Scotland. Hutt was awarded the Companion of the Order of Canada in 1969, and in 1973 a tour took him to Denmark, Holland, Poland and Russia, where his portrayal of King Lear in Moscow brought a lengthy standing ovation. His other memorable Stratford roles included *Tartuffe*, highly praised in the *New York Times*, and his Lady Bracknell in *The Importance of Being Earnest*. Hutt spent five years as Theatre London's artistic director and many seasons as associate director at Stratford. In 1989 he starred for the first time at the Shaw Festival in Niagara-on-the-Lake. Not long after, Hutt received the Order of Ontario.

### CHARMION KING

Toronto-born and educated, Charmion King became involved early with theatre, taking part in school and church plays, but it was at the University of Toronto's Hart House she became certain she wanted to make theatre her career. While there, she was offered a Warner Brother's screen test, which she declined. In addition to the Straw

Hat Players and the New World Theatre Company, King also appeared with the Niagara and Peterborough Summer theatres, the Bermudan Theatre and the International Players in Kingston. In 1951 King made the decision to leave Canada long enough to receive some training, which she felt was sorely needed. She explained:

> I had been working and working, but I really had no [training].... My choice was New York or England. I thought it is better to live in Britain where no one had any money. You don't have this awful thing in New York where you were either rich or poor, and I was the latter, and it just draws a lot of your strength.... I just adored it [England]. I came back in 1953 because I suddenly got terribly homesick. Television had begun at that time and I got a wire, "Would I do a television show?"

King agreed and became very busy at once, appearing on television, at the Stratford Festival and on radio. She was a leading lady with the Crest Theatre and was the first female head of Canadian Actor's Equity in 1959. In the early 1960s, King all but retired for a time following her marriage to fellow-actor Gordon Pinsent. The 1970s found her back on stage at the Shaw Festival and on film in W.O. Mitchell's *Who Has Seen the Wind*. In 1990 at Hart House Theatre she reprised an earlier role in *Arsenic and Old Lace*, opposite her old friend Kate Reid.

## FÉLIX LECLERC

Félix Leclerc went on to become famous as a songwriter and poet, but he began as a radio scriptwriter at CHRC in Quebec City, and then for Radio-Canada, where one of his most popular series was *Je me souviens*. Leclerc was also heard in many radio drama series. In 1948, he and two friends founded VLM, a short-lived theatre that presented his own plays throughout Quebec. Leclerc became well known in Canada only after he succeeded elsewhere, selling more than 300,000 copies of his music record, *Le P'tit Bonheur*, during the first year he lived in France at the beginning of the 1950s.

An acknowledged separatist, Leclerc supported Quebec independence following the war measures crisis in October 1970. He was at René Lévesque's side the night the Quebec Federalists defeated the sovereignty-association referendum on May 20, 1980. Leclerc was made a member of the Order of Canada in 1985 and the following year received France's highest honour, Chevalier de la Légion d'honneur.

## JANE MALLETT

Jane Mallett, who was born in London, Ontario, and raised in Saskatchewan, became interested in theatre while attending the University of Toronto, where she worked at Hart House with the Players' Club. Mallett followed this with two seasons at the Empire Theatre, an old professional stock company in Toronto. She also appeared at Bala in John Holden's company and in the 1930s began a long and profitable career in radio. Mallett's work in radio was recognized in 1976 when she received ACTRA's John Drainie award for distinguished contribution to broadcasting. For ten years in the 1930s and '40s, Mallett presented her own revue, *Town Tonics*, an annual production of skits and monologues which played all around Ontario in small town theatres. Mallett's most distinctive characteristics, a growly voice and throaty, suggestive laugh, made her very popular with the public. The voice was actually a result of an operation in the late 1940s which removed a nodule on her vocal chords. Over the years she had to overcome other handicaps, including a broken hip (which had to be replaced with an artificial one in the 1960s) and a bone disease which reduced her height by a number of inches. In 1957, concerned over the plight of performers, Mallett helped found the Actor's Fund of Canada, which supports actors in financial need.

## PETER MEWS

Peter Mews was born in Toronto and received his first professional experience in summer theatre with the John Holden Players in 1940. His first major theatre job was with the *Army Show* from 1943 to 1946. After graduating from art school he gained employment making mannequins, and for three years he ran his own company. His skill and knowledge of art and design made him a valuable addition to the New Play Society, where Dora Mavor Moore put his talents to good use, often having him design the sets. "I enjoyed it," Mews said, "and it also gave me an insight into what the designer needed in order to apply his design in a way which would help the actors."

Through the years, Mews appeared with many theatres, including Stratford in its first two seasons and the Shaw and Charlottetown Festivals. It was while with this last group that Mews became involved with his most memorable role, one that he played across the country and performed for many years—Matthew in *Anne of Green Gables*.

## (JAMES) MAVOR MOORE

(James) Mavor Moore, who was born and raised in Toronto, played a part in every area of the entertainment world, as director, actor, producer and writer. He worked both on and behind the stage, as well as with radio, television and film. Following his graduation from university in 1941, he became a producer for the CBC and directed many of Canada's war-time shows. He then spent two years with the Canadian Army Intelligence Corps, specializing in psychological warfare.

"I came out of the Army early in 1945," Mavor Moore remembered. "I was brought back to head up the broadcast program to the troops—Radio Overseas—that section of the CBC's international service which was just then starting up in Montreal."

Moore then had a brief sojourn in Vancouver as chief CBC producer for the Pacific region. His subsequent return to Toronto in the fall of 1946 paved the way for his involvement with his mother's theatre, the New Play Society. From 1950 to 1953 he was the chief television producer in Toronto as the new medium launched in Canada. As an author, his writings include *Sunshine Town*, a 1955 musical adaptation of Stephen Leacock's *Sunshine Sketches of a Little Town*; *Who's Who*; and *Johnny Belinda* (a musical based on Elmer Harris' play), produced at the Charlottetown Festival and eventually televised. In 1980 the Charlottetown Festival premiered *Little Lord Fauntleroy*, which Moore adapted from the book by Frances Hodgson Burnett. His awards include the Order of Canada, the John Drainie Award for excellence in broadcasting and the $50,000 Molson Prize from the Canada Council in 1986 for his contribution to the arts.

### SAM PAYNE

Sam Payne was, without doubt, one of the busiest and most mobile actors in Canada during the post-war years. Speaking of his early interest in theatre, Payne said, "I started when I was quite young, fourteen or fifteen. I had always been involved with it—that was my life. Some kids do other things like hockey. I did theatre."

While working with the Vancouver Little Theatre, he met a girl who had come from London's Royal Academy of Dramatic Art (RADA) and was impressed by her training. It was 1935 and Payne quickly left for England and RADA. After working his way through his first term doing odd jobs, he won a scholarship. After graduation, he spent three years in England, working both in the West End and with regional repertory and touring companies. Payne also began his long association with radio and appeared on television and in a number of British films. With war threatening, Payne returned home and worked on the amateur stage and with Theatre Under the Stars. In 1947 he moved east and hooked up with Toronto's radio community and performed with both the New Play Society and the Earle Grey Players. Weekend visits to Ottawa led to acting with the Ottawa Stage Society and its successor, the Canadian Repertory Theatre. After jumping from east to west and back every year, Payne finally returned to Vancouver permanently in 1953.

### DENISE PELLETIER

Denise Pelletier was born in Saint-Jovite, Quebec, and studied theatre as a teenager after responding to a newspaper ad for the Montreal Repertory Theatre. Her professional career began in radio with *Vie de famille*. She also appeared on stage with L'Équipe, Les Compagnons de Saint-Laurent, Théâtre du Nouveau Monde (she was with them for Stratford's 1956 appearance), and the Montreal Repertory Theatre. Her later career included Théâtre du Rideau Vert and La Nouvelle Compagnie Théâtrale. She also played in *Dance of Death* by August Strindberg at the Stratford Festival in 1966. Known as one of the greatest actresses of that era, Pelletier will be best remembered for two roles: Cecile Plouffe in the French and English versions of Quebec's first television drama series, *The Plouffe Family*; and Sarah Bernhardt in a one-woman play called *La Divine Sarah*. It was her last role in a stellar career cut short during a heart operation in 1976. One of only a few in those post-war years who could act fluently in both languages, Pelletier always gave credit to Charles Rittenhouse for her abilities with the English language. She was given the Order of Canada in 1969, received the Andrew Allan award from ACTRA in 1974 and, shortly before her death, was awarded the Molson Prize of $20,000 from Canada Council.

## CHRISTOPHER PLUMMER

Arthur Christopher Orme Plummer was born in Toronto on December 13, 1929, but his heart always belonged to Montreal. It was there that he grew up, spending much of his time in night clubs during the early hours of the morning. Plummer remembered it well:

> Growing up in Montreal was great because it was during the jazz age and I was a fan of all that. Every great entertainer in the world came to Montreal in those days. I saw them all. . . . It was a very international town back in the forties and late thirties and it had its own sort of real European kind of personality that has slightly disappeared since. It really was a swinging town in those days, there were at least 400 night clubs. . . . I hung around the clubs all the time, it was great fun. From about fifteen, I used to sit at the bar. I always looked older so I could lie about my age beautifully. Montreal was sort of loose and free in those days. You could nurse a whiskey or a beer twenty-four hours a day, it never closed. What happened to those days? It was a great time and I will never forget it.

The great-grandson of Canadian Prime Minister Sir John Abbott, Plummer was raised by his mother and aunts, summering in the very "proper" atmosphere of Senneville, a Montreal suburb. He credits his mother for the direction his life would take: "My mother, Belle Abbott Plummer, really introduced me to the theatre by taking me to everything from when I was about six years old," Plummer said. "She took me to opera, to concerts. I was very musical and I loved music. Actually almost first and foremost I loved music and then the theatre. I had been lucky enough to have a brush with everything including the paint brush because I studied under Arthur Lismer [one of the Group of Seven]."

Right from the beginning, Plummer was not comfortable playing himself. It was always easier assuming someone else's personality, and for a young boy talented in the art of mimicry, theatre was definitely the way to go:

> I began because, a lot of actors say this, and I think it is true of all of us who begin because we are shy. There was something that was difficult about meeting people in the old days. I remember as a child all the guests that came to our house, an enormous number of people, which frightened the hell out of me. I used to run upstairs when I heard someone coming in, and hide to avoid confrontation. Terrifying, the pain of meeting someone. So then one kind of overcame this by performing in a room. In order to hide that fear, you had to be someone else. You didn't want to be yourself, because you were so insecure, so you played some other creature even in front of the family, they didn't recognize me. They would look at me so strangely, they thought I was insane.

He hated the routine of school, which bored him, but loved reading. Plummer's family was passionately interested in literature and passed their love of it on to the youngster. "They loved their books," he recalled. "We did after-dinner readings at home. It was one of those reading-aloud families. Then of course I couldn't wait to get on when I discovered that I could read, I thought, much better than anybody else. I was so appalling, arrogant—even around the family. Books were always a part of growing up and television had not yet been invented, thank God. It was radio and literature and music, music that really stirred me."

In fact, Plummer was an accomplished musician, and life might have led him to become a classical pianist if it were not for his introduction to the stage. He was sixteen years old when he portrayed Darcy in Helen Jerome's *Pride and Prejudice* on the stage at a Montreal high school. Theatre then became his great love. "I was really hooked, instantly," he said. "I mean I knew what I wanted to do, there was no question." When asked if it was the feeling he got on stage or the audience reaction that convinced him, Plummer answered this way:

> Both. It was a sort of marriage and it worked. What better tonic for a potential show-off than having it work for you at sixteen. Hearing the audience laugh and being able to make them laugh was such a tonic. When I was able to find that I could possibly charm people to thinking in my direction, I knew it was the most comfortable profession to get into because then I truly could be someone else and one day get paid for it. I was very lucky to have a mother who was interested because I came from a family that was, although artistic in a sense, a very conservative lot. My mother was a free spirit. . . . She finally converted the whole family and they were resigned to my desperate fate.

Plummer's "desperate fate" was to become one of Canada's biggest and most versatile talents. Even at the start, his talent was evident to those around him in the business. At sixteen he looked much older, with a rich, distinctive voice and a profile that showed a dash of First Nations blood.

He would not be ignored and if he was, Plummer's uneven temperament and penchant for getting into trouble quickly brought attention back his way. He had little humility and expected to succeed. In the brashness of youth, Amelia Hall recalled, he once addressed a Canadian Repertory Theatre (CRT) audience, thanking them and saying he hoped to appear before them again one day—"in a far, far better company."

By the time he joined the CRT at eighteen years of age, Plummer had already appeared with the Shakespeare Society, Brae Manor Theatre, Montreal Repertory Theatre and the Open Air Playhouse. Because of his mature looks, he was a natural to play older or character roles, which thrilled the young actor. "I was always playing older parts because I love character work. I didn't want to look handsome. Yuck. It's boring. I wanted to change my face, be somebody else, so I enjoyed that more than those boring, romantic leading men," said the man who, much to his chagrin, went on to become best-known as the handsome Captain von Trapp in *The Sound of Music* movie.

After his CRT stint, Plummer appeared with many groups, including the largely Canadian theatre in Bermuda. He also did a number of radio dramas and serials, in both French and English, before leaving Canada in 1953 for his second attempt to conquer New York. He lived well through the 1950s, and when funds diminished, someone would always help him out. It was usually his mother, as Plummer explained:

> I had expensive tastes. My poor mother had to fork out so much money. I just had charge accounts everywhere, thinking the world was my oyster. My mother, who could not afford it, had to pay. I was always so grateful to her and wanted to show, to prove to her that I was okay, and I did without my knowing it. She knew [before her death] I was going to do *Henry V* at Stratford [1956] and she'd seen the Broadway production of *The Lark* and knew I had kind of made it. I made her life miserable but somehow she was rewarded by having lived long enough to know that I was a success. And that was very important to me.

Plummer won a Theatre World Award in 1954 for his performance in *The Dark Is Light Enough* by Christopher Fry. It was the first in a series of awards he would receive through the years, including Tony wins for the musical *Cyrano* in 1973 and William Luce's *Barrymore* in 1997. Other Tony nominations included *Inherit the Wind*, *King Lear* and *Othello*. Plummer's biggest theatre success in the 1950s was his first appearance at Stratford in 1956, playing the lead in *Henry V*. Although staying mostly with theatre in the 1950s, he tentatively began his film career with *Stage Struck* and *The Fall of the Roman Empire*, but it was not until Plummer made *The Sound of Music* in 1964 that his face was widely known. The movie became one of the most-watched films in the history of entertainment and, although he once called it "The Sound of Mucus," Plummer said he never hated the movie: "It is not true that I didn't like *The Sound of Music*. I think it was a very well-made film. I didn't find my part very exciting. I had been spoiled by doing so many marvellous roles and von Trapp . . . but the film, I thought for the kind of film it was, was superbly made. I always respected it for what it stood for. We were all walking on egg shells [to make it good] but it did work."

Although Plummer continued with theatre, much of the 1960s was given over to trying to establish himself in the movies. One of his most triumphant pieces of work in that decade combined theatre and television as he appeared in *Hamlet*, filmed at Elsinore in Denmark in 1964. It was also in the late '50s and '60s that his celebrated temper got a little out of control and Plummer acquired a reputation of being difficult to work with. In spite of the fact that he mellowed considerably through the years, Plummer never lost his desire for professional perfection, from himself and everyone around him. From 1970 on, Plummer followed the pattern of making movies or TV miniseries until his lust for the theatre returned and found him once again before the footlights. Among his movie credits are *Murder by Decree*, *A Beautiful Mind*, *The Insider*, *Up* (voice), *On Golden Pond* (for television), *Beginners* and *The Last Station*. His performances in the latter two saw him nominated for Academy Awards. And in 2012 he won the Oscar for best supporting actor in *Beginners*.

Plummer always remained a Canadian. He had a great fondness for his homeland and returned to work in Canada whenever the opportunity arose, in spite of the fact he seldom received the kind of good reviews from the press that he'd received so often in earlier days of the theatre. "In those days Canadians were very supportive," he said of his early years. "It's when you arrive that they leave you alone or get a bit mean or oddly jealous. It's not quite jealous, I don't quite know what it is. It's always been a dilemma to me. . . . The minute I had sort of made it, established myself . . . . I'm not the only one and I'm not being self-pitying about it, I'm just amazed. I've never expected to get a good review [in Canada] since."

Things changed in that regard when he returned to Stratford in the 1990s. He had long wanted to perform there again, and he did so with his one-man show on the life of John Barrymore, which he subsequently took to Broadway in 1996. He also starred at Stratford in *Caesar and Cleopatra* and a fiftieth-anniversary production of *King Lear*, which was subsequently taken to Broadway to glowing reviews in 2004. Among his stage appearances outside Canada, Plummer starred on Broadway in *Macbeth* and *Othello*. The latter, in 1982, was one of his greatest successes, as his portrayal of Iago caused one New York critic to call it "quite possibly the best single Shakespearean performance to have originated on this continent in our time."

Plummer loved Shakespeare. As a boy he spent hours in the woods reciting passages to his dog or he would grab his "poor mother in the kitchen and do the whole of Donald Wolfit [Shakespearean actor] for her." He said it was easy to fall into Shakespeare. It all came easily to Plummer, much to the chagrin of some of his fellow actors. "That is what drove [other actors] crazy," Thor Arngrim remembered, "because he [Plummer] was such a brilliant actor. With Christopher there was nothing to it, he could do it drunk, sober, hung over, no rest, anything. It was easy for Christopher."

His later career saw Plummer working harder than ever, at a breathtaking pace. "I would be very bored if I didn't work," Plummer said. "I don't like too long a time hibernating or vacationing. I'm anxious to get on with it. It's a fascinating profession and you discover things all the time. . . . Now I can be more versatile than ever. I am now at this lucky age . . . those days of vanity are over and it's a big, big release. It really is."

## CHARLES RITTENHOUSE

Born in Montreal, Charles Rittenhouse grew up in Winnipeg where he attended the University of Manitoba before moving east to do his masters at McGill University. Except for two years studying drama at Yale University, Rittenhouse devoted himself solely to the theatre scene in the Montreal area. He was a sometime actor and frequent director, and in the latter category he worked with the Montreal Repertory Theatre, Brae Manor Theatre and Montreal's Shakespeare Society. Rittenhouse used his nurturing magic on young actors in the schools. He was also an editor of more than forty textbooks and an adapter of numerous plays for radio, many of which were produced by CBC's *Wednesday Night*. It was in his capacity as supervisor of English and drama for Montreal's Protestant schools that Rittenhouse had his strongest influence.

His passion for the theatre inspired young students, and he became a mentor to many of them, including John Colicos, William Shatner and Christopher Plummer. "He was a wonderful character," Plummer said of Rittenhouse. "He was the earliest influence [on me] as far as the school system was concerned." Charles Rittenhouse and his friend Herbert Whittaker were acknowledged in a 1947 *Saturday Night* magazine article as "two men who always seem to be all over the theatrical lot in Montreal."

## JEAN-LOUIS ROUX

There came a time when Jean-Louis Roux decided changes had to be made in his life:

> I quit Le Nouveau Monde in 1963 because I wasn't happy anymore with the choice of the plays, or maybe it was a lack of courage, I don't know. Maybe I felt I wouldn't be able to do much about it because Jean and André [Gascon] were very powerful in the company. Duplessis was dead, the Liberals were in power and well, in the sixties you know what happened. It made us probably very conscious of what we could do with theatre. At least it made me conscious of what we should do with theatre. Since I felt it was impossible to do it with Nouveau Monde I decided to leave. For three years I didn't even set foot in a theatre.

Roux survived by writing and working in television, where he had become well-known to French and English audiences during the 1950s, playing the intellectual son in both language versions of *The Plouffe Family*. Ironically, it was his old friend Jean Gascon who was the ticket back to the stage in 1966. Gascon worked with artistic director

Michael Langham at Stratford that summer and Roux phoned him and asked if he needed him for that season because he wanted to find out if he could still enjoy the stage. Gascon said yes, and after re-discovering his love for the theatre, Roux was asked by Gascon to take over the directorship of Théâtre du Nouveau Monde. As had been the case with Roux earlier, it was now Gascon who had become disgruntled and discouraged about theatre in Montreal, and he was moving permanently to Stratford. Roux agreed to take over and stayed until 1982.

Roux received the Molson Prize in 1976 and from 1977 to 1980 he was chairman of the board of the National Theatre School for which he had been a founding member in 1960. Following his resignation from Théâtre du Nouveau Monde, Roux became the director-general of the National Theatre School until 1987 when he left amid controversy over his opposition to suggestions of moving the English section from Montreal to Toronto. Like Gascon, he felt the French and the English actors had a lot to learn from each other.

He was a member of the Canadian Senate from 1994 to 1996 and was appointed lieutenant governor of Quebec in 1996, but it was a short-lived reign. In an interview Roux had voluntarily admitted that while he was nineteen and a university student he had worn a swastika on his lab coat as a protest against conscription. It was one of many protests at the time, involving many individuals who went on to become prominent Quebecers, but the information was used against him, and he resigned only months after the appointment. After a lifetime in the arts, Jean-Louis Roux was appointed chair of the Canada Council in 1997.

## LISTER SINCLAIR

Born in India to Scottish parents, Lister Sinclair came to North America from England in 1939 to attend the World's Fair in New York and visit Niagara Falls, after which he intended to return to the U.K. as a student at Cambridge on a scholarship. The outbreak of war scuttled his plans, stranding both his mother and him in Canada.

Always interested in theatre, Sinclair found that his enthusiasm for it became stronger when he attended the University of British Columbia and started working with the Players' Club. In the beginning he confined his talents to acting but then the pen took over. "I guess many actors get into writing the same sort of way, namely that what you think of yourself can't possibly be any worse than this crap they are handing you to do. So that's really how I got started. I wrote a couple of one-act plays for UBC."

Sinclair then moved to Toronto to take his masters degree, and there he wrote his first play, *The Abominable Assassination*. He wrote primarily for the radio with an occasional stage play thrown in. Among his own plays, his favourite was *Socrates*, which was performed at Jupiter Theatre as well as on radio. "The ones I liked best, that I am most interested in, were some of the later ones, particularly the verse ones," Sinclair said. "There is, for example, a nativity play for agnostics called *The View from Here Is Yes*. Good piece. I've done it quite a lot."

The *New York Times* once cited Sinclair and fellow Canadian Len Peterson as two of the four best radio playwrights on the continent. Known as "the Armpit" in his early days because of his shaggy beard and scruffy appearance, Sinclair was intensely private about his personal life. With an ability to turn an interview around on the interviewer, he had a passion for absorbing facts, which he passed on to others—whether they wanted to hear them or not. Sinclair had read all of Charles Dickens and Mark Twain by the time he was six. He studied math and physics later on, and spoke English, French, German, Gaelic, Spanish and Italian. He was known for his one-liners. One of Sinclair's best was a response to Andrew Allan the day they met. Allan offered him a cigarette and Sinclair declined, saying, "No thanks, I don't indulge in non-cooperative vices." He gave up performing as an actor "about 1950" but appeared behind the microphone on various CBC radio shows through the years, even becoming executive vice-president of the CBC for a couple of years in the early 1970s. He later spent a number of years as host of the national CBC radio program *Ideas*. He was awarded the Order of Canada in 1985.

### BERNARD SLADE

Born in St. Catharines, Ontario, in 1930, Bernard Slade Newbound spent his teenage years in Britain with his parents before they all returned to Canada when he was eighteen. He dropped the "Newbound" part of his name and started summer theatre work with Jack Blacklock. In 1953 Slade married one of his co-stars in the theatre, Jill Foster. Slowly he drifted away from performing and into writing, using his acting knowledge to good advantage. When Slade submitted a script called *The Prizewinner* to the CBC, and did not hear back from them, he sent it through an agent in New York to NBC, which promptly bought it for $2,000. Now that the script's worth had been proven elsewhere, the CBC suddenly decided to buy the script as well, professing disappointment that Slade had submitted it elsewhere while they were "considering" it. The sale in the United States was the turning point for Slade, who realized his talents lay in writing, not acting. It was not until Slade moved to the U.S. that he made it big. He quickly found work writing for the series *Bewitched*, and in the ensuing years he created *The Partridge Family*, *Bridget Loves Bernie* and wrote the first seven episodes of *The Flying Nun*. Although these made him a wealthy man, it was his Broadway play successes that gave Slade critical acclaim. His two biggest hits were *Tribute* and *Same Time, Next Year*, both of which were transferred to the big screen.

## MURRAY WESTGATE

Murray Westgate acquired bigger and better parts in radio after he left Everyman Theatre in 1947, but he kept his theatre interest alive by working with the Vancouver Little Theatre and Juan Root's Island Theatre. When theatre work in Vancouver began to dry up, Westgate followed the direction of a number of his friends—"the great exodus"—he called it, and moved to Toronto. In addition to his work in radio, he performed on stage with the International Players in Kingston, and with Jupiter Theatre and the New Play Society in Toronto. Film work began coming his way, too, and it was an industrial film for Imperial Oil that led to Westgate's famous commercials as a gas-station attendant during *Hockey Night in Canada* broadcasts. In these commercials, he seemed so friendly and so much like the guy next door that when Westgate said good night and happy motoring, the audience really believed he worked at the gas station. This proved embarrassing on several occasions when a real gas attendant recognized him at the pumps and told him to help himself. There was no self-serve back then, and Westgate did not have the first idea how to pump gas. For sixteen years he had a captive audience on Saturday nights, and then in 1968 suddenly it was over. "It was a mixed blessing," Westgate said of his Imperial Oil job, "but I don't regret it."

The parts were scarce for a while after his Saturday night employment ended, and Westgate survived mainly on radio, where he had met and married actress Alice Hill. His radio shows included *The Craigs* and *Jake and the Kid*. Slowly television and movies opened up to him again, and in 1979 Westgate won an award from ACTRA for *Tyler*, a drama in the series *For the Record*. He also appeared on television in *Seeing Things* in the 1980s. His movie roles included *Two Solitudes*, *Blue City Slammers* and *The Rowdyman* with Gordon Pinsent.

# ACKNOWLEDGEMENTS

There are many people to thank who helped bring this book to fruition. Firstly, there is John Drewery, Dorothy Davies and Rudy Horwood, who many years ago helped me secure the Canada Council grant that started this project. The Canada Council itself deserves a vote of thanks for believing in my vision of Canadian theatre in the post-WWII period. Thanks also go out to my mother, Anne Caza (I wish you were still here to see the book in print); to my father (I finally did it, and an important time in your life is recorded); to my publisher, Ronald Hatch, who has stayed the course; to the librarians at the old Vancouver Public Library; and those in the theatre division of the Toronto Public Library.

I am grateful to the following actors who shared their time and their stories with me, for without them, this book would never have been written. I am honoured to have met all of them: Thor Arngrim, Yvette Brind'Amour, Vernon Chapman, Robert Christie, Dorothy Davies, Donald Davis, Ted Follows, David Gardner, Amelia Hall, Barbara Hamilton, Don Harron, Peggy Hassard, Arthur Hill, Eric House, William Hutt, Charmion King, Paul Kligman, Betty Leighton, David Major, Lois McLean, Peter Mews, Mavor Moore, Sam Payne, Toby Robins, Jean-Louis Roux, Lister Sinclair, Peter Sturgess, Murray Westgate, Herbert Whittaker, and two actors who gave me multiple interviews and great encouragement—Christopher Plummer and Joy Coghill.

Finally, I want to thank all the cats in my life who have supported me, encouraged me, and who continued to believe in this project through the years even when my own faith stumbled—you know who you are.

# NOTES

1. Letter from Robertson Davies to Amelia Hall, dated May 27, 1946.
2. "The Diary of Samuel Marchbanks," *Peterborough Examiner*, March 4, 1950.
3. Sydney Butler, ed., *Arts in our Lives* (Vancouver: Brock House Writers, 2002), 40.
4. Sydney Butler, 41.
5. Sherrill Grace & Jerry Wasserman, eds., *Theatre and AutoBiography* (Vancouver: Talonbooks, 2006), 232.
6. *The Critic*, January 1952: 6.
7. *The Critic*, January 1952: 6.
8. Diane Mew, ed., *Life Before Stratford: The Memoirs of Amelia Hall* (Toronto: Dundurn Press, 1989), 95–96.
9. Christopher Plummer, *In Spite of Myself: A Memoir* (New York & Toronto: Alfred A. Knopf, 2008), 63.
10. Diane Mew, 98.
11. Diane Mew, 106.
12. *The Evening Citizen*, December 3, 1948.
13. Christopher Plummer, 62.
14. *Ottawa Journal*, May 12, 1973.
15. *Ottawa Journal*, May 12, 1973
16. Herbert Whittaker, *Whittaker's Theatricals* (Toronto: Simon & Pierre, 1993), 158.
17. Robertson Davies, *Happy Alchemy* (Toronto: McClelland & Stewart, 1997), 140.
18. Robertson Davies, 150.
19. Diane Mew, 72–73.
20. Herbert Whittaker, 77.
21. Robert Cushman, *Fifty Seasons at Stratford* (Toronto: McClelland & Stewart, 2002), 14.
22. Robert Cushman, Foreword.
23. Keith Garebian, *William Hutt: A Theatre Portrait* (Oakville: Mosaic Press, 1988), 94.
24. Grace Lydiatt Shaw, *Stratford under Cover* (Toronto: NC Press, 1977), 76.

# SELECT BIBLIOGRAPHY

Anthony, Geraldine, ed. *Stage Voices: Twelve Canadian Playwrights Talk About their Lives and Work*. Toronto: Doubleday Canada, 1978.

Appleford, Robert, ed. *Aboriginal Drama and Theatre*. Toronto: Playwrights Canada Press, 2005.

Boss, Allan. *Identifying Mavor Moore: A Historical and Literary Study*. Toronto: Playwrights Canada Press, 2011.

Butler, Sydney, ed. *Arts in our Lives*. Vancouver: Brock House Writers, 2002.

Chapman, Vernon. *Who's in the Goose Tonight: An Anecdotal History of Canadian Theatre*. Toronto: ECW Press, 2001.

Cushman, Robert. *Fifty Seasons at Stratford*. Toronto: McClelland & Stewart, 2002.

Davies, Robertson. *Happy Alchemy: On the Pleasures of Music and the Theatre*. Toronto: McClelland & Stewart, 1997.

Edmonstone, Wayne E. *Nathan Cohen: The Making of a Critic*. Toronto: Lester and Orpen, 1977.

Garebian, Keith. *William Hutt: A Theatre Portrait*. Oakville: Mosaic Press, 1988.

Grace, Sherrill and Jerry Wasserman, eds. *Theatre and AutoBiography: Writing and Performing Lives in Theory and Practice*. Vancouver: Talonbooks, 2006.

Guthrie, Tyrone, Robertson Davies and Grant Macdonald. *Renown at Stratford: A Record of the Shakespeare Festival in Canada*. Toronto: Clarke, Irwin & Company, 1953.

Hall, Amelia Wells and Diane Mew, eds. *Life Before Stratford: The Memoirs of Amelia Hall*. Toronto: Dundurn Press, 1989.

Hamelin, Jean. *The Theatre in French Canada (1936–1966)*. Quebec: Dept. of Cultural Affairs, 1986.

Harron, Martha. *Don Harron: A Parent Contradiction*. Don Mills: Collins Publishers, 1988.

Kennedy, Brian. *The Baron Bold and the Beauteous Maid: A Compact History of Canadian Theatre*. Toronto: Playwrights Canada Press, 2004.

Lydiatt Shaw, Grace. *Stratford under Cover: Memories on Tape*. Toronto: NC Press, 1977.

Moore, Mavor. *Reinventing Myself: Memoirs*. Toronto: Stoddart Publishing Co., 1994.

Nardocchio, Elaine F. *Theatre and Politics in Modern Quebec*. Edmonton: University of Alberta Press, 1986.

Plummer, Christopher. *In Spite of Myself: A Memoir*. New York. Toronto: Alfred A. Knopf, 2008.

Ratsoy, Ginny, ed. *Theatre in British Columbia*. Toronto: Playwrights Canada Press, 2006.

Sperdakos, Paula. *Dora Mavor Moore: Pioneer of the Canadian Theatre*. Toronto: ECW Press, 1995.

Wagner, Anton, ed. *Establishing Our Bounderies: English-Canadian Theatre Criticism*. Toronto: University of Toronto Press, 1999.

Wallace, Robert and Cynthia Zimmerman. *The Work: Conversations with English-Canadian Playwrights*. Toronto: Coach House Press, 1982.

Wasserman, Jerry. *Spectacle of Empire: Marc Lescarbot's Theatre of Neptune in New France*. Vancouver: Talonbooks, 2006.

Whittaker, Herbert. *Setting the Stage*. Montreal & Kingston: McGill-Queen's University Press, 1999.

———. *Whittaker's Theatricals*. Toronto: Simon & Pierre, 1993.

Yeo, Leslie. *A Thousand and One First Nights*. Oakville: Mosaic Press, 1998.

## ABOUT THE AUTHOR

Susan McNicoll's lifelong love of history has been the main focus of her writing career, which began with five years as a reporter for the *Ottawa Journal* in the 1970s. The majority of her five published works, which include *British Columbia Murders* (2003 & 2009) and *Ontario Murders* (2004 & 2009), involve accounts of historical murders with most of the material being taken from the actual trial transcripts and other source documents. She is proud that another book, *Jack the Ripper* (2005), is more an investigation of his five victims and their lives in Victorian England than the killer himself. Susan also writes family histories on private commission, using interviews, historical documents and photographs to create a family portrait. For *The Opening Act*, she spent some ten years interviewing many of the major theatre directors and actors active in the period after the Second World War, and has amassed a treasure trove of information about theatre during this time. Although her work to date has been in the non-fiction realm, Susan is currently working on a series of spiritual fables based on the four seasons of healing. She makes her home in Vancouver, B.C.

# INDEX

*Citations of photographs are in bold*

Marquis imprimeur inc.

Québec, Canada
2012

Imprimé sur du papier Silva Enviro 100% postconsommation traité sans chlore, accrédité ÉcoLogo et fait à partir de biogaz.